Explorations

Second Edition

Explorations

CONDUCTING EMPIRICAL RESEARCH
IN CANADIAN POLITICAL SCIENCE

Keith Archer and Loleen Berdahl

OXFORD
UNIVERSITY PRESS

OXFORD
UNIVERSITY PRESS

8 Sampson Mews, Suite 204, Don Mills, Ontario M3C 0H5
www.oupcanada.com

Oxford University Press is a department of the University of Oxford.
It furthers the University's objective of excellence in research, scholarship,
and education by publishing worldwide in

Oxford   New York

Auckland Cape Town Dar es Salaam Hong Kong Karachi
Kuala Lumpur Madrid Melbourne Mexico City Nairobi
New Delhi Shanghai Taipei Toronto

With offices in

Argentina Austria Brazil Chile Czech Republic France Greece
Guatemala Hungary Italy Japan Poland Portugal Singapore
South Korea Switzerland Thailand Turkey Ukraine Vietnam

Oxford is a trade mark of Oxford University Press
in the UK and in certain other countries

Published in Canada by Oxford University Press

Copyright © Oxford University Press Canada 2011

Previous edition published in 1998 by ITP Nelson

Library and Archives Canada Cataloguing in Publication

Archer, Keith, 1955–
Explorations : conducting empirical research in Canadian political science / Keith Archer &
Loleen Berdahl. — 2nd ed.

Previous title: Explorations : a navigator's guide to quantitative
research in Canadian political science, 1998.
Includes bibliographical references and index.

ISBN 978-0-19-543232-9

1. Political science—Research—Textbooks. 2. Political statistics—
Textbooks. I. Youngman, Loleen II. Archer, Keith, 1955– .
Explorations : a navigator's guide to quantitative research in
Canadian political science III. Title.

JA71.5.A72 2011   320.072   C2010-906636-7

Cover image: Kheng Ho Toh/Veer

Printed and bound in Canada.
3 4 5 — 15 14 13

CONTENTS

4   Defining the Political World: Measures   67

5   Research Ethics: People behind the Numbers   96

PART II   RESEARCH DESIGN   121

6   Observing the Political World: Quantitative and Qualitative Approaches   123

18 Multivariate Analysis: An Introduction to the Deep End of the Pool   323

19 Analyzing Qualitative Data   349

20 Writing the Report   358

PREFACE

Many students in political science, and indeed in the social sciences more broadly defined, try to avoid research methods courses because they dislike or even fear math. Some resent being confronted with the very numbers and math that they had designed their undergraduate program to avoid. Others are simply anxious about their ability: 'Will this be the course that kills my GPA?'

Let's begin, then, with some basic reassurance. To paraphrase former American president F.D. Roosevelt, you have nothing to fear but fear itself. If you passed math in grade 10, you have more than enough mathematical skill to handle the material in this text. If you can add, subtract, multiply, divide, and plug numbers into simple equations, you are as ready as you need to be. The content of this text is primarily *conceptual*. Our goal is to give you the necessary tools to think clearly about research issues in political science, to understand both the power and limitations of quantitative data. True, the math is there, but it is there as a form of conceptual understanding more than as a form of calculation.

Some contemporary research methods books shy away from mathematical computations altogether, recognizing that most students will be working with computer-based statistical packages that will effortlessly do the calculations for them. However, it is our belief that some hands-on familiarity helps students to acquire greater conceptual confidence. Statistical tests and measures can be difficult to understand in the abstract; thus, we will provide simple illustrations to give you the opportunity to work through the basic formulas. It is not our expectation that you will abandon the computer-based programs in favour of pencil and paper, but rather that you will have some first-hand experience with the statistical terminology you will encounter in your own reading and research. You will be more comfortable with that terminology if you have had this opportunity.

In the chapters to come we will take you through the steps involved in empirical research. How should you conceptualize a research problem? What evidence, or data, should you bring to bear on the problem? How do you measure the concepts you wish to address? How do you describe the research findings? What statistical tests might be used? Under what ethical guidelines should you operate? Throughout the chapters we will try to engage you actively in the text material by providing opportunities for you to test your own thinking and comprehension. These opportunities, identified as *Apply Your Understanding,* are not meant to be formal exercises for which there are right and wrong answers. Rather, they provide the chance to think about the material and to apply it in situations familiar to most readers. The same objectives guide the group discussion topics raised at the end of each chapter.

Throughout the text we will constantly be bringing real data into play through sections that we have identified as *Expand Your Knowledge.* These are real-life illustrations frequently drawn from the kinds of surveys and reports that you run across daily in newspapers and on television. Others, and perhaps the more important, will come from the political science and social science literature. Our objective in both cases is the same: to illustrate how empirical research methods can be used to enrich and expand our understanding of the political world and, in some cases, to illustrate how mistakes can be made.

There is, then, an *applied* character to the text. But this should not imply an avoidance of normative issues. We recognize that an interest in normative issues—the shoulds and oughts of politics—is what draws many students into political science. We also recognize that normative questions cannot be reduced to empirical questions; knowing how the world *is* does not tell us how it *should be*. At the same time, a great deal of normative debate in politics and political science draws upon empirical evidence and understanding. Should there be seat-belt laws? Prohibition of smoking in public places? Controls on violence in television programming? Limitations on campaign spending in federal or provincial elections? Our answers to such questions depend *in part* upon assumptions about empirical effects. Thus, a nuanced empirical understanding of the political world is a means to a richer normative debate and not a way of avoiding such debate.

While this text emphasizes the benefits of using the scientific method in understanding and evaluating the empirical—or observable—world, it is also important to remain mindful of the limitations of the scientific method, particularly as they relate to the social sciences. Although the scientific method purports to be a way of understanding the world on the basis of observable facts, we will show that at times these facts themselves are a matter of dispute. There are many possible reasons to explain different perceptions of reality, and these will be introduced and explored throughout the text.

Underlying this assumption about the importance of empirical understanding is the reality that research skills are essential in the contemporary labour market. An ability to design, conduct, and, more commonly, *assess* empirical research is no longer a frill; it is rapidly becoming a necessity. Research literacy is as essential to today's job market as literacy itself was to the job market of earlier generations. We are convinced that of all the courses you take, research methods courses are the most immediately relevant to getting and keeping a job.

Finally, we would like to emphasize the thematic intent of the book's title, *Explorations*. It is not our intent to give the last word on empirical research methodology, for the field is rich, vast, and complex. Rather, we hope to open some doors, to provide you with a rough understanding of empirical research in political science. Our goal is to equip you with both the basic skills you need to handle research material and an appreciation of the strengths and weaknesses of empirical research. The text, then, is no more than a preliminary exploration. The destinations identified for each chapter are not final destinations but rather way stations on what, for many readers, will undoubtedly turn out to be a much longer journey. For those readers for whom the way stations turn out to be the final destination, we trust that you will find the exploration to have been interesting and helpful as you continue to run up against political issues and debates throughout your life.

We would like to thank the reviewers who took time to comment on the manuscript of this text: John E. deRoche, Cape Breton University; Laura Stephenson, University of Western Ontario; and Elizabeth Goodyear-Grant, Queen's University.

We would also like to thank the reviewers who took time to comment on the manuscript of the first edition of *Explorations*: Grant Amyot, Queen's University; Gerald Bierling, McMaster University; and David Docherty, Wilfrid Laurier University.

The first edition of *Explorations* was co-authored by Roger Gibbins. We would like to thank Roger for his work on the first edition and for supporting our revision of the text. We also extend our appreciation to Daniel Rubenson (Ryerson University), Natasja Treiberg (University of Alberta), Linda Trimble (University of Alberta), and Jared J. Wesley (University of Manitoba) for their contributions to the second edition. And finally, we would also like to thank our respective families for their support during the revision process: Lisa Hurst-Archer, Justin (and Alison), Caitlin (and Jeff), Ben, Will, and Isaiah Archer; and Troy, Katie, and Zoë Berdahl.

PART I
CONDUCTING POLITICAL SCIENCE RESEARCH

Many of the students reading this book will be enrolled in their first course in political science research methods. Some might even be coming to this course, and this book, with a sense of trepidation stemming from a concern that political science research involves 'math.' Many of the students that we've taught in our research methods courses over the years have expressed such concerns. So, let's be frank about this at the outset. This book will introduce a number of techniques that can be used to assess the strength of relationships between variables, and we will often represent these relationships by using quantitative data. This means we will be counting people's responses and grouping them to assess how strongly one characteristic is related to another. A number of statistical techniques will be introduced that will help summarize these relationships, and these statistics are based on mathematical formulas.

This book, therefore, includes some math. However, political science research involves much more than conducting tests of the relationships between variables. We begin with a broader discussion of the use of the scientific approach to the study of politics. Many readers of this book are enrolled in a course in a Department of Political Science. Although a couple of generations ago such a department might have been called Political Economy or simply Politics, today it is more common to refer to the discipline as well as the university or college department as Political Science. The book

begins in Chapter 1 by considering what such a label implies for the ways in which people in this academic discipline gain knowledge and understanding of their subject matter.

The discussion then turns to the matter of applying the scientific method to the study of politics. In Chapter 2 we consider the role that theory plays in our empirical models and examine the degree to which we can use quantitative methods to identify causal relationships in politics. This chapter introduces the idea of testing hypotheses as a way of conducting empirical research and identifies a number of alternative models for such hypothesis testing.

Chapters 3 and 4 raise the question of the way in which political scientists define concepts in the research and also the way in which such concepts are 'operationalized' as variables that can be measured. We will see that the language used in political science research must be precise so that when a term is used to describe a phenomenon, there is as little confusion or disagreement as possible regarding the meaning of that term. As we'll see, achieving this goal is more difficult in practice than it might seem.

This section concludes in Chapter 5 with a discussion of ethics as it relates to conducting research on human beings. There is a requirement in conducting research that our research subjects be treated with respect and dignity and that a number of safeguards need be in place to ensure compliance with such an expectation.

These discussions in Part 1 of the book set the stage for the more detailed discussions that follow in Part 2, concerning research design and data collection, and Part 3, focused on data analysis. The goal is to ensure that students have an understanding of each of the stages of the research process, and that by following the steps outlined in the three parts of the book, students are able to be more informed consumers of political science research. It is also expected that students will begin to develop the tools to conduct their own political science research projects.

Chapter 1

THE SCIENTIFIC APPROACH TO POLITICS

DESTINATION

By the end of this chapter the reader should

- understand the idea of *science* in political science;
- know the basic postulates of science;
- understand the general methodology of science as applied to the more specific study of politics;
- know the distinction between normative and empirical studies; and
- appreciate some of the limitations of the scientific method and some of the critiques of the scientific methodology that have emerged.

One of the goals of an undergraduate education, and in particular one of the goals of a course in research methods in the social sciences, is to help students think critically. By this we mean that propositions or arguments are not accepted unless they are accompanied by sufficiently compelling evidence. Critical thought therefore involves weighing and evaluating the merits of evidence marshalled in support of an argument. Researchers ask whether they understand the evidence in the same way that others do and whether they interpret the implications of the evidence in the same way as others. If the evidence is found wanting, either because it fails to provide sufficiently strong support or because it does not bear directly on the argument, then the argument can be rejected. Thus, the ways in which we *perceive* and *interpret* evidence are two key aspects of critical thought.

One of the goals of the **scientific approach to politics** is to use critical thought as a guide to our perceptions of the political world. Boldly stated, the scientific study of politics attempts to provide a method whereby observations of the political world can be relatively independent of the observer. Stated more cautiously, it can help in determining not only when political perceptions differ but also why they differ.

Not surprisingly, this book takes the view that it is useful and worthwhile to pursue the goals of **scientific analysis**. However, we also accept the premise that most political research falls well short of the goal of providing similar observations and interpretations of political reality. Thus, a good deal of our attention will be focused on understanding why political scientists are so often in disagreement about so many of the most fundamental questions of politics. This is not meant to suggest that little progress has been made over time in our understanding of politics. On the contrary, much knowledge has been gained. In some areas of political science, including the study of voting, elections, and political belief systems, the scientific approach has so transformed both political practice and research that they are unrecognizable from earlier generations. Nonetheless, the scientific approach to politics is not a simple template or cookie cutter that can be applied holus-bolus to any political problem or research question. Its application requires detailed and careful attention from students and researchers alike.

An example of an issue over which there is considerable disagreement may help illustrate the role of the scientific approach. One of the most common features of political life in advanced industrial democracies is the persistence of female underrepresentation in legislative assemblies. Every national legislature in the Organisation for Economic Co-operation and Development (OECD) has fewer women, and usually a lot fewer women, than men. In the 2008 Canadian general election, for example, only 69 of the 308 MPs (22.4 per cent) elected to the House of Commons were women, up from 18.0 per cent in 1993. Hence the *fact* that women are underrepresented in legislatures can scarcely be disputed. Far more controversial, however, are the *explanations* that account for this finding. Some would argue that women are underrepresented out of choice, that women are less inclined than men to seek elective public office. This explanation can be further broken down into the propositions (1) that women and men are socialized to have different preferences and/or (2) that women and men have different responsibilities throughout the life cycle that, for instance, place a greater onus on women for child-rearing, thus freeing men to engage in other activities, including participating in political parties and seeking election. Yet another possible explanation for differential rates of seeking election is the systematic bias against strong women candidates that may exist in political parties. That is to say, the parties themselves may present barriers to otherwise willing female candidates, making it difficult for them to win nomination for office, particularly in highly competitive ridings.

Which of these three explanations for the underrepresentation of women in legislatures is the most accurate and informative?[1] The answer is important because it can have profound implications for public policy. If female underrepresentation is caused mainly by the parties systematically excluding women, then the solution (assuming one believes, as we do, that this is a problem) may be quite different than if it stems largely from gender-specific differences in the life cycle or gender differences in socialization. (Of course, each of these explanations may contain a partial truth about the causes of differences in political representation.) The key feature of the scientific approach to politics is that it requires the formulation of testable hypotheses and the marshalling of empirical data that can either confirm or fail to confirm the hypotheses. It provides a way of applying empirical data to normative questions and public policy debates.

EXPAND YOUR KNOWLEDGE

Women's Representation in the Canadian House of Commons

The issue of gender representation in legislative assemblies has been the subject of a considerable body of empirical research. The proportion of women in the Canadian House of Commons was extremely low until 1984, when there was an unusual surge in the number of women elected to the Canadian House of Commons. This surge increased the number of elected women MPs from 10 in 1979 (3.5 per cent) and 14 in 1980 (5.0 per cent) to 27 in 1984 (9.6 per cent). In an article published in 1994, Donley Studlar and Richard Matland addressed the 1984 surge. The empirical question they asked was whether the 1984 increase was a fluke stemming from the unexpectedly large number of Progressive Conservative MPs elected from Quebec. This question stemmed from the assumption that the Conservatives had nominated female candidates in Quebec ridings they expected to lose, but then won. After statistical analysis, the authors concluded that 'it becomes difficult to credit the conventional wisdom that the rise of women in the Canadian House of Commons in 1984 was the product of an accident, a fluke in which intended Conservative sacrificial lambs were surprisingly elevated because of a massive swing of the Quebec electorate toward the Progressive Conservative party. Such an explanation ignores the broader patterns of candidacy underlying the rise of women in 1984' (1994, 77).

By submitting the 1984 election results to an empirical test, the authors were able to show that what might have been considered an idiosyncratic event in Canadian politics could better be seen as confirmation of much broader currents of change common to most Western democratic states.

EMPIRICAL AND NORMATIVE ANALYSIS

The goal of *all* political analysis is to advance our knowledge and understanding of the political world. There are two dominant forms of political analysis: normative and empirical. **Normative analysis** is prescriptive in nature and addresses how society and political life *should be*. This is the realm of political theory and philosophy. Because it entails the discussion of ideals, normative political analysis is infused with value judgments and preferences. Normative discussions invoke convictions and feelings, things that are terribly important but are also difficult to measure and observe empirically in day-to-day life. In addition, people often disagree about the 'truth' of normative statements, for they bring different values, priorities, and moral perspectives into play.

For example, consider the debate on capital punishment. Both sides of the debate are presented as fact, in statements such as 'It is wrong to kill anyone, even murderers' and 'It is wrong to allow those who take life to continue life.' Yet which position one sees as true depends upon one's own values and beliefs; the distinction is normative, not factual. We can identify normative analysis by the use of value-laden terms such as 'good', 'bad', 'right', 'wrong', 'should', 'must', and 'ought'. Many political debates concern normative issues, since people often disagree about what ends should be sought and the best means for reaching such ends.

The second branch of political analysis is **empirical research**. Empirical political analysis is descriptive in nature; the goal is to describe and to explain the political world *as it is*, rather than as it should be. Whereas normative analysis is self-consciously 'value' based, empirical research purports to be more 'fact' based. Factual evidence is gathered from the physical and social worlds; unless a phenomenon can be observed (experienced through the senses), it cannot be considered admissible evidence (Singleton et al. 1988, 31). Knowledge obtained from methods other than observation—such as faith, intuition, or common sense—is not considered empirical knowledge. This is not meant to discredit other ways of knowing, but rather to emphasize the distinction between empirical and nonempirical knowledge. Empiricism requires observation and therefore measurement. In addition, empirical facts must be independently observed and agreed upon by many people. This quality is known as **intersubjectivity**. How one observes an event or a phenomenon is ultimately subjective; as those who have witnessed a car accident can attest, there are often two, three, or even six sides to every story. By requiring that more than one person observe and give a similar account of the event, we are able to increase objectivity. Intersubjectivity also requires that more than one observation occur; in the scientific process this is known as **replication**. Researchers seek out evidence that confirms the findings of other researchers, thus 'double-checking' the observations of others. The more people who observe a phenomenon and the more times it is observed, the more willing we are to accept it as fact. An empirical statement does not indicate preferences or values, but rather presents observable facts.

A key issue for empirically based research is the degree to which facts exist independently of the observer. We made reference a moment ago to the fact that witnesses to an accident often report different versions of the 'facts' of the case. Quite literally, they have perceived the same events very differently. On a matter such as a traffic accident with the attendant legal and financial implications, it may very well be in the interest of those concerned to perceive things differently: neither driver wishes to be charged with a traffic offence or to have his or her insurance premiums rise. Thus, there may be an incentive for perceptions of reality to be distorted, either consciously or unconsciously.

The view of some researchers is that this particular example of the filtering of 'facts' among motorists in a traffic accident is generalizable in perceptions of the social and political world. In this view, 'facts' are not completely objective, but instead perceptions of fact are influenced or mediated by the social and political context of the observer. To the extent that this is true, it may be difficult to fully separate facts and values, or the empirical and normative aspects of the study of politics.

There are other ways in which normative and empirical analysis overlap in the study of politics. Empirical research is used to question the conclusions of normative analysis, and normative analysis often employs empirical facts in its arguments. Consider, for example, environmental debates. Environmentalists state empirical facts—changing climate conditions, endangered species—before stating normative positions: we *should* reduce emissions, clean up the oceans, and so on. Opposition to the environmental movement's normative positions also contains appeals to empirical fact. For example, Julian Simon (1995, 11) strongly asserts, 'Every measure of material and environmental welfare in the United States and in the world has improved rather than deteriorated . . . there is every scientific reason to be joyful about the trends in the conditions of the Earth.' Some of the most contentious environmental debates occur when there is no concrete, agreed-upon empirical evidence; for example, Do harp seals really deplete cod stocks? Is the global temperature increasing, or are we just witnessing short-term fluctuations around a constant norm? While this text will be concerned with empirical research, the reader should note how frequently empiricism is used in normative debates.

EXPAND YOUR KNOWLEDGE

Normative and Empirical Approaches to Democracy: Robert Dahl

An interesting example of the difference between the normative and empirical approaches to political analysis is seen in the work of Robert Dahl, who devoted much of his long academic career to the study of democracy. Initially, he worked as an empiricist, seeking to explain how democracy works. In *Who Governs?* (1961), Dahl explored the distribution of power in New Haven, Connecticut. He found that although power appears to be concentrated in political elites, interest groups have great influence on the decisions elites make, leaving government acting more as a referee between conflicting interests than as a powerful decision-maker with interests of its own. Dahl assumed that all relevant social interests could form groups to lobby the government and that all groups have political weight, and from these assumptions he concluded that democratic politics is not elite dominated. The school of thought that asserts that democracy is a contest among numerous groups and 'potential' groups is known as the pluralist school, which has been challenged empirically on many fronts. Critics include public choice theorists, who argue that not all interests are equally likely to form lobby groups, and neo-Marxists, who argue that powerful corporate interests have greater status than noneconomic elites in the battle between interests.

Two decades later, the normative component of Dahl's writing emerged more clearly. In *Democracy and Its Critics* (1989), Dahl distinguishes between the ideal and practice of democracy. Political orders based on democratic practices—such as free elections, inclusive suffrage, freedom of expression, and representative government—are defined as 'polyarchies', rather than as democracies. Polyarchy can be empirically observed: does a country have democratic institutions? If yes, it is a polyarchy. Dahl reserves the word 'democracy' for the ideal toward which all polyarchies strive; it is the system under which liberty and self-development flourish. Dahl writes (1989, 322): 'In my view, neither political equality nor the democratic process is justified as intrinsically good. Rather, they are justified as the most reliable means for protecting and advancing the good and interests of all persons subject to collective decisions. . . . [Political equality is] an essential means to a just distribution of freedom and to fair opportunities for self-development.' Thus, Dahl's later work clearly makes normative judgments: liberty is *good*, and given that democracy is the best means to liberty, democracy *should* be pursued.

APPLY YOUR UNDERSTANDING

Normative and Empirical Statements

Identify the following statements as either normative statements or empirical statements:

1. Seat-belt usage decreases automobile-related fatalities.
2. Seat-belt usage ought to be mandatory.
3. Democracy is the best system of government available.
4. Democratic systems, on average, have better human rights records.
5. In terms of demographic weight, women are severely underrepresented in legislatures.
6. The electoral system should be changed to ensure a more representative legislature.

In assessing these statements, note the impact that specific words can make. In the fifth statement, for example, does the addition of the adverb 'severely' affect your categorization of the statement as normative or empirical? Can 'better' in statement four be assessed in empirical terms, or is it inherently normative?

WHAT IS SCIENCE?

At its root, **science** is a set of rules that help us understand the world around us. The rules describe *how* we know, not *what* we know. Science, therefore, is a *method for acquiring knowledge* rather than the knowledge itself. We would call something science not because of the subject that was being studied, but because of the *way* in which it was being studied. If a study is done according to the rules of science, then it is science. The scientific method consists of formulating hypotheses about the causal relationship between variables and empirically testing the hypotheses. The goal is to ensure that many observers, acting independently, will make similar observations, and draw similar conclusions, about the cause-and-effect relationship.

NATURAL AND SOCIAL SCIENCES

By understanding science as a method of gaining knowledge, it is possible to extend the application of the scientific method beyond the natural sciences of physics, chemistry, and the like to include the social science areas of human interactions in social relations. This has given rise to the development of social scientific research in the areas of anthropology, archaeology, economics, political science, sociology, and others. (Whether psychology is a natural or social science depends upon the branch of the discipline.) As we will see, applying the scientific method to social relations brings with it a number of attendant problems, some related to science generally and others more specific to studying people. While researchers need to be aware of these limitations, they usually find that the advantages of the scientific approach far outweigh its disadvantages.

One significant difference between much of the research that takes place in the natural versus social sciences is the amount of control that the researcher has over the research setting. The laboratory, a site for highly controlled experiments, remains a mainstay of much research in the natural sciences. As a result, researchers have a high degree of success in isolating the few variables selected for study. In the social sciences, by contrast, the laboratory is replaced for the most part by field research, whether through survey research, participant observation, focus group analysis, or other methods. These methods provide a variety of ways in which researchers attempt to control for extraneous factors, but in general they are less efficient in doing so than are controlled laboratory experiments. The result is that alternative independent variables may confound the analysis.

A second difference between the natural and social sciences is the level of agreement within the scientific communities about the meaning and measurement of concepts. For example, in physics, researchers share a common understanding of such terms as mass, density, heat, and speed. According to Thomas Kuhn in *The Structure of Scientific Revolutions*, such agreement characterizes mature sciences, enabling the progression from one **paradigm** (a framework for understanding) to another. By contrast, the social sciences are characterized by considerable disagreement over the definition and measurement of key terms. For example, disagreement persists—and perhaps always will persist—over the definition of terms such as democracy, effective representation, and social class (a topic explored in more detail in Chapters 3 and 4).

A third difference between the natural and social sciences is the degree of determinacy of the results. In the natural sciences, the goal is to derive laws of behaviour. In the social sciences, though, the presence of human agency—free choice—means that outcomes are never completely determined. Thus, instead of deriving laws of behaviour, the social sciences use probability in stating the generalized form of causal relationships. For example, social sciences tend to use probabilistic phrases such as 'young people are less likely than the middle-aged to participate in politics' rather than deterministic phrases such as 'young people participate less in politics than do the middle-aged'.

There are a number of features of the scientific method that make it an attractive **epistemology**, or approach to knowledge. One strength is that it attempts to remove, or at least to minimize, the effect of the observer on the observed. Two people working independently of each other to explore a given topic, and using the same methodology under similar conditions, should perceive the same result. In this respect, the scientific method begins with the assumption that no single observer is uniquely suited to perceive the real world in ways that are denied to all others. Thus, because of the independence of results from observers, no observer is inherently better able to acquire scientific knowledge. This principle points to the central place that replication has in science. If the results of a scientific study cannot be independently verified, they are not accepted as an addition to the body of knowledge in that area of inquiry. Therefore, it is essential that results of scientific research are reported in ways that enable others to verify them through replication, or the repeated testing of the empirical relationships.

A second strength of the scientific approach results from its orientation toward cause and effect. In all scientific research, there is some outcome, or set of outcomes, that one wishes to explain. This outcome, or effect, must be clearly stated and defined. There must also be at least a minimal amount of **variance** to be explained. This means that there must be some change over time or across space or differences in outcome patterns across cases in the sample. Thus, for example, one could not explain why people voted (voter turnout) in an election if everyone voted; there is no variance in electoral participation to explain. The causes of voting (or nonvoting) could be examined only if a comparative referent was introduced by including a set of nonvoters in the database.

The task of the research then becomes one of finding which characteristics cause people (or cases) to vary in outcome. Research will usually involve testing the strength of alternative causes of an outcome. Continuing with the example of the likelihood of voting, one could speculate that education may be a factor that affects turnout: people with a higher level of education are more likely to vote than those with lower education. This is called a research **hypothesis**. We are proposing (hypothesizing) that increased education leads to an increased tendency to vote. At the outset of the research we do not know whether or not this hypothesis is true. But for a variety of reasons (other research that we have read, our personal experience, our intuition) we believe this may be true. However, there will be other probable or at least possible causes of voting turnout that we also wish to examine. For example, an alternative hypothesis is that people with higher incomes are more likely to vote. Still another is that people who are more interested in politics are more likely to vote.

Each of these hypothesized causes of voting focuses on the characteristics of individuals. If, however, one was using cross-national data, then different characteristics of the political system could also be used to explain differences in turnout. For example, one might hypothesize that voting is more likely in those systems that minimize the costs of voting, such as those that register voters automatically. In addition, the perceived closeness of the race, the frequency of elections, the differences between political parties or between governing coalitions also could lead to differences in turnout rates. By highlighting the importance of the cause-and-effect structure of research hypotheses, the scientific approach ensures that research remains targeted at evaluating alternative causes of phenomena and rejecting those that are less powerful.

A third strength of the scientific approach is that it can be used not only to explain but also to *predict* events or outcomes. The approach assumes that there is an order and a structure to the real world and that through a careful application of the methods of science the order can be known and understood. This assumption of patterned behaviour, based on relationships of cause and effect, implies that we can gain knowledge of the present and, through that knowledge, predict future behaviours or events. And, of course, both the explanations of present events and the predictions about the future are themselves subject to further empirical verification.

Fourth, the scientific approach tries to draw lawlike generalizations about the real world. Our understanding of specific events or outcomes, although useful in its own right, is of greater value to the extent that it reveals a more enduring quality about relationships among phenomena. Thus, for example, although it may be highly useful to know what effect, if any, the federal government's expenditures had on spiralling inflation and unemployment during the 1970s, it is even more useful to know the general effect that government spending has on inflation and unemployment. Does the effect of the 1970s hold across time? Across countries and different economic systems? This impulse to generalize is a core feature of the scientific project. The lawlike generalizations are formulated as **theories**; we will explore theory development in Chapter 2.

The scientific method is often referred to as **positivism**. The principles underlying the positivist approach in social science can be traced back to eighteenth-century sociologist Auguste Comte (Neuman 1994, 58). Positivism is based on empiricism and determinism: it is believed that almost everything can be objectively measured (empiricism) and that every event has an explanation or a cause (determinism). The postulates of science are extrapolations of these positivist principles.

Summary: Strengths of the Scientific Method

1. It attempts to minimize the effect of the observer on the observed.
2. It directs our attention to the dynamics of cause and effect.
3. It can be used not only to explain but also to predict.
4. It seeks lawlike generalizations that can be applied to the political world across time and space.

EXPAND YOUR KNOWLEDGE

Postmodernism

The assertion that the effects of the observer on the observed can be minimized is hotly contested by the proponents of **postmodernism**. The underlying premise of postmodernism is that reality is socially constructed and that the observer cannot be separated from what he or she purports to see. Furthermore, not only will one construction of the world differ from another, but there is also no method, and

(continued)

certainly no scientific method, that enables us to determine which perspective is accurate or correct. Indeed, postmodernism calls into question such notions as 'accurate' or 'correct;' the perspective that prevails will be the one backed by those with power. In this sense, power defines the nature of reality.

Postmodernism has had a dramatic impact on the arts, cultural studies, the humanities, and the social sciences. Although the tenets of postmodernism are themselves hotly contested, they should be taken into account by anyone hoping to be conversant with contemporary political and cultural dialogue. For an excellent conceptual introduction, see Pauline Marie Rosenau, *Post-Modernism and the Social Sciences: Insights, Inroads, and Intrusions* (Princeton: Princeton University Press, 1992).

POSTULATES OF SCIENCE

The scientific method asserts that knowledge can best be acquired by following certain rules or sets of rules that can lead to the formulation of lawlike generalizations about the social and political world. This methodology is predicated on certain beliefs (**postulates**) about nature and about how nature can be known. If we do not accept these beliefs, then the scientific method itself becomes less compelling. Furthermore, in an ironic twist on the usefulness of the scientific method, these postulates themselves are not testable through the scientific method. Although this foundational paradox has led some to reject the validity of the scientific method, others are prepared to accept, or at least to turn a blind eye to, this incongruity while judging the usefulness of scientific research by its output.

We find that all empirical research is premised on the following six postulates (see Nachmias and Nachmias 1987, 6–9):

1. Nature Is Orderly. Earlier we discussed the characteristic feature of scientific research as centring on cause-and-effect relationships. Such an orientation has meaning only when one accepts the belief that natural phenomena are ordered in causal sequences. The belief that everything has a cause, that nothing is random, is known as **determinism**. In some aspects of our lives, a belief in the ordered sequencing of events is noncontroversial. For example, in baseball we know that a home run ball results from the force of its impact with a baseball bat, which causes the ball to travel over the fence. The scientific method can be used when nature is ordered in such a way, and applying the scientific method to social and political reality implies a belief in a similar type of ordering. It implies, for example, that people do not protest at random or that revolutions do not occur by chance alone. In short, political attitudes, beliefs, and behaviours are not random occurrences. This does not imply, of course, that all people respond identically when faced with similar situations, for we know this is not the case. (One of the reasons for variation may be that people experience similar situations in dissimilar ways; thus, one could say that the situations differ.) Nonetheless, use of the scientific method in political science implies a belief in the causal ordering of social and political reality, even if our understanding of that ordering is very limited at this time.

2. *We Can Know Nature.* The belief that nature is orderly is devoid of empirical implications if the order cannot be revealed to us. Consequently, science postulates that through a rigorous application of the scientific method, the pattern of natural phenomena can be revealed. This belief also implies that no one has a privileged position in the search for knowledge. An awareness of the pattern assumed by a causal relationship does not spring from one's special gifts of perception, nor is the structure of reality divinely revealed. Instead, knowledge about nature is available in equal measure to anyone and everyone. Furthermore, such knowledge results from an application of the scientific method, not from the personal characteristics of the observer. Some may use that method with greater precision, insight, or creativity than others, but it is ultimately the method itself that reveals the patterned structures of natural and social phenomena.

3. *Knowledge Is Superior to Ignorance.* The third postulate of science, that knowledge is superior to ignorance, is based on the assumption that our awareness of the world around us can be one of two types: we can be ignorant about that reality or about the underlying causes of that reality, or we can understand them correctly and have knowledge of them. Ignorance of reality is a recipe for superstition about cause and effect and an invitation to paralysis in the face of social problems. The position of science is that it is always preferable to have a correct understanding of nature than to misunderstand it. Part of the reason for this is that if one wishes to alter the present or future reality, one must at a minimum understand how that might be achieved. For example, a strategist for a political party could increase her party's standing in the electorate only if she correctly understands why people support one party over another. A further reason for the superiority of knowledge to ignorance is the belief that knowledge and understanding can be ends in themselves. Knowledge is important not only because it is instrumental in helping us solve problems; we believe that knowledge is desirable in and of itself. A greater understanding of our world and environment, be it social, political, physical, intellectual, or otherwise, is believed to be part of the task of being human.

4. *Natural Phenomena Have Natural Causes.* The fourth postulate of science is that natural phenomena have natural causes. Another way of describing this is to say that those aspects of social and political reality that we can perceive can be explained by other things that we can perceive. The postulate holds that attitudes and behaviour in the natural world are not produced by supernatural, or spiritual, forces. Thus, once again, all observers can equally observe the natural world as well as the causal influences within the natural world. As Agent Scully observed on the 1990s television series *The X-Files*, 'nothing happens in contradiction to nature, only in contradiction to what we know of it.'[2]

If it is true that all natural phenomena have natural causes, then one might ask, 'Why have we not been able to isolate these causes more completely and strengthen our lawlike generalizations?' The reasons for this are complex and will be discussed at many places throughout this book. It should only be noted at this point that one of the most important reasons for the limited success of the social sciences to date concerns problems of measurement and measurement error. There are some aspects of the natural world that cannot be measured very accurately or reliably; thus, their linkage to social and political behaviour remains highly underdeveloped. In other cases, our knowledge is simply too incomplete. For example, the importance of DNA in the inheritance of physical characteristics is well known. Yet at this time we do not know the degree to which one's attitudinal and behavioural characteristics are transmitted through DNA. Is there a genetic link in the development of political ideologies? In participatory strategies? In aggressive behaviour? We do not know the answer because essential research has not yet been completed, although research has begun. For example, political scientist James Fowler and his team are researching genetics and voting behaviour. As *Scientific American* (2007) reports, 'Their analysis of voting histories for 326 identical and 196 fraternal twins suggests that genetics was responsible for 60 percent of differences in voting turnout between twin types, with the rest coming from environmental or other factors.'

A second question that arises from the postulate of natural phenomena having natural causes is the role of spirituality in the uncovering of nature. Does one have to be an atheist to use the scientific method? The answer is no. Although it is possible to interpret the scientific method, and in particular this fourth postulate of science, as a denial of God, one could also understand the divine presence as providing the limits of the scientific method. This latter view sees divine presence as part of the residual category in scientific research. A **residual** is everything outside the explanatory factors in a model. Thus, spiritual factors are included along with other influences that cannot be identified, isolated, and measured as causal influences. To identify the impact of spiritual or divine phenomena, one would need to use a research method other than the scientific method. At this time, the residual element in our understanding of the social and political worlds is immense and thus provides ample room for spirituality to be brought into play.

5. *Nothing Is Self-Evident.* The postulate that nothing is self-evident is an affirmation that knowledge is not derived *a priori* or by intuition. Everything is subject to empirical testing through the scientific method. This idea that nothing is self-evident was captured eloquently by René Descartes, a sixteenth-century philosopher and one of the founders of the scientific method. Descartes began his inquiry by denying the existence of everything and then accepting only those propositions that could be *proven* to be true. He went so far as to deny his own existence until it could be proven otherwise. Descartes's proof of his existence was expressed in his famous assertion, 'I think, therefore I am.' That is to say, because I am doing human things, like thinking, therefore I am human and my existence is confirmed,

although others challenged the logic of his demonstration. Another way to think about this postulate is to assume that nothing is beyond scientific investigation. There are no aspects of the natural world, including the social and political world, that are outside the domain of science. Nothing is off-limits. Whether the area of inquiry relates to the causes of war, the development of political ideologies, the stability of government, or the determinants of political participation, the scientific method can be used in uncovering the natural order. Furthermore, science challenges other ways of knowing, such as knowledge gained through communication with supernatural forces, as invalid. If knowledge is not subject to the rules of science, which in turn make it available to all who apply those rules, then it is rejected.

6. *Knowledge Is Derived from the Acquisition of Experience*. The last postulate of science is that knowledge is acquired through a continuous application of the scientific method. It stems from repeated observation, careful testing, and a replication of the results under varying conditions. This postulate would also seem to imply that scientific knowledge is cumulative, each step building upon preceding steps. However, there are several alternative views about the advancement of knowledge. One is that the development of scientific thought is paradigmatic, that it comes by leaps and bounds rather than by gradual, incremental change. A paradigm is a body of knowledge within which investigators agree on the general ordering of nature. Some suggest that advances in science come about as monumental shifts in paradigms; one worldview is replaced by another when incremental gains in new knowledge gradually erode existing paradigms to the point of collapse. Paradigm shifts often entail a considerable amount of struggle against an established orthodoxy until a new view ultimately prevails.[3] This suggests that there is always a prevailing view within the scientific community, and individuals either subscribe to that view and conduct 'normal science' or fight to replace that view, while struggling against the institutional strength of the orthodox paradigm. (Postmodernists, for example, would see themselves as struggling against the positivist paradigm embedded in this text.) A second argument is that scientific advances themselves tend to be random occurrences and that science is more often characterized by disorder than by order. Nonetheless, whether scientific advances occur through cumulative incremental change, paradigm shifts, or at random, there is a general agreement that the critical factor is the accumulated experience that accompanies the continual application of the scientific method.

Summary: Basic Postulates of Science

1. Nature is orderly.
2. We can know nature.
3. Knowledge is superior to ignorance.
4. Natural phenomena have natural causes.
5. Nothing is self-evident.
6. Knowledge is derived from the acquisition of experience.

EXPAND YOUR KNOWLEDGE

Thomas Kuhn and *The Structure of Scientific Revolutions*

Thomas Kuhn's publication *The Structure of Scientific Revolutions*, first published in 1960 and then republished in 1970, had a profound and far-reaching impact on our understanding of the social dynamics of knowledge in both the natural and social sciences. Kuhn argued that while science routinely progressed through incremental, piecemeal increases in knowledge—what he calls normal science—incrementalism does not account for major paradigm shifts such as that from an Earth-centred to a Sun-centred solar system and from Newtonian physics to quantum mechanics. These paradigm shifts, which were indeed revolutionary, could be understood only by looking at the sociology of knowledge. Knowledge, in other words, is socially constructed; we see the world not only through our instruments but also through paradigms that are the products of complex social, cultural, and political interactions. Paradigm shifts do not emerge effortlessly from incremental change but rather are the consequence of power struggles between competing paradigms and the proponents of such paradigms. He writes: 'a new theory, however special its range of application, is seldom or never just an increment to what is already known. Its assimilation requires the reconstruction of prior theory and the re-evaluation of prior fact, an intrinsically revolutionary process that is seldom completed by a single man and never overnight' (1970, 7).

Kuhn's work changed the way in which we see science and thus in itself constitutes a paradigm shift of far-reaching proportions.

THE METHODOLOGY OF SCIENCE

Thus far in our discussion we have insisted on the need to use the scientific method to acquire knowledge about nature, including knowledge about the nature of social and political life. This empirical approach can be used to gain knowledge about things as they are, which is to say, knowledge of social and political reality. Such empirical knowledge can be contrasted with normative knowledge, or knowledge about things as they ought to be or as we would wish them to be. This contrast in the study of politics is usually reflected in the differences between political philosophy and empirical political science. Political philosophy typically focuses on normative questions: What is the good life? What is the meaning of justice? What is the most desirable social order? It often focuses on questions of what is right and wrong, good and bad. Empirical political science, in contrast, is generally more concerned with discovering why things are as they are. Why are some countries more stable than others? More successful at managing their national economy than others? Why do people vote as they do? Although values may underlie some questions of empirical research (for instance, the researcher might prefer political stability to instability, or he may prefer lower unemployment to lower inflation), the research itself cannot and does not claim to provide insight into normative issues. Empirical research cannot be used to conclude that increased inflation is superior to increased unemployment, although it could draw out some of the implications of either event or reveal who has the power to impose their preferred policy options. One can use the results of empirical research to pursue preferred policy outcomes, but the preferences for outcomes are themselves not empirically derived.

The methodology of science is a set of sequential steps that guide the research enterprise. Because all scientific research uses these essential steps, any particular research project is linked by the scientific method to the larger research enterprise. In beginning a project, therefore, it is useful to think of oneself as part of a broader research community, with your research building on previous research in a particular area and representing a continuation of investigations into that topic. Likewise, the research that you produce is also subject to further replication, and subsequent research may either reject or accept the conclusions drawn in your study. Note, however, that your conclusions cannot be *proven* by subsequent research.

Steps in the Scientific Method

1. *Identify the Problem.* All scientific research begins with a problem, which involves variation on some outcome or event. Why do some people support sovereignty in Quebec while others are opposed? Why do people support some parties rather than others? Why do some people calculate their income tax honestly and others cheat? Why are some countries more stable than others? When does conflict escalate into war? The 'problem', or the outcome, in social scientific research is called the dependent event and is measured by the **dependent variable**. It is the thing we are trying to explain.

The dependent event has a number of important features. First, it must contain sufficient variation that can be explained. If all people thought alike or behaved alike, or if all countries behaved alike, there would be little for social science to explain. Fortunately, human attitudes and behaviour are full of inconsistencies and variability, thus making social and political relations fertile ground for scientific research. Nonetheless, it is important in identifying the problem to explore in your research that you cast the problem in such a way that you highlight the variation you wish to explain. Second, the dependent event must be susceptible to a clear definition, and it must be measurable. These topics and the problems associated with them are discussed in detail in Chapters 3 and 4. For the moment, it should be recognized that empirical research requires that the dependent event be defined with enough precision and specificity that it can be linked to previous research. Likewise, the dependent variable must be measured in such a way that other researchers are able to replicate your study. As we will see, the issues of concept definition and operational measurement can create serious difficulties in empirical research, making close attention to these issues an essential component of useful and generalizable findings.

2. *Hypothesize the Cause of the Problem.* The goal of empirical research is to explain variation with respect to the dependent event. One can begin to explain the dependent event by proposing, or hypothesizing, causes of the observed variation across cases or across time. Hypothesized causes are called independent concepts and are measured by **independent variables.** The word 'independent' implies that the variation in this concept is independent of, or not caused by, variation in the dependent event. The relationship between independent and dependent variables is hypothesized to be a causal sequence from the independent to the dependent variable, and not vice versa. A hypothesis is an expected or proposed relationship of the type 'A causes B'.

For example, it has often been observed that older people are more likely than younger people to hold conservative political views. Thus, there is a relationship, or **correlation**, between age and political thinking. Since empirical research is concerned with identifying causal relationships, it is necessary to ask which of these factors is the independent variable and which is dependent. In this case, it seems fairly obvious that political ideology cannot affect chronological age. One does not become older if one becomes more conservative. Therefore, to the extent that there is a causal relationship between age and ideology, age must be the independent variable and ideology the dependent variable. Right? Not necessarily. Social and political phenomena are often bound together in highly complex relationships. To continue with this example, some research has shown that affluence is negatively related to mortality rates (more affluent people live longer) and to ideology (they are also more conservative). Thus, it may be that age and ideology are related, but not according to the simple 'aging' hypothesis offered above. It may be that mortality rates are different for groups that fall predominantly into left-wing and right-wing camps (affluent versus nonaffluent). Those to the right tend to outlive those to the left, although this does not mean that you can extend your lifespan by changing your political beliefs. Therefore, there are more conservative old people not because they have changed their ideology, but because of the presence of a third variable, mortality rates.

An important component of proposing a causal hypothesis is to identify the theory that underlies the effect of the independent concept on the dependent event. When we speak of 'theory' in this sense we refer to generalized statements about the causes of attitudes or behaviour. An example may help illustrate the point. Suppose we want to explain why people voted Conservative, Liberal, New Democrat, Bloc Québécois, Green, or something else (including abstainers) in the last federal election. How do we explain variation on voting preference? One of the first things we must do is decide which theory of political choice will guide our research. One theory is that voting in Canada is determined mostly by short-term factors and is therefore very unstable. An alternative theory is that people hold relatively firm political allegiances, and voting is characterized more by stability than by change. Of course, it is possible to design a research project that tests both of those theories.

Nonetheless, it should be obvious that the selection of independent variables will depend heavily upon which theory one is testing.

3. *Provide Clear Definitions of the Concepts.* **Concepts** are abstractions used to describe the characteristics of a group or an individual case according to a given criterion or quality. Empirical research begins and ends at the abstract, conceptual level in which generalizations are made about social and political life. Some of the concepts that traditionally interest political scientists include, among many others, political participation, social class, political stability, ideology, conflict, and political culture. To conduct research on any of these topics, one must be prepared to define with a great deal of precision the characteristics or features of that abstraction. Most readers are probably not surprised to learn that there can be considerable disagreement within the scholarly community about the meaning of many concepts. For example, one study reported that the concept 'culture' had been defined in more than 250 different ways (Eulau 1963) and that study itself does not reflect a wealth of conceptual development over the past five decades.

An example can illustrate the difficulties that arise when trying to get researchers to agree on the meaning of concepts. Consider the concept of political participation. Several questions emerge when we attempt to define this important concept. Is political participation one thing, or is it a bundle of quite different activities? Do participatory activities differ in degree or in kind? That is, should participatory activities be thought of as being more or less participation or as different types or modes of activities? How far does the domain of the term 'political' extend? Is political participation limited to electoral participation, or does it include other activities that can influence political decision-making? Does it include volunteer work for a community association or women's shelter? What about strikes and work stoppages? Are activities directed in the first instance at private market-oriented actors included as political participation? What about strikes among public sector workers or among those employed by Crown corporations or mixed enterprises? Is there a difference between legal and illegal forms of political participation? Empirical political scientists, together with Canadians more generally, may disagree in their answers to these questions. For researchers, those differences are likely to be reflected in different definitions of the concepts under study.

The problem for social science research more generally is that it is difficult to advance our knowledge and understanding of a concept when researchers are working with different definitions. At the same time, it is not possible to 'require' that researchers agree on common definitions. Part of the research enterprise itself is to provide the intellectual freedom for researchers to pursue research in a manner that they themselves define as suitable and appropriate. The requirement to publicize the results of one's research in independent, peer-reviewed journals and books ensures to a degree that researchers are held accountable for their research decisions. It also emphasizes once again the importance of the idea of a scholarly community conducting a common research enterprise.

4. *Operationalize the Concepts.* An empirical research project moves from the general or conceptual level to the specific and concrete. This movement from concepts to variables is called **operationalization.** It involves obtaining a specific measurement of the concepts with respect to the data that have been collected. More specifically, it involves assigning a numerical score on a variable to each case in the data set. For some concepts the process is straightforward and noncontroversial. The concept of sex is a good example of a simple concept for most research. Typically, the researcher thinks of sex as being a dichotomous variable, and respondents are scored as male or female. This standard view assumes that people are differentiated into either of two distinct categories. However, this dichotomy may be too simplistic. For example, it is well known that all humans possess both masculine and feminine hormones. Although, in general, men have more masculine hormones and women have more feminine hormones, some men have more masculine hormones than other men, while some women have more feminine hormones than other women. When one considers sex in these more biological terms, it becomes a continuous variable with everyone having a specific mixture of masculine and feminine aspects. If we turn from sex to *gender,* the measurement situation becomes considerably more complex. Gender is a more socially constructed concept than is sex and, as a consequence, defies simple dichotomization.

Other concepts may be even more intractable in operationalizing because of their multidimensionality. The concept itself may be a combination of attributes on several different criteria. Political participation appears to be a multidimensional concept because of the distinct ways that one can participate in politics. Social class would have a strong claim on multidimensionality because of the different components of the social hierarchy and the variation that may exist across those components, complexities discussed more fully in Chapters 4 and 5. At this stage the key thing to remember is that a variable should reflect as closely as possible the abstract concept that it represents. Recall that research begins and ends at the conceptual level; the conclusions will relate to the abstract concept and not to the particular variable that was used in this single study. To the extent that the variable does not accurately reflect the concept, then the conclusions derived from the research will be distorted.

5. *Gather Empirical Data.* All empirical research includes a test of a hypothesis. This test requires that data be collected on both the independent and dependent variables, as well as on intervening variables, or those that cause a spurious relationship (the latter two types are discussed more fully in Chapter 2). There are many different types of data and research design strategies that can be used in the data collection phase. In Chapters 8 through 13 the methodologies involving survey research, population data, content analysis, experimental design, interviews and other data collection strategies are discussed at length. There is no single right or wrong approach to data-gathering; each method has its advantages and disadvantages. The key consideration for any researcher is to gather data that best

suit the purposes of her specific research questions. Faculty members and students alike often find it expedient and cost-effective to conduct *secondary analysis* on data that have already been gathered by other researchers. In view of the wealth of such data today, as well as their ready accessibility through data libraries and archives, this strategy is also becoming increasingly attractive to all researchers.

6. *Test the Hypothesis or Hypotheses.* One of the defining characteristics of scientific research is that hypotheses are **falsifiable**. It must be possible, through both the logic of analysis and the design of the research, to demonstrate the absence of a causal relationship between the concepts being examined. If it is not possible to disprove the hypothesized relationship, then the research cannot claim to have been conducted scientifically. Although the emphasis during the research design portion of a research project is on developing and justifying hypotheses about the causal relationship between concepts, the emphasis shifts during the empirical part of the project.

Empirical testing requires that the research hypothesis is inverted, or is replaced by its opposite, called the **null hypothesis**. The null hypothesis states that the two concepts, or variables, are independent of each other and are not causally related. While researchers typically expect the null hypothesis to be false and the research hypothesis to be true, the empirical test is conducted on the null hypothesis for an important reason. The research hypothesis can never be proven to be true; although data can and often do support the research hypothesis, they never prove it unequivocally. This is because another experiment or another empirical test could provide a context in which the hypothesis is disproved. Thus, research hypotheses can be disproved by a single test, whereas they cannot be proven even with a large number of repeated tests. The null hypothesis, on the other hand, is either *accepted* or *rejected*. The null hypothesis that there is no causal relationship between two variables is accepted if an empirical test shows they are independent. Likewise, the null hypothesis is rejected if the empirical test reveals that the variables are related to each other. Therefore, testing hypotheses involves deciding whether to accept or reject the null hypothesis, a matter discussed at greater length in the next chapter.

Recall at this point that the researcher is conducting a single empirical test on a hypothesized relationship between two variables. The research is important but not so much for what it reveals about the particular variables in the time and place at which the data were gathered. Instead, it is important to the degree to which the variables represent more general concepts in a more generalized temporal and spatial dimension. We can think about the generalized setting as representing the true relationship between concepts. The empirical test is taken as a measure or proxy of that true relationship.

7. *Reflect Back on Theory.* When drawing conclusions about the research, one moves back once again from the operational level to the conceptual level. Variables are recast in their generalized form, and conclusions are drawn about the nature of the causal relationships. At this stage, the researcher is able to evaluate the theoretical

aspects of the research in light of the empirical evidence. Were the hypotheses confirmed? Which hypotheses and in what ways? What are the implications for the theoretical underpinnings of the study? Does the theory need revision in light of the research? What generalizations can be drawn from the study? Are there policy implications from the results of the research? In what direction should future research in this area be pursued? Remember that one of the chief goals of empirical research is to draw lawlike generalizations about social and political phenomena. These generalized statements find reflection in the theories developed to understand and explain politics. The later stages of empirical research, therefore, require that one step back from the specific empirical findings and reflect upon the more general patterns of interaction and causality. The continual process of testing, refining, and adjusting theoretical statements of causality forms an essential step in the ongoing research enterprise.

8. *Publicize the Results*. An old saying around universities is that one must either publish or perish. Like many such aphorisms, there is more than a grain of truth to this saying. The weight of one's scholarly publications is the key indicator of academic performance at many universities, and a full curriculum vitae is often richly rewarded. However, although publication certainly fulfils an important institutional function, it serves the more important function of enabling the scholarly community to engage in an ongoing research dialogue. Indeed, one of the responsibilities of researchers is to engage in this dialogue. It is necessary not only to maintain an active research agenda but also to place the results of those efforts into the public domain for debate, discussion, challenge, and verification.

All levels of scholarly inquiry have outlets for such dialogue. For undergraduate students the dialogue typically occurs between student and course instructor. Part of the learning process at universities is to accept criticisms of your work, and part of the responsibility of instructors is to provide criticism of students' work in a way that strengthens and improves research. For graduate students, the feedback from course instructors is supplemented with feedback from their supervisory committees on independent or quasi-independent research projects in the form of master's theses or doctoral dissertations. For research scholars, including professors, the outlets for publicizing the results of research include scholarly journals, research institute monographs, public lectures or displays, and books. Typically, it is expected that the prepublication stage includes some form of blind **peer evaluation process**.

9. *Replicate the Results*. The final step in the process of empirical research is to repeat the study by using either the same data or data gathered at a different time or in a different setting. This is known as replication. Since the goal of empirical research is to draw lawlike generalizations, research results are valuable to the extent that they can be generalized. If similar empirical tests conducted at other times and places fail to produce the same result, one is not able to generalize from the initial test. The importance of replication also reinforces and highlights

the need for researchers to systematically and completely describe each stage of the analysis, from the design of the study to defining concepts, gathering data, operationalizing measures, testing the relationships, and drawing conclusions. Only then can the research be replicated and each stage of the research opened to critical examination.

Summary: Steps in the Scientific Method

1. Identify the problem.
2. Hypothesize the cause of the problem.
3. Provide clear definitions of the concepts.
4. Operationalize the concepts.
5. Gather empirical data.
6. Test the hypothesis or hypotheses.
7. Reflect back on theory.
8. Publicize the results.
9. Replicate the results.

APPLY YOUR UNDERSTANDING

Youth and Political Participation

You are a researcher looking at the question, 'Do young people participate politically at levels lower than the rest of the population?' What concepts need to be defined before you begin your study? How would you define them? If you do find that young people participate less, what reasons might explain this difference?

EXPAND YOUR KNOWLEDGE

Federal Theory and Empirical Research

Canadian scholars of federalism, and particularly one the country's leading scholars in the field, Alan Cairns, have argued that the passage of the 1982 Charter of Rights and Freedoms had a pervasive and even profound impact on the Canadian political culture. The effect has been to heighten the political identities and influence of those groups able to claim constitutional status through their recognition within the Charter. These 'Charter Canadians' have changed the nature of constitutional discourse, disrupted executive federalism, and enhanced the role of the courts in the definition and

(continued)

application of public policy. This theoretical contribution by Cairns has been accepted as close to dogma by many students of Canadian federalism.

Others, however, have argued that while these changes may indeed have occurred, it is a mistake to attribute them to the introduction of the Charter. Instead, and drawing upon the postmaterialism theorizing of Ronald Inglehart, it is suggested that these changes in Canadian politics reflect broad patterns of social and ideological change that have swept across all Western democracies since the end of World War II. Those individuals coming of age in the era of postwar affluence, Inglehart argues, are less concerned about material well-being and success and are more concerned with aesthetic values and self-expression. The idiosyncratic effects of the Charter, therefore, pale beside the impact of these broader currents of postmaterial change. (Note that **postmaterialism** is not the same as postmodernism.)

This challenge to the Charter thesis was put to an empirical test by Ian Brodie and Neil Nevitte (1993). Employing data from the 1981 and 1990 World Values Surveys, they found that their "new politics theory" outperformed the "citizens' constitution theory" of Cairns when it came to explaining such things as confidence in political and legal institutions. Their article and the rejoinder by Cairns (1993) provide a useful illustration of the dynamic interplay of theory and empirical data.

CRITICISMS AND LIMITATIONS OF THE SCIENTIFIC APPROACH TO POLITICS

We noted earlier in the chapter that the scientific approach is also known as positivism. It should be mentioned that some people argue that the scientific approach has limited utility for the study of society and politics and recommend alternative approaches to replace positivism. Recall that positivism assumes that reality can be measured empirically, that measurements can be made objectively, and that nature is orderly—every effect has a cause, every event is determined by a prior event. It is these three ideas—empiricism, objectivity, and determinism—that have been subject to criticism. Fortunately, the criticism has been largely constructive; by pointing out the weaknesses of the scientific model, the critics encouraged positivist researchers to refine and adapt their methods.

Many people have difficulty applying the idea of determinism to human behaviour, and for good reason. Determinism suggests that there exists no choice, while most of us know that humans have free will. A pencil has no choice but to submit to the force of gravity; we, on the other hand, have control over our thoughts, feelings, attitudes, and behaviour. Thus, we cannot with certainty predict the actions or reactions of an individual. However, when we look at aggregates of individuals— groups—we can often make generalizations. Social scientists have been able to note *patterns* in human behaviour, patterns that are linked to outside phenomena. For example, we may find that most people whose parents are liberal are also liberal; thus parental ideological views influence those of the child. At the same time, there are always some people who do not fit the pattern: some children of liberals are conservative. Having a liberal parent will increase one's probability of being liberal but does not determine liberalism.

A second criticism is that not all aspects of reality can be empirically measured. How does one measure beliefs, thoughts, and attitudes? We cannot get inside people's heads and see exactly what is going on; therefore, we must rely on the information they give us, either through their words or their actions. Even when we can access information about beliefs, there are difficulties in quantifying such beliefs and comparing this information across individuals. Did Bob and Sue mean the same thing when they each classified themselves as 'highly religious'? Are our subjects being honest with us—and with themselves—when they respond to controversial questions? There are many practical difficulties in measuring reality, and we continually need to ask ourselves if we are in fact measuring what we believe we are measuring. These difficulties, moreover, go well beyond measurement error; they also include disagreements about the meaning of such terms as full employment, unemployment, pay equity, and democratic government. This issue is known as **validity** and will be explored further in Chapter 4. The challenge to researchers is to select indicators that most closely tap the concept they wish to measure. In some cases, this can be a difficult task.

The objectivity of the scientific method is also called into question by some critics. It is argued that true neutrality is impossible, that there is no system of study that is value-free. The beliefs and values of the observer will always play a role in the interpretation of the facts, it is argued; thus research always contains a measure of subjectivity. This subjectivity can be positive, since it allows the researcher to be sensitive to the context within which political action (or inaction) occurs, but it can also be the source of inadvertent bias. This criticism is particularly noteworthy for researchers who study a variety of cultures and societies. Political scientists who wish to consider the role of context for their subject often address this criticism by using **qualitative** approaches to their studies. Qualitative research will be explored in depth in Chapter 6.

Other criticisms are more ideological in character. For example, some feminist, postmodern, and class theorists argue that 'positivism defends the status quo because it assumes an unchanging order instead of seeing current society as a particular stage in an ongoing process' (Neuman 1994, 66). Attempts to objectively describe and explain the status quo are seen by some as a defence of the status quo, because there is often an implicit assumption that the identified reality is natural and immune to change. Such criticisms vividly demonstrate the fact that political science (and social science in general) lacks a single paradigm to which all can appeal. There is no common overriding view of how the social world is or of how to best measure that world. Even if we can agree on the principle of causality, there is confusion over what are the important social determinants. Some political economists point to the class system or the structure of the international political economy, feminists point to the gendered nature of social and political institutions, and so on. This poses a serious limitation to the advancement of science: if knowledge is to be cumulative, it requires some degree of paradigm agreement (Baxter-Moore et al. 1994, 88). On the other hand, it can be argued that the variety of approaches to the study of politics is an advantage, since it ensures that a diverse set of perspectives and interpretations of the social world is considered.

In conclusion, we would argue that despite the criticisms noted, the scientific approach to politics is the best means by which we can work to understand the very complex social world around us. Admittedly, political science has far to go; the discipline is just over one hundred years old. Attempts to compare such a 'young' science to 'older' sciences such as biology and physics are perhaps unfair; think of how little was known about the human body when the study of anatomy was in its infancy stages. The goal of our journey is to advance our comprehension of politics and society. Although the final destination, 'truth', may seem far away and beyond our reach, we must keep in mind that we have only really just begun the journey.

APPLY YOUR UNDERSTANDING

Science and Politics

List the pros and cons of using the scientific method in the study of politics. How do the methods and principles of the scientific method fit with your own conception of politics? Can you think of situations in which the scientific method would be particularly appropriate? Particularly inappropriate? How does the study of political and social life differ from the study of the natural world?

WORKING AS A TEAM

1. There are some people who argue that the study of politics, and society in general, can never be considered a 'true' science. They suggest, furthermore, that 'political studies' is a more appropriate label than 'political science'. Do you feel the terms 'social science' and 'political science' are misleading? Can the study of humans in aggregate be a science? What are the pros and cons of 'political science' as the name for our discipline? Can you think of a better or more appropriate name?

2. With your discussion group, consider the advantages and disadvantages of applying the scientific method to the volatile public policy question, 'Should Canadians support capital punishment?' Are there limits to the application of empirical approaches, or can almost all questions benefit from empirical study? What questions do you see as beyond the reach of the scientific method?

SELF-STUDY

1. How might the concept of 'socialism' be approached in normative political analysis? What are the types of questions that might be asked? How might it be approached in empirical political analysis? Again, what questions might be asked? Is either approach superior for increasing our understanding of socialism? What are the strengths and limitations of each? If you were asked to write a term paper on 'socialism in the contemporary world', would you adopt a normative approach, an empirical approach, or some blend of the two? How would you justify your choice?

2. What hypotheses would you advance to explain current levels of electoral support for the federal government? Can you offer five or six competing hypotheses? From where do these hypotheses emerge? From your readings? Political science classes? Your political instincts? Your favourite political blogger? Editorials in the *Globe and Mail*? If you had to rank your hypotheses in order of plausibility, which would strike you as the most compelling? The least compelling? What evidence would you need in order to test these hypotheses and to choose among them?

NOTES

1. The three explanations discussed do not exhaust the range of possible explanations. Comparative research extending beyond the OECD experience could be particularly helpful in revealing other possibilities.

2. October 4, 1996.

3. In the time of Nicolaus Copernicus (1473–1543), challenging the Earth-centred paradigm of contemporary physics could be quite literally a matter of life and death.

Chapter 2

THEORY-ORIENTED RESEARCH AND THE ISSUE OF CAUSALITY

DESTINATION

By the end of this chapter the reader should

- have a sound understanding of the role theory plays in empirical political research;
- know the distinctions between basic and applied research, and inductive and deductive research; and
- appreciate how theories are developed and applied in empirical research and how causal explanations can be both advanced and confused.

When we think of research, most of us picture a laboratory, with men and women in white coats examining test tubes, seeking the cure for cancer, or at least for the common cold. However, as Chapter 1 has argued, the scientific approach can be extended beyond the natural sciences and the laboratory to include the social sciences and the broader social world. In the natural sciences, the scientific approach is used to increase knowledge of the physical world; in the social sciences, it is used to advance knowledge of the social world. This chapter will explore the different research approaches that political scientists use to augment our understanding of politics and society. In particular, the role of theory in political science research will be explored, and within this context we will see why cause-and-effect relationships are difficult to establish in the political realm.

BASIC AND APPLIED RESEARCH

Empirical researchers differ in the reasons they have for conducting studies. Some research is directed at answering specific questions or solving immediate problems. For example, what is the best way to implement a new home-care program? What are the costs and benefits of an employee-training program? How effective has a teenage anti-smoking campaign been? How can a particular political party strengthen its appeal among young voters? When research is directed at finding answers to specific problems, with immediate practical usage, it is known as **applied research**. Examples of applied research include cost-benefit analyses, social impact assessments, needs assessments, and evaluations of existing programs or policies, all of which provide job opportunities for social science graduates. Applied research is frequently used by governments, businesses, marketing agencies, political campaign organizers, hospitals, and educational facilities to help fine-tune their programs, products, and strategies. Given that such agencies must work with limited resources, it is important that their money and time are put to the most effective and efficient usage. Applied research is used to maximize effectiveness and efficiency, and to do so over the short haul.[1]

The federal granting councils (the Social Sciences and Humanities Research Council, the Natural Sciences and Engineering Research Council, and the Canadian Institutes of Health Research), together with the federal and provincial governments, and universities and colleges, have increasingly advocated for the societal mobilization of research conducted in Canada's publicly funded postsecondary institutions. Whether referred to as 'knowledge mobilization' or 'knowledge translation', the goal of such advocacy is to increase the salience of applied research for the benefit of Canadians.

A limitation of applied research is that it is usually descriptive in nature; it indicates how things are but does not explain *why* they are that way. Thus, applied research addresses a single question in a very narrow manner and may fail to advance our knowledge of the larger political and social world. However, the fact that applied research is relatively narrow in scope also may be viewed as an advantage. Since applied research is outcome-oriented, the question posed in an applied research project may be how a general process applies in a particular setting. For example, consider a project whose purpose is to reduce the incidence of gang membership in the downtown east side of Vancouver. The researchers may begin with the general proposition that greater social interaction in a safe and supportive environment reduces the incidence of gang membership among 'at-risk' youth. They may then identify and apply various kinds of opportunities for social interaction among at-risk youth in the downtown east side of Vancouver and assess the effectiveness of each in deterring gang membership. The solutions found in this community, for example, among 15- to 24-year-old males in Vancouver's east side, may not be effective among similar groups of at-risk youth in Calgary, Toronto, Montreal, or Halifax, but the finding that they work among the target group in Vancouver is sufficient. Therefore, the relative limited application of the results to one specific community in this applied research project would be sufficient to justify the research.

Basic research, on the other hand, has as its primary goal the broadening of our understanding of political life. Seeking to advance general knowledge, basic researchers (usually academics) examine theories about politics and attempt to formulate explanations and generalizations by empirically testing hypotheses. For example, basic research might address why there are so few women in elected politics and from this research develop a number of explanations and theories. These explanations are not immediately translated into policies to address the problem, but rather add to our foundational understanding of the impact of gender in the political realm. Basic research is *theory-oriented research,* and much academic research falls into this camp.

Thus, in basic research, knowledge is pursued for the sake of knowledge. This is not to say, however, that basic research does not have practical implications. The ideas that emerge from basic research are frequently utilized in applied research, although the importance of basic research may not immediately be seen. We must remember that knowledge is cumulative and continually advancing. W. Lawrence Neuman notes that 'Today's computers could not exist without the pure research in mathematics conducted over a century ago, for which there was no known practical application at the time' (1994, 21). Over time, 'irrelevant' research findings can have a great impact upon our lives.

Some of the biggest research projects in the history of the Canadian social sciences have combined applied and basic research. In 1989, the Royal Commission on Electoral Reform and Party Financing (the Lortie Commission) launched a sweeping study of campaign-related issues. Twenty-three volumes of research studies, containing more than one hundred separate reports, were published in the early 1990s, and these volumes provided much of the core Canadian political science knowledge in this area at the time and for years to come. The Royal Commission on Aboriginal Peoples, which reported in late 1996, provides another example. Its research reports constitute a massive amount of applied and basic knowledge with respect to Aboriginal peoples. A third example is the Royal Commission on the Future of Health Care (the Romanow Commission, 2002), which was informed by research papers, public opinion analyses, and discussion papers, as well as a series of consultations. In all three cases, the marriage of applied and basic research was complementary and mutually reinforcing.

APPLY YOUR UNDERSTANDING

Basic and Applied Research

Consider that you are gathering documentary evidence in a study of Canada's 'national identity'. What type of questions would you seek to answer if you were conducting basic research? Applied research?

Theory: Relationships between Concepts

As academic researchers, our primary goal is to advance theory. Before discussing how we develop a political theory, we should first consider what exactly a theory is and what elements a theory contains. A **theory** is an integrated set of explanations

EXPAND YOUR KNOWLEDGE

Action Research

When applied research is conducted for social purposes defined a *priori*, it may fall outside our definitions of scientific research. This **action** or **advocacy research** often begins with a premise that one group is socially or economically disadvantaged and proceeds to draw the implications of that disadvantage, or to assume the causes of the disadvantage. For example, for feminist action research, the cause of disadvantage could be the male hegemonic power structure. For Aboriginal action research, the cause of disadvantage could be the Eurocentric, materialistic power structure. For labour action research, the cause of disadvantage may be the corporate power structure. But action research need not be based only on the support of the socially disadvantaged; instead, it could be action research conducted in reaction to the perception of a group receiving too much support. For example, conservative (re)action research could begin from the premise that the government (through the legislature, the courts, or the administration) acts in support of the disadvantaged. Thus, the governmental/interest group power structure may be the source of the problem. Whether action, or advocacy, research stems from the ideological left or right, it is inconsistent with the scientific method to the extent that it violates the fifth postulate of science discussed in Chapter 1, namely, that nothing is self-evident. If something is taken as an empirical fact, it must be demonstrably true. In other words, a demonstration of the sources of power must be a part of the overall research enterprise.

of the political and social worlds. We attempt to understand the complex political world by simplifying reality into theories. A theory identifies a general pattern of behaviour, and from these generalizations we can both make predictions and empirically test hypotheses derived from the theory. For example, we might theorize that support for ideological conservatism varies with social economic status. From this we can make predictions, for instance, expecting two individuals with differing social economic status to show dissimilar support for a conservative party, and we can test the theory with empirical data by seeing if the generalizations fit with our observations. As Jarol B. Manheim and Richard C. Rich note, '[t]heories are simply intellectual tools . . . theories are neither true nor false in any absolute sense, but only more or less useful' (1981, 17). Thus, basic research is continually testing hypotheses based on theories to maximize their explanatory power.

Hypotheses are statements of the relationships between concepts, or more specifically, are proposed explanations for an observable phenomenon. Thus, for example, one can hypothesize that an increase in political interest leads to an increase in political participation. A **proposition**, on the other hand, states that if the hypothesis is true, then the following predicate of a subject also is either true or false. Continuing with the example above, the following proposition can be stated: if an increase in political interest leads to an increase in political participation, then Canadians with a high level of political interest will display relatively high levels of political participation (that is, relative to Canadians as a whole). Therefore, the proposition follows from the hypothesis. However, whether the hypothesis is true or false is not known and will be known only after empirical analysis is conducted.

A **concept** is a defined term that enables us to organize and classify phenomena. Politician, region, discrimination, power, income, and sexism are all examples of concepts. Obviously, a concept can be either concrete or abstract, which means that some concepts require more elaborate definitions than others if they are to be measured. For example, age is a simple concept; a person's age is equal to the present year less the year they were born. Equality, on the other hand, is a very complex idea, and political scientists differ in how they define this concept. It should also be noted that many concepts have built-in assumptions about how people interact (Neuman 1994, 37). For example, the concept of sexual discrimination assumes (1) that people distinguish between men and women and (2) that these distinctions influence how they behave. If sex is relevant in hiring, and if one sex is preferred over the other, then sexual discrimination occurs. If an assumption is not upheld—if sex is irrelevant in hiring decisions—sexual discrimination does not exist.

In addition to allowing us to classify phenomena, concepts enable us to make comparisons through categorization. Categories designate the *variation* that occurs within a concept. Income can be classified as high, medium, or low; religion can be classified as Protestant, Catholic, Jewish, Muslim, Hindu, Buddhist, or other. All concepts contain a degree of variation; thus, when we measure concepts empirically, we refer to them as **variables.** We are able to see variation in a concept by identifying the different values, or categories, that exist.

The simplest way to classify concepts with discrete values is to identify the dominant categories that exist within the concept, that is, identify the significant points where variation occurs. An example of this treatment is seen in Max Weber's theory of authority. Weber argued that there exist three types of authority: charismatic, traditional, and legal. Charismatic authority is derived from the unique qualities of an individual leader. Traditional authority derives from established patterns: doing things in a certain way because they have always been done that way. Legal authority derives from the legal specification of the duties (Albrow 1970, 37–40).

When classifying ordinal variables, we often use a **continuum.** We order values of the concept along a dimension, ranging from low to high or from less to more. In his classic work, *An Economic Theory of Democracy* (1957), Anthony Downs arranged political ideologies along a single-dimension continuum. This 'left–right spectrum' organizes political ideologies in terms of positions toward the desired role of the state in the economy. Socialism is located to the left on this spectrum, liberalism is positioned in the centre, and conservatism to the right. Downs argued that both political parties and individuals can be located on the spectrum; in fact, a party's location is dependent upon where voters are located. Parties seek to maximize the number of votes they receive and therefore position themselves at the point on the ideological spectrum where the greatest number of voters is located.

EXPAND YOUR KNOWLEDGE

The Conventional Left–Right Spectrum

Left -- **Centre** ------------------------------- **Right**

Full government ownership of the means of production	No government ownership of the means of production
Extensive government regulation	No government regulation
Extensive redistribution of income	No redistribution of income

There are other means of classifying concepts that should be considered. The **ideal type** is one such means. In this approach a nonexistent ideal is outlined, and observed cases are then compared with this ideal. An example would be Weber's ideal type bureaucracy, organized hierarchically with all rules, procedures, and responsibilities defined impartially (Albrow 1970, 37–40). Although Weber does not suggest that the ideal type bureaucracy exists in reality, it does serve as a model against which to compare existing organizational systems. A final means of classifying concepts is the **typology** (Manheim and Rich 1981, 171), wherein the relationship between two or more concepts is expressed in a way that leads to the creation of new concepts (Neuman 1994, 38). One well-known typology in political science is Aristotle's typology of regimes. Political systems are divided along two dimensions: the number of rulers and the beneficiaries. Note that each of these two concepts has categories of its own: 'number of rulers' takes three values (one, few, many), while 'beneficiaries' has two values (citizens and rulers). The resultant categories—monarchy, tyranny, aristocracy, oligarchy, polity, and democracy—are the different values of the concept 'regime'.

We have outlined concepts and the different means for classifying values within a concept. In addition to concepts, a theory requires relationships, or **correlations**, between concepts. Two concepts are correlated if a change in one occurs when there

EXPAND YOUR KNOWLEDGE

Aristotle's Typology of Regimes

Number of Rulers	Beneficiary	
	All Citizens	**Rulers**
One	Monarchy	Tyranny
Few	Aristocracy	Oligarchy
Many	Polity	Democracy

Source: Nicolas Baxter-Moore, Terrance Carroll, and Roderick Church, *Studying Politics: An Introduction to Argument and Analysis* (Toronto: Copp Clark Longman Ltd., 1994).

is a change in the other. For example, age and voting are correlated if people of different ages tend to vote for different parties. Variations occur simultaneously within each concept; thus, the two are said to *covary*. However, a theory does not just state that concepts are correlated, but also indicates the *direction* of the correlation. A **positive correlation** occurs when an increase in value in one concept is accompanied by an increase in the value in the other concept. Similarly, a decrease in the value in one concept is accompanied by a decrease in the value in the

APPLY YOUR UNDERSTANDING

Examples of Theory

Consider the two political science theories that follow. For each, identify the key concepts and the key propositions (relationships between the concepts). Which has a broader scope?

Michels's Iron Law of Oligarchy

Robert Michels, a loyal socialist, studied the inner dynamics of the German Social Democratic Party. Although the party was committed to participatory decision-making, Michels (1962) found that within the party a leadership elite emerged. He reasoned that this was due to the need for organization: in order for a political party to operate efficiently, an elite must emerge to take charge and keep the party on track. Michels also found that the leadership elite often pursued its own interests, rather than those of the party as a whole; in other words, an oligarchy had emerged. Given that a revolutionary democratic party was the last place Michels expected to find self-interested leadership, he concluded that *any* need for organization will be met by the creation of oligarchies, despite contrary claims of democracy: 'the government, or . . . the state, cannot be anything other than the organization of a minority . . . and can never

be truly representative of the majority. The majority is thus permanently incapable of self-government' (1962, 351). He summarizes this process in the statement, 'Who says organization says oligarchy.' This broad assertion is known as the 'iron law of oligarchy'.

Brodie and Jenson's 'Defining the Political' Theory

There are a number of different approaches to the study of political party development. In the mobilization approach, parties 'are strategic actors engaged in defining the issues of importance in political conflict and in mobilizing voters behind their issue positions' (Archer et al. 1995, 417). This theory is put forward by Janine Brodie and Jane Jenson (1980), who argue that Canadian political parties have effectively written social class out of the political realm. Political parties are able to control what social cleavages are seen as 'important' through the issues they champion. By refusing to focus on issues of social class, the Canadian parties, including the CCF (Co-operative Commonwealth Federation)/NDP, keep class issues from becoming politically relevant. It is in this way that political parties 'define the political'.

other. Thus, the direction of change is the same on each variable. If voter turnout increases when age increases, this is a positive correlation. A **negative correlation** indicates that the direction of change is inverse: an increase on one concept is related to a decrease on the other. A negative correlation does *not* mean that there is no relationship between the two variables; negative refers to the direction rather than the existence of the relationship. To return to the previous example, a negative correlation between voting turnout and age would occur if an increase in age accompanies a decrease in voting. Of course, in order for a relationship to have direction, it must be possible to order the values of the concepts involved. When *either* of the concepts in a relationship cannot be ordered (when either is measured by a nominal variable; see p. 77 for a discussion of nominal, ordinal and interval variables), the correlation cannot have direction. In such cases, we simply note that the concepts, for example, voter turnout and religious affiliation, are correlated.

Overall, a hypothesis will state the relationships between concepts by providing a statement of the *proposed cause* of an observable phenomenon, and the underlying theory will attempt to explain *why* these relationships exist. A proposition is then a statement of fact that follows from the accuracy of the hypothesis, such that if the hypothesis is true, then the following condition will prevail. Some theories are quite broad in scope, making sweeping generalizations about social and political life. Other theories are less ambitious, seeking, for example, to explain events in a single country rather than all countries.

DEVELOPING AND TESTING THEORIES

How does one develop a theory? There are two approaches: inductive and deductive. **Inductive** approaches move from data to theory: we begin by observing the world and from our observations develop generalizations and conclusions. For example, if we observe that members of the Canadian Union of Public Employees (CUPE) are more likely than nonmembers to support the NDP, we might generalize that union membership is correlated with ideological position. (The validity of such generalizations may depend upon the specific union to which members belong; members of the Canadian Auto Workers may be different from CUPE members.) Induction, then, involves the progression from empirical evidence to generalization. Inductive research is often exploratory: we begin with an open mind and look for patterns in behaviour. An example of inductive theorizing is seen in Alexis de Tocqueville's *Democracy in America* (1863). Tocqueville visited the United States to assess the desirability of the republican system for France. He found that America was characterized by social equality (a lack of aristocracy) and political equality. However, the high levels of equality were correlated with mediocre leadership: the popularly elected representatives were not the best and the brightest men in the country. Tocqueville feared that the love for equality and majority rule would lead to the 'tyranny of the majority', in which majority interests are pursued at the expense of minority liberties. Tocqueville concluded by theorizing that increased levels of political equality lead to decreased leadership quality and that democracy threatens the rights and liberties of minorities. Thus, Tocqueville began with an observation and from that observation generalized about the nature of democracy.

Deductive theorizing moves the other way, from the general to the specific. We are engaging in deductive research when we begin with specific assumptions, or hypotheses, and set out to test them in the real world. For example, we may assume that union members will support left-wing parties because of common policy agendas. This proposition leads us to gather data to see if our theory holds: we might survey union members and ask their ideological position or test the degree to which supporters of left-wing parties are sympathetic to concerns of union members, such as the right to collective bargaining. If the evidence confirms our hypothesis, then our theory is supported. Deductive research is often referred to as **hypothesis-testing**, discussed in more detail later in this chapter. Obviously, deductive research requires that we have a source for our assumptions. Sometimes our source is merely logic: the theory makes sense. Other times, our source is pre-existing research or theorizing: the literature suggests that a relationship or pattern exists, and we seek empirical evidence to test it. Take, for example, Tocqueville's theory that democracy is correlated with mediocre leadership. We could test this theory by looking at the quality of leadership in a single country or across countries and time. Is Canada governed by intellectual or economic elites or by 'ordinary people'? And, if the latter, is a reduction in the quality of leadership an inevitable result?

One way to distinguish between inductive and deductive reasoning is to consider the analogy of a wheel. One can think of the centre of the wheel as its most specific or particular point, and of the extremity of the wheel as the more general point. Outward movement along the spokes is a movement from the particular to the general, and inward movement is from the general to the particular. Using this analogy, inductive reasoning is that which moves from the centre to the periphery, from the specific to the general, whereas deductive reasoning moves in the opposite direction, from the periphery to the centre, or from the general to the specific. It should be noted that inductive and deductive research play off each other. We might notice a pattern in society and from that observation make the broad generalizations necessary to develop a theory (inductive research). Then we might seek to test hypotheses derived from the theory more directly by gathering data from different sources (deductive research). This process of data collection may lead us to note new or different patterns, from which we might generalize into different theories (inductive research). We would develop hypotheses based on the new theories (deductive research), then test them empirically, and so on. Inductive research tends to be more *exploratory* and broader in scope, whereas deductive research tends to be more directed and narrower in scope.

APPLY YOUR UNDERSTANDING

Inductive and Deductive Research

Consider the relationship between age and political conservatism. How would you examine it *inductively*? What are the observations you have made, and what theories can you develop? How would you examine the relationship *deductively*? What hypotheses could you test? How did you develop these hypotheses? How might you test the hypotheses?

HYPOTHESIS TESTING

With deductive research we seek to test our hypotheses empirically. Before discussing how we do so, first consider exactly what a hypothesis is. Recall that a hypothesis states a relationship between two concepts; propositions state logical 'if *x*, then *y*' statements that flow from the hypotheses, and propositions are combined to create theories. When we empirically test theories, propositions are reduced to their antecedent hypotheses, and concepts are defined more specifically as variables. Simply stated, then, a hypothesis is a *testable statement of relationship* between two variables. It is a statement, not a question. Usually, a hypothesis will state a *direction* (positive, meaning that variables change in a similar direction, or negative, meaning that variables change inversely) and will contain a *comparison*. Consider the hypothesis, 'High-income earners are more likely to support conservatism than low-income earners.' A relationship is stated between two variables: income and support for conservatism. The direction of the relationship is positive: as income increases, support for conservatism increases. And the hypothesis includes a comparison: high-income earners are compared with low-income earners. Is the hypothesis empirically testable? Yes, we could measure attitudes toward conservatism among the general population and see if there are differing levels of support among different income groups.

Summary: Characteristics of a Hypothesis

1. It states a relationship between two variables.
2. It states the direction of the relationship if possible.
3. It states a comparison between values of the independent variable.
4. It is empirically testable.

When we formulate hypotheses, we must ensure that they are empirically testable, which means that we do not use normative statements. A hypothesis does not state preferences or judgments. Often, we will have to reformulate our ideas to make them empirically testable. This can be done by making our assumptions more explicit and by ensuring that all the elements of a hypothesis—relationship, comparison, direction, testability—are present. If we start with 'democratic regimes are better than authoritarian regimes' (a comparison), we need to consider what we mean by 'better'. What is regime type being related to? Perhaps we are interested in human rights, and we believe that 'democratic regimes have better human rights records than authoritarian regimes'. Now we have included a relationship (between human rights and regime type) and a direction (as democracy increases, human rights records improve). This is now a testable hypothesis, rather than a normative statement.

In political analysis our goal is to test our hypotheses or, more specifically, to see if and to what extent those hypotheses are supported by empirical data. We gather empirical data to see if the evidence agrees with or contradicts our hypotheses. As support grows for a particular hypothesis, we gain more confidence in it and are more inclined to see it as 'true'. However, we never state that we have 'proven' a hypothesis. The reason for this is the importance of skepticism in the scientific method. Recall that science avoids any notions of certainty: if we are certain, we assume perfect knowledge, something scientists are reluctant to claim. There is always the chance that further knowledge will develop, that new information will be discovered, information that may place our 'truths' into question. This has happened many times in the history of humankind: it was once believed that the Earth was flat, the Sun revolved around the Earth, heavy objects fell more rapidly than light objects, and atoms were indivisible. Modern scientists and social scientists wish to avoid such errors and therefore refuse to make statements of absolute certain 'proof'.

Consequently, the process of hypothesis-testing involves examining whether the hypothesis can be shown to be false. In a formal sense, although the development of the hypothesis is based on formulating a 'testable statement of relationships' between variables, when testing a hypothesis we focus instead on the **null hypothesis**. As we noted in Chapter 1, the null hypothesis states that *no* relationship exists between two variables. For example, a null hypothesis might state 'there is no relationship between age and party identification'. Before we can conclude that support exists for our hypotheses (for example, 'as age increases, support for conservative parties increases'), we must first reject the null hypothesis. By rejecting the null hypothesis, we have established that some sort of relationship exists, and we are free to consider questions of direction.[2] For these reasons, when writing our research hypothesis, we first state a null hypothesis (no relationship exists, identified by H_0) and then state an **alternative hypothesis** (the relationship we think exists, identified by H_a).

Hypothesis-testing can be seen as the gradual elimination of alternative explanations. If we are trying to identify determining factors in party identification, for example, we might consider age, income, religion, region, parents' income, parents'

EXPAND YOUR KNOWLEDGE

Hypothesis Testing

Time 1: Which of the eight potential hypotheses in competition to explain a dependent variable is best?

$$H_1 \; H_2 \; H_3 \; H_4 \; H_5 \; H_6 \; H_7 \; H_8$$

Time 2: Research tests the hypotheses and shows support for some but rejects others.

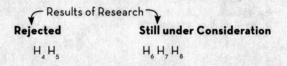
Results of Research

Rejected	**Still under Consideration**
$H_1 \; H_2 \; H_3$	$H_4 \; H_5 \; H_6 \; H_7 \; H_8$

Time 3: Future research tests remaining hypotheses in contention.

Results of Research

Rejected	**Still under Consideration**
$H_4 \; H_5$	$H_6 \; H_7 \; H_8$

New hypotheses developed and added for consideration: H_9

Time 4: Future research tests hypotheses still in contention.

Results of Research

Rejected	**Still under Consideration**
H_6	$H_7 \; H_8 \; H_9$

New hypotheses developed and added for consideration: $H_{10} \; H_{11}$

Time 5: New hypotheses are developed and enter into the competition. Research now tests the previous as well as the new hypotheses.

Results of Research

Rejected	**Still under Consideration**
$H_7 \; H_9$	$H_8 \; H_{10} \; H_{11}$

Source: Neuman, W. Lawrence, *Social Research Methods: Qualitative & Quantitative Approaches*, 2d ed. 'Hypothesis Testing', pp. 101–102, © 1994 Allyn & Bacon. Reproduced by permission of Pearson Education, Inc.

party identification, and gender. Testing might find that age and region do not appear to contribute to party identification. We would then drop hypotheses related to these variables and continue testing the remaining factors. Over time, others would probably drop from contention and new hypotheses emerge; we might, for instance, also choose to test the impact of education and marital status. Some hypotheses would continue to hold up after repeated testing, while others would be eliminated. Those that stay in contention and have the greatest empirical support are considered to be the best explanation *at that point in time* (Neuman 1994, 100). Thus, if after repeated testing, income and parents' party identification remain correlated with party identification, we can say with confidence that the hypotheses are *supported*. We do not, however, state that the hypotheses have been proven.

APPLY YOUR UNDERSTANDING

Developing Hypotheses

Create null and alternative hypotheses for relationships between

1. political conservatism and support for deficit reduction;
2. age and political party membership/ involvement;
3. regime type and economic system;
4. economic system and distribution of wealth;
5. gender and support for national child-care.

CAUSALITY

Until now, we have been looking for relationships between variables: does a relationship exist, and if so, what is the direction of that relationship? However, while recognizing correlations is important in the social sciences, we often wish to go further; more specifically, we want to know *why* two variables, A and B, are related. Does A cause B, or is their covariance accidental? Or is there a third variable, C, that causes both A and B? Recall from Chapter 1 that an important assumption of the scientific approach to politics is determinism: the belief there exist cause-and-effect relationships and that social scientists can, through research, discover the form of these relationships. Of course, few would argue that the underlying causes of human actions are either clear or certain, but the goal in social science is to find *patterns* of behaviour and propose causes to explain those patterns.

Recall also that causal relationships involve cause and effect. Variable X causes variable Y when a 'change in X (sooner or later) produces change in Y', or (because some Xs don't change) 'Ys tend to line up with fixed values of X' (Davis 1985, 9). How do we determine which variable is the cause and which is the effect? When one event precedes another in time, it is clear which is the cause and which is the effect. We give a plant water and light and it grows. We cast our ballots and a legislature is elected. When one event occurs in reaction to another, we have **temporal order.** The reacting variable (the effect) is dependent upon the preceding event (the cause): the life of the plant depends upon the supply of water and light, and the composition of the legislature is dependent upon the votes cast. As we noted in Chapter 1, the influenced variable is known as the dependent variable. The influencing variable—the cause—is called the independent variable: its values are independent of the dependent variable. The availability of water and light does not depend upon the existence of a single plant; the future composition of the legislature does not determine our individual vote, although our expectations about its composition might do so. Some independent variables are descriptive characteristics of the individual, qualities such as age, sex, race, and religion. These variables are known as **prior conditions** and precede in time such dependent variables as political beliefs and behaviours.

We can graphically represent causal relationships with causal models. Figure 2.1 a) illustrates a simple causal relationship: age (the independent variable) influences income (the dependent variable). The small '+' above the arrow tells us that the relationship is positive; in other words, the two variables change in the same direction. As age increases, income increases. Relationships between a single independent variable and the dependent variable are **bivariate**; there are only two variables being considered. Some causal relationships involve more than one independent variable; these relationships are **multivariate**. Figure 2.1 b) illustrates a causal relationship among three variables. Both age and education are independent variables, while income is the dependent variable. Note that both relationships are positive.

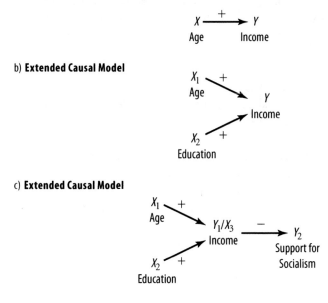

a) **Basic Causal Model**

b) **Extended Causal Model**

c) **Extended Causal Model**

FIGURE 2.1 Causal Models

When there is a chain of influences, with many variables interacting, our causal models become more complex. Figure 2.1 c) illustrates a more elaborate causal model: both education and age are positively related to income, while income is negatively related to support for socialism. As income increases, this model suggests, support for socialism decreases. Note that in this example, income is a dependent variable to age and education, but an independent variable with respect to support for socialism. Causal models help us visualize the relationships between variables; when a large number of variables are involved in a theory, a causal model can often simplify very complex relationships.

Errors in Causal Reasoning

Not all relationships are causal, although unfortunately many people confuse correlation with causation. For example, if there is a rise in crime at the same time as there is a rise in the number of single mothers, some will argue that single motherhood causes crime. However, the world is not that simple. It is entirely possible that a third factor, such as poverty, causes both crime and single motherhood. When a relationship between two variables can be accounted for by a third variable, it is known as a **spurious** relationship. To test for a spurious relationship, we need to examine whether the relationship between variable A and variable B exists without the influence of variable C. If the relationship exists without C, it may be a causal correlation; if **controlling** for C causes the relationship between A and B to disappear, the relationship is spurious. We control for the effects of other variables by holding the values of the third variable constant. (See later in this chapter for a more extended discussion of spurious relationships.) Returning to our example, we would need to know whether the relationship between single motherhood and crime can be attributed to a third variable: poverty. Thus, we test if the relationship exists in all socioeconomic groups or if it is isolated to the poor alone. If the relationship between single motherhood and crime disappears when poverty levels are held constant, we have found a spurious relationship; if it exists in all socioeconomic groups, it may be a causal relationship. To be confident that the relationship is causal, we need to be able to eliminate as many alternative explanations of the relationship as possible.

Once we know that a causal relationship is possible, we need to consider the order of that relationship. Sometimes social scientists find that it is difficult to ascertain which variable is the cause and which is the effect. When temporal order is not clear—when events appear to occur simultaneously—**causality** is difficult to establish. We noted that a correlation between single motherhood and crime might be seen as moving from the former to the latter; in other words, it might be posited that single motherhood causes increased crime rates. However, it is possible that the relationship could work in the opposite direction: perhaps crime causes single motherhood. For example, violent crime could lead to fathers being killed or imprisoned, leaving the mother alone to raise the children. Many of the relationships we seek to explore in social science can seem like chicken-and-egg dilemmas. When we cannot clearly determine cause and effect, we have less confidence that a causal relationship exists.

Another common error in causal reasoning is that temporal order necessarily implies causality. This fallacy is similar to assuming that correlation is equated to causation. Just because variable X precedes variable Y is not sufficient grounds to argue that X causes Y; again, we must ensure that some other variable Z does not cause Y. Controlling for other possible causes is the only way we can suggest with confidence that X causes Y. Unfortunately, we can never rule out all possible alternative explanations for social and political behaviour. In addition, temporal order can be difficult to establish in the social sciences. For these reasons, theory is particularly important to political analysis. Many of the gaps in our knowledge are filled by clear reasoning and logic; good data alone are seldom sufficient.

Finally, we should note the **ecological fallacy.** To understand this concept, imagine a study of electoral support for a local referendum on the amalgamation of municipal governments. In order to test the hypothesis that support for amalgamation will decline as personal income increases, the researchers collect data on average family income and percentage voting 'no' in the referendum for each polling district. And, as the hypothesis predicts, polls with relatively high family incomes were more likely to vote no in the referendum than were polls with relatively low family incomes. The researchers then conclude that high-income *voters* are more likely to oppose amalgamation than are low-income *voters*. In coming to this conclusion, the researchers are committing the ecological fallacy. They are assuming that what is true of the polling district—the ecological unit of analysis—is equally true of individuals within the polling districts. They are assuming that because high-income districts are more likely to vote no, so too are high-income individuals. In fact, however, there need not be any relationship between district characteristics and the determinants of individual voting behaviour. There could be no relationship between family income and voting preference for individuals *within* each district, and yet there could still be a relationship between income and vote when the level of analysis shifts from individuals to the polling district. The lesson is that we must be careful in projecting ecological characteristics onto the behaviour of individuals.

Spurious Relationships

By modelling carefully, it is possible to increase confidence that the relationship observed in the data is a result of the impact of the specified independent variable on the dependent variable. One of the most significant errors of analysis occurs where a relationship is *spurious*, and this fact is not detected by the analyst. A relationship is spurious if it exists because of the influence of a third variable. In the example in Figure 2.2, assume that the bivariate analysis showed a relationship between variable A and variable B. Given the way in which the relationship was modelled, the conclusion would be that A causes B. Now, assume that a third variable, C,

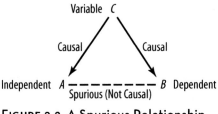

FIGURE 2.2 A Spurious Relationship

influences both *A* and *B*. In this instance, *C* causes *A* to vary and *B* to vary. Thus, the initial variation that was observed between *A* and *B* was not causal but instead was a byproduct of the effect of *C* on both *A* and *B*. After taking into account the presence of *C*, we would conclude that the relationship between *A* and *B* is spurious.

Intervening Variables

An **intervening variable** is one that comes between an independent and a dependent variable, but the direction of causality flows from the independent variable to the intervening variable to the dependent variable. The use of intervening variables is one way of providing further elaboration to a theory. For example, assume the initial hypothesis is that education leads to participation in politics: the higher one's level of education, the more likely he or she is to have a high level of participation. But why is this the case? What is it about having a higher level of education that leads one to have a higher level of political participation? A variety of theories could be introduced to explain this relationship, each of which could include specifying an intervening variable. For example, one theory is that people participate in politics when the cost to them of doing so is not too high. Higher levels of education provide people with a greater understanding of politics, which reduces the 'cost' of becoming informed about the parties during an election campaign. Therefore, the hypothesis follows that people with higher levels of education will participate in politics because the cost to them of doing so is lower than for people with lower levels of education. Thus, in the model in Figure 2.3, variable *C* is knowledge about the parties and/or the political process. This model could be extended by including other variables that intervene between level of education and level of political participation. These could include such things as a larger number of social contacts with people actively involved in politics (therefore being more likely to be asked to participate), having a

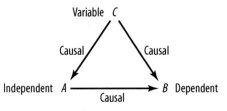

FIGURE 2.3 An Intervening Variable

higher income, and therefore taking a greater interest in governmental decisions as they affect the allocation of resources, and other intervening factors.

Note the difference between an intervening variable and a spurious relationship. In the former, the original independent variable is important, because it causes variation in the intervening variable, whereas in a spurious relationship the initial independent variable is not important, because the direction of causality is reversed. In each of the examples of intervening variables, education was hypothesized to affect the intervening variable; that is, higher levels of education led to greater political knowledge, more social contacts, or a higher income, which in turn led to higher levels of political participation.

Reinforcing Variables

A reinforcing variable is one that can strengthen and magnify the relationship between an independent and a dependent variable. For example, assume we are examining the effect of gender on attitudes toward abortion. We might find that women are more likely than men to agree that abortion is a matter that should be decided between a pregnant woman and her doctor. A reinforcing variable in this model could be attitudes toward feminism. People who hold views favourable to feminism also are more likely to agree that abortion is a matter that should be decided between a pregnant woman and her doctor. Since women are more likely to be feminists (that is, to hold views favourable to feminism) than are men, attitudes toward feminism reinforce the relationship between gender and attitudes toward abortion. However, attitudes toward feminism don't replace the effect of gender; instead they complement and reinforce this relationship. This means that the causal connection between gender and attitudes toward abortion persists even after the effect of the reinforcing variable is taken into account. The causal line from *A* to *C* indicates that gender is hypothesized to have an effect on attitudes toward feminism but that in the case of a reinforcing effect, it is expected that a direct effect of gender on attitudes toward abortion will persist even after controlling for feminism. In short, the attitudes toward feminism strengthen rather than replace the direct effect that gender has on attitudes toward abortion. When the two variables are reinforcing, such as in this example, the impact of the independent variable on the dependent variable is larger among women who hold feminist attitudes than among those who do not.

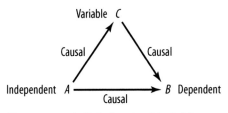

Figure 2.4 A Reinforcing Variable

Multiple Independent Variables

We also could model a set of causal relationships in which a number of independent variables can have an effect a dependent variable. This type of modelling is quite common when using multiple regression analysis, because this technique allows us to examine the effect of each of the independent variables under the *ceteris paribus* assumption, that is, assuming all other things are equal. Thus, for example, we could examine the effect of attitudes toward party leaders, attitudes toward political issues, and party identification on voting to see which of these variables is the most important determinant of voting. Such an analysis would try to answer the question 'Are Canadian elections little more than television-oriented popularity contests among the party leaders, or are they the result of policy discussions and debates among the parties and candidates?' To what extent does the government receive a mandate to implement a policy agenda following a Canadian election? Understanding the nature of causality among these competing models provides insight into the character and meaning of Canadian elections, and of course also provides strategic information that can be used by the parties in formulating their election campaigns.

The caution to bear in mind when modelling and empirically testing relationships with multiple independent variables is that the assumption of independence between the causal or independent variables may not reflect the true relationships between these variables in the real world. For example, from the preceding discussion, is it sensible to assume that attitudes toward party leaders, attitudes toward political issues, and party identification are independent of one another? Is it sensible to think that in Quebec politics there is no relationship between attitudes toward Quebec sovereignty, attitudes toward Bloc Québécois leader Gilles Duceppe, and support for the BQ? Of course, not all independent variables will be strongly related to one another. But be aware of the assumptions that accompany the modelling of the relationships in your analysis. If there is reason to think that the independent variables are related to one another, you may wish to reconsider the way in which you have conceptualized the relationship to take into account this interrelationship.

This chapter has explored the role of theory in political analysis. Most of the following chapters will explore different ways that we make empirical observations of the social world in our efforts to test our theories and advance our knowledge of the political world. In the next chapter, we turn our attention to defining political concepts.

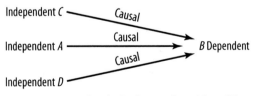

FIGURE 2.5 Multiple Independent Variables

WORKING AS A TEAM

1. With your discussion group, discuss what you consider to be the major causes of the decline in voting among young Canadians. Identify two or more hypotheses that purport to account for the decline in voter turnout among youth.

2. Consider the hypotheses that your discussion group identified. What theory or theories can be said to underlie these hypotheses?

SELF-STUDY

1. Identify a hypothesis that you would be interested in examining. Discuss how using a deductive versus inductive approach, you would examine this hypothesis.

2. State a hypothesis. Map the hypothesis by identifying which is the independent and which the dependent variable. Identify a possible spurious relationship that can be tested and map the relationship. Map a relationship with two separate intervening variables.

NOTES

1. A notable form of applied research is *feminist action research* (Reinharz 1992). Indeed, the argument has been made (Lather 1988) that research is feminist *only* if it is linked to action, to attempts to repudiate the status quo. This does not mean that action research is unable to enrich our conceptual or theoretical understanding of the world; it only means that such enrichment cannot be the sole or perhaps even the primary justification for research projects. Research is seen as an essential part of a larger process of social transformation.

2. As Chapter 16 will discuss, hypotheses sometimes include a specific directionality. Two-tailed tests are used to reject the null hypothesis if no direction is specified, if, for example, the hypothesis is simply that some relationship exists between age and conservatism. One-tailed tests are used when the direction of the relationship is specified by the hypothesis.

Chapter 3

DEFINING THE POLITICAL WORLD: CONCEPTS

DESTINATION

By the end of this chapter the reader should

- appreciate the importance of clear conceptual definitions when conducting empirical research;
- appreciate the difficulties in arriving at clear and consistent conceptual definitions;
- know some rules of thumb that can be applied to the development of conceptual definitions; and
- be familiar with issues of measurement with respect to the political world.

The goal of empirical political science is to conduct research in such a way that lawlike generalizations can be made about the political world. Although it is no doubt interesting to know why one voter—say Cheryl Smith of Richmond, British Columbia, voted for the Green Party in the 2008 federal election—it is of greater interest to know what are the determinants of voting more generally in Canadian federal elections. The factors that can impinge on voting include many characteristics, such as voters' gender, age, ideology, partisan identifications, attitudes toward party leaders, and the like. But the importance of these factors varies over time and over political space. For example, gender may be more important as a predictor of voting behaviour in the 2010s than it was in the 1960s, as women contest more ridings in which their party stands a chance of winning, as political discussions become more relevant to women, or as women become more likely to lead political parties. Likewise, ideology may be a more important determinant of voting in a province such as Ontario, where the parties themselves appear more ideologically distinct, than in Nova Scotia where the major parties seem to have a higher level of consensus.

To develop lawlike generalizations about the political world, it is necessary to devise models that enable a comparison of alternative possible causes. We began exploring causal models in Chapter 2. The basic structure of such a model is presented in Figure 3.1. In this simple model, there is one hypothesized causal factor and one outcome. The hypothesized causal factor is labelled 'A', and the outcome is labelled 'B'. Following the discussion from the previous paragraph, B represents the concept that we wish to explain, namely, voting in Canadian federal elections. A represents the hypothesized cause of that outcome, such as attitudes toward the

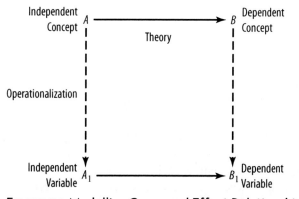

FIGURE 3.1 Modelling Cause and Effect Relationships

party leaders. These two concepts are joined by a causal arrow, which runs from
A to B. Thus, it is read as attitudes toward party leaders cause Canadians to vote
for one party over another in an election. In this model, 'attitudes toward party
leaders' is the **independent** concept, and voting is the **dependent** concept. Recall
that in empirical research a dependent concept is the outcome that we are trying
to explain. In brief, we hypothesize that variations in this concept are based on, or
depend upon, variations in other elements *inside* the model. Another way of saying
this is that the variance is **endogenous** to the model. Thus, in the present example,
variation in voting is hypothesized to stem from variation in attitudes toward leaders. The independent concept is the hypothesized cause of the outcome. Variations
in the independent concept are hypothesized to depend upon factors *outside* (that
is, **exogenous** to) the model.

Concepts can be independent or dependent, depending upon the topic of the
research and the way in which the causal structure is specified. Although the independent concept in the model under consideration is attitudes toward party
leaders, this concept could be dependent in a different research program. For example, in a separate research study, one might hypothesize that women were more
likely than men to view NDP leader Jack Layton in positive terms. In contrast, men
may be more likely than women to view another party leader positively, such as
Conservative leader Stephen Harper. Thus, 'attitudes toward party leaders' in this
example is the dependent concept and the hypothesized cause of variation (that is,
the independent concept) is respondents' gender.

Underlying the hypothesized causal connection between attitudes toward party
leaders (A) and voting (B) in Figure 3.1 is a **theory** about the causes of voting. A
theory can be defined as 'a statement of what are held to be the general laws, principles or causes of something known or observed' (*Shorter Oxford English Dictionary*,
2167). Therefore, the theory provides a more generalized statement of the cause of
some outcome. We explored the idea of theory in Chapter 2 and found that theories
are statements about the relationships between concepts. In the present example,

the theory accounting for the relationship between attitudes toward party leaders and voting could be that politics in the electronic age is delivered to people in their living rooms via television or social media sites. Since television coverage of politics focuses on party leaders and their images (as opposed to a detailed discussion of political issues and policies), we expect attitudes toward leaders to have an important impact on voting preferences. If the results of the research do not support the hypothesized relationship between attitudes toward leaders and voting, then our theory of political behaviour based on media images of party leaders is not supported. Particularly in the social sciences, *statements about causality arise from theorizing.* Thus, our theories, and the concepts embodied in our theories, are extremely important.

The initial stages in developing an empirical research project involve identifying the concepts that will be studied, specifying a hypothesized causal relation, and proposing a theory underlying the relationship. At this stage of the research, these **concepts** are defined as relatively abstract entities. To conduct the empirical

APPLY YOUR UNDERSTANDING

The Difference between Concepts and Variables

Do you understand the difference between concepts and variables? The preceding discussion suggested that the key difference is that a concept is abstract, whereas a variable is concrete. Let's see if we can take this a step further. To say that a concept is abstract does not imply that it is fuzzy or vague. Quite the contrary, we are suggesting that empirical political researchers try to define concepts as precisely as possible. However, even a concept that is defined very precisely can be measured in a variety of ways. A variable is the way in which the concept has been measured in this particular study. When we say a variable is concrete and specific, we mean that the researcher can actually assign a value to every 'case' in the study. Any clearer?

Consider the concept 'attitudes toward party leaders'. What is meant by this concept? Can you provide a specific definition of the concept? You might ask, what kinds of attitudes? In a study of the 1988 Canadian federal election, Richard Johnston and his colleagues suggested that the relevant attitudes toward party leaders concern their 'character' and 'competence'. Do you agree with their definition of this concept? How might assessments of the character and competence of party leaders be measured? Johnston et al. suggest that these dimensions can be measured (that is, they can be changed into variables) by asking people four questions concerning competence and another four concerning character. The answers to these questions can be combined into 'mean' (average) character and competence ratings for each of the party leaders (Johnston et al. 1992, 174–84). (See Chapter 15 for a discussion of 'means'.) Are there other ways of conceptualizing 'attitudes toward party leaders'?

research, one needs to move from the level of concepts to the level of **variables** (designated as A_1 and B_1 in Figure 3.1). Whereas concepts are abstract representations of a phenomenon, variables are the concrete manifestations of that phenomenon in the current research project. Research on the variables will provide the evidence on which to draw conclusions about the hypothesized relationship between concepts. Variables are sufficiently specific that values can be assigned to each person or case in the data set. A variable gets its name by virtue of the fact that these values can vary across the cases.

In effect, much of the statistical component of empirical research involves comparing the variation in one variable with the variation in another. As we will see in subsequent chapters, there are many statistical methods available to test the strength of the relationship between variables. It is important to note, however, that statistical techniques largely are able to assess the strength of association, not the direction of causation. The latter is a matter primarily of research design, in which the researcher hypothesizes a direction of causality and underpins this hypothesis with a more general theory of the causal relationship.

Since empirical analysis is conducted on variables, but we wish to make generalizations about the concepts, it is important that the variables are an accurate reflection of the concepts. We wish to ensure that the relationship between the variables mirrors the relationship between the concepts. This can be accomplished only if the variable is both a precise and an accurate measure of the concept. A discussion of the ways to ensure precision and accuracy in measurement, through the process of operationalization, is taken up in Chapter 4.

CONCEPTUAL DEFINITIONS

In everyday conversation, we often use terms in a way that presupposes that others understand and agree with our conceptualization. Indeed, effective communication requires that a particular word has the same meaning for each person involved in the dialogue. Yet, there is often a degree of ambiguity in our conventional use of words. Some of the ambiguity stems from the differences in meaning attached to words when they are used in different contexts. For example, emerging from an 11 a.m. lecture, a student might be overheard saying, 'Let's go over to the Student's Union building. I'm starving.' In this context, the word 'starving' might imply that the student hasn't eaten in the four hours since breakfast, when he had a coffee, some toast, and a piece of fruit. Over lunch, the student might read in the newspaper about a drought in East Africa and learn of the rising death toll of the local population through starvation. Obviously, the comment about his state of hunger upon leaving the classroom was not meant to be equated with the life-threatening condition that starvation presents to many people in the world. In conversation we are often willing to tolerate a certain measure of ambiguity in conceptual definitions while still being able to communicate effectively.

There are other instances in which such ambiguity in everyday language use can lead to ineffective or lack of communication. As a teenager prepares to leave the house on a Saturday night, she might say to her parents: 'I'm going out with a group from school. See you later. I'll be home early!' This type of statement is a recipe for miscommunication, since parents and teenagers almost universally have a different understanding of the statement 'I'll be home early.' Unless the term 'early' is defined more precisely, the chances are good that misunderstanding will arise. In fact, in this instance, there may be so much difficulty in coming to a shared understanding of the meaning of the term 'early' that communication might be facilitated by doing away with using the terms 'early' and 'late' in this situation altogether, instead using a term that is defined in such a way that both parties agree. Thus, it may be preferable to say 'I'll be home at 11 o'clock' or 'I'll be home at midnight.' The parents and the teenager would then have a common understanding of the time at which she is expected home. Of course, there may be a downside to using this level of precision, if the intent of the teenager is to come home at 1 o'clock in the morning. From the teenager's perspective there may be advantages to arguing over whether 1 o'clock is 'early' or 'late' compared with explaining why she is home two hours after the agreed-upon time of 11 o'clock.

The problem of lack of clarity in conceptual definitions plagues those engaged in empirical political research as well. One of the features that continues to differentiate research in the social sciences from that in the natural sciences is the relative lack of agreement in the former around the meaning of concepts. If the goal of research is to test theories of political attitudes and behaviour, and the expectation is that multiple observers will independently arrive at the same observations and conclusions, then it is important to have consistent understandings of the concepts under study. As we will see, however, such consistency is an elusive goal, as the following examples illustrate.

Example: The Impact of Education on Voting

What impact does education have on voting? To begin exploring this question, we can map a causal relationship as in Figure 3.2. Education is the independent concept (the hypothesized cause) and voting is the dependent concept (the hypothesized effect). Notice as well that there is a theory underlying this hypothesized relationship. The theory might be that higher educational achievement leads people to feel themselves a greater part of the political community and thereby inspires them to higher levels of political activity. Thus, the higher the level of educational

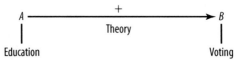

FIGURE 3.2 The Impact of Education on Voting

achievement, the higher the level of political activity, such as voting. Since this is a positive relationship (an increase in the value of one concept leads to an increase in the value of the other), we include a $+$ over the causal arrow.

To proceed with this research, it is necessary to define the terms 'education' and 'voting'. The theory being tested concerns the impact of education on level of political activity. In this instance, voting is conceptualized as indicative of a certain amount of political involvement or activity. The research is concerned not about whether the person voted for the Conservatives, Liberals, NDP, Green, or Bloc Québécois, but simply whether or not he or she voted. Thus, we may wish to refer to this concept as 'voting turnout' rather than simply 'voting'. Furthermore, voting turnout could be conceptualized either as a **categorical** or a **continuous** concept. A categorical concept is one in which the characteristics of the concept are separate and distinct. A continuous concept is one in which the categories are joined or connected in a sequential manner. For example, examining voting turnout in a single election, we see that the characteristics would be that one voted or that one did not vote. This is indicative of separate or distinct activities, and therefore it is a categorical concept. In contrast, voting turnout could also be conceptualized as being a 'disposition to vote' and therefore best measured over time. For example, one could ask in what percentage of federal elections in which the voter was eligible to vote did he or she in fact vote. This conceptualization would result in the creation of a continuous measure of voting, with responses ranging from 0 per cent to 100 per cent. We will see later that there are important implications in the selection of statistics regarding which approach to follow. At this juncture, the key point to remember is that these different possible conceptualizations of voting turnout could result in researchers lacking consistent definitions of an important concept in their research.

Once we have settled on a definition of voting turnout, we must also define education. On the surface this seems straightforward and uncontroversial: level of education increases with the number of years of formal schooling. Yet slightly below the surface lie a number of questions and concerns that challenge this simple conceptual definition. One of the most obvious concerns is with regard to the change over the past two generations in the meaning of what constitutes a high or a low level of education. Prior to a major expansion in the Canadian postsecondary education system in the 1960s, a university-level education was relatively uncommon. Indeed, even the successful completion of a high school diploma was viewed as a mark of significant educational achievement as recently as the period just prior to World War II. Today, a university-level education has become much more widely available, and it is a much more common achievement. What are the implications of this change for the way in which 'level of education' is conceptualized? On the one hand, we might agree that people today are simply more highly educated than in the past. From this perspective, level of educational achievement is an absolute quality—what is high for one generation is high for others. On the other hand, the conclusion might be that level of education is a relative quality and that those who achieve high levels of education relative to their age cohort should be considered to have high educational achievement. Such a conclusion would imply that level of educational achievement must be adjusted for the time at which the person was enrolled in the school system.

A second, and possibly more complicating, issue concerns our understanding of how one might achieve a high level of education. At the outset it was suggested that level of education corresponds with the number of years attending an (accredited?) educational institution. But does education always take place within an educational institution? It would seem self-evident that a considerable amount of 'learning' takes place both inside and outside the classroom. What role does the classroom experience play in the overall educational process? Such questions are raised not to stretch beyond credulity the meaning of the concept of education, but instead to indicate some of the important debates that are currently taking place at universities across the country. Educators are beginning to ask whether university credits can be given for certain kinds of 'life experiences', thereby acknowledging that much learning takes place outside the classroom. If university credit can be obtained for certain life experiences, are these not part of a person's education even if one has not applied for and obtained university credit? If university credit is not viewed as the prime indicator of one's level of educational achievement, then is it possible to arrive at a uniform agreement on the meaning of education? Thus, the issue of whether to include life experiences as a component of educational attainment goes to the very heart of the difficulties often faced in the social sciences of agreeing on the meaning of social concepts.

The third complication that arises in developing a definition of the concept of 'education' concerns the connection between years of education and the level of educational achievement. In the secondary education system, there is a difference in courses of study between advanced academic streams (that is, the International Baccalaureate program), the regular academic stream, and the lower stream. Does the completion of 11 years of schooling in different academic streams equate to the same level of educational achievement? Of course, in the postsecondary education system, such differences in fields of study are even more pronounced. Students might attend a technical training institute (that is, a business college), a technical college, an arts and sciences community college, or a university, including a university with graduate and professional training. Does enrollment at any of these institutions for a similar period of time provide the student with a similar level of educational achievement? We might anticipate a negative answer to this question—two years as a university student provides a higher level of educational achievement than two years at a technical college. One would need to adjust the definition of educational achievement accordingly. Even within the university, one might ask whether students studying in different areas are obtaining the same level of educational achievement. For example, is two years of study toward an engineering degree similar to two years of study toward a Bachelor of Fine Arts, a Bachelor of Arts, a Bachelor of Science, or a Bachelor of Commerce? Furthermore, what impact does different level of performance within the program have on level of educational achievement? Does a student who has completed 15 university courses with an A average have a higher or lower level of educational achievement than a student who has completed 18 courses with a C average?

These might seem like very 'technical' issues. Some readers may be thinking that the preceding discussion makes overly complex two relatively simple and straightforward concepts. Everyone knows, you may be thinking, what is meant by the terms 'education' and 'voting'. We will discover, in fact, that what may appear

EXPAND YOUR KNOWLEDGE
Changing Definitions of Educational Achievement

In their provocative book, *Transforming Higher Education*, Michael Dolence and Donald Norris (1995, 31–2) contrast postsecondary education by using the model inspired by the Industrial Age with that of the Information Age:

> Under the Industrial Age model, colleges and universities and the training organizations of corporations traditionally created separate, vertically integrated organizations to impart learning. All of the factors of production were included and provided to a largely resident and essentially captive group of learners—geographically isolated learners were served by visiting faculty or remote delivery of instruction. The clustering of the factors of production on the campus was the key competitive advantage. Under this factory/physical campus model of learning, the barriers to entry were huge, and two basic classes of participants existed: providers and learners. During the Industrial Age, higher education has held a virtually exclusive franchise on teaching and certifying mastery in its core areas of interest.
>
> In the Information Age, network scholarship will eliminate much of the advantage of vertical integration and the physical concentration of scholarly resources. Not only can learners be anywhere, they can acquire learning and knowledge from sources in any location or mixture of locations. Owning the physical facility where faculty and other expertise reside will not be a critical differentiator in the eyes of many learners. On the other hand, developing the ability to provide expertise, learning, and knowledge to networked learners will be essential. The capacity to measure demonstrated competence and to certify learning in a way that will be accepted by employers will also be a key differentiator. New learning support roles—facilitators, knowledge navigators, and learner/service intermediaries—will become increasingly important.

self-evident to you may not be self-evident to others. What is perhaps most important to recognize is the need to be as specific as possible in providing a definition of the key concepts in the research in which you are going to be engaged. Many of the most interesting debates in political science literature are debates over the meaning of concepts. Such debates can only take place, however, if researchers provide clear definitions of the concepts that are included in their analyses.

APPLY YOUR UNDERSTANDING

Conceptual Clarity

Is there something unusual about the concepts of 'voting' and 'education' that led to the confusion about their meaning, or is this problem of conceptual ambiguity common in the social sciences and in political science? To answer that question, think of some examples of concepts that could be used in political science research, and ask yourself whether you could provide one and only one definition of the concept.

Try it with the concept of 'age'. Winston Churchill once said that a person who was a conservative at 20 years old had no heart, whereas a person who was not a conserva-tive at 40 years old had no brain. Thus, he suggests a connection between aging and political belief systems. To examine this hypothesis, one would have to define aging. Can you provide a definition? Do you foresee any problems with this definition? Do you suppose the process of 'aging' takes place at the same rate, and in the same way, for all people?

How about the other variable in this model—political belief systems? What do you mean by the term 'conservative'? Or 'liberal'? Do you think all researchers would agree with your definitions?

Example: Party Identification

Party identification was one of the more important concepts to emerge from early studies of voting and elections in the United States. In reporting on some of the first studies undertaken on samples of the American electorate during the 1950s, Angus Campbell and his collaborators (1960) at the Center for Political Studies of the University of Michigan developed an attitudinal model of voting. They described the model as consisting of a 'funnel of causality'. At the wide end of the funnel were the factors that exist in the more distant past or that are further removed (in cognitive space) from the voting decision. As one approaches the narrow end of the funnel, one finds the factors that are most relevant, immediate, and important in the voting decision. These factors invariably are a set of political attitudes and beliefs that impinge directly on the vote. For Campbell et al. the three most relevant such factors were party identifications, attitudes toward party leaders, and attitudes toward

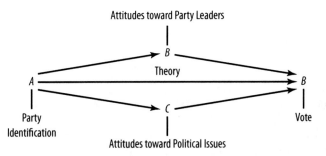

Party
Identification

Attitudes toward Party Leaders

Attitudes toward Political Issues

Vote

FIGURE 3.3 The 'Michigan' Model and the Determinants of Voting

political issues. These factors coexist in the sequence outlined in Figure 3.3. This model indicates an important role for party identification in two respects. First, it is one of the three variables that have the most immediate *direct effect* on voting decisions. Second, it is even more important because of the role it plays in influencing the other two prime determinants of voting. In other words, party identification has an important *indirect effect,* through its impact on attitudes toward political issues and on perceptions of the party leaders.

Before turning to a discussion of party identification, it is noteworthy that the dependent concept in Figure 3.3, 'vote', differs from the concept 'voting' in Figure 3.2. Whereas the previous discussion centred on voting turnout, in the present example vote refers to vote choice. That is, the concern is not with whether or not a respondent voted, but for which party he or she voted. In the United States, of course, the main options are to vote for the Democratic or Republican parties, although there is some indication that a broader range of choices may be emerging. In Canada, the options at the federal level would include Conservative, Liberal, New Democrat, and Bloc Québécois among the parties with seats in Parliament, together with a host of other parties that do not control parliamentary seats.

The concept of party identification that emerged from the 'Michigan' studies derives directly from the empirical findings of the research. In particular, Campbell and his collaborators found that only a very small minority of American voters actually join political parties and pay membership fees. Nonetheless, a large majority of Americans think of themselves as being either a Democrat or a Republican. Furthermore, they found that this psychological attachment tended to develop relatively early in life, was often passed from one generation to the next through the socialization process, and was highly stable for most voters unless there was a particularly tumultuous set of political circumstances. Party identification also tended to exert a strong influence on other political attitudes and beliefs, such as feelings toward the candidates or evaluations of political issues (as outlined in Figure 3.3).

Research on the determinants of voting in other advanced industrial democracies borrowed heavily from the pioneering studies in the United States. This is certainly true of Canadian scholarship.[1] The first book-length treatment of Canadian

EXPAND YOUR KNOWLEDGE

American Responses to the 'Michigan' Model of Party Identification

The findings of Campbell and his colleagues regarding the long-term determinants of voting and the stability of party identification generated considerable debate within American political science. Many saw in the Michigan model an argument for irrationality in voting, that voters were guided more by the beliefs of their forebears than by an understanding of the issues at stake in American elections. In one famous response, V.O. Key (1966) declared that 'Voters are not fools!'

Others, such as Norman Nie, Sidney Verba, and John Petrocik (1976) argued that the findings of Campbell et al. in *The American Voter* (1960) were accurate for the time at which the study was conducted (the data are mainly from the 1952 and 1956 American National Election Studies), but that the 1950s was a relatively quiet period in American domestic politics, during the presidency of former general and war hero Dwight Eisenhower. The more turbulent 1960s and 1970s period, which saw dramatic increases in the number of protests, demonstrations, sit-ins, and riots in response to the civil rights movement and the Vietnam War, was accompanied by greater instability of party identifications.

The question of the stability of party identification in the United States, and the 'rationality' of the electorate, continues to generate interest and research.

voting behaviour that used the principles of social psychology as developed by Campbell and colleagues was Harold Clarke, Jane Jenson, Lawrence LeDuc, and Jon Pammett's *Political Choice in Canada*, published in 1979. Similar to the findings of Campbell et al. in their studies of the American electorate in the 1950s, Clarke et al. found that most Canadians in the 1970s also had a psychological attachment to a political party. However, in contrast to the American findings, which emphasized the stability of party identification and its long-term impact on other political phenomena, Clarke et al. found that party identification in Canada tended to be somewhat more complex. Indeed, they argued that whereas party identification in the United States varied along the single dimension of strength of attachment (that is, the range extended from strong Democrat through weak Democrat, independent, weak Republican, to strong Republican), in Canada the psychological attachment to a political party was **multidimensional**. A multidimensional concept is one in which more than one factor, or dimension, exists within a concept. Clarke et al. suggested that psychological attachments to a political party in Canada consist of three major dimensions: strength, consistency, and stability. Furthermore, they argued that the character of the psychological attachment to a political party in Canada is sufficiently different from that developed by Campbell et al. in the United States to warrant a different name. They used the name 'partisanship'.

The different conceptualization of partisanship stems from the differences that Clarke et al. observed in their study of Canadian voters in the 1970s. They

EXPAND YOUR KNOWLEDGE

A Comparison of the Conceptualization of Party Identification and Partisanship

Party Identification (US)	Partisanship (Canada)	
Strong Republican	Strength	Strong identifier
Fairly strong Republican		Weak identifier
Weak Republican		Nonidentifier
Independent		
Weak Democrat	Consistency	Same federally and provincially
Fairly strong Democrat		Different federally and provincially
Strong Democrat	Stability	Never changed identification
		Changed identification

found, for example, that many Canadians hold different partisan attachments at the federal and provincial levels of government. It was not uncommon for a voter to think of herself as a Liberal when asked about federal politics, but to think of herself as a Conservative at the provincial level. Indeed, in many provinces different parties compete at the two levels of government. At the time of their study, the main federal/provincial inconsistency was among the provincial Social Credit and federal Liberals and Conservatives in British Columbia, and among the provincial Parti Québécois and federal Liberals in Quebec. More recently, the federal and provincial distinctiveness between political parties has become even more pronounced, with the emergence of parties such as the Bloc Québécois, and during the 1990s, the Reform and Canadian Alliance parties, which competed only at the federal level. Supporters of these parties are not able to hold 'consistent' identifications at the two levels of government. In contrast, cross-level inconsistency of party identification is much less common in the United States. Since Clarke et al. found that cross-level inconsistency had an important bearing on the character of the psychological attachment to a party, they included this dimension as a component of the conceptualization of partisanship.

The other dimension added to partisanship was stability of attachment to a party. Once again, this reconceptualization grew out of empirical research on the character of party attachments. Recall that the 'Michigan' formulation of party identification stressed its stability and suggested that it was a long-term attachment to a party passed intergenerationally through the socialization process. In

EXPAND YOUR KNOWLEDGE

Consistency in Party Identifications

A debate between David Elkins and Jane Jenson in 1978 regarding the meaning of party identification illustrates the importance of clarity in conceptual definitions: Elkins's view (1978, 419-21): 'Concepts are like wines; some do not travel well. Thus, a frequent problem concerns whether phenomena with the same label in two societies are really the same. Party identification is a concept which is particularly interesting in this regard. . . . [E]xhibiting different identifications in different party systems should not be considered evidence of inconsistency. . . . Jenson et al. do treat contrary federal and provincial party identifications as a form of inconsistency.'

Jenson's view (1978, 437-8): 'Concepts do not travel; theories do. The distinction is an important one because the concept party identification and its measurement in different contexts provides students of voting with one of a class of problems in comparative analysis. Comparative analysis implies a search for and the development of general laws about human behaviour, laws which are valid across political systems. The way that this search is carried out is through the development, confirmation and modification of theory. . . . The more general and abstract the language, the more comparable phenomena that can be found. The more specific and historical the language, the more different things that will be observed.'

important respects, the transmission of party identification was viewed as similar to the transmission of religious affiliation. Many Americans and Canadians think of themselves as having a religious affiliation, whether or not they formally hold membership in a church congregation. For most, this religious affiliation did not result from a period of detailed and systematic study of the major religious texts—the Koran, the Torah, the Bible, and others. Instead, most people learn about religion from their parents and become adherents of a religious faith through the socialization process. Similarly, the Michigan model of party identification suggested that most voters do not become party identifiers as a result of a long period of detailed and systematic study of the major political ideologies and parties. Party identifications, like religious affiliations, are passed through the socialization process.

Empirical research on voting in Canada suggested that this process of intergenerational transmission of party identification is much less pronounced than it was in the United States in the 1950s. Although many voters did receive political 'cues' from their parents as they were socialized into the political system, these political cues seemed far less powerful in influencing attitudes toward other political phenomena, such as attitudes toward political leaders or issues. Furthermore, for many Canadians, partisan affiliation seemed to change in response to the parties' changing issue agenda or changing leadership. That is, the causal relationship between partisan attachment and attitudes toward issues and leaders appeared to be in the opposite direction: from perceptions of the leaders to partisan attachment as well as vice versa.

This multidimensional conceptualization of partisanship developed in response to empirical applications of the concept of party identification to a study
of Canadian voting behaviour. Partisanship is thus defined as a psychological attachment to a political party, which can vary along the dimensions of strength,
stability, and consistency of attachment. Those voters with strong, stable, and consistent attachments to a party are referred to by Clarke et al. as 'durable' partisans,
whereas those without one or all of these qualities are called 'flexible' partisans.
Durable partisans resemble in many respects the 'party identifiers' discussed by
Campbell et al. in their research on public opinion and voting in the United States;
these voters have a long-term, stable tie to a party, and this tie colours their perception of the political world, including their attitudes toward the party leaders and
their understanding of political issues and events. However, in Canada only about
one in three voters is a durable partisan. The rest of the electorate consists of flexible partisans, for whom partisan affiliation is less stable and more likely to change
in response to short-term political issues and events. Approximately two in three
Canadian voters are flexible partisans, providing Canadian elections with considerable opportunities for change in response to short-term electoral phenomena.
The 1993 federal election, which saw the 'emerging' success of two parties (Reform
and the BQ) and the near-obliteration of two 'old' parties (PC and NDP), provided
a case in point of the dramatic changes that are possible when flexible Canadian
partisans go to the polls.

While Harold Clarke and his colleagues argued that party identification in
Canada is best understood by the more complex term of 'partisanship', analyses by
subsequent teams of researchers conducting the Canadian Election Studies adopted a
different tack of definition and measurement. In the study *Letting the People Decide,*
Richard Johnston and his collaborators suggested that a key difference between the
way in which party identification was conceptualized in the United States and Canada
was in the way in which respondents could self-identify as not identified with a
party, or as politically independent. Whereas studies in the US always provided
respondents with the option of identifying as independents, the Canadian studies
to that point had not included political independence as one of the options offered
when measuring a person's party identification. The result, according to Johnston
et al., was that 'more Canadian than American non-partisans were induced to give
what appeared to be a party commitment. This inflated the percentage appearing
to identify with some party and made the identifier group appear quite unstable
over repeated measurements.' The measurement solution to this conceptual problem was to include the option 'none of these' in the question probing respondents'
party identification. Thus, individuals were asked whether they thought of themselves as Liberals, Conservatives, New Democrats, some other party, or none of
these. Not surprisingly, the percentage of respondents indicating that they were not
partisans increased from an average of approximately 20 per cent between 1965 and
1984, to 35 per cent in 1988 (Johnston et al. 1992, 82, Table 3-1).

The reconceptualization of party identification among the Canadian Election Study team continued when Andre Blais and his collaborators (2001) conducted an analysis of the measurement of party identification through a comparison of election study data in Britain, Canada, and the United States. According to Blais et al., party identification has two key components—it is a self-definition among individuals (that is, one does not need to hold a party membership, or vote a certain way to identify with a party), and there is a time horizon associated with the identification, in that it consists of an enduring attachment. Using question-wording experiments in the election surveys of the late 1990s in the three countries, Blais et al. found that the observed incidence of party identification changed considerably according to the question set used. Specifically, they recommended the adoption of a question set that included items that touch on both of these elements. In terms of the self-identification element, they found that using a term such as 'normally', when asking about a party self-image, helped direct the respondent to an enduring attachment rather than attachment of the moment. They also recommended the use of a cue that enables respondents to indicate that they have no attachment, to ensure there is not an inflated assessment of respondents with a party identification. Both of these recommendations can be seen in the way respondents to the 2008 Canadian election study were asked about their party identification, with the following wording: 'In federal politics, do you *usually* think of yourself as Liberal, Conservative, NDP, Bloc Québécois, Green, or *none of these*' (emphasis

APPLY YOUR UNDERSTANDING

Multidimensional Concepts

One of the prime goals at the stage of formulating conceptual definitions is to achieve clarity of concepts. This is not to say, however, that the concepts should be simple. As the discussion of party identification and partisanship indicated, concepts in the social sciences may be complex and multidimensional. Consider the following concepts. Devise a definition of each concept that includes only a single dimension. Then offer a multidimensional definition of that concept:

- political participation
- interest in politics
- assessment of party leaders

- neoconservative ideology
- feminism
- environmentalism

How did you do? Were you able to develop both unidimensional and multidimensional definitions? You can check how well your definitions match the definitions of these concepts among social scientists working in the area. One way of doing so would be to search for one of these key terms in an academic journal database. Find a recent article identified in the database, and look for the author's definition of the concept.

added). Thus, in key areas of research in public opinion and voting, there is an on-going dialogue between the way concepts are defined and subsequently how they are operationalized and measured with questions in our election study data sets.

SOURCES OF CONCEPTUAL DEFINITIONS

It is clear that one of the perennial difficulties in the social sciences is defining con-cepts in such a way that all researchers, and all observers, agree on their meaning. If we wish to conduct research with the goal of formulating lawlike generalizations about the social world, agreement on the meaning of terms would appear to be a basic precondition. Unfortunately, the reality in the social sciences is that agree-ment on the meaning of terms remains elusive. Furthermore, there is no indisput-able guide to which one can turn for the single, authoritative definition of a concept. One can refer to the political science literature, but, as we have seen, that literature is as likely to document disagreement as it is consensus. This does not mean, how-ever, that concepts either have no meaning at all or that they have any meaning one wishes to ascribe, as suggested by the Mock Turtle in *Alice in Wonderland*:

> 'Of course not,' said the Mock Turtle. 'Why, if a fish came to me, and told me he was going on a journey, I should say "With what porpoise?" '
> 'Don't you mean "purpose"?' said Alice. 'I mean what I say,' the Mock Turtle replied, in an offended tone.[2]

Instead, it is to suggest that debate over the meaning of concepts can itself be an important topic of scholarly inquiry. Within the debate, inductive reasoning, extrapolation, and intuition all come into play.

INDUCTIVE REASONING

Although most studies begin with a literature review, an account of the conceptual and empirical terrain mapped out to date, this should not suggest that a researcher can define concepts only in ways in which they have been defined by previous research. Quite the opposite. It is both possible and at times highly desirable to focus a research project on the development of alternative conceptual definitions. Perhaps the most common method of doing so is through the use of **inductive reasoning**. By inductive reasoning we mean using empirical evidence to help form the definition of a concept. An illustration of this can be drawn from the example of party identification given earlier in this chapter. When Clarke and his colleagues were examining Canadian voting behaviour in the mid-1970s, they began with the conceptualization of party identification as it was developed in the United States. However, their early studies of this phenomenon in Canada indicated several im-portant differences: they found that many Canadians held different identifications

EXPAND YOUR KNOWLEDGE

Inductive Reasoning and Reconceptualization

The preceding argument is that evidence from a research project can lead to a new and different definition of a concept. A good illustration of this can be seen in some of the research on political participation. One of the early empirical studies of political participation in the United States was conducted by Lester Milbrath (1965), who argued that there was a hierarchy of participation. The hierarchy, in Milbrath's view, was shaped as a pyramid, with many people near the bottom, exhibiting low levels of participation, and with decreasing numbers of people as one moved up the hierarchy. Milbrath labelled those at the high end of the pyramid 'gladiators', those in the middle 'participants', and those at the low end 'spectators'.

In a later study, Sidney Verba and Norman Nie (1972) found that political participation was not arrayed in such a hierarchical fashion. In particular, they found many people involved in protest activities such as marches, demonstrations, or sit-ins, including those who were highly involved in such participatory activities, often were not involved in more conventional types of political participation, such as voting, donating money to a political party, or running for elective office. This finding led to the conclusion that there were different types or 'modes' of participation and that these modes may be relatively independent of one another. Furthermore, different factors may account for the level of activity in different modes of participation. Thus, the empirical evidence led to a reconceptualization of political participation.

at the federal and provincial levels, and they found that party identifications were not as stable in Canada as they were reported to be in the United States (see Jenson 1975; Jenson 1978; Clarke et al. 1979; LeDuc et al. 1984). Thus, evidence from the application of the concept led to its reconceptualization.

Extrapolation

An alternative method of changing a conceptual definition is to *extrapolate,* even borrow from other fields of study. Political scientists have developed certain conceptual tools for understanding political phenomena, as have economists, sociologists, psychologists, and other social scientists for their fields of study. At times, the concepts developed for one of the social sciences may have important applicability to others. One well-known example of this type of conceptual borrowing can be seen in Anthony Downs's (1957) adoption of a 'rational' approach to voting. (Recall that Downs was introduced in Chapter 2.) An economist, Downs attempted to explain voters' decision-making and the relative ideological positioning of political parties using the **deductive reasoning** that is popular in economic analyses. The deductive method begins by the identification of one or more postulates, followed by the derivation of expectations and conclusions based on the postulates. The postulate often used in economic analysis, and used by Downs in his study, is that voters and the leadership of political parties are rational (that is, self-interested, utility-maximizing) decision-makers. The justification for this extrapolation from economics to politics is that this method has a number of insights for economic decisions involving the marketplace and therefore could provide insight into political decisions involving power, influence, and authority. Whether it does so is a matter of ongoing empirical investigation.

Intuition

Each of the ways of justifying conceptual definitions discussed thus far relies to a considerable extent on how *other* researchers have operationalized a concept. But what about the ideas that are quite unique and independent to *you* as a researcher? What if you have thought about a concept in a way that no one else has thought about it before? Is it not possible to bring one's own creativity to a research project, to define concepts in new ways that speak more directly to one's experience and imagination? The answer to the latter question is a qualified yes. One certainly should not feel restricted to using concepts whose definitions appear less helpful and informative than others that could be imagined. Concepts should be defined to best capture the essence of the quality that is being examined.

However, our experience is that students often do not fully appreciate the scope of previous research on a topic. A vast and continually growing amount of research has been conducted and published on topics in political science. The chances are reasonably good that the ideas that occur to you regarding the best definition of a concept, or the best explanation for variation in a dependent concept, have been examined by others in a different context. What may appear very new to you as you begin to think of yourself as someone engaged in empirical political science may well have occurred to others as well. Thus, two cautionary flags should be raised. First, it is important to check the literature thoroughly for examples of other research that has used conceptual definitions similar to those in your study. To acknowledge the work of the previous researchers and to connect your findings to those of the broader research community, it is important to provide citations to the previous research. Second, if you are truly the first researcher ever to define a concept in a particular way, it is important to thoroughly search the literature and to highlight the differences between how you have defined the concept and how it has been defined in previous studies. It is also important to explain why your conceptual definition is superior to that used in the previous studies.

In summary, defining concepts in clear and concise ways is an important part of using the scientific method. It is useful to begin from the premise that other political scientists may think about this concept differently than you do. Therefore, to avoid misunderstanding about the topic of the research, it is helpful to provide clear definitions of the concepts that will be used in your study. It is also important to recognize that your study will be part of 'the literature' in an area of study, so it is useful to provide cross-references to other studies related to yours, and that are points of departure for your work.

WORKING AS A TEAM

1. One of the central elements of democratic theory, and one of the most common elements of contemporary political debate, is the concept of *equality*. Discuss in your group various meanings that might be attached to this concept.

2. Can you produce a conceptualization to which everyone can agree?

SELF-STUDY

1. Think of a concept that may be of interest in political science research (political ideologies, political belief systems, voting, political stability, democracy, etc.). Identify three journal articles in which this concept was examined. Describe the way in which the authors define the concept in the three studies. Provide a critique of the conceptual definitions.

    Concept:
    First article:
    (author, year, title, journal, volume, issue, page)
    Definition:
    Second article:
    (author, year, title, journal, volume, issue, page)
    Definition:
    Third article:
    (author, year, title, journal, volume, issue, page)
    Definition:
    Critique of the three definitions:

2. Participation in politics is variously called 'political participation', 'political involvement', or 'political activity'. It is sometimes defined as a single, simple concept, as a number of (possibly unrelated) simple concepts, and as a complex, multidimensional concept. Find an example of each type of definition in the literature on political participation. Discuss the usefulness of each.

    a. Political participation:
       Single, simple concept:
       Multiple, simple concepts:
       Multidimensional concept:
    b. Political involvement:
       Single, simple concept:
       Multiple, simple concepts:
       Multidimensional concept:
    c. Political activity:
       Single, simple concept:
       Multiple, simple concepts:
       Multidimensional concept:

NOTES

1. For a discussion of the more general pattern of the influence of American scholarship on research in Canada, see Cairns (1975).

2. Lewis Carroll, *Alice's Adventures in Wonderland and Through the Looking Glass,* with notes by Martin Gardner (New York: Random House, 1990), 26.

Chapter 4

DEFINING THE POLITICAL WORLD: MEASURES

DESTINATION

By the end of this chapter the reader should

- understand the process of operationalization and appreciate the research concerns brought to that process;
- know the distinctions among concepts, variables, and indicators;
- be familiar with nominal-, ordinal-, and interval-level variables and with issues of accuracy in the measurement of political phenomena; and
- have some experience with the logic behind and creation of scales and indices.

As political scientists, we often find that questions of interest to us are stated as abstractions. For example, Which political system is better? Which economic system promotes the greatest social equality? What is the best means to provide health care? When we approach these matters from an empirical rather than a normative position, we seek factual evidence that can be applied to these abstract questions. In order to obtain such evidence, we first need to transform the concepts embedded in our questions into a form where they can be tackled empirically. The first step in doing so, as outlined in the previous chapter, is a conceptual definition. With that definition in hand, we can then turn to the matter of measurement.

For example, consider the grading of university students. Universities reserve the grade A for those students whose course performance is 'excellent'. However, 'academic excellence' is an abstract concept; thus, how will a professor know which students have earned an A and which have not? In the interests of fairness, the professor needs to quantify academic performance so that all students are comparable. She may decide that students should be judged on three areas: subject knowledge, research skills, and writing ability. Now she needs some method to measure student performance in these three areas. Examinations, homework assignments, and term papers are all methods that might be used. This process—moving from an abstract concept (academic excellence) to a concrete measure (midterm examination mark)—is known as **operationalization**. As we will see, it is not a simple process and at times can be a very contentious one. Think, for instance, of the potential conflicts and controversies that can swirl around the measurement of academic excellence even in a class such as this one! Seldom can we fall back on widely shared rules to make the decisions that have to be made.

This chapter explores the use of conceptual definitions to select variables and the use of indicators to locate individual cases among the different values of the variable. In addition, we will explore how to select and create the best possible variables and indicators for our research questions. It is in this process of operationalization that the conceptual rubber hits the empirical road.

APPLY YOUR UNDERSTANDING

Operationalizing University Objectives

Universities often come under a good deal of public scrutiny with respect to the objectives of postsecondary education. In their own defence, universities often argue that the public and, more particularly, politicians, fail to understand that the objectives of a university education entail more than the acquisition of marketable skills.

Suppose, then, your own premier says, 'Fine, I will accept your university's definition of its own mission [which might be to produce graduates with a capacity for independent and critical thought and with the research and analytical skills necessary for success in the twenty-first century]. Now, show me the evidence that the university is in fact producing such individuals. Show me proof that universities are not simply taking in bright students, aging them four or five years, and then releasing them back into society with no significant increase in their capacity for independent and critical thought, and without the necessary research and analytical skills. In short, show me that the government and public are getting good value for publicly funded postsecondary education.'

Given this challenge, how would you operationalize the university's objectives? How would you measure whether students are, in fact, getting better with respect to their ability to think, and whether they are acquiring the appropriate research and analytical skills? What impact has your own education to date had in these respects, and how would you measure this impact? How might you prove that the government and public are getting good value? Or do we simply ask to be taken on faith? Will such a plea carry much weight in an environment of fiscal constraint?

CONCEPTS, VARIABLES, AND INDICATORS

It is important at the outset to be clear on the difference between a concept and a variable. Recall that a concept is an idea or a term that enables us to classify phenomena; equality, order, social class, political culture, and region are all examples of concepts. Obviously, concepts can be relatively abstract (for example, liberty) or relatively concrete (for example, region); the more abstract a concept, the more difficult it is to find a definition that is acceptable to one's peers. When we transform our conceptual definition into a quantifiable, observable phenomenon, we have a **variable**.

The distinction between concepts and variables might best be seen by way of an example. 'Education' is a concept; we might, for instance, define education as 'formal training to develop mental abilities and skills'. 'Level of education' is a variable that can empirically distinguish between different levels of training. How is the variable 'level of education' different from the concept 'education'? The variable, unlike the concept, can take on different **values**. We might choose to divide level of education into categories (for example, low, middle, and high), or we may look at the actual years of education completed by individuals and compare them on a precise basis. The point to stress is that the variable empirically captures *the variation within the concept*. This is a fine but nonetheless important distinction.

Ultimately, our goal is knowledge about the concepts themselves. As we have seen, concepts are the building blocks of theory, and *theories use propositions to state the relationships between concepts*. Variables are our means of tapping and quantifying these concepts, and *hypotheses state the relationships between variables*. We test hypotheses in an effort to find support for our propositions and, by extension, for our theory. It is important to note, however, that as we move from concepts to variables, some degree of meaning or understanding is invariably lost (Manheim and Rich 1981, 45). This is because we are limited by our variables to those aspects of the concept that can be measured empirically. Often, concepts include intrinsic values or meanings that cannot be captured fully by empirical research. For example, many of the benefits that are thought to spring from postsecondary education are not easily captured by empirical measurement. You may be a more thoughtful individual with your degree in hand, but demonstrating this to others can be a difficult task.

APPLY YOUR UNDERSTANDING

Moving from Concepts to Variables

For the following concepts, (1) provide a precise conceptual definition, and (2) select three variables to measure each concept. Do you find it easier to select variables for the more abstract concepts, or are the concrete concepts easier to work with? How do your variables differ from the concepts? What is lost by being limited to only three variables?

What is lost when you move from concept to variable?

- environmentalism
- political interest
- democracy
- economic growth
- family values

EXPAND YOUR KNOWLEDGE
Abuse of Women in Canadian University and College Dating Relationships

A widespread public discussion of the distinction between conceptual and operational definitions in the social sciences occurred with the release in 1993 of a study examining the abuse of women in Canadian university and college dating relationships. The conclusions of the study, widely reported in the media at the time, were shocking: 35 per cent of Canadian students reported having been physically abused, 45.1 per cent had been sexually abused, and 86.2 per cent had been psychologically abused in a dating relationship (DeKeseredy and Kelly 1993, 148–53). These results were so inconsistent with the conventional understandings of the prevalence of abuse of women in dating relationships at Canadian universities and colleges that their release was greeted with widespread disbelief in much of the popular commentary. The study's operationalization of the concept 'abuse' was also challenged in the scholarly community. The researchers' response to their critics presents a very revealing portrait of the challenges facing researchers working in highly sensitive areas within the social sciences.

DeKeseredy and Kelly define 'abuse' as follows: 'Any intentional physical, sexual, or psychological assault on a female by a male dating partner was defined as woman abuse' (1993, 146). Thus, they identify three types of abuse. The authors also distinguish between the 'incidence' of abuse (a situation that has occurred in the last 12 months) and the 'prevalence' of abuse (has occurred since they left high school) (138). Since 'prevalence' covers a longer period of time, the prevalence data invariably are higher than incidence data. The study also compared the responses of male and female respondents, but only regarding the behaviour of men toward women, not vice versa.

Let's illustrate with the data on the prevalence rates of psychological abuse:

Type of Abuse	Men (N = 1,307)		Women (N = 1,835)	
	%	N	%	N
Insults or swearing	62.4	747	65.1	1,105
Put her (you) down in front of friends or family	25.9	322	44.2	742
Accused her (you) of having affairs or flirting with other men	40.9	495	52.6	901
Did or said something to spite her (you)	65.2	773	72.2	1,216
Threatened to hit or throw something at her (you)	8.0	97	20.6	346
Threw, smashed, or kicked something	30.6	373	37.3	652

The data under the column for men indicate the percentage of men who said they did one of these behaviours to a woman they were dating in the period since they left high school. The data for women are the percentage of women who reported they had these behaviours done to them by a man they were dating in the period since they left high school. When these six questions were combined, DeKeseredy and Kelly found that 86.2 per cent of women had experienced at least one of these behaviours since high school. Based on their operational definition of abuse, they concluded that 86.2 per cent of women had been psychologically abused, and 80.8 per cent of men had been psychologically abusive with a dating partner in the period since high school (1993, 153).

The reaction to this conclusion from the scholarly community was swift and strong. In the following issue of the *Canadian Journal of Sociology*, commentaries appeared by Gartner (1993) and Fox (1993). Gartner challenged the validity of the term 'abuse' as operationalized by DeKeseredy and Kelly (we discuss validity in more detail later in this chapter). She argued that the questions used to measure psychological abuse are derived from a commonly used battery of questions called the Conflict Tactics Scales. These questions are introduced to respondents 'by noting both the normality of disagreements and conflicts between partners in a relationship and the range of different ways disagreements are dealt with' (1993, 314). The term 'abuse' is not used in the questions themselves. Furthermore, as the name of the scale implies, the questions are designed to measure 'conflict tactics', which may go both ways in a relationship, and not abuse. This latter point is important, Gartner argues, because previous research shows that 'women and men are about equally likely to use verbal aggression' (1993, 316). Similarly, Fox argues that the use of 'global' measures of abuse combine the least with the worst offences (for example, an unwanted kiss with rape) (1993, 322). Both Gartner and Fox argue that conflating the two risks trivializes the more serious offences (Gartner 1993, 318–19; Fox 1993, 322).

In a set of responses to their critics, DeKeseredy (1994) and Kelly (1994) justify their operational decisions. However, in a revealing description of the publication of the findings, Kelly provides an eye-opening account of her experiences with this study: 'Once the data were collected, there was immediate pressure to release them. From the onset, I was concerned about the release of the psychological abuse items. . . . [W]e agreed to initially release only the marginals for the physical and sexual abuse items and not to release the aggregate of all abuse items and the psychological abuse items until the data had been fully analyzed. Unfortunately, the data were released without my consent, against our express agreement, and in a form that, in my view, distorted the value of the research. . . . [T]he bulk of the media attention was to the combined total abuse figures and the psychological abuse items' (1994, 83).

This saga stands as stark testimony of the importance of having consistency between conceptual and operational definitions in the social sciences. It illustrates the accuracy of the old adage 'The devil is in the details.'

When we choose variables, we strive to select those that most accurately capture our concepts and thereby reduce the amount of meaning that is lost. One way to do so is to use *multiple* variables to tap the same concept. Often, many variables can be seen as legitimate measures of a given concept and particularly of more complex concepts. Consider the concept of 'political participation', which we will define here as 'acting with the intent of directly influencing the political system'. One variable that might tap political participation is voting: did the individual vote in the last election or not? Voting is empirically measurable and can take on different values (did or did not vote).[1] However, other variables also provide insight into political participation; party membership, political campaign contributions, lobbying, letter writing, and protest activity are all aspects of political participation.

As Figure 4.1 on page 72 shows, each of these variables captures a piece, but only a piece, of the concept. Some, such as community participation, may capture part of the

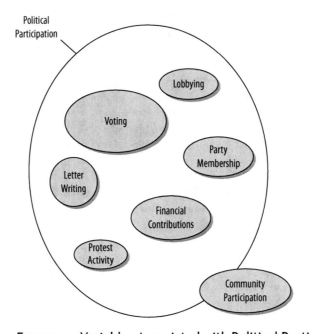

FIGURE 4.1 **Variables Associated with Political Participation**

Source: Adapted from Lawrence Neuman, *Social Research Methods,* 2d ed. (Boston: Allyn & Bacon, 1994).

concept, even though the bulk of community participation is nonpolitical in character. In Figure 4.1, therefore, 'community participation' falls largely outside the conceptual domain of 'political participation'. And, even with a number of variables at our disposal, there will still be 'spaces left', conceptual aspects of participation that remain untapped. These spaces are represented by the unshaded parts of Figure 4.1. Ideally, only small sections of the conceptual domain will be left uncovered by our selected variables.

Our discussion of grading in the introduction to this chapter provides another example of multiple variables: subject knowledge, research skills, and writing ability are all variables that can be used to quantify the concept of 'academic excellence'. In such cases, when we have multiple variables that appear to measure the same concept, there are likely to be a number of *dimensions* to the concept. The ability to write, for instance, is not the same as knowledge of the subject matter, although we hope there is some relationship (some *positive* relationship!) between the two.[2] We can sometimes combine variables into an index or a scale, which will act as a **complex multiple indicator**. By using multiple variables to quantify the conceptual definition, we are able to capture more fully the meaning of the concept, as Figure 4.1 suggests. This allows us to be more confident when we use the variables to draw conclusions about the concepts. However, as the study of woman abuse in dating relationships illustrates, simply choosing more variables to measure a concept is not necessarily a prescription for better measurement if the variables lack validity (see the discussion of validity later in this chapter).

Once we have selected the variables to measure a concept, we still need ways to gather information about the variables. The measures are referred to as **operational definitions** or **indicators**. Indicators are the means by which we assign each individual case to the different values of the variable.[3] In the example used in the introduction to this chapter, the grades recorded for examinations, homework assignments, and term papers could be used as indicators for the various dimensions of academic excellence.

Let's consider the variable 'support for feminism'. We might understand support for feminism to vary from high through moderate to low support. But what observable facts indicate support for feminism? How do we know whether Jane shows high, moderate, or low support? Possible indicators of support might include stated support in surveys for either feminism or feminist goals, membership in feminist organizations (recorded in membership lists), or financial support for feminist lobby groups (recorded in donation lists). In a study of 1,006 Alberta respondents conducted by Keith Archer and Roger Gibbins, feminism was measured in part by responses to the following questions:

- Do you agree or disagree that society would be better off if more women stayed home with their children? (51.5 per cent agreed.)
- Do you agree or disagree that we have gone too far in pushing equal rights in this country? (50.6 per cent agreed.)
- How important is it to guarantee equality between men and women in all aspects of life? (61.0 per cent thought it was very important, 31.8 per cent somewhat important, and 7.1 per cent not important.)

Or consider the variable 'economic development'. Some commonly used indicators of economic development are GDP (gross domestic product) and GDP per capita, infant mortality rates, literacy rates, and the proportion of GDP spent on research and development. Information from these indicators can be used to classify countries as 'developed' or 'developing'.

There may be multiple indicators of a single variable. For example, in the Alberta survey discussed earlier, three indicators have been brought into play. Just as multiple variables may allow us to tap more of a concept, multiple indicators may allow us to tap more of a variable. The various indicators, however, will not yield exactly the same results. (If they did, we would need only one.) The United States, for instance, has a poorer record than most Western states with respect to infant mortality, but a better record than most with respect to per capita GDP. Nonetheless, all indicators should point in the same direction; developed countries tend to have higher scores across the board than do developing countries.

To illustrate this point, consider a very simple illustration and then a much more complex illustration. The first comes from a questionnaire administered to grade 10 students who had just completed a summer volleyball camp. The students were asked a very rudimentary question: 'Did you enjoy the camp, yes or no?' While the organizers of the camp were pleased that the vast majority of the students said yes, the questionnaire did little to tap the various dimensions of enjoyment. Did students enjoy the coaching? The food? The level of competition? The chance to meet new friends? The social atmosphere? Did they enjoy some elements more than others? What did they like least and most? By asking only one question, and an extremely simple one at that, the organizers missed the opportunity to acquire the type of information that might enable them to plan a better camp the next time around. In short, they needed more than a single indicator of enjoyment.

Next consider social class. As a concept, social class has played an extraordinarily important role in the evolution of social science theory. It is one of the truly 'big' concepts, particularly in economics, political science, and sociology. However, it is not easy to capture the theoretical richness of class concepts with empirical indicators. Theoretical nuance is inevitably lost. Certainly one indicator is not sufficient; knowing, for instance, an individual's annual income, education, or occupation alone will not suffice. Class is more than money, more than income, more than occupational location, although all three have a significant role to play. Nor is it easy to pull together multiple indicators, for they do not always move in sync. Education and income are positively correlated, as are education and occupation and occupation and income, but there are many exceptions to the general rule of positive association. It is the relationship between these variables that affects a person's class position.

The multidimensionality of class can be illustrated by a couple of examples. Imagine two individuals who each earn $150,000 per year. If social class were measured solely by *annual income,* they would both be considered as having a high social class. Now, imagine that one of them earned this income as a physician and the other by selling cocaine. Because these two occupations have such a different *status* in Canadian society, it is no longer apparent that they both have a high social class, even though they have identical incomes. Indeed, the drug dealer has a relatively low social class despite a high income. This type of finding, of course, is not limited to instances in which people are engaged in illegal activities. As a second illustration, assume two respondents who have each graduated from law school, which gives them a high score on a variable measuring education. Imagine that one of them practices corporate law and earns $250,000 annually, while the other works at an inner city legal aid clinic and earns $30,000 annually. Which of these lawyers has the higher social class? In answering this question, be careful to stay within the definition of the concept being measured. Some (idealistic?) students might well prefer to work for a legal aid clinic, and such a position might be viewed as more socially relevant and, for them, more enjoyable. But the question was, which individual has the higher social class? If social class is defined as a multidimensional concept, comprising levels of education, income, and occupational status, and in which a higher score on each component corresponds with a higher class position, then the answer is simple: the corporate lawyer has the higher social class.

In summary, variables are a means of translating concepts into observable and quantifiable phenomena; indicators are the means or operations used to determine the exact values of our variables. As we move from concept to variable to indicator, we move from broad abstraction to narrow precision. Figure 4.2 presents a fairly simple visual representation of how indicators, variables, and concepts fit together, whereas a more complex example using multiple indicators and variables is seen in Figure 4.3 on the next page. In each figure the objective is to support the *proposition*, that is, the relationship between the two concepts. Hypotheses, variables, and indicators are the tools we use to test the proposition.

Given the importance of selecting proper variables and indicators for our concepts, a justification of their selection should be part of any research report. Choices will always be involved, and you need to be able to justify the choices made. By explaining the logic behind our operationalization and demonstrating the linkages between indicators and variables and between variables and concepts, arguments and conclusions are more readily defended. In addition, the need to explain one's choices in operationalization improves the process: when we know we must defend our selections to our peers, we are more likely to take every precaution to avoid criticism.

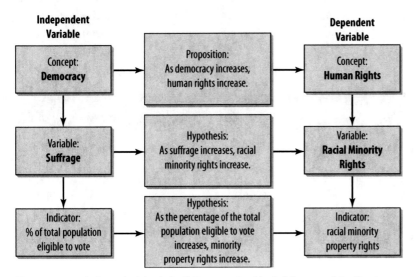

FIGURE 4.2 A Simple Model of Concepts, Variables, and Indicators

Source: Adapted from Jarol Manheim and Richard Rich, *Empirical Political Analysis: Research Methods in Political Science* (NJ: Prentice-Hall, 1981).

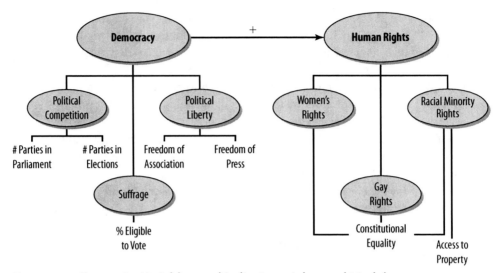

FIGURE 4.3 Concepts, Variables, and Indicators: Advanced Model

In this context, it is important to recognize that much of the research done by both students and faculty involves secondary analysis of existing data sets. In such cases, the primary selection of indicators has already been made by others. If, for example, we are using data from the Canadian Election Studies, we are locked into the measures selected by the CES research teams. Thus, our choices are limited, and we may end up using indicators that are not quite what we would like them to be. This is not to imply that our own design of indicators would necessarily be better, but only that researchers who rely on secondary analysis must use indicators that may have been designed for other research purposes and agendas.

APPLY YOUR UNDERSTANDING

Moving from Variables to Indicators

Using the most recent Canadian Election Study or a comparable survey, can you find indicators of the following variables?

- support for environmentalism
- political interest
- social class
- attitudes toward party leaders
- party affiliation

Using the same study, select five additional survey questions. What concepts or variables do you believe these questions were intended to tap? List all possible uses for each of the five questions.

PRECISION IN MEASUREMENT

Our indicators allow us to distinguish between the values of a variable. When indicators are designed, the issue emerges as to how precise the distinctions should be between categories of a variable. There are three basic **levels of measurement** that capture the different levels of precision that variables can take: **nominal**, **ordinal**, and **interval**. As we will see in later chapters, the level of measurement selected will largely determine the type and power of statistical measures available for analysis: the higher the level of measurement, the more powerful the statistics that are available.

What do we mean by precise? Think about the difference in precision between describing someone as 'young' and describing the same person as '21 years of age'. Both descriptions can be used for the same individual, but the latter is more precise than the former. The designation 'young' omits a great deal of information: we do not know the cutoff point between 'young' and 'not young', nor do we know where this person sits within the category: is she at the upper limit of the category (as she would be if the category 'young' ended at age 22), or does she still have a few years to enjoy being 'young' (as she would if the category ended at age 30)? If we were to pursue precision to the extreme, we would have an overabundance of information; age could be specified to the year, date, and even time of birth. Fortunately, such detail is neither required nor desirable for most variables and most research questions. For example, if we are interested in the impact of age on support for neoconservatism, we might expect people in their twenties to differ from those in their forties or fifties, but we would not expect to find significant differences between those who are 26 and 27. Our goal in research is to form generalizations about groups of people, and that goal by necessity requires that we categorize individuals on the basis of similar and different characteristics. If we pursue such high levels of precision that we end up with an extremely small number of cases in each category, we will be unable to notice patterns or relationships between variables. Overall, we should strive for the highest level of measurement that *is useful for the research question at hand*.

Recall that concepts can be conceptualized as either categorical or continuous. Categorical concepts have characteristics that are distinct and unconnected, while continuous concepts have characteristics that are sequentially connected. Similarly, variables can be distinguished between those that have discrete categories and those whose categories can be placed on a continuum; religious affiliation would be an example of the former, age of the latter. Categorical concepts will result in the selection of nominal-level variables, whereas continuous concepts lend themselves to either ordinal- or interval-level variables. We will outline each level of measurement in turn.

Nominal-level variables are those whose categories cannot be ordered or ranked. Religion, region, and gender are examples of nominal variables, as are 'yes–no' distinctions. (For instance, 'Do you agree in principle with assisted suicide for terminally ill patients?') Differences exist between the categories of the variable, as, for example, between males and females, and numerical values can be assigned to the categories (for example, male = 1; female = 2), but there is no mathematical relationship between these values. The values are arbitrary and may be assigned arbitrarily (for example, male = 2; female = 1). With a nominal-level variable, the numerical values represent differences in kind (for example, Liberal = 1, Conservative = 2, NDP = 3, BQ = 4, and Green = 5), not in degree. Thus, while the categories of nominal variables are distinct, they cannot logically be ordered. To appreciate how common nominal-level variables and indicators are in political science research, imagine how hamstrung we would be if we could not distinguish survey respondents on the basis of their language, region, sex, religion, or partisan identification.

Ordinal-level variables allow for the ranking of categories. The ranking in an ordinal-level variable is *relative* to the position of the other categories; we do not know the exact distance between the categories, but we can organize the categories along a continuum. 'Strongly agree – agree – disagree – strongly disagree', 'poor – fair – good – excellent', and the 'A – B – C – D – F' grading system are all examples of ordinal rankings.

It is common to encounter rank-ordered data in the social sciences, and most people have an intuitive understanding of data presented in this way. However, there are a number of precautions that must be kept in mind when working with rank-ordered data. The first is that we cannot assume that the distance between ranks is the same. For example, if you were asked to rank-order your first five destinations for a midsession holiday, there may be a much larger perceptual gap between your first and second choices than between your fourth and fifth choices. You might *really* want to go to your first choice but be relatively indifferent between choices four and five. Second, and perhaps of greater importance, any rank order always has a bottom, a lowest, or a worst, but being ranked last does not necessarily indicate the absence of quality. Let's look briefly at two illustrations.

Many universities use student evaluations of faculty teaching to generate decile ratings; some instructors are ranked in the tenth decile, meaning that their student scores are higher than those received by 90 per cent of their peers, while others are ranked in the first decile, meaning that 90 per cent of their peers had better student perceptions. However, this does not mean that first-decile teachers are necessarily poor teachers; it means only that 90 per cent of the other instructors are viewed by students as *better* teachers. It is possible, therefore, that students in Professor Filibuster's class might describe him as a competent and effective teacher, yet still have their assessments place him in the first decile in comparison with his peers. Ten per cent of the professors *have to be* in the first decile. When individuals are rank-ordered, someone must finish last regardless of the quality of their performance. The last place athlete in an Olympic event is still an excellent athlete.

A second illustration comes from a decision to rank-order public and Catholic schools in the Calgary system by their pass rates and to release these rankings to the press. Parents, therefore, can see where their children's school, or potential school, is placed. Is it first, second, or last? The problem is that very small differences in the pass rate can have a major impact on rank order. For example, among grade 6 classes in the Catholic system, the difference in pass rates between the number one ranked school and the tenth ranked school was only between 100 per cent and 98.4 per cent. The school that ranked twentieth still had a pass rate of 96.0 per cent, while the pass rate for the school ranked thirtieth had 'plummeted' to only 93.2 per cent. Thus, relatively minor differences in the measure used to determine rankings can have a substantial impact on the rank ordering. Students, teachers, and parents associated with the school ranked twentieth in the system could well be depressed by their comparative position, even though the substantive difference between their own school and the school ranked first was negligible. In a similar fashion, the first-decile teacher may feel depressed and incompetent, even though most of his students may feel he is doing an effective job.

Interval-level variables can also be placed on a continuum, but unlike ordinal variables, the categories are separated by a standard unit. The distance between 1 and 2, for instance, is the same as the distance between 3 and 4. Thus, with interval data, the value of 4 is twice the size of 2, and 8 is twice the size of 4. Note that this was not the case with ordinal-level data. With ordinal data, 4 is larger than 2, but it is uncertain how much larger it is.

Let's illustrate this difference by comparing an ordinal- and an interval-level measurement of attitudes toward the performance of the government. A 5-point Likert scale is a common way of deriving an ordinal-level attitudinal measure in the social sciences. Respondents could be asked the following:

> On a scale of 1 to 5, where 1 is 'strongly disapprove', 2 is 'somewhat disapprove', 3 is 'neither approve nor disapprove', 4 is 'approve', and 5 is 'strongly approve', how would you rate the performance of the government?

In response to this question, respondents' scores on the 'government rating' variable would range from 1 to 5. The higher the score, the more positively the respondent feels about the government. But notice that the size of the units on this variable is not constant. That is, the difference between 1 and 2 (strongly disapprove and somewhat disapprove) is not the same as the difference between 2 and 3 (somewhat disapprove and neither approve nor disapprove). By extension, the value of 4 is not twice the value of 2, in the sense that people scoring 4 are not twice as supportive of the government as those who score 2. Because of this, and to anticipate our discussion in Chapter 15, it would not be appropriate to compute an 'average', or mean, score based on this question. A mean assumes a constant value between categories.

In addition, the issue of giving 'meaning' or 'context' to data, an issue that was at the heart of the dispute over the 'woman abuse' data discussed earlier in the chapter, also adds a measure of subjectivity to social sciences data. For example, some would say that money is an interval-level variable or indicator in the social sciences. A dollar is a dollar, and 10 dollars is half of 20 dollars. But it is also true that money has a different meaning for people, depending upon the context of their social and economic situation. A government policy designed to increase individual taxes by a flat rate of $1,000 across the board would have a different meaning for people earning $200,000 annually than it would for people earning $25,000 annually. Although the amount is the same, its value varies. Therefore, even 'hard' interval-level data in the social sciences can take on ordinal-level characteristics.

Despite these obvious concerns with interval-level data in the social sciences, researchers often assume that their data are interval-level, or sufficiently close to

EXPAND YOUR KNOWLEDGE

Feeling Thermometers

Researchers sometimes try to impose an interval scale by defining a response set in such a way that it appears to have a standard unit between categories. One frequently encountered illustration of such a pseudo interval-level variable is the '**feeling thermometer**'. For example, in Canadian Election Studies prior to 1988 (when the studies switched from face-to-face interviews to telephone interviews), the feeling thermometer was introduced with the following set of instructions:

> You will see here a drawing of a thermometer. It is called a feeling thermometer because it helps measure people's feelings toward various things. Here is how it works. If you don't have any particular feeling about the things we are asking about, place them at the 50-degree mark. If your feelings are very warm toward a particular thing, you would give a score between 50 and 100—the warmer your feelings, the higher the score. On the other hand, if your feelings are relatively cool toward something, you would place them between 0 and 50. The cooler your feelings, the closer the score will be to zero. (Clarke et al. 1979, 406)

Feeling thermometers can be used to compare politicians, parties, interest groups, countries, or virtually anything.

Feeling thermometers are attractive because respondents are able to use them with respect to a multitude of different objects. However, we cannot assume that the difference between a thermometer rating of 20 and 30, for instance, is the same as that between 70 and 80; the feeling thermometer is not a true interval-level variable. An interval-level scale would presuppose that all respondents internalize feelings of like or dislike by using a standard scale, and intuitively this is not to be the case. The trouble is that this differentiation of scales among respondents appears to occur for all attitudinal variables: even if researchers are definitive in the meaning of a response set, it still must be interpreted by the respondents. That process of interpretation, or internalization of the scale, adds a subjective component to its interpretation. It should also be noted in the specific case of the feeling thermometer that most respondents convert the thermometer to a 10-point scale; 40 and 50 are used more frequently than are 43 and 47.

approximate interval-level data. The reason, as we will discuss in much more detail in subsequent chapters, is that interval-level data are amenable to much higher-level statistical techniques and, in particular, provide opportunities for multivariate statistical techniques that offer more analytical insight than do the bivariate techniques common to nominal- and ordinal-level data analysis. The challenge is to understand the assumptions that underlie the data analysis, and to discern to what extent the data analytical techniques violate those assumptions, and with what effect. Understanding that process calls for a combination of both the art and science of data analysis.

Notice the precision differences between the levels of measurement. Nominal-level variables have categories, ordinal-level variables have categories that can be ranked, and interval-level variables have categories that can be ranked with a specified distance (or interval) between the categories. As we stated earlier, there are statistical advantages to using the highest level of measurement available. These incentives can lead some researchers to 'artificially' create interval-level variables where nominal- or ordinal-level variables would be more appropriate. For example, instead of using a single nominal-level variable to represent the regions of Canada, one could create a series of 'dummy' interval-level variables, such as Atlantic versus non-Atlantic, Quebec versus non-Quebec, etc. Sometimes it is desirable to move *down* in precision, moving, for instance, from interval- to ordinal-level variables. If we do not have enough cases within the categories, we cannot detect patterns, leading us to group interval-level data. In addition, grouped data can be easier to read in a contingency table because of the reduced number of categories. Finally, the calculation of certain measures of strength (addressed in Chapter 17) is easier with grouped data than with interval-level data.

The decision to group data presents the researcher with yet another decision: on what basis should data be grouped? Consider the variable 'age'. If we have 100 cases, with ages measured in years, how should we construct groups? Should we have three groups—young, middle, old—or perhaps four groups—young, young–middle, middle–old, old? What should be the cut-points between groups? Do we group the data to create equally sized age categories, for example, 0–19, 20–39, 40–59, 60–79, and 80–99, or do we categorize age according to our knowledge about life cycle and cohorts, for example, under 30, 30–65, over 65? Perhaps we should divide the data so that there are roughly the same number of cases in each category; for example, put the first 33 cases in 'young', the next 33 in 'middle', and the final 34 cases in 'old'. However you choose to group the data, it is recommended that you have some theoretical justification for your choice.

One question that should always be asked is, 'How have other researchers measured this variable?' Is your operational definition consistent with the literature in the area? If so, there usually is no need to provide a detailed justification. However, if the operational definition differs from the literature, be sure to highlight this fact and discuss its implications with regard to the comparability of the findings. In short, engage in the scholarly dialogue.

APPLY YOUR UNDERSTANDING

Levels of Measurement

What is the most appropriate level of measurement for each of the following variables? Explain why.

- party identification (values = Liberal, Conservative, NDP, BQ, and Green)
- ideological position (values = left, centre, right)
- unemployment rates (values = 0 per cent to 100 per cent)
- development (values = preindustrial, industrial, postindustrial)
- regime type (values = democratic, fascist, communist, authoritarian)
- population (values = 10,000, 20,000 . . . 10 billion)

APPLY YOUR UNDERSTANDING

Grouping Interval-level Data

You are interested in the relationship between age and active involvement in political parties. In order to pursue this interest, you have access to the following data set. How might you group respondents into age categories? What categories, what break points might you use, and how would you justify your choices?

Age	Number of Cases	Age	Number of Cases
18	8	31	2
19	16	32	0
20	4	33	2
21	8	34	3
22	12	35	1
23	7	36	0
24	11	37	2
25	7	38	1
26	10	39	3
27	6	40	4
28	4	41	1
29	1	42	0
30	5	43	3

ACCURACY IN MEASUREMENT

As we noted earlier, conclusions about a theoretical proposition are only as good as the variables and the indicators of those variables upon which the conclusion is based. Do the indicators measure the variables? Do the variables represent the concepts? Are the measures stable, or are different results obtained with repeated use of the measures? To the degree that we have confidence in the measures, we can have confidence in the conclusions. When we are considering the *accuracy* of indicators and variables, we need to look at two issues: *validity* and *reliability*.

Something is **valid** if it does what it was intended to do; thus, an indicator is valid if it measures the variable, and a variable is valid if it represents the concept. Essentially, **validity** refers to the 'degree of fit' between the indicator and the variable or between the variable and the concept (Neuman 1994, 130). Consider, for example, indicators of 'support for feminism in Canada'. One might use the number of members in NAC (the National Action Committee on the Status of Women) as an indicator of support. However, this indicator would be inappropriate: NAC mostly comprises member organizations, such as women's shelters and the YWCA, rather than women who expressly join NAC itself. It is possible, therefore, that many members of NAC are not even aware of their membership. Changing the indicator of support for feminism to the number of member organizations in NAC would produce a more appropriate measure. But would the measure be complete? How would we deal with groups of very different sizes? What about the individual men and women in the population who support feminism and/or feminist principles but who may not belong to organizations falling under NAC's umbrella? And what about all the members of women's groups not affiliated with NAC? A convincing argument could be made that a study of feminism in Canada would need to look further than NAC alone.

To ensure valid measurements, and thus valid conclusions, we need to select or create measures that are both '*appropriate* and *complete*' (Manheim and Rich 1981, 58). The first step in doing so is acquiring knowledge: the more we know about our subject matter, the more certain we can be that our measures are appropriate and complete. Such knowledge keeps us from making avoidable errors. To continue our example, basic knowledge of Canadian feminism would allow one to know that the antifeminist lobby REAL (realistic, equal, active, for life) Women would be inappropriate on a list of feminist organizations. The second step to increasing the completeness and appropriateness of our measures is testing and evaluating the measures. Here there are a number of tests:

- **Face validity**: *on the face of it*, is the measure logical? Does it appear to measure the concept? Can you justify your selection of the measure? Would other people see the logic in the selection? For example, few of us would accept ownership of a pet as a measure of animal rights activism. Face validity tests help address the question of appropriateness.

- **Convergent validity**: this is a comparison of indicators designed to measure the same variable. Logically, if two indicators are measuring the same variable, they should yield similar results for most cases. Thus, most individuals who score 'high' on one measure of conservatism should score 'high' on a second measure of conservatism. Since we are using one indicator as a criterion against which the other is measured, it is often preferable that we use a 'tried-and-true' measure as the criterion.
- **Discriminant (divergent) validity**: this test is the opposite of convergent validity. If two indicators predict opposing or very dissimilar views, they should yield different results for most cases. For example, imagine an indicator of feminist views—do you agree or disagree that 'women and men should have equal access to education and employment opportunities'—and an indicator of antifeminist views—do you agree or disagree that 'we would all be better off if women stayed home to raise children'. In this case, we would expect a negative correlation between the indicators: most people who agree with one can be expected to disagree with the other. If, on the other hand, we were to find a positive association (those who agree with the former also agree with the latter), we would have reason to question the validity of our measure.
- **Predictive validity**: does use of the measure help us to predict outcomes? To test predictive ability, we need to pilot test the measure in an appropriate population. For example, if we have a measure designed to tap attitudes about gun control, we could pilot test this measure among self-identified NRA (National Rifle Association, a strong anti-gun-control lobby in the United States) supporters. We would predict that strong opponents of gun control by our measure would be more likely than others to belong to the NRA. If they are not, we have reason to believe that the measure may be flawed.

It should be emphasized that indicators and variables are not themselves valid, but rather are valid (or invalid) with respect to the purpose at hand. Validity is a question of 'fit'; the same measure may have a poor fit with one concept yet a good fit with another. Also, it must be noted that perfect validity is an impossible ideal; we cannot find a variable that perfectly represents its concept or an indicator that perfectly measures its variable. This is inevitable given the losses in meaning that occur as we move along the continuum from concept to quantification. The very nature of operationalization requires that concepts and variables be simplified and, in the process, made less valid. Thus, when we discuss validity, we are considering a continuum between 'less valid' and 'more valid'.

One solution to the perpetual existence of validity problems is to use multiple variables and indicators. The goal here is to have the strengths of one compensate for the weaknesses of the other. Louise White (1994, 155–6) writes:

[I]t should be clear that neither variables nor their indicators are totally valid or totally invalid and that most pose some validity problems. . . . Because it is hard to find measures that are as valid as we would like, it is preferable to rely on two or more variables to measure our concepts, and two or more operational definitions to measure our variables. Usually, no single variable can do justice to a concept or reflect its full meaning, and no single operational definition can do justice to the variables we select.

The use of multiple variables and indicators ensures that the least amount of conceptual meaning and nuance is lost.

EXPAND YOUR KNOWLEDGE

Controversies in the Validity of Measures: Seymour Martin Lipset's *Continental Divide*

In *Continental Divide: The Values and Institutions of the United States and Canada* (1990), Seymour Martin Lipset argued that the differences between Canada and the United States can be attributed to our different histories: '[t]he United States is the country of the revolution, Canada of the counterrevolution.' Among other things, the historical background of 'counterrevolution' has led Canadians to demonstrate greater deference to authority and elites. Canadians, he argues, are a more lawful and peaceful people. Lipset cites differences in rates of violence, crime, and drug abuse, as well as differences in attitudes toward both police authority and gun control as indicators of the Canadian 'deference to authority'.

But do behavioural indicators such as crime rates provide a valid measure of a predisposition such as deference? Lipset's critics argue that his indicators are often inappropriate and that he fails to take into account important national differences in institutional arrangements. What is at issue, then, is whether Canadians behave differently than Americans (for example, have a lower crime rate) because of their attitudinal predispositions (for example, greater deference to authority) or because of the institutional environment in which they behave. This in turn boils down to a debate over the validity of different indicators.

The second factor to be considered when assessing the accuracy of our measures is **reliability**. A measure is reliable if it is *consistent* regardless of circumstances such as time or subpopulation. Thus, if consecutive weighings on a doctor's scale result in identical or near-identical weights (for example, 70 kg), the scale is reliable. If you step on the scale and it registers 70 kg on Monday, 95 kg on Tuesday, and 45 kg on Wednesday, the scale is clearly unreliable. Note that reliability does not ensure validity; a scale that is consistently 5 kg low is reliable because it provides the same response with repeated measures (that is, 70 kg each time). However, it is not valid because it fails to measure what it purports to measure (your weight).

Another way of thinking about the difference between validity and reliability in measures is to consider the distribution of errors. **Random errors** exist when a measure is inaccurate, but the inaccuracy is not systematic. **Nonrandom errors** are systematic errors. For example, consider a 100-point feeling thermometer scale of assessments of the prime minister. If asked to rate the prime minister on this scale, a respondent might place him at 65, which represents a feeling of 'warmth' toward the prime minister. But if asked the same question the next day, the same respondent, feeling just as warmly toward the prime minister, might place him at 70. A

EXPAND YOUR KNOWLEDGE
The Reliability and Validity of IQ Tests

How can circumstances such as time and subpopulation affect reliability? An example of an unreliable test over time appears to be the IQ (intelligence quotient) test. IQ tests have long been used to predict not only academic performance but also performance in the broader social and economic worlds. IQ tests are designed to measure *innate* intelligence, in other words, raw mental ability. Further, the measurement of IQ is based on the assumption that intelligence is normally distributed in all cultures and all generations: within each population, there is expected to be a small number of low intelligence individuals, a large number of moderately intelligent individuals, and a small number of highly intelligent people. If IQ is a reliable measure of intelligence, the distribution of IQ scores should be similar between cultures and across generations.

It has been assumed that the tests are independent of academic training, that they measure some innate ability (or lack thereof) rather than the quantity or quality of individuals' formal education. However, research by New Zealand academic James R. Flynn suggests that IQ measures may be far more reflective of environmental circumstance than we have come to believe (Ambrose 1996, D1):

> [The Flynn effect shows] that IQ scores in industrialized nations have shot skyward in recent decades. If intelligence were strictly innate as many psychologists have contended, a rise of this magnitude wouldn't be possible. Geneticists concur on that much, and one conceivable conclusion of this is that people are being made dramatically smarter by environmental factors. That would mean that IQ tests primarily indicate intellectual development at a given moment . . . and not a predetermined learning ability. Or possibly people are only getting better at taking the tests and not in the scope and creativity of their intellects, which is a way of saying IQ test results should be viewed as meaningless.

Given that IQ scores are highest in developed countries where educational levels are greater, and within such countries IQ scores have been increasing over generations, the reliability of IQ tests is put into question. These results also suggest that the IQ tests are not valid; rather than testing raw intelligence, they appear to be testing *educated* intelligence. Obviously, nature and nurture are not easily separated.

Source: Jay Ambrose, 'We're Smart Enough to Know How Dumb IQ Tests Are,' *Globe and Mail*, 3 August 1996, p. D1.

month later, that same respondent might rate him at 62, and the next month at 65 again. The respondent, with the same feelings toward the same individual, exhibits slight changes in ratings simply through random error: sometimes the score is a little higher, sometimes a little lower. Now imagine you lived in a country that had an authoritarian regime, and you felt your safety was threatened if you were seen to be critical of the government. If you were surveyed for your feelings toward the political leader, you might choose to inflate your rating (to 100 points on this scale!) for fear that you would be punished if you revealed your true feelings (perhaps you really rate this person at 0). Furthermore, each time you were asked this question, you would respond in the same way. This kind of error is nonrandom, or systematic, error; the error is always in the same direction. A measure is reliable if it is free from random error (that is, there may be nonrandom error in a reliable measure). A valid measure is free from both random and nonrandom error.

For an indicator to be reliable across subpopulations, it must receive similar results across all subgroups. For example, if a measure performs differently for men and women, there is a reliability problem. It is possible that men and women are interpreting the question differently or that different social or cultural factors are interfering with the measure. We often hear that women respond to problems by empathizing, whereas men respond to the same problems by suggesting solutions (one indicator of the popularity of this theory is the success of 'self-help' books such as John Gray's *Men Are from Mars, Women Are from Venus*). If such generalizations are true, it is possible that men and women would respond differently to a stated problem. Or consider survey questions concerning body weight and height. Many young women are socialized to feel they should understate their weight, whereas many young men feel they should overstate their height. If such a phenomenon occurred, the measures would suffer from reliability problems.

A number of steps can be taken to reduce reliability problems (Neuman 1994, 129). First, as with validity, multiple indicators are useful. Again, the idea is to allow the strengths of one measure to compensate for the weaknesses of the other. Second, our measures will be more reliable if we are clear in our purpose when designing questions or selecting indicators. It is important that indicators are unidimensional. Consider the question, 'Are you satisfied with the food and service at this restaurant?' A response of yes may mean that the respondent is happy with both service and food, or it may indicate that he is happy with one but not both. With such 'double-barrelled' questions, it is difficult to assess what exactly is being measured. A third suggestion for increasing reliability is to select the most precise measures available.

Unfortunately, there are occasionally tradeoffs between validity and reliability: as we decrease abstraction, we increase reliability, but in doing so, we decrease validity (White 1994, 158). Of course, our goal is to find measures that maximize both validity and reliability. The balance to seek is a measure that is sufficiently exact that it is reliable, yet sufficiently abstract that it captures the meaning of the concept and therefore is valid.

In all circumstances, indicators can benefit from pilot testing and/or replication (Neuman 1994, 130). Pilot tests can be used to pretest a survey instrument within a convenience sample. (Sampling is discussed in Chapter 8.) The purpose of a pilot test is not to tabulate statistics and draw conclusions about population parameters, but to test the validity and reliability of the measures. (In addition, pilot tests can help 'troubleshoot' within the research design itself.) Often, if measures are found to be particularly useful and accurate, they are replicated in future studies by other researchers. The reasons for this are threefold: (1) the measures have proven themselves in terms of validity and reliability; (2) replicating measures allows researchers to test the conclusions of others with different samples; and (3) replicating measures allows researchers to detect changes and patterns over time.

APPLY YOUR UNDERSTANDING

Assessing the Accuracy of Our Measures

Suggest three possible survey questions that could act as indicators of the variable 'liberalism', indicators that would enable you to distinguish between 'liberal' and 'illiberal' respondents. How would you assess the validity of each indicator? What steps would you take, and to what conclusions would you come? How would you assess the reliability of the indicators? Would you describe the measures as more valid or more reliable? Formulate three final indicators of liberalism that you feel are accurate measures.

What about survey questions that might serve as indicators for nationalism? Populism? Environmentalism? Neoconservatism? Racism?

DESIGNING SURVEY QUESTIONS

One of the most common research designs in political science is survey research; we use telephone polls, mailed questionnaires, web surveys or (less frequently) in-person surveys to gather the information necessary to test hypotheses. In survey research, indicators are the survey questions themselves. Thus, to design accurate indicators, we need to select or design valid and reliable survey questions. Survey research is conducted not only by governments and polling firms but also by private businesses, nonprofit organizations, educational and health providers, community associations, and campaign management teams. It is quite likely that many political science students will have the opportunity to participate in the design of a survey at some point in their lives.

When designing a survey, we need to be mindful that all the information necessary for that study must be captured within the survey instrument. Thus, we will need not only questions addressing attitudes, behaviours, and opinions but also questions designed to solicit demographic information such as age, income, and education. All variables of interest—be they dependent, independent, or control variables—must be included in one instrument. Ideally, we will begin by making a list of all the relevant variables and all the indicators needed to measure these variables. This helps us ensure that all information is gathered and also prevents us from gathering unnecessary or useless information. There may be a desire when we design surveys to ask questions on every issue from A to Z, but this temptation should be avoided. Time restraints—yours and the participant's—preclude such an approach, as do ethical considerations. We want to keep our survey instruments directed at the question at hand; they should not be seen as 'fishing expeditions'. If we cannot separate the necessary variables and indicators from those that are superfluous, we need to work on our theory.

The researcher needs to choose a question format. **Closed questions** force the respondent to choose among the presented alternatives, for example, 'Which of the following do you prefer: (1) Coca-Cola; (2) Pepsi Cola; (3) another cola brand; or (4) noncola beverages?' **Open questions** allow the respondent to provide her own response, without prompting from categories, for example, 'Which cola brand do you prefer? _____.' There are advantages and disadvantages to each format.[4] Closed questions have a number of design advantages: respondents can answer the questions quickly; it is easy to compare the responses of different individuals; and data entry is less complex. In contrast, open questions present a number of data problems: there are many possible answers to any given question, making data entry difficult; respondents will spend more time on open questions, making the questions less efficient; and comparisons between individuals can be complicated. However, open questions have the advantage of allowing a greater range of answers; the respondent is not limited to or biased by preset response categories and may provide answers that lead the researcher into new theoretical waters. Closed questions often ask the respondent to give a simple response to a very complex issue (Neuman 1994, 233) and, by providing categories for the respondent, may encourage the statement of opinion or knowledge where none exists.

Selection of question format tends to vary with the type of survey instrument. Telephone polls typically rely on closed questions, while mail and web questionnaires are more likely to employ a mixture of open and closed questions. Many surveys begin with open-ended questions designed to capture the respondents' 'top of the head' impressions before respondents are contaminated by subsequent questions. For example, if the survey is designed to measure public attitudes toward climate change, it would not make sense to ask respondents 'What is the most important issue facing Canadians today?' after they had already been exposed to extensive questions about climate change. Front-end, open-ended questions are also used to warm up respondents for the more detailed questions that follow. They try, in short, to establish a conversational format.

When designing questions, there are a number of steps researchers should take to increase indicator accuracy. First, use *neutral language*. It is important that questions are designed in a way that does not bias or 'lead' respondents. For example, questions such as 'All reasonable people agree that policy A is bad. Do you support policy A?' or 'Policy Q will put millions of people out of work. Many children will go hungry as a result of policy Q. Do you support policy Q?' are biased questions. When we use scales (for example, 'strongly agree – agree – disagree – strongly disagree'), it is important that we ensure that the response categories are balanced between positive and negative. For example, a scale with categories 'excellent – very good – good – satisfactory – poor' is unbalanced; there are three positive categories, one neutral, and one negative.

Second, be clear. To ensure reliable questions, we must first ensure that all respondents interpret the question in the same way. This necessitates that we are specific regarding the exact information sought. Consider the question, 'What is your income?' It is not clear if this means annual income, monthly income, or weekly income. Is the researcher interested in family income, household income, or individual income? Net or gross (pretax) income? In addition to being specific, clarity requires that we keep our questions simple. Avoid double negatives, keep your sentences relatively short, and use common language. It is important not to use jargon or assume detailed knowledge; not everyone knows the definitions of GNP and GDP or the content of policy Q. Finally, clarity demands that each question be limited to only one topic. So-called double-barrelled questions, such as 'How do you feel about the government's policies on military defence and international trade?' will lead to reliability problems.

Third, avoid **response sets**. Some respondents tend to be yea-sayers, who agree with virtually any statement placed before them, while others tend to be nay-sayers, who disagree with virtually every statement. It is important in such cases that personality predispositions do not push respondents toward a particular policy position on the questionnaire. For example, if you have five agree–disagree statements designed to test respondents' support for environmentalism, and for each statement 'agree' is indicative of a pro-environment position, then yea-sayers will tend to show up as environmentalists and nay-sayers as opponents of environmentalism. It is useful, then, to have batteries of questions where respondents must move back and forth between agreement and disagreement in order to register a consistent position, and where respondents who agree (or disagree) with everything end up in the middle of the scale.

Fourth, keep response categories **mutually exclusive** and **exhaustive**. We need to ensure that all relevant responses (including 'no opinion' or 'don't know/refused') are provided for by our response categories. In addition, there should be no overlap between categories. Consider, for example, the problems with the following response categories for the question 'What is your annual personal net (after-tax) income: (1) $10,000–$25,000; (2) $25,000–$40,000; or (3) $40,000–$65,000?' Clearly, not all possible responses are included. There is no room for those whose incomes are below $10,000, for those whose incomes are above $65,000, or for those individuals who refuse to answer the question. Thus the categories are not exhaustive. A second problem is that there is overlap between the categories. Should an individual whose income is $40,000 be placed in category (2) or category (3)? The categories are not mutually exclusive; it is possible for an individual to be placed in two categories, rather than just one. A better set of categories for the same question would be: (1) under $10,000; (2) $10,000–$24,999; (3) $25,000–$39,999; (4) $40,000–$65,000; (5) over $65,000; and (6) don't know/refused.

Fifth, select the **highest reliable level of measurement**. When possible, we should select interval-level measures above ordinal-level measures. As we have seen, it is possible after data collection to move from interval- to ordinal-level data through the grouping of data. The reverse, however, is not true: we cannot go from age categories to exact ages. Thus, using higher-level measurements allows us greater flexibility when it comes time to analyze our data. That said, there are some questions, such as income, where we may be inclined to use grouped categories in the question itself, rather than exact numbers. This is because there are some topics about which respondents prefer to be more ambiguous and for which precise answers may be impossible in any event.

Sixth, pay close attention to **question order**. Remember that respondent reactions to a particular question will be shaped by preceding questions, which provide the context for the question. Thus what comes first will contaminate what comes after. For example, imagine a survey measuring both intended vote in the next provincial election and public reaction to health-care spending cuts. If the health-care questions come first, then respondents may be in a different mindset when the voting intention question comes up than they would be if asked at the outset how they would vote 'if a provincial election were held today'. It is also useful advice to leave intrusive questions to the end of the questionnaire. Some respondents, for instance, may be very touchy when asked about their income or marital status, and may even terminate the interview. If this happens near the end of the interview schedule, most of the information is already in place and therefore the loss is minimized.

Seventh, try to **minimize defensive reactions** by making the respondent as comfortable as possible. Remember that respondents are under considerable social pressure in an interview situation; they want to appear to be knowledgeable and thoughtful. This can create a situation where respondents would rather fabricate a response than not have an opinion or appear not to know the answer. In some cases, therefore, it is important to assure respondents that a socially incorrect response is all right. For example, questions that ask respondents whether they voted in the last election are sometimes prefaced with a set of acceptable excuses for not voting. It is acknowledged that some people may have been ill, had car or child-care problems, or were called out of town on short notice; the message is that not voting is a perfectly understandable event and that respondents should not be embarrassed by admitting they did not vote. If these steps are not taken, the result is likely to be an inflated estimate of turnout rates. This in turn would make a comparison of voters and nonvoters difficult, since some of the latter, in fact, would be lumped in with the former in the statistical analysis.

Of course, following all of these steps will not guarantee a problem-free research instrument. For one thing, a host of research design and measurement issues will undoubtedly remain. How, for example, should missing data be handled? In measuring political and social attitudes, should we use odd-numbered scales that provide a middle response category for respondents, or should we use even-numbered scales, which force respondents to lean toward one pole or another? For example, scales measuring respondents' self-location on the left–right spectrum could provide either six or seven response categories. In the latter case, a response of 4 provides an option for respondents who do not want to identify themselves with either the left or right. However, if a 6-point scale is used, such respondents are forced to choose either 3 (slightly left) or 4 (slightly right).

Finally, we must remember that a fair amount of error and noise is inevitable in survey research. After all, we are dealing with very human subjects who will occasionally fake answers or lie and who will respond to aspects of the interview situation—the sex or age of the interviewer, the artistic quality of the questionnaire, the time of day or night, distractions in the room—as much as they will to the specific questions being posed. The potential sources of error are perhaps best illustrated by questions concerning family income. Some respondents will refuse to disclose their income, while others will inflate it to impress the interviewer. Some people will not know their income; they may, for instance, know their hourly wage but not their after-tax annual income or the precise income of their spouse. As a consequence, there is a good deal of noise associated with survey measures of income, noise that then may make it difficult to measure the impact of income on political attitudes or behaviours.

In any case, researchers should always ensure that their questions are as polite and courteous as possible. Respondents have voluntarily given their time to the research project and should be treated with respect.

Summary: Characteristics of Question Design

1. Use neutral language.
2. Be clear.
3. Avoid response sets.
4. Keep response categories mutually exclusive and exhaustive.
5. Select the highest reliable level of measurement.
6. Pay close attention to question order.
7. Minimize defensive reactions.

CREATING INDICES

We noted earlier in the chapter that social scientists will often use a number of variables to capture one concept and a number of indicators to capture one variable. After the data have been collected, indicators can be combined into an **index**, a single measure of the concept or variable in question.

Index construction generally follows a number of conceptual steps. First, we want indicators that are strongly associated or correlated with one another; this is illustrated by the bold line between indicators 1 and 2 in Figure 4.4 on page 94. (At the same time, we do not want a degree of association so strong that the indicators are obviously measuring exactly the same portion of the variable.) Second, we want to cover as much of the conceptual terrain as possible and, therefore, the more indicators, the merrier. However, and as indices B and C in Figure 4.4 illustrate, the more indicators we include in the index, the weaker the association is likely to be between those indicators. Thus, as our index gets more comprehensive in its conceptual coverage, it also becomes less internally coherent. The trick, then, is to balance the competing needs of broad conceptual coverage and internal coherence. Indices that combine three to six indicators are common in political science research, whereas larger indices are much less common.

An example of indices is seen in work by Neil Nevitte and Roger Gibbins (1990). In their analysis of a mailed survey of senior university undergraduate students in Australia, Britain, Canada, New Zealand, and the United States, Nevitte and Gibbins constructed a number of ideological indices. One researcher measured respondent orientations toward feminism and incorporated answers to the following questions:

- Respondents were asked to locate themselves on a 7-point scale between two statements: 'women would be better off if they stayed at home and raised families' and 'women would be better off if they had careers and jobs just as men do'.
- Respondents were asked to locate themselves on a 7-point scale between another pair of statements: 'if women tried harder they could get jobs equal to their ability' and 'discrimination makes it almost impossible for women to get jobs equal to their ability'.
- Respondents were asked if they agreed or disagreed with the following statements:
  - It is the right of a woman to decide whether to have an abortion.
  - If a company has to lay off part of its labour force, the first workers to be laid off should be women whose husbands have jobs.
  - Lesbians and homosexuals should not be allowed to teach in schools.
  - There should be more laws that aim at eliminating differences in the treatment of men and women.

By combining the responses to these six questions, the researchers were able to create a much more powerful measure of orientations to feminism than would have been provided by any one of the questions alone.

In conceptual terms, the creation of indices is a reasonably straightforward operation. In practice, however, it brings into play many of the statistical techniques and measures of association addressed in later chapters.

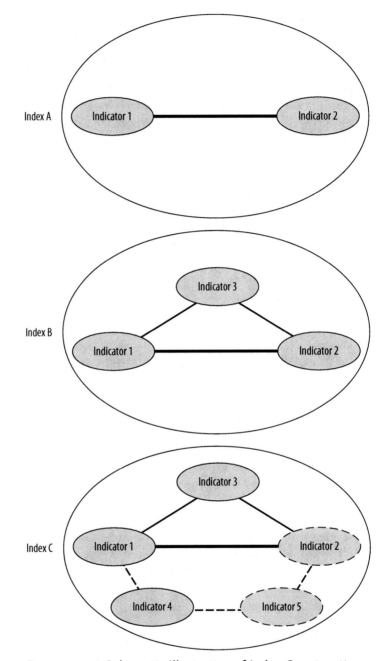

FIGURE 4.4 A Schematic Illustration of Index Construction

WORKING AS A TEAM

1. With your group, examine the code book for one of the recent Canadian Election Studies or a similar survey research instrument. Are there questions that appear to be reasonable candidates for an index of liberalism? Feminism? Conservatism? Environmentalism? What conceptual steps would be involved in the creation of such an index?
2. How would you go about designing a questionnaire to measure teaching effectiveness in a course such as this one? What questions would you ask? Would they be open-ended or closed questions? What would be the advantages and disadvantages of each type? Which strategy would work best: using generic questions that would enable you to compare this course and its instructors to other courses and instructors, or course-specific questions that would enable you to probe the idiosyncratic aspects of this course and its instructor?

SELF-STUDY

1. You have been provided with the research opportunity to explore, through survey research, the relationship between environmentalism and the more general ideological predispositions captured by conventional left–right scales. Your theory is that support for environmentalism is correlated with ideological position; more specifically, you suspect that as support for the 'left' increases, support for environmentalism also increases. In preparation for this research, work through the following steps of operationalization:

    a. State your theoretical proposition. What are the main concepts? Provide a conceptual definition for each.
    b. Identify two variables that could be used to quantify each concept. Identify the level of measurement for each variable.
    c. Identify two indicators for each variable. Provide the complete wording for the survey questions, including all response categories.
    d. Select one of the four variables and discuss how you would assess the accuracy of both indicators for that variable.

NOTES

1. Note that surveys that measure voting rates often suffer from 'vote inflation': a higher proportion of the sample reports having voted than was the case in the population at large. For example, while the turnout rate in Canadian general elections hovers around 75 per cent, the reported turnout rate in Canadian Election Studies is often 10 per cent higher. This distortion may be caused by voters being more likely than nonvoters to respond to the survey or by nonvoters in the sample being unwilling to admit that they did not vote.
2. The relationship between independent variables is referred to as multicollinearity. Two independent variables that are themselves related will tend to overlap in their predictive power. For example, we would expect that both knowledge of the subject matter and writing skill will predict academic excellence.
3. You should note, however, that the distinction between variables and indicators is often ignored; literature references to variables are often references to what we have termed indicators.
4. For a more complete list of the advantages and disadvantages of each format, see Neuman (1994, 233).

Chapter 5

RESEARCH ETHICS: PEOPLE BEHIND THE NUMBERS

DESTINATION

By the end of this chapter the reader should

- understand the ethical considerations that lie behind the choice of research topics and methodologies;
- appreciate the concerns relating to anonymity, confidentiality, and informed consent; and
- be familiar with how ethical considerations are handled in the social sciences.

As readers are drawn into the complexities of statistical analysis in the chapters to come, it will be easy to forget that the numbers encountered in quantitative analysis represent real people. For example, in a table showing that 44.1 per cent of 950 respondents in a survey of the Ontario electorate intend to vote for the Progressive Conservative candidate in the next provincial election, it is easy to forget that this represents 419 discrete individuals who were disrupted from their everyday routine to answer a survey, who made assumptions about the survey's legitimacy, and who were assured that their anonymity and confidentiality would be respected. In this chapter, we expose readers to some of the ethical issues and dilemmas that confront political scientists as they engage in a wide variety of research activities relating to the collection, analysis, and publication of data. As you will see, any assumption that quantitative research is immune from ethical considerations because we are dealing with *numbers rather than people* should be quickly discarded.

Ethical considerations emerge from a number of directions. To some degree, they govern the topics we decide to study and, consequently, our choice of research subjects. Ethical considerations may determine the research methodologies we employ. Indeed, the most vigorous ethical standards tend to come into play with respect to data collection: the samples we select, the information provided to subjects or respondents, the precautions taken to ensure confidentiality, and the avoidance of risk. Ethical considerations also come into play in the relationships we have with colleagues, both in specific research projects and within the broader scholarly community. Finally, ethical considerations may determine what we do with research results. Of particular concern is the manner in which research findings can shape the political debate over public policy in democratic states.

The intent of the chapter is to bring this range of ethical considerations into play before readers become entangled in the more technical aspects of political science research. By doing so we also hope to bring the human face of empirical research into sharper focus.

RISK ASSESSMENT AND THE MEDICAL MODEL

Many of the ethical guidelines currently employed in the social sciences find their roots in medical research. When research is being conducted on the introduction of new medications or on the use of alternative treatments or therapies, there can be a significant potential risk to human subjects. For instance, whether an experimental drug has unwanted side effects is not an 'academic question' to the subjects in whom those side effects might become manifest. If a new treatment is being tested to see if survival rates following heart surgery can be increased, it is not a matter of indifference to patients whether they are subjected to the new or old treatment. In the early days of medical research, however, research subjects were often recruited without their consent, much less informed consent. Patients who were institutionalized were particularly exposed to research risks. In light of this history, medical researchers have now developed elaborate protocols to ensure that research subjects are fully informed about the nature of the research and the risks to which they may be exposed, and to ensure that participation is voluntary. These protocols have come to provide the model for similar protocols within the social sciences.

Underlying these protocols is the first principle of medical practice: *do no harm*. This is a principle to which social scientists should also adhere. Any potential research gain with respect to description or theory must be carefully weighed against potential risks to research subjects, to the communities from which they are drawn, and, at times, to the researcher himself or herself. As an example of this last risk, Julie Brannen (1988) draws our attention to the psychological costs that may emerge for researchers doing in-depth interviews on sensitive topics. Unlike professional confidants such as counsellors, psychotherapists, and priests, social science researchers lack their own confessors who can help them come to grips with the troubling information to which they may have been exposed.

But wait, you might say, surely the potential risks in social science research are much less serious than they are in medical research, and thus the ethical considerations less acute. For example, it is hard to argue that a respondent to a national Ipsos Reid survey is exposed to the same level of risk as the research subject in a new chemotherapy treatment program. Asking someone his or her opinion on issues of the day seems almost risk-free compared to administering new drugs or food additives. However, while most forms of social science research, and particularly most forms of survey research, are *relatively* benign in their potential impact on participants, it would be a mistake to assume that ethical considerations are absent or even that the potential of risk to research subjects is absent. The nature of the risk may be quite different from that addressed by the medical model, but risk is not absent. Social science research is with human subjects, and such research cannot escape a concern for the welfare of those subjects. As Bruce Chadwick et al. explain (1984, 15–16), 'Whereas the chemist may wish to see which substance or combination of substances will change the composition of the compound under study, the social scientist must make sure that his or her research does not result in any permanent change, damage, or injury to the persons studied.'

Risk, it should be stressed, is not always self-evident. Take, for example, the risk associated with self-knowledge. Imagine you have become an unwitting participant in a hypothetical experiment designed to see if people will come to the aid of strangers in real-life situations. The researchers have set up a situation in which individuals walking down the street are confronted by strangers apparently experiencing different degrees of distress. In one case it might be someone pretending to be lost, in another case someone who is ill or is being attacked. The researchers want to see if you will come to the stranger's aid and to what extent intervention might be determined by the characteristics of the subject, the 'victim', and the event. Let's imagine further that you decide not to intervene and keep walking. At the end of the block a member of the research team stops you, informs you about the experiment, and, in the debriefing, assures you that no one was in fact in distress. Thus, to a degree your mind is set at ease in that you do not have to worry about what might have happened to the individual you ignored. However, you also have to confront what might be some disturbing new knowledge: you have been shown to be the kind of person who ignores strangers in distress. This self-knowledge may be enlightening, but it may be the kind of enlightenment that you would just as soon have done without. In effect, you have been damaged; you have a diminished sense of your own personal worth, the effects of which may be long-lasting. The question, then, is whether the researchers had the right to inflict this cost. Was the research ethical?

The message here is self-evident but important. Any proposed research must be assessed not only in terms of the possible advance of descriptive knowledge and/ or theoretical insight. It must also be assessed in terms of risk to subjects, communities, and at times to the research team. This assessment is first and foremost an ethical exercise.

SELECTING THE RESEARCH TOPIC

Ethical considerations begin with the selection of the research topic. As Duelli-Klein (1983, 38) points out, our decision about *what* to investigate always precedes the methodological issues of how the research might best proceed. In this context, we must acknowledge the emphasis that universities and colleges place on freedom of intellectual inquiry. If *academic freedom* means anything, it surely means

APPLY YOUR UNDERSTANDING

Animal-Testing

A great deal of medical research entails testing on animal subjects, generally as a prelude to testing on human subjects. Not surprisingly, animal-testing has been the source of much ethical and political debate centring not only on technicalities—are the test animals being treated as humanely as possible, is everything possible being done to minimize pain and discomfort?—but also on whether such testing should be done at all.

Fortunately, perhaps, very little political science research involves animal-testing. Indeed, no cases come to mind. However, the debate on this subject can be a useful way to 'prime the pump' for ethical considerations that are relevant for political science research. Consider, then, the following research

dilemma. A firm has developed a new food additive that may ameliorate lactose intolerance for hundreds of thousands of people in Canada and millions around the world. To ensure that the additive is safe for human consumption, the firm first intends to feed large amounts of the additive to research rats for four weeks and then to dissect the rats to determine if any abnormalities have shown up in larger than expected numbers. The research program, therefore, will necessitate the death and dissection of literally thousands of rats. Does this strike you as a reasonable price to pay, given the potential of the new additive? Would your opinion change if the research animals were cats? Beagles? Chimpanzees?

the freedom to pursue research topics that the individual researcher feels are interesting and important. This freedom of inquiry extends beyond academics; it should be a guiding principle for student research. However, this does not exempt researchers from ethical constraints on the conduct of their research, nor does it preclude a concern with the *social relevance* of the research. Furthermore, while researchers may be free to pursue any topic that strikes their fancy, funding agencies are under no compulsion to provide the financial support that may make the research possible. In fact, funds are most likely to be allocated for projects with some social relevance; research driven solely by intellectual curiosity or theoretical concerns faces an uphill, although by no means impossible, battle for funding.

The definition of what is and is not socially relevant takes us quickly into the ethical domain. There are no empirical criteria by which we can determine social relevance; the issue is a normative one. Admittedly, media coverage and the political agenda may send strong cues regarding the relative importance of various issues, and we might use these cues to identify some research topics as having greater social relevance and thus funding appeal than others. However, social relevancy implies something more than salience; it suggests that certain topics *should* be pursued and perhaps that others *should not*.

Much of the discussion in this respect has entailed a variety of problems, both ethical and methodological, that arise when researching *sensitive topics*. But what do we mean by such a term? Broadly defined, socially sensitive research includes studies 'in which there are potential consequences or implications, either directly for the participants in the research or for the class of individuals represented by the research' (Sieber and Stanley 1988, 49). This, however, is a very general definition that could embrace virtually the entirety of public policy research. A tighter definition, focused on the presence of risk, is provided by Raymond Lee and Claire Renzetti (1990, 513): 'a sensitive topic is one which potentially poses for those involved a substantial threat, the emergence of which renders problematic for the researcher and/or the researched the collection, holding, and/or dissemination of research data.' Lee and Renzetti go on to explain that research is more likely to be threatening '(a) where research intrudes into the private sphere or delves into some deeply personal experience; (b) where the study is concerned with deviance and social control; (c) where it impinges on the vested interests of powerful persons or the exercise of coercion or domination; or (d) where it deals with things sacred to those being studied which they do not wish profaned'. There is no suggestion that research *not* be conducted in such areas. Rather, the point is that ethical considerations are likely to be brought into bold relief when research is conducted in the circumstances identified by Lee and Renzetti.

APPLY YOUR UNDERSTANDING

Putting Research Subjects at Risk: The Milgram Studies of Obedience

At times the risk to research subjects can come through increased self-awareness; we may find out that we are not as nice or compassionate as we thought we were. A good example of this risk comes from Stanley Milgram's (1963) famous experimental research on obedience.

Milgram recruited male subjects, aged 20 to 50, from the community to participate in a study of memory and learning, or at least so they were told, at Yale University. Subjects heard that the objective of the study was to determine the impact of punishment on learning and were then 'randomly assigned' to be either the 'teacher' or 'learner' in the experiment. In fact, the subjects were always the teacher, and an accomplice of the experimenter was always the learner. The learner was strapped into an electric chair apparatus in one room, after which the teacher was conducted to an adjoining room where there was an electric shock generator with switches ranging from 15 to 450 V. The switches also had qualitative labels ranging from 'slight shock' to 'extreme intense shock', 'Danger: severe shock', and 'XXX'. The task of the teacher was to administer electric shocks to the learner whenever a mistake was made. Moreover, the teacher was told to move to a higher level of shock each time a mistake was made. If the teacher resisted an increase in the level of shock, the researcher provided prods such as 'it is absolutely essential that you continue'. The learner, who could be heard but not seen, and who was not actually being shocked, began to indicate discomfort at the 75 V level. At 120 V he shouted the shocks were painful, at 150 V he asked to be released, at 180 V he screamed he couldn't stand the pain, at 270 V he screamed in agony, and after 330 V made no sound at all (Nachmias and Nachmias 1987, 79).

The experiment was designed to determine at what level of shock obedience would end and the teacher would refuse further participation in the experiment. In one of his experiments, 26 of 40 participants administered shocks up to the maximum of 450 V (Nachmias and Nachmias 1987, 79).

Milgram's work became so famous because many subjects, when prodded by the researcher, administered very high levels of shock. The 'shock' to readers was that American males were obedient to the point of administering severe and dangerous electrical shocks to compatriots in a university-based research experiment.

What do you think about the ethics of this experiment? Was the knowledge gained sufficient to compensate for the risk to subjects? Were the subjects really at risk? How would you feel if you ended up administering severe electric shocks to a fellow student in a study of memory and learning? In the study itself, 'subjects were observed to sweat, bite their lips, groan, and dig their fingernails into their flesh' (Milgram 1963, 375); some had uncontrollable seizures. If a similar piece of research was proposed today, do you think it would receive ethical clearance at your own institution? Are there conditions that might be imposed to reduce ethical concerns?

It should also be noted that Lee and Renzetti acknowledge potential risk to the researchers themselves as an ethical consideration. In rare instances this risk may involve the physical safety of the research team. In less extreme circumstances it may entail legal action, including the potential of research material being subpoenaed. (Research material is not protected by the conventions of client confidentiality that apply to medical files and legal counsel.) A more general risk is that of 'stigma contagion' for those researching unpopular topics. As Lee and Renzetti illustrate (1990, 521), 'those involved in the study of sexual deviance have frequently remarked on their stigmatization by colleagues, university administrators, and students.'

Within political science, such stigmatization could be a concern for researchers studying the extremes of the political left and right, particularly if their research was seen as empathetic rather than critical. It might also be a concern for those investigating public policy in areas of high social sensitivity such as immigration, same-sex marriage, abortion, or Aboriginal self-government. As a consequence, there is a good chance that researchers will avoid topics that carry the risk of stigmatization. But when this happens, we may all be losers:

> Adverse publicity that could destroy a researcher's career may keep researchers from investigating sensitive topics. Yet, scientific knowledge is especially important precisely because the topics are sensitive ones. Without scientifically based knowledge, fear, prejudice, and ideology dominate public policy and public opinion. (Neuman 1997, 460)

Here it is worth noting that matters of social relevance are of greater importance to some forms of political science research than they are to others. Researchers interested in the complex dynamics of voting behaviour, for example, have not been overly preoccupied with the social relevance of their work; the primary concern is to advance theoretical understanding of voting behaviour and electoral choice in democratic societies. Feminist researchers, on the other hand, place a great deal of emphasis on applied or 'action' research. Indeed, Patti Lather (1988) argues that feminist research must be action-oriented, that the research and the feminist thought on which it is based must be directed to social and political change. Feminist researchers also emphasize the importance of involving research subjects in the research enterprise, thereby blurring the distinction between the researcher and the researched. As Shulamit Reinharz (1992, 181) explains:

> In feminist participatory research, the distinction between the researcher(s) and those on whom the research is done disappears. To achieve an egalitarian relation, the researcher abandons control and adopts an approach of openness, reciprocity, mutual disclosure, and shared risk.

As suggested above, part of the hard reality of contemporary social science research is that the availability of research funding may drive the choice of research topics. It is always worth asking, therefore, whether there is an ethical dimension to the proclivities of funding agencies, whether the unavailability of funding squeezes out research that, on ethical grounds, may have some claim to priority. It should be noted, however, that in many cases funding agencies have been instrumental in elevating ethical standards. The primary funding agency for social science research in Canada, the Social Sciences and Humanities Research Council (SSHRC), has been particularly aggressive in requiring that both universities and individual researchers give careful attention to ethical concerns. SSHRC also insists that researchers address the social relevance of proposed research and recently has advocated greater attention to **knowledge mobilization**, or the application of social sciences research to social problems. While grant applications are not assessed exclusively on the basis of social relevance, and funding basic research is part of SSHRC's mandate, social relevance remains an important factor in the funding formulas.

APPLY YOUR UNDERSTANDING

Tri-Council Policy Statement

In 1998 the three federal granting councils, the Natural Sciences and Engineering Research Council (NSERC), the Social Sciences and Humanities Research Council (SSHRC), and the Canadian Institutes for Health Research (CIHR) jointly sponsored a statement on the ethical conduct of research, known as the Tri-Council Policy Statement (TCPS). The policy is overseen by the Interagency Advisory Panel of Research Ethics. The TCPS established a framework for the application of ethical guidelines for research on human subjects by researchers in Canada. Beginning in 2008, the TCPS went through a period of revision and public consultation, the result of which is a substantially revised edition of the TCPS. This document provides guidance to Research Ethics Boards established at universities and colleges across the country in their institutional review of research protocols. The revised TCPS is based on the application of three core principles, a partial description of which is taken from this excerpt from the *Revised Draft Second Edition of the TCPS*, dated December 2009:

Core Principles

Respect for human dignity has been an underlying value of the *Tri-Council Policy Statement: Ethical Conduct for Research Involving Humans* (TCPS or the Policy) since its inception. Despite clear recognition of its centrality in research ethics, the term lends itself to a variety of definitions and interpretations that make it challenging to apply.

Respect for human dignity requires that research involving humans be conducted in a manner that is sensitive to the inherent worth of all human beings and the respect and consideration that they are due. In this Policy, respect for human dignity is expressed through three core principles—respect for persons, concern for welfare, and justice. These core principles transcend disciplinary boundaries and therefore, are relevant to the full range of research covered by this Policy.

Article 1.1 The guidelines in this Policy are based on the following three core principles:

> Respect for Persons
> Concern for Welfare
> Justice

These principles are complementary and interdependent. How they apply and the weight to be accorded to each will depend on the nature and context of the research being undertaken.

Respect for Persons

An important mechanism for respecting participants' autonomy in research is the requirement to seek their free and informed consent. This requirement reflects the commitment that participation in research, including participation through the use of one's data, or biological or reproductive materials, should be a matter of choice

(continued)

and that, to be meaningful, the choice must be informed. An informed choice is one that is based on as complete an understanding as is reasonably possible of the purpose of the research, what it entails, and its risks and potential benefits, both to the participant and to others.

Concern for Welfare
Concern for welfare means that researchers and Research Ethics Boards (REBs) should aim to protect the welfare of participants, and, in some circumstances, to promote that welfare. To do so, researchers and REBs must ensure that participants are not exposed to unnecessary risks. Researchers and REBs must attempt to minimize the risks associated with answering any given research question.

They should attempt to achieve the best possible balance of risks and potential benefits in a proposed research study. Then, in keeping with the principle of respect for persons, participants or authorized third parties make the final judgement about the acceptability of this balance to them.

Justice
Justice refers to the obligation to treat people fairly and equitably. Fairness entails treating all people with equal respect and concern. Equity requires distributing the benefits and burdens of research participation in such a way that no segment of the population is unduly burdened by the harms of research or denied the benefits of the knowledge generated from it.

Source: Interagency Panel on Research Ethics, *Revised Draft Second Edition of the TCPS* (December 2009).

PROTECTING RESEARCH SUBJECTS AND RESPONDENTS

The ethical guidelines governing social science research throw up three interconnected lines of defence around research subjects and respondents: confidentiality, informed consent, and the right to withdraw. We will examine these in turn.

Generally speaking, the assurance of respondent **confidentiality** is a routine aspect of social science research. In survey research, for instance, confidentiality is assured primarily through **anonymity**; respondents' names, addresses, or phone numbers are virtually never part of the data record. Although researchers are interested in the characteristics of their respondents—their age, sex, regional location, income, etc.—they have no interest in their specific identification. It may be very important to know that the research subject is a single white female working at a part-time job and living in Toronto, but it is not important to know her name, phone number, or address. These would only come into play in the initial selection of the sample or if a survey supervisor wanted to telephone respondents to ensure that the interview had actually been conducted and had not been fabricated by a member of the research staff or employee of the data collection firm. When names are collected at the time of the interview, it is only to enable the researcher to ascertain that the interview was, in fact, completed. Names are stripped from the survey as soon as authenticity is confirmed. Only in panel studies will names be kept as part of the record, and even here the information is coded so that specific identifiers can be isolated from the primary data set that will eventually enter the public realm. 'John Smith' becomes 'case 1383' before any data are released.

In elite interviewing (discussed in Chapter 13), the identity of respondents is a more contentious issue. An interview with a deputy minister in the federal government takes on additional weight because the opinions expressed are expressed by a deputy minister. If anonymity is respected, the interview material becomes less useful. The upshot of this is that the protection of anonymity for individuals holding public office is not required *if* the individual agrees to an on-the-record interview and *if* that agreement is conveyed through signed consent that explicitly waives anonymity. In the event that such consent is not provided, the researcher has little alternative but to fall back on descriptions like 'a senior public servant said . . .' or 'an unnamed but senior Liberal Party strategist revealed . . .'. Even then, the researcher must be careful that the description provided does not inadvertently reveal the individual's true identity. A published report that described an interviewee as a 'greying deputy minister with a decided limp and sinister goatee' would not protect the interviewee's anonymity.

EXPAND YOUR KNOWLEDGE

Anonymity and Confidentiality

Social science researchers are obligated to protect both anonymity and confidentiality. As Neuman (1997, 452–3) explains, the two are not the same thing:

> *Anonymity* means that subjects remain anonymous or nameless. . . . *Confidentiality* means that information may have names attached to it, but the researcher holds it in confidence or keeps it secret from the public. . . . A researcher may provide anonymity without confidentiality, or vice versa, although they usually go together. Anonymity without confidentiality means that all details about a specific individual are made public, but the individual's name is withheld. Confidentiality without anonymity means that information is not made public, but a researcher privately links individual names to specific responses.

In many cases, research topics will not place subjects at risk and therefore may not bring questions of anonymity and confidentiality into bold relief. For example, imagine a conventional public opinion survey in which one thousand randomly selected respondents are asked to identify 'the most serious issue facing Canada today'. If by chance it was disclosed that one of the respondents was Ms Irene Brown of 115 Bonavista Crescent in Regina and that she had identified unemployment as the most serious problem, it is unlikely that this disclosure would place Ms Brown at serious risk. Embarrassment, perhaps, but not risk, and even embarrassment would be unlikely unless the survey addressed some aspects of personal behaviour or opinion on sensitive topics. Indeed, it is difficult to imagine to whom such information might be disclosed; there is no ready media or commercial market for the identity of respondents to national surveys. However, if the survey focus was more localized, and if, therefore, there was a chance that the researchers might know the respondents, then breaches of anonymity and confidentiality become more serious. This is particularly so if the research touches on topics with greater sensitivity than 'the most serious issue facing Canada today'. Imagine, for instance, research in which participants in an AIDS treatment program or a program designed to control spousal abuse were being questioned about their satisfaction with the program. In this case, the inadvertent release of a participant's name could have a serious impact on that individual's employment, community status, and personal relations.

The protection of confidentiality is often woven into broader procedures designed to ensure **informed consent**. Simply put, this means that potential participants (or, in the case of minors, their legal representatives) should be fully informed *in writing* of the nature of the research project, the identity of the researchers, the potential use of the research findings, and any risks to which participants might be exposed. Potential respondents or subjects should also be advised that they are under no obligation to participate in the research project; there must be no 'force, fraud, deceit, duress, or other forms of constraint or coercion' (Liemohn 1979, 159; cited in Chadwick et al. 1984, 19). Willingness to participate is conveyed by signing the informed consent form, thus signifying that the participant is proceeding with a full understanding of the research project and any risks that might attend the project. The signed consent form is kept on record as evidence that participants in the research project were, in fact, participating under conditions of informed consent and without coercion.

At times, signed informed consent forms can be problematic. For instance, they are impossible to use in telephone interviews, particularly when respondents are also being assured that their anonymity is being fully protected. Researchers must therefore fall back on an oral statement along the lines described above and upon oral and therefore undocumented consent. It is assumed that the respondent's decision to continue with the interview rather than hanging up is implicit evidence of consent, but not necessarily fully *informed* consent. Many of the same considerations come into play with mailed questionnaires, which are generally returned in a way that does not identify the respondent. Anonymity is thereby protected, but a signed consent form is precluded. Here again, the respondent's willingness to return the completed questionnaire, rather than throwing it away, is taken as evidence of consent. The issue that remains is whether the consent was informed consent.

EXPAND YOUR KNOWLEDGE
Informed Consent and Response Rates

Some researchers may fear that elaborate informed consent procedures will adversely affect response rates in survey research. Potential respondents, it is thought, are more easily retained if the researcher moves quickly to the 'meat' of the survey. Conversely, it can be argued that informed consent may positively affect response rates by reassuring potential respondents about confidentiality, anonymity, and the legitimacy of the research project.

The empirical evidence in this regard is at best quizzical. Eleanor Singer (1978) conducted a study of the impact of various informed consent procedures on response rates with an American national probability sample of 2,084 potential respondents. She found that the amount of information provided about the survey to potential respondents had no impact on survey response rates. Variability in the assurance of confidentiality (some respondents were assured of complete confidentiality, while the matter was not even mentioned to others) had no impact on response rates to the survey, although an assurance of confidentiality increased *item response rates* to questions dealing with sensitive issues or personal behaviour. Finally, she found that a request that potential respondents sign an informed consent form reduced the response rate to the survey; 71 per cent of those not asked for a signature completed the survey, compared to 64 per cent who were asked for a signature before the interview and 65 per cent who were told they would be asked for a signature after the interview.

Informed consent means explaining the nature of the research to potential participants. However, there are limits to that explanation; if participants are informed about the specific research hypotheses, their behaviour may be affected as a consequence. For example, a research project may be interested in the relationship between partisanship and support for environmental protection and may therefore include questions on both topics in a mailed questionnaire or telephone survey. If respondents know that the relationship between the two is of particular interest to the researcher, they may modify their answers to the environmental questions in order to ensure that their own party is portrayed in the best possible light. As Allan Kimmel (1988, 76) observes:

> Few researchers feel that we can do entirely without deception, since the adoption of an overly conservative approach could deem the study of important research areas hardly worthy of the effort. For instance, a study of racial prejudice accurately labeled as such would certainly affect subjects' behavior. Deception studies differ so greatly in the nature and degree of deception that even the harshest critic would be hard pressed to state unequivocally that all deception has potentially harmful effects or is otherwise wrong.

The use of deception in research is a particularly sensitive topic, as illustrated with the Milgram experiments discussed above and with Kimmel's comments about the risk of informing respondents of the true purpose of a research project. The TCPS on research ethics provides a framework for assessing the ethical character of research at publicly funded institutions such as universities and colleges. The framework calls for the establishment of Research Ethics Boards (REBs), and such boards exist at virtually all public universities and most public colleges in Canada. The TCPS identifies instances in which research poses **minimal risk** to participants, which is defined as a level of risk consistent with that experienced in everyday life. Ethics reviews are expedited in instances where the risk is minimal. Furthermore, the TCPS indicates that where the project has been identified as minimal risk, a REB may approve a project involving deception, as long as the following five conditions prevail:

- the research is minimal risk;
- the deception is unlikely to harm the respondent;
- it is not possible to conduct the research without deception;
- where possible and appropriate, participants will be fully debriefed; and
- no therapeutic, clinical, or diagnostic interventions are involved.

Source: Interagency Panel on Research Ethics, *Revised Draft Second Edition of the TCPS* (December 2009, Article 3.7).

Informed consent on surveys is often framed in a very bland or abstract fashion: 'We are interested in determining public opinion toward a number of current public policy issues, and to that end we would like to ask you a few questions.' More

EXPAND YOUR KNOWLEDGE
Confidentiality and the Internet

Survey work conducted through the Internet confronts conventional ethical considerations and opens up new ethical terrain.

A questionnaire sent out to potential respondents via the Internet faces the same informed consent dilemma that mailed and telephone surveys confront: it is impossible to document consent without forcing the respondent to reveal his or her name, thereby abandoning anonymity. Moreover, one cannot 'sign off' over the Internet. Problems of anonymity and confidentiality are further compounded by the nature of e-mail responses. In an Internet survey of western Canadian university students conducted by Carey Hill for her MA thesis in political science at the University of Calgary (1998), potential respondents were asked to respond through the conventional reply cues on e-mail systems. However, the electronic replies invariably included an identification tag for the sender, a tag giving the sender's e-mail address and therefore university location. Respondents were assured that the tag would be removed from the questionnaire once it had been downloaded and printed, but respondents had no option but to rely on Ms Hill's ethical standards. They could not remove the identification tag themselves. It should be noted that Ms Hill also informed potential respondents of the potential risk. If the risk of breached confidentiality was deemed to be serious, individuals receiving the questionnaire through the Internet could simply not reply.

specific information about the research hypotheses, information that would distort the data collection exercise, is not included. The rather insipid information provided by such an informed consent statement, which Singer (1983, 185) describes as a 'deceit' condition, is justified in part by the rationale that the risks to respondents from a generalized survey instrument are minimal and in part by the assumption that the identification of specific research hypotheses would be of little additional use to potential participants trying to assess the risks of participation.

In this context it is worth mentioning the ethical problems that arise in providing informed consent for *participant observation*. This technique, which is discussed in more detail in Chapter 14, entails the researcher working within a group or institution without the members of the group or institution being aware that the researcher is there *as a researcher* and that her observations will be used later in published research findings. In some cases, participant observation is the only possible research approach for target populations. As Lee (1993, 143) explains, participant observation avoids problems of reactivity: 'Because they do not know they are being studied, research participants are not threatened by the research and do not change their behaviour even though to outside eyes it may be considered deviant.' However, the ethical problems associated with covert observation are so great that it is seldom used by academic researchers. It is difficult to construct a defensible argument for lying to or misleading people in the interests of social science research. In the context of the present discussion, the point to emphasize is that participant observation negates the principle of informed consent; subjects are not only uninformed about the research, but cannot give their consent. At the same time, it should be recognized that in many cases participant observation only becomes apparent after the fact. A researcher, for instance, may work within a political party or community group *as a citizen* and only later realize that the participation can be blended into subsequent research programs, theoretical explorations, or teaching anecdotes. In such cases, the opportunity for informed consent has passed; the researcher is simply drawing upon life experiences.

The third line of defence for research subjects is the **right to withdraw** from the research exercise at any time. This, of course, is an option that cannot be extended to subjects in participant observation, which is just one more ethical problem that this research strategy encounters. It should also be noted that the right to withdraw may not be easy to exercise. Note, for example, a 1978 letter to the *American Sociologist* cited by Robert Broadhead (1984, 121). The letter was written by a senior university administrator who had been interviewed by a graduate student:

> In spite of the fact that I was very annoyed at being taped without my permission as well as by the questions and felt increasingly defensive and put down, I did not attempt to terminate the interview. Afterwards I realized how difficult it was to cut off an interview while it is

APPLY YOUR UNDERSTANDING

Discussion of Signed Student Teaching Evaluations

Most universities provide a mechanism by which students are able to assess faculty teaching. If student assessments are to be of assistance in improving teaching, it is imperative that they be returned at some point and in some form to faculty members. What is less clear, however, is whether such assessments should be anonymous or signed. Student assessments of teaching are considered program evaluation or assessment rather than research and therefore do not fall under the rubric of the TCPS and REBs. However, they do raise important issues of anonymity, which is the point under discussion here.

The argument for anonymity hinges on the assumption that students are under some degree of risk, that they might face retaliation by faculty members who were negatively assessed. Such retaliation could be manifest through grading in subsequent courses, negative letters of reference, or rumour mongering. Anonymity reduces the risks to which students are exposed by participating in teaching evaluations. There is a chance, moreover, that in the absence of anonymity students might inflate their assessments of faculty teaching in order to minimize the risk of retaliation.

However, the argument can also be made that anonymity strips students of any responsibility for their actions. Students, in short, could strike out at instructors through the teaching assessments and could do so with impunity and for reasons unrelated to teaching performance itself. There would be no check, for instance, on negative assessments driven by personal malice, sexism, or racism. One possible consequence would be that anonymous assessments might be more negative on balance than would be signed assessments.

What do you think? Should the primary concern be to protect the student by using an anonymous instrument? Or should equal concern be placed on protecting instructors by forcing students to take responsibility for their assessments? Is there a middle ground?

in process. It caused me to reflect on the coerciveness of the interview situation. If as an agency administrator I did not feel free to terminate an interview with a graduate student, it must be almost impossible for the typical subject being interviewed by a 'social scientist' to do so when the perceived status differences are reversed.

It can be difficult to hang up on someone or to ask an interviewer to leave your house or office. It could be equally difficult for students in a classroom to withdraw from a study being conducted by the course instructor. Thus, although informed consent statements should always include the right to withdraw at any time, this right may not be as effective a means of protection as we often assume. When the right to withdraw is extended, everything must be done to make it possible for participants to exercise that right should they choose to do so.

COMMUNITY CONSENT VERSUS INDIVIDUAL CONSENT

To this point, the discussion of informed consent has centred on the researcher obtaining the informed consent of the individual research subject. However, the revised TCPS makes special reference to the 'unique status of Aboriginal peoples of Canada', and discusses the implications of applying the three core principles of research ethics—respect for persons, concern for welfare, and justice—to research on Aboriginal peoples. Upon considering the application of the core principles, the TCPS concludes that researchers are obligated to 'engage' the relevant community regarding the research and to seek the community's consent in conducting the research. Therefore, in a research program involving Aboriginal peoples, the guidelines of the TCPS indicate that researchers should obtain both the informed consent

EXPAND YOUR KNOWLEDGE
Forms of Engagement of Aboriginal Communities

The *Revised Draft Second Edition of the TCPS* indicates that researchers working with Aboriginal subjects should engage the community in providing consent to the research program. The TCPS recognizes that there are many different settings and contexts in which Aboriginal peoples can participate in the research project, and therefore the engagement of the community can take a variety of forms. The following is the general statement of forms of engagement in the TCPS:

> Forms of Engagement
> Community engagement as defined in this Policy can take varied forms. In geographic and organizational communities that have local governments or formal leadership, engagement would normally take the form of review and approval of a research proposal by a designated body prior to recruiting participants. In less structured situations (for example, a community of interest), a key consideration for researchers, prospective participants and REBs is determining the nature and extent of community engagement required. In some situations, the determination may be that the welfare of relevant communities is not affected, and consent of individuals is sufficient. Communities lacking infrastructure to support community engagement should not be deprived of opportunities to participate in guiding research affecting their welfare. (See Article 9.14.)
>
> Article 9.2 The nature and extent of community engagement in a project shall be determined jointly by the researcher and the relevant community and shall be appropriate to community characteristics and the nature of the research.

of each of the individuals involved as research subjects, as well as the informed consent of the Aboriginal community that is the subject of the study.

ETHICAL CONSIDERATIONS IN RESEARCH DESIGN

As we have already discussed, research projects should be designed with a close eye to matters of informed consent, confidentiality, and the protection of anonymity. It is also important that research projects be constrained by the requirements of theory or policy analysis. Even informed consent does not give researchers a blank cheque with respect to the violation of privacy; we should only ask what we need to ask. As Neuman (1997, 445) explains:

> Ethical research requires balancing the value of advancing knowledge against the value of noninterference in the lives of others. Giving research subjects absolute rights of noninterference could make empirical research impossible, but giving researchers absolute rights of inquiry could nullify subjects' basic human rights. The moral question becomes: When, if ever, are researchers justified in risking physical harm or injury to those being studied, causing them great embarrassment, or frightening them?

In matters of questionnaire design, this means restricting oneself to questions that can be justified by the theoretical underpinnings of the study. It is important not to ask respondents a barrage of questions just in the hope that something interesting might later emerge from the data analysis. Such fishing expeditions strain the boundaries of ethical behaviour. If, for example, survey respondents are to be asked about their family income or church attendance, there should be a reason for doing so, and a reason that extends beyond 'most surveys always ask such questions'. In particular, questions that pry into the private lives of respondents, or that may potentially embarrass respondents, must be asked only if there is a compelling research reason to do so. Even then, every effort should be made to avoid embarrassment and to avoid a situation in which the social pressure of the interview situation compels respondents to reveal information or preferences that they would rather not reveal. Here it is not enough to simply assume that respondents are under no compulsion to answer and that if they do so then no harm has been done. There are very real social pressures at work. It should also be noted that interviews that intrude on sensitive matters without a valid justification may generate questionable data. The fact that respondents answer does not mean that they answer truthfully. Therefore, close attention to ethical parameters may yield better research instruments.

Some would argue that survey research itself may be an inappropriate research strategy. Ann Oakley, for example (cited in Finch 1984, 72), criticizes survey research on two grounds: first, for imposing a hierarchical relationship between interviewer and interviewee and second, for objectifying women. Oakley not only maintains that survey research will fail to produce good sociological work on women; she also objects to the technique on the basis of feminist ethics.

Research designs should be respectful of participants' privacy and time. As Allan Kimmel (1988, 139) recommends, 'Research subjects should be considered as another 'granting institution', granting us their valuable time in return for our generation of valuable scientific knowledge.' Research that is not designed with adequate attention to ethical considerations may yield poor data, particularly if participants are trapped in an uncomfortable situation. Failure to pay due regard to ethical concerns may also 'poison the well' for future researchers, which is why sales promotions beginning with the claim that 'we are conducting a survey to determine . . .' are so anathema to social scientists. Research participants who are once bitten will be twice shy.

ETHICAL CONSIDERATIONS IN DATA ANALYSIS

In most cases, ethical issues arise before the data analysis begins or after the data analysis has been completed and the researcher is considering how best, or even if, to disseminate the research findings. However, data analysis itself is not totally immune from ethical considerations. In Chapter 16 we will be discussing the choice of *confidence levels* and therefore the risks of making different kinds of errors. As will be seen, our tolerance for different kinds of errors is not without ethical implications if the research is addressing public policy issues. As Kenneth Bailey (1978, 381) notes, researchers can act unethically 'by revealing only part of the facts, presenting the facts out of context, falsifying findings, or offering misleading presentations . . .'.

A relatively minor but still interesting issue arises with respect to interview transcripts. When extracts from recorded interviews are used in published research findings, assuming of course that the respondent has given written permission for the taped material to be used in this way, the researcher must decide how faithful she will be to the transcript. The problem is that people's spoken language is quite different from written text. In speech, and thus in transcripts, people often use incomplete sentences, strangely constructed sentences, and odd grammatical configurations, all of which may be perfectly understandable within the context of speech, where the listener has access to visual cues, tone, and emphasis. However, if the spoken words are converted directly to written text, the respondent can appear to be illiterate, bumbling, and incoherent. There is, then, an almost irresistible compulsion to clean up the transcript, to transform the irregularities of the spoken word into more polished written text. But to do so is to alter the data and to change not only the form but perhaps also the nuanced meaning of the spoken word.

There is an established convention of asking respondents to review quotations before publication. This ensures that the quote corresponds with the interviewee's meaning. However, it also opens up the possibility that the interviewee will change his or her mind and, therefore, that the quote eventually used does not correspond with the quote given at the interview itself.

Janet Finch draws our attention to another issue, and that is the possibility that the data analysis may be used against the interests of the group from which respondents were drawn. The concern in her case arises initially from interviews with women and with the 'exploitative potential in the easily established trust between women, which makes women especially vulnerable as subjects of research' (1984, 81). Finch then goes on to discuss problems in protecting the *collective* interests of women, protection that cannot be provided by protecting the anonymity or confidentiality of particular women who might participate in a research project. Indeed, Finch raises the possibility of *betrayal*:

> I do not really mean 'betrayal' in the individual sense, such as selling the story of someone else's life to a Sunday newspaper. I mean, rather, 'betrayal' in an indirect and collective sense, that is, undermining the interests of women in general by my use of the material given to me by my interviewees. It is betrayal none the less, because the basis upon which the information has been given is the trust placed in one woman by another.

Even if the researcher is able to avoid the betrayal that Finch identifies, there is no guarantee that the research material will not be used by others in a way that is contrary to the collective interests of women. The point, then, is that ethical considerations cannot be confined to the mechanics of data collection and analysis and cannot be addressed solely by protecting the interests of research participants.

ETHICS AND COLLEGIALITY

Many of the ethical considerations that are important to the social sciences have less to do with the relationship between researcher and research subject than with relationships *within* the research communities. Ethical considerations extend to how we use the work of others, how we recognize the contributions of others, and how we report research findings.

Students first confront this ethical domain when they learn about the perils of *plagiarism*. It is unethical to take credit for the work, wording, or ideas of others as if they were your own. It is essential, therefore, to acknowledge our sources. If this is not done, then the scientific enterprise is also thrown into risk, for there is no way to trace the evolution of ideas and evidence. Plagiarism is a serious offence within universities and within the broader social science community.

The avoidance of plagiarism is best seen as a minimal condition of ethical behaviour. The respect shown for one's colleagues should go beyond acknowledging the use of their work and ideas. It should extend to fostering a cooperative research environment where ideas and data are shared openly and quickly, where methodologies are fully transparent, and where current research is effectively connected to the work that has gone before.

EXPAND YOUR KNOWLEDGE

Integrity in Research and Scholarship

The Canadian Institute of Health Research (CIHR), the Natural Sciences and Engineering Research Council of Canada (NSERC), and the Social Sciences and Humanities Research Council of Canada (SSHRC) have issued a tri-council policy statement on research integrity. The core of this statement addressed the appropriate ethical considerations to be addressed within the research community and among researchers. Five basic principles are identified by the councils:

- recognizing the substantive contributions of collaborators and students; using unpublished work of other researchers and scholars only with permission and due acknowledgment; and using archival material in accordance with the rules of the archival source;
- obtaining the permission of the author before using new information, concepts, or data originally obtained through access to confidential manuscripts or applications for funds for research or training that may have been seen as a result of processes such as peer review;
- using scholarly and scientific rigor and intensity in obtaining, recording, and analyzing data, and in reporting and publishing results;
- ensuring that authorship of published work includes all those who have materially contributed to, and share responsibility for, the contents of publications, and only those people; and
- revealing to sponsors, universities, journals, or funding agencies, any material conflict of interest, financial or other, that might influence their decisions on whether the individual should be asked to review manuscripts or applications, test products or be permitted to undertake work sponsored from outside sources.

Source: CIHR, NSERC, and SSHRC, *Integrity in Research and Scholarship: A Tri-Council Policy Statement* (January 1994).

ETHICAL CONSIDERATIONS IN THE PUBLICATION OF RESEARCH FINDINGS

Much of the research done in the social sciences is applied research; the intent is not only to map and understand social reality but also to shape that reality. As Donald Warwick and Thomas Pettigrew (1983, 335) explain:

> Front-page newspaper headlines about economic indicators, voting analyses, national scores on school achievement tests, and a myriad of

other topics tell the story. Social science is now taken seriously in public policy. No longer are social science findings and theories of great
interest only to those in the discipline. Such work now has *the potential
to affect the lives of citizens* [emphasis added].

As a consequence, the publication of social science research and the injection
of that research into public policy debate bring us face to face with ethical concerns. The argument that empirical research is normatively neutral provides at best
a weak defence against ethical considerations, particularly when it is remembered
that once the research is in the public domain, it can be used for quite different
purposes than originally intended.

The intensity of ethical debate may depend upon the form through which research findings are disseminated. The most common form of dissemination for
academic research is through scholarly publications such as the *Canadian Journal
of Political Science* or *Canadian Public Policy*. However, dissemination can also take
place through the popular press, and indeed the argument can be made that social
scientists have an obligation for broad public dissemination. Helen Roberts (1984,
210–11), for example, argues that a strategy of broad dissemination helps fulfil the
responsibility to inform respondents about the research findings, increases the general credibility of the social sciences, and increases the impact of research findings
on political elites and public policy audiences. At the same time, dissemination
through the press often strips away the subtle interpretation that is so important
to scholarly inquiry. Issues that are not black-and-white are portrayed that way,
because the academic's fascination with endless shades of grey is not shared by
journalists and those who write the headlines. There is, then, an unavoidable risk
that popular dissemination will distort the research findings. There is also an unavoidable risk that the findings will be used for political and social ends with which
the researcher does not approve. However, lack of dissemination means that the
research is not subjected to critical review by other researchers in the field.

One of the more commonplace ethical considerations that arises from the
dissemination of survey research findings is their potential impact on social behaviour. Here, the most prominent example comes from pre-election surveys,
which might credibly be thought to influence voter behaviour. As a case in point,
the 2008 federal election saw considerable variation among polling firms in the
predicted vote for the major parties. The result of the election on October 14 is
that the Conservative party received 38 per cent of the vote compared with 26 per
cent for the Liberals. An Angus Reid Strategies poll conducted October 9 through
12 came very close to the actual result, with the Conservative vote estimated at
37 per cent and the Liberal vote at 27 per cent. Therefore, the actual difference
between the two parties on election day was 12 percentage points, and the estimated difference according to Angus Reid was 10 percentage points. However,
not all polling firms had the same degree of accuracy with their polls. The polling

firm Ipsos pegged the Conservative support at 34 per cent and Liberal support at 29 per cent. Similarly, the Strategic Counsel estimated Conservative support at 33 per cent and Liberal support at 28 per cent. Thus, both of these latter polling firms were estimating a difference of 5 percentage points, substantially at odds with the 12 percentage point difference that emerged on election day. It may be that some of the error is due to the fact that voters might still have been deciding on which party to support during the period between the end of polling and election day, and the fact that both the Ipsos and Strategic Counsel polls ended before the Angus Reid poll is consistent with this explanation. Nonetheless, this degree of inaccuracy in some of the major polls, coupled with the reasonable expectation that poll results can influence the expectations, and therefore the behaviour, of the electorate, raises concerns about the widespread use of polls during election contests.

Concern over the impact of surveys on electoral behaviour has led to some legislative constraints. In Canada, for example, it is illegal to publish survey findings within 48 hours of the onset of a federal election. What remains unclear, however, is the *direction* of survey effects. Our ethical concerns may depend upon whether we believe that surveys lead to a **bandwagon effect**, whereby undecided voters opt to support whatever party is placed in the lead by the polls, or an **underdog effect**, whereby voters opt to rally behind the losing side. Somewhat ironically, survey research has failed to provide conclusive evidence of either effect, leading to the comforting belief that maybe the effects cancel out (see Pickup and Johnston, 2008, on bandwagon and underdog effects).

It is important that published research provide sufficient methodological information about such things as sampling procedures, the nature and size of the sample, the source of funding, and the wording of specific questions. If this information is not provided, it is difficult to have any confidence in the findings, nor is replication possible. Ideally, the research data themselves—data sets, questionnaires, code books, field notes—will be available to other researchers for secondary analysis. Data that are not released into the public domain within a reasonable period of time can become suspect. It should be noted, however, that the failure to release data can often be traced to a variety of factors that have nothing to do with an attempt to conceal information. The researcher may have been slower with his own analysis than anticipated, may lack the funds to clean up the data for release, or may simply have become overcome with other work.

One of the more difficult problems encountered in the social sciences has to do with the publication of negative findings. It is relatively rare, for example, to see studies of regionalism in Canada that conclude that regionalism has no effect on political values and behaviours, or studies of gender politics that show that gender has no impact. Negative findings lack the appeal of positive findings; they are like a story in the morning paper saying that nothing happened yesterday. It is not the stuff from which headlines are made. Yet as Marie Jahoda points out (1981, 211), if negative findings are not published, we may 'accept theories on the strength of one statistically significant divergence from the null hypothesis'.

At times the dissemination of research findings may be constrained by prior commitments relating to confidentiality. If, for example, access to particular informants has been secured only through the promise that identities and some forms of information not be revealed, then the researcher may be unable to publish exciting findings.

APPLY YOUR UNDERSTANDING

Disclosure of Research Findings

Imagine you are taking an undergraduate course on sociobiology. Everyone in the class has been asked to undertake a specific research topic and to report back through a class presentation. Your research project involves looking at instances of rape in the animal world. After reviewing a reasonable slice of the published research material, you conclude that rape is a 'natural act'. (Whether the research in the field supports such a conclusion is not at issue here.) Are there ethical considerations that should be brought into play in presenting this finding to the class? Can a case be made that you should not report the findings? Is there any likelihood that the research findings might affect the behaviour of students in the class? That it might heighten perceptions of risk?

SUMMARY

In bringing this chapter's discussion to a close, it should be stressed that ethical guidelines for social science research are now more than normative, although the normative codes of ethical behaviour that have been adopted by most professional associations are certainly important. Ethical guidelines are generally embodied in specific institutional documents and policed by ethics review committees. It is therefore imperative that researchers of all types, including students building 'fieldwork' into term papers and honours theses, know their institution's policies and procedures. 'Behaving ethically' is no longer simply a matter of principled behaviour on the part of the researcher, although it is that above all else. It is also a matter of meeting clearly specified institutional requirements that generally entail some form of external review. Given the very serious consequences that can follow from a failure to observe ethical guidelines and the accompanying procedures, it is imperative that researchers familiarize themselves with the institutional environment. When in doubt, ask. If still in doubt, ask again.

This chapter has not identified all of the ethical issues and concerns that political scientists are likely to encounter as they go about their work; we have tried only to highlight a number of particularly important concerns. Our intent throughout has been to bring into focus the people behind the numbers. It should also be noted in conclusion that ethical guidelines are not meant to muzzle the engagement of political scientists in public policy debate. As Warwick and Pettigrew (1983, 356–7) remind us, 'policy researchers, like other citizens, have every right to express their policy opinions'. At the same time, there is a need to separate the roles of policy advocate and social scientist, to distinguish between empirical research and the normative conclusions one might draw from that research and wish to inject into the political arena.

WORKING AS A TEAM

1. Virtually all universities and colleges have formal ethical guidelines in place for social science research. Find copies of the relevant guidelines for your own institution and discuss their coverage.

2. Do the guidelines seem relevant to political science research? Are there concerns that are not addressed by the guidelines or that are addressed inappropriately in the context of political science research?

SELF-STUDY

1. Imagine that a political debate has erupted within your community over levels of immigration and what contributions immigrants make to Canadian society. A group to which you belong supports increased levels of immigration and is determined to show that opposition to immigration is a minority opinion within the community. You are commissioned to do a survey of community opinion and find, to your surprise and distress, that the majority of respondents oppose increased levels of immigration. Unfortunately, the press has learned that the survey took place and is pressing you for the results. What are the ethical issues involved in releasing or not releasing the survey findings?

2. Researchers have demonstrated the possibility of cloning a wide array of livestock (sheep, cattle, pigs, etc.). Can such findings be extended to the cloning of human beings? If so, should researchers be allowed to proceed, at least to the point of testing the technology? And who should make this decision? Should it be the scientists themselves? Their employers? The government?

PART II
RESEARCH DESIGN

When conducting research, political scientists must pay explicit attention to **research design**. Researchers need to be clear about their research questions and hypotheses, and about their concepts and measures. They need to specify their population and sample. And they need to make important decisions about data collection and data analysis. Earlier decisions—research questions, concepts, population—influence decisions about data collection. Decisions about data collection, in turn, influence how the data are analyzed.

We begin this section with an overview of quantitative and qualitative approaches. We then consider two questions that are pertinent to all research designs, be they quantitative or qualitative: first, will the study consider a single case, or employ a comparative approach; and second, how will the research select the cases that will be included in the analysis?

After considering these overarching issues, the section turns to a number of short chapters on various data collection techniques. We start with the chapters on quantitative data collection: surveys, government data (such as the Census and electoral returns data), experiments, and content analysis. We then consider qualitative approaches: elite interviews, observation research, and focus groups. In each chapter, we note the strengths and limitations of the data collection method, as well as the ethical considerations facing the researcher.

Conscious attention to research design helps the researcher ensure that she will in fact obtain the necessary empirical data to answer her research question and/or test her hypothesis. For this reason, political scientists must devote sufficient time and attention to questions of research design.

Chapter 6

OBSERVING THE POLITICAL WORLD: QUANTITATIVE AND QUALITATIVE APPROACHES

Jared J. Wesley, University of Manitoba

DESTINATION

By the end of this chapter the reader should

- appreciate the parallels between the casual ways in which we all view the political world and the more systematic methods used by social scientists;
- know the epistemological and methodological distinctions between quantitative and qualitative research; and
- be able to explain what trustworthiness is and what steps researchers can take to increase trustworthiness.

Whether studying voter turnout and voting behaviour, laws and institutions, cultures and ideas, or any other topic, all political scientists confront the same set of fundamental questions when designing their research. Does my study seek to uncover broad generalizations about the political world, or am I seeking a narrower, more in-depth understanding of a particular phenomenon? Will my examination involve a large number of individuals, groups, or countries, or will I focus on a smaller number of cases? Do I have a predefined set of hypotheses I wish to test, or is my study more exploratory in nature?

Answers to these questions determine the most effective methodological approach to pursue. In particular, they establish whether the research should proceed in the 'quantitative' or 'qualitative' tradition—whether the study should involve a more deductive process of counting and statistical analysis, or a more inductive method of nonnumerical interpretation.

Previous generations of political scientists viewed these two traditions as incommensurable. Many in the discipline believed in a hard-and-fast connection between quantitative methods and the tenets of **positivism**, on one hand, and qualitative methods and **interpretivism**, on the other. According to this perspective, quantitative positivists believed in the principles of inherency and verifiability, which put them at odds with the belief among qualitative relativists that all reality was socially constructed. In this environment, researchers toiled in opposing camps—either parallel, but separate, in their pursuit of knowledge, or each actively seeking to undermine the others.

Indeed, until recently, heated debates between quantitative and qualitative researchers constituted one of the deepest divisions in the political science community. The chasm was broadest during the so-called behavioural revolution, a period consuming the second half of the twentieth century. With the advent of the computer and the development of mass survey techniques, quantitative approaches came to dominate the discipline. Qualitative methods were overshadowed, their decline the product of researchers' preferences, trends in postsecondary education, and—to a more limited degree—non-acceptance by some positivist puritans.

Today's discipline is not entirely immune to these tensions.[1] As Manheim et al. (2002, 318) describe, 'Some quantitatively oriented scholars regard at least some qualitative work as so dependent on the perceptions of the individual researcher and so focused on specific cases as to be unverifiable and essentially useless. In contrast, some qualitatively oriented scholars judge quantitative methods to be so incomplete in their representation of reality as to be empirically misleading.' Fortunately, while many empirical researchers continue to work under one tradition or the other, most have come to appreciate the value of the other approach. Unlike their forebears, most present-day political scientists perceive benefits in both quantitative and qualitative research, and an important element of interdependence in their relationship. As Brady and colleagues (2004, 10) put it:

> *In the social sciences, qualitative research is hard to do well. Quantitative research is also hard to do well. Each tradition can and should learn from the other.* One version of conventional wisdom holds that achieving analytic rigor is more difficult in qualitative than in quantitative research. Yet in quantitative research, making valid inferences about complex political processes on the basis of observational data is likewise extremely difficult. There are no quick and easy recipes for either qualitative or quantitative analysis. In the face of these shared challenges, the two traditions have developed distinctive and complementary tools [emphasis in original].

Instead of struggling for methodological supremacy, most political scientists seek to 'refine and develop the battery of techniques on offer, and above all to be as explicit as possible about the implications of the methodologies we employ' (Laver 2001, 9). Most researchers strive to develop strengths, or at least awareness, in a variety of different methodological techniques.

APPLY YOUR UNDERSTANDING

Evidence in Political Science Research

Think for a moment about the types of 'evidence' we consider as political researchers. When measuring the level of democratic satisfaction in a particular community, for example, what type of data could we collect? We could use objective indicators, like electoral participation rates or the prevalence of violent political protests, for instance. Alternatively, we could use subjective indicators, gleaned from interviews, surveys, focus groups, or letters to the editor.

Now ask yourself, What would these various types of evidence look like? Would the data consist of numbers and statistics (such as turnout figures or 'feeling thermometer' ratings)? Or would the data take a nonnumerical form, as in the words of the respondents or the nature of political protests? How would the analysis differ, depending upon whether the data were collected quantitatively or qualitatively? How would this choice affect the research process, itself, or the nature of its findings?

QUANTITATIVE AND QUALITATIVE APPROACHES TO EMPIRICAL RESEARCH

Empirical research is based on observation and interpretation, and includes two distinct traditions. The first, which typically comes to mind when one thinks of empirical research, is the **quantitative** approach. As the root of the word suggests, this approach seeks to understand political life through the study of a large quantity, or number, of cases. A **case** is a single unit, which could be individuals, legislatures, organizations, nation-states, court decisions, or whatever the unit of interest may be. Because of time and financial constraints, one can rarely conduct an in-depth study of large numbers of cases; thus, quantitative research tends to have greater breadth than depth. The research tends to be quite *structured;* for example, a survey researcher will ask the questions listed on her polling sheet and nothing more.

The second approach to empirical analysis is known as **qualitative research.** As its word root suggests, the emphasis here is on quality, or detail. Qualitative researchers attempt to learn about politics through a more thorough study of a small number of cases. In this way, qualitative research complements quantitative research, emphasizing depth over breadth. Qualitative research is equally rigorous but less structured than quantitative research, which allows the researcher to explore the subtleties of individual beliefs or group dynamics. For example, an interviewer may be intrigued by something his subject mentions and may choose to follow this point with a spontaneous line of questioning.

Three common misconceptions surround the relationship between the quantitative and qualitative traditions. First, despite common impressions, no research topic is inherently qualitative or quantitative. Researchers can study any subject—from political participation to military intervention—by using either approach. Granted, certain topics have been approached more quantitatively (voting and elections come to mind), whereas others have fallen largely under the purview of qualitative scholarship (including Indigenous politics and gender studies). Yet, the subject matter, itself, does not determine which tradition should be employed. Second, specific methodologies do not belong solely to one tradition or the other. Surveys can be quantitative or qualitative, as can interviews, focus groups, content analysis, observation research, or any other mode of inquiry. And third, while analysts are likely to develop certain preferences and skill sets, it is becoming increasingly uncommon (and unpopular) to refer to individuals as being purely quantitative or qualitative researchers. Instead of specializing in only one tradition or methodology, political scientists are expected to approach their research with entire 'toolboxes' at their disposal. This means learning different methods, qualitative and quantitative, depending upon the task at hand.

Indeed, the choice between the two traditions depends upon the specific *research question* guiding the study. As Laver (2001, 9) suggests, 'different theoretical problems will always demand different types of data.' Because quantitative research involves numbers, frequencies, intensities, and other measurements of degree, it is particularly well suited to questions of How much? How often? and How many? By contrast, qualitative research deals best with questions involving conditions, norms, and values (Tashakkori and Teddlie 2003, 317). As King et al. (1993, 4–5) put it, '[T]rends in social, political, or economic behavior are more readily addressed by quantitative analysis than is the flow of ideas among people or the difference made by exceptional individual leadership.' In other words, while all questions in political science involve some sort of comparison, quantitative research is best equipped for 'judgments of which phenomena are "more" or "less" alike *in degree*', whereas qualitative research is best suited to examining differences '*in kind*' (King, Keohane, and Verba 1993, 5).

APPLY YOUR UNDERSTANDING

Quantitative and Qualitative Methods

Consider the question, *Why do some people support universal health care?* How would you address this question from a quantitative approach? Whom would you study? What type of questions might you ask? How would your study and questions differ if you were conducting qualitative research? What specific advantages and limitations do you see to each approach?

Epistemological Differences

While most political scientists have accepted the value of, and even tried to bridge the divide between, the two approaches, certain core differences between quantitative and qualitative research remain. First, there are important **epistemological** and methodological distinctions between the quantitative and qualitative traditions. In Chapter 1, we introduced the positivist approach to science and discussed its application in the social sciences. We also noted that positivism is not without its critics and that alternative approaches take more of an interpretative position (often referred to as 'postpositivism'). Quantitative approaches are often associated with positivism, and qualitative approaches are often associated with postpositivism, but in practice the lines are not always so clearly defined. When it comes to the two traditions, most scholars do not sit solely in one 'camp' or the other. Some will employ quantitative methods in one study and qualitative tools in another; some will combine both traditions in a single analysis. Moreover, although there is a *tendency* to associate quantitative research with the positivist approach to political life, and qualitative analysis with the interpretivist (or naturalistic), most political science research fits somewhere between these two extremes (Bryman 2004, 442). In this spirit, although the following descriptions of the epistemological differences refer to two sides of a continuum, readers should keep in mind that most social scientists occupy the middle ground (see Table 6.1).

Primary Intent

The primary purpose of most quantitative analysis is to test hypotheses. Researchers employing this approach enter the data collection, processing, and analysis stages with predefined postulates, which they actively seek to disconfirm. By contrast, most qualitative scholarship approaches the investigation with broader research questions in mind. Specific expectations are both developed and assessed during the process of observation and analysis (Neuman and Robson 2007, 336). To be sure, quantitative analysis proceeds from research questions, just as some qualitative research seeks to test hypotheses. The difference in intent is more a matter of degree than kind. In general, researchers applying the quantitative method

TABLE 6.1 Epistemological Differences between the Two Traditions

Element of Research	Quantitative Tradition	Qualitative Tradition
Primary intent	Test hypotheses	Address questions
Ultimate objective	Generalizability	Specificity
General approach	Manipulative	Naturalistic
Position of researcher	Distanced	Instrumental
Theory development	Primarily deductive	Primarily inductive

approach the process with answers they seek to verify or disprove, whereas those pursuing a qualitative route approach the process with problems they seek to understand or address (Altheide 1996, 15).

Ultimate Objective

The ultimate objective of most quantitative analyses is to produce widely applicable results, whereas most qualitative studies aim to shed intense light on a specific context. The former often generate generalizable findings based on a wide range of cases. Proponents refer to this as a 'broad', **large-N** approach, while critics call it 'shallow'. By conducting **'small-N'** studies, qualitative research designs produce more detailed understandings of specific cases. Some deem this analysis to be 'deeper', others 'narrower', than quantitative research. Again, it is important to note that while quantitative analysis enables researchers to examine a large number of cases, not all quantitative studies involve a large-N. The same is true of qualitative analyses; although it may require more resources, some qualitative studies involve the examination of many cases.

General Approach

Most quantitative scholarship treats 'reality' as something that can be both measured and configured. Real-world observations are converted into numerical form, and then manipulated statistically to produce findings. Qualitative research tends to take a more 'naturalistic' approach, adapting analytical techniques to the environment rather than vice versa (Guba and Lincoln 1985). To put it crudely: in quantitative research, nature submits to the method; in qualitative research, the method is more likely to submit to nature.

For these reasons quantitative research is often described as being 'harder' than qualitative research. This difference lies not in the level of difficulty or complexity associated with the former (although some may portray it as such). Rather, quantitative research is commonly viewed as nearer to the physical ('hard') sciences than the ('soft') arts- or humanities-focused brand of qualitative research (see Brady, Collier, and Seawright 2004, 10–11; Guba and Lincoln 1994, 105–6).

Position of Researcher

Most quantitative analysis aims to limit the researcher's own personal imprint on the findings. Although often recognized and acknowledged, researcher biases are actively minimized during the investigation, because they are seen as contaminants of objective inquiry. Such prejudices are deemed more benign (or, at least, less malignant) in most brands of qualitative research. There, researcher biases are more likely to be perceived as unavoidable elements of interpretive inquiry, rather than as pollutants. Researchers are typically the instruments of qualitative study; they are the agents of quantitative research (Merriam 2002b, 5).

Theory Development

Chapter 2 introduced the distinction between deductive and inductive research. While both the quantitative and qualitative traditions combine deduction and induction in their analyses, they do so to differing degrees (Punch 2005, 196–7; Neuman and Robson 2007, 111). Quantitative analyses tend to apply existing theories to the data at hand in order to deduce patterns among predefined variables, whereas the qualitative method is more conducive to an inductive process whereby themes and explanations emerge from the data. All told, and as noted earlier, quantitative research is more closely connected to the positivist school of social science, wherein theory precedes observation. In qualitative research, ('grounded') theory tends to emerge from observation—a notion closer to the interpretivist or postpositivist approach to social science (Creswell 2003, 182; see Babbie and Benaquisto 2002, 378–9; Punch 2005, 209; Ryan and Bernard 2003, 278–80; Strauss and Corbin 1994).

Methodological Differences

The broader epistemological divisions influence the narrower, methodological differences between quantitative and qualitative analyses (see Table 6.2). To reiterate, the following discussion treats the two traditions as poles on a spectrum; most political science research is conducted in the middle ground between these two extremes.

Data Format

Quantitative analysis deals in numbers and qualitative research does not. By definition, quantitative analysis requires the 'quantification' of political phenomena. Behaviours, ideas, and other observations must be converted into numbers by means of counting or scoring. Qualitative scholarship approaches political life

TABLE 6.2 Methodological Differences between the Two Traditions

Element of Data	Quantitative Tradition	Qualitative Tradition
Data format	Numerical (frequency, amount, salience, intensity)	Nonnumerical (words, images)
Data reduction	Variables (operationalized a priori)	Themes (emergent)
Substance of data	Meaning is inherent	Meaning is contingent
Data recording	Standardized instrument	Variable instrument
Data processing	Mathematical	Conceptual
Data reporting	Statistical, graphical	Verbal
Standards of evidence	Probability	Plausibility

differently, treating phenomena in terms of words, images, symbols, and other nonnumerical forms.

Data Reduction

The desired format of the data leads those employing quantitative and qualitative methods to pursue different means of reducing their 'raw materials' into manageable portions. In quantitative analysis, data reduction involves categorizing observations according to a series of predefined criteria. Phenomena are counted or ranked based on the means by, and extent to, which they 'vary' in terms of certain attributes. In other words, observations are filtered through a set of **variables**, with specific values being assigned to them. As outlined in Chapter 4, this variation may be expressed in nominal, ordinal, or interval form. Crucially, these categories are determined prior to the data reduction process, such that the resulting data set is the product of how each variable was defined and which variables were studied.

By contrast, scholars employing qualitative methods make sense of their observations through the identification of themes. This may be achieved through a wide range of techniques, with various researchers referring to the process as one of 'soaking', 'chunking', 'puzzle-solving', or 'concept-mapping'. Regardless of the terminology, all researchers in the qualitative tradition search for patterns in their data, as they group different observations according to certain nonnumerical relationships. This may involve linking similar ideas or respondents under given 'schools of thought', or combining related concepts into distinct 'pillars' of understanding.

In this sense, regardless of the tradition they apply, all researchers impose orderliness on their data. They simply approach this data-reduction process from different perspectives, using different tools. As one group of methodologists explains, 'Quantitative researchers conceptualize and refine variables in a process that comes before data collection or analysis. By contrast, qualitative researchers form new concepts or refine concepts that are grounded in the data' (Neuman and Robson 2007, 336–7).

Substance of Data

A guiding, if unstated, premise of quantitative analysis holds that meaning is intrinsic to the data itself. Given the operational definition established a priori, the nature of a given observation is inherent, intersubjective, static, and **univocal**. This differs from the qualitative approach, whose practitioners insist that meaning is more contingent, or subject to the unique perspectives of the observer and the diverse qualities of the observed. As such, to most qualitative social scientists, observations are necessarily subjective, dynamic, and—ultimately—**equivocal**.

Data Recording

Based on these perspectives, data collection is pursued quite differently in the quantitative and qualitative traditions. For the former, meaning is inherent in the data, which allows analysts to use a standardized recording instrument (for example, a closed questionnaire or code sheet). Qualitative research is more 'flexible' in terms of recording data (Babbie and Benaquisto 2002, 381; Neuman and Robson 2007, 111). In this tradition, meaning varies from observation to observation, and observer to observer. A more inclusive form of data collection is necessary to allow for these variations. Hence, qualitative analyses employ open-ended questionnaires, interviews, and coding techniques.

Data Processing

Quantitative research applies proven statistical formulae, correlation coefficients, regression analyses, tests of significance, and other mathematical procedures in an effort to reveal the regularities of political life. Conversely, qualitative approaches provide a 'softer' approach of 'extracting' distinct themes and motifs. Hence, whereas the data reduction, processing, and analysis stages are distinct and sequential in quantitative analyses, all are subsumed under the qualitative coding process. Qualitative data coding is described in Chapter 19.

Data Reporting

Findings in quantitative analyses are depicted largely in numerical terms, in the form of graphs, tables, charts, and other figures. By contrast, analysts working in the qualitative tradition use words, not numbers or statistics, to express research findings verbally. Again, these are generalizations. Nearly every qualitative analysis invokes numbers, or speaks in terms of frequency or intensity, just as almost all quantitative scholarship 'qualifies' its findings with reference to quotations or other nonnumeric evidence. Suffice it to say, however, just as quantitative research formats, reduces, and manipulates data in numerical terms, so, too, does it report findings in terms of numbers. The same applies to qualitative analysis, which informs through words and concepts.

Standards of Evidence

A final distinction between the quantitative and qualitative traditions lies in their differing definitions of 'proof' or 'evidence'. According to the tenets of post-positivism, social scientists need not—indeed cannot—establish their conclusions with absolute certainty. Rather, their aim is to approximate 'truth', limiting the scope of their findings based on certain disciplinary standards. Grounded in numbers and mathematics, quantitative research relies on statements of statistical significance and other measures of **probability** to establish the boundaries of its conclusions. Conversely, qualitative research reports the **plausibility** of its findings, based not on statistical odds but on the conceivability and fitness of the results to the real world; rather than mathematical tests, analysts marshal evidence and logic to establish the soundness of their findings (Neuman and Robson 2007, 336; Manheim, Rich, and Willnat 2002, 317). Although closely related, 'probability' and 'plausibility' are by no means synonymous.

Summary

Each tradition has its advantages and limitations. One advantage of the quantitative approach is that the large size of the group studied allows us to make generalizations from the sample to a larger unit, such as society as a whole. The ability to make generalizations is more limited in qualitative research, because of the small size of the group being studied. In addition, quantitative research is often seen as more objective than qualitative research. The research methods employed in qualitative analysis require a greater degree of interpretation on the part of the researcher and are therefore more subjective. However, qualitative research allows for a richer understanding of the political phenomena being studied. Political research often concerns individual beliefs, attitudes, and behaviours, topics that cannot be completely explored by quantitative research. For example, one of the most insightful studies of ideological belief systems in the United States (Lane 1962) was based on in-depth interviews with only 15 male respondents in New Haven, Connecticut. Although the researcher was unable to make empirical generalizations to the American population at large, he was able to provide vivid insights into how the 'American Common Man' tries to make sense out of a complex political world.

As noted earlier, how one chooses between the two approaches depends upon the research question and objectives of the study. If one wishes to develop generalizations that are broad in scope, the quantitative approach may be more appropriate. If one desires a greater understanding of the phenomena in question, with less concern for generalizability, the qualitative approach is best. Of course, in political science we often wish to achieve both ends. The solution, then, is to combine the two research strategies, allowing the strengths of one to complement the strengths of the other. For example, a researcher might combine a large-*N* quantitative telephone survey with a series of in-depth, qualitative interviews with a small subset of respondents. The survey allows her to ask an identical set of questions to a large sample, while the interviews allow her to explore the issues in depth with a smaller group of individuals. Combining research approaches, or **triangulation**, is discussed later in this chapter.

EXPAND YOUR UNDERSTANDING

Considerations in Selecting Research Methodologies

When selecting a particular data collection methodology, the researcher has to consider both the goals of the study and the feasibility of the research design. By considering these issues, the researcher can limit the number of (inevitable) research problems that will arise and can ensure a greater degree of confidence in his final conclusions.

Research projects vary in their goals. Some projects attempt to tackle a new subject area in order to promote inductive theory or to provide the descriptive facts necessary for applied research. Others seek to explain why events occurred, what caused their appearance, and so on. There are six basic types of questions we can ask: who, what, where, when, why, and how. 'What' questions usually fall into the category of **exploratory research**; the researcher merely wishes to get an idea of what is happening in an unexplored aspect of the political world (Neuman 1994, 18). Exploratory research often benefits from qualitative methodologies, which allow the researcher the greatest insights into group dynamics and individual motivations. **Descriptive research** addresses questions of 'who', 'where', 'when', and 'how'. We use descriptive research to get an accurate account of a situation; thus, it is often useful for applied research, such as policy studies. Exploratory and descriptive research studies create knowledge that provides the basis for **explanatory research**, which addresses the question of 'why'. Explanatory research focuses on questions of causality, and experiments are the ideal method for this type of research.

Another factor to consider is **feasibility**. Not all research projects are possible, despite our best intentions or level of interest in the topic. Resources—time, money, personnel, equipment— are always scarce. Some populations are difficult to access, making research near-impossible and at times dangerous. Some research involves ethical dilemmas that cannot be resolved easily. When selecting a research method, the researcher must be practical; although in theory one approach may be optimal for the study, the reality may be that the research is only feasible if another approach is taken. In research, as in the rest of life, there are often gaps between what we want to do and what we can actually do.

TRUSTWORTHY RESEARCH

Having established the core differences between quantitative and qualitative scholarship, our focus now turns to the common ground between them. In this spirit, although they may use different terminology, both traditions rely on similar standards to judge the respectability of their research.

The core question at the heart of all political research, both qualitative and quantitative, is, *How do we ensure that the knowledge generated through political science is legitimate?* For most scholars employing quantitative methods, the answer is relatively straightforward: their research must achieve three standards of accuracy: validity, reliability, and objectivity. Many purely qualitative researchers, particularly postmodernists and other relativists, reject these notions entirely. For them, all explanations of social life are constructed and subjective, and, thus, no universal standards of 'proof' or 'truthfulness' can be applied. Finding middle-ground between these two approaches, most political scientists today agree that—while attaching slightly different labels and imposing unique measurement requirements—the qualitative and quantitative traditions share a common set of expectations of scholarly research.

Criteria for Trustworthiness

This view is best captured by Guba and Lincoln's (1985) concept of '**trustworthiness**'. Building on their seminal account, the following discussion outlines the four essential elements of all legitimate social science research: authenticity, portability, precision, and impartiality (see Table 6.3).

Authenticity

At its basic level, **authenticity** connotes a correspondence between the observation and the observed. To what extent is the recorded data a genuine reflection of reality? In this sense, 'the goal is to demonstrate that the inquiry was conducted in such a manner as to ensure that the subject was accurately identified and described' (Marshall and Rossman 1989, 145). In quantitative research, this notion is known as **measurement validity**—or 'the degree to which the measurement of a concept truly reflects that concept' (Bryman 2004, 541). Because they harbour more reservations about the intersubjectivity of 'accuracy', in general, many scholars toiling in the qualitative tradition prefer the term '**credibility**' to 'validity'. To have integrity or authenticity, a qualitative account must provide a tenable, believable depiction of the subject under study. In other words, the observation and data must 'fit' the world being described—an evaluation that depends less upon the true nature of reality than the judgment of the reader (Krippendorff 2004, 314).

Portability

A second important criterion for assessing the trustworthiness of a social scientific study is its **portability**. Most researchers acknowledge that, in order to make a substantive and substantial contribution to knowledge, studies must move beyond the explanation of a small number of cases. The results ought to connect to broader questions about social life; they ought to be 'portable', or applicable in some way to other environments. Researchers working in the quantitative tradition refer to this as **external validity**—or the degree to which 'the results of a study can be generalized beyond the specific research context in which it was conducted' (Bryman 2004, 539). This is often established through the specification of operationalized

TABLE 6.3 Criteria for Trustworthiness

Criteria	Quantitative Tradition*	Qualitative Tradition*
Authenticity	Measurement validity	Credibility
Portability	External validity	Transferability
Precision	Reliability	Dependability
Impartiality	Objectivity	Confirmability

*Columns adapted from Guba and Lincoln (1985).

variables, causal models, and regression models, which may be repeated in other contexts. Many researchers employing qualitative methods prefer the term '**transferability**', reflecting the view that a study's findings must be transposed in order to establish their portability. In this sense, 'the burden of demonstrating the applicability of one set of findings to another context rests more with the investigator who would make that transfer than with the original investigator' (Lewis and Ritchie 2006, 145). As Merriam (2002a, 28–9) suggests:

> the most common way generalizability has been conceptualized in qualitative research is as reader or user generalizability. In this view, readers themselves determine the extent to which findings from a study can be applied to their context. Called case-to-case transfer by Firestone, 'It is the reader who has to ask, what is there in this study that I can apply to my own situation, and what clearly does not apply?'

Precision

The inability of researchers conducting qualitative research to replicate their results constitutes the most crucial point of contention among followers of the two traditions. **Replicability** is a fundamental component of the positivist approach to social science. To confirm its **reliability**—'that quality of measurement method that suggests the same data would have been collected each time in repeated observations of the same phenomenon' (Babbie and Benaquisto 2002, 497)—any finding in quantitative research must be repeatable.

Because the process of qualitative research is more fluid and dependent upon the researcher's role as an instrument in the process, findings cannot be reproduced in the same sense as quantitative ones (Lewis and Ritchie 2006, 270). This is not to say that qualitative research ignores the value of **precision**. Rather, the focus shifts from the more intersubjective notion of 'reliability' to the standard of '**dependability**'. As Merriam (2002a, 27) argues:

> Replication of a qualitative study will not yield the same results, but this does not discredit the results of any particular study; there can be numerous interpretations of the same data. The more important question for qualitative researchers is *whether the results are consistent with the data collected.* . . . That is, rather than insisting that others get the same results as the original researcher, reliability lies in others' concurring that given the data collected, the results make sense—they are consistent and dependable [emphasis in original].

Thus, provided that the research process is clearly specified and transparent, readers may assess its precision by asking the question, 'Is it reasonable to assume that, given the opportunity to repeat the exercise under the same conditions, a researcher would have reported the same results from the same observations?' If yes, the qualitative study is verifiable and dependable in the same way that a quantitative analysis is replicable and reliable.

Impartiality

Last, but certainly not in terms of importance, most social scientists agree that research should produce **impartial** knowledge about the world, as opposed to normative opinions or value-laden wisdom. As Marshall and Rossman (1989, 147) put it, 'How can we be sure that the findings are reflective of the subjects and the inquiry itself rather than the product of the researcher's biases or prejudices?' In attempting to minimize their own biases, researchers employing quantitative methods aim to protect a study's **objectivity**—a term clearly at odds with the interpretive principles of qualitative scholarship. The latter are more likely to acknowledge (even embrace or test) their personal biases as unavoidable elements of the research process (King, Keohane, and Verba 1993, 14–15; Merriam 2002b, 5). As a result, all qualitative inquiry contains some element of subjectivity. Instead of objectivity, when striving for trustworthy results, the qualitative tradition demands that readers ask, 'Can these findings be *confirmed* by another individual, independent of the original researcher's predispositions?' This is the essence of '**confirmability**'.

Neither of the two traditions is beyond reproach when it comes to producing trustworthy results. Preserving validity is the greatest challenge for students employing quantitative methods. For example, the coding of platforms and speeches has the potential to reduce complex, living texts to a series of simpler, colder numbers. The opposite issue confronts analysts in the qualitative tradition. By delving into the deeper meaning of these documents, relying upon more 'intuitive, soft, and relativistic' modes of interpretation, they risk compromising the dependability, transferability, and confirmability of their findings (Creswell 1998, 142) (see also Manheim, Rich, and Willnat 2002, 315). Hence, on their own, neither the quantitative nor qualitative tradition stakes claim to a superior method. Both have their own advantages and drawbacks. Fortunately, their weaknesses are offset by their complementary strengths, and common tools are available to preserve the trustworthiness of their research.

EXPAND YOUR UNDERSTANDING

Internal and External Validity

When conducting quantitative research, the researcher must always ask, 'How valid is my research design?' **Validity**, in this sense, refers to how useful our design is in advancing the knowledge we are trying to obtain. There are two broad forms of validity that we need to be concerned with when considering research design: internal validity and external validity. **Internal validity** concerns the validity within the study: are we measuring what we believe we are measuring (measurement validity)? Are our conclusions supported by the facts of our study? Have we ruled out alternative explanations and spurious relationships? Internal validity can vary with the degree to which we can control our study. If we are able to hold conditions constant, we can rule out alternative factors, and thus our conclusions are more likely to be supported. In such a case, we have high internal validity. If, on the other hand, there are many factors that we cannot control and therefore many alternative explanations that may compete with our conclusions, we have low internal validity. In a nutshell, low internal validity means that we have less confidence in our conclusions about the study, whereas high internal validity means that we have a strong degree of confidence.

Note that with internal validity, we are concerned with the validity of the study itself. Questions of **external validity** are concerned with the legitimacy of generalizations made from the study. Was the study representative, or was it a 'rogue' or 'fluke' study, a one-in-a-million occurrence? Can our study allow us to make generalizations about the 'real world', or are the conclusions applicable only to the single study? When conducting theory-oriented research, we desire high external validity, since we wish to use the studies to make generalizations about the larger political world. Quite often there are tradeoffs between internal and external validity. The more 'realistic' one's study is, the greater the external validity. However, as realism increases, the researcher's level of control over the study decreases, thus reducing internal validity. How the researcher addresses such dilemmas will depend upon her research objectives.

Ensuring Trustworthiness

There are numerous ways for political scientists to bolster the authenticity, portability, precision, and impartiality of their research.[2] Many of the following tools are available to quantitative and qualitative scholars, regardless of tradition or method. Although leading methodologist John Creswell (1998, 203) recommends adopting at least two legitimacy checks, students would be wise to incorporate as many of the following practices as possible to ensure the trustworthiness of their analyses (see Table 6.4 on page 138).

Triangulation

By selecting a research approach, we are choosing to see the world in a particular way. As Kathleen Driscoll and Joan McFarland (1989, 185–6) write, 'Techniques of data collection and analysis are not neutral. . . . Each technique's usefulness and its limitations are structured by its underlying assumptions. Adopting a research technique means adopting its underlying conceptual framework.' Each research design privileges some forms of information over others. Perhaps the best analogy is a line of sight (Berg 1989, 4). If we stand in front of an object, we get one impression of it; standing behind the same object can lead to different observations. Similarly, standing above or below the object gives further nuance to our understanding. To best understand the object, to get the most complete picture, we should take in as many perspectives as possible. The same holds true for understanding political

TABLE 6.4 Ensuring Trustworthiness in Political Science

Checks	Authenticity	Portability	Precision	Impartiality
Triangulation	•	•	•	•
Detailed findings	•	•	•	
Established techniques	•	•		
Report method	•		•	
Discrepant evidence	•		•	•
Publish data	•		•	•
Member checks	•			•
Intense exposure	•			
Research teams		•	•	•
Pilot studies and training			•	
Report biases				•
Peer assessment	•	•	•	•

and social phenomena: comprehension grows as we approach data collection in a variety of ways. The combination of multiple research strategies in social research is known as triangulation. As the image of the triangle suggests, triangulation implies the use of *three* different methods of data-gathering, although a researcher may, in fact, choose to use only two or more than three. Research strategies are combined to maximize the variety of data collected.

'Triangulation' is the foremost means of protecting the legitimacy of political research, although the definition of the term is somewhat ambiguous.[3] Some view triangulation as the concurrent use of a number of different methods in a single research study. This may involve combining content analysis with interviews or direct observation, for example. To others, this combination may take place through separate studies, either consecutively or in tandem (Boyatzis 1998, xiii). Still others believe triangulation can be achieved by using existing literature to provide 'supplemental validation' of research findings (Creswell 1998).

Moreover, the complementary strengths of qualitative and quantitative research have pushed many dualists to develop 'hybrid' approaches as a 'third way' of conducting social science research (Tashakkori and Teddlie 2003, x). Whether to compensate for the weaknesses of a single approach, or to address a particularly complex topic, an increasing number of social scientists are adopting a broader perspective on research (Creswell and Clark 2007). Some refer to this as **mixed-**

methods research—'the use of both qualitative and quantitative method in one study or sequentially in two or more studies' (Hesse-Biber and Leavy 2006, 316). For qualitative researchers, this may mean '**quantizing**' their verbal analyses, by buttressing their findings with reference to frequencies and other quantitative measures (Hesse-Biber and Leavy 2006, 326–30) (see Gerring 1998). By the same token, quantitative researchers may '**qualitize**' their data, contextualizing their findings with direct quotations from various documents or sources (Hesse-Biber and Leavy 2006, 330–3; see also Neuman and Robson 2007, Chapter 16).

Whatever the definition, the purpose of triangulation is clear: by invoking multiple data sources to support their findings, researchers may substantiate the overall trustworthiness of their work.

Detailed Findings

Only by providing a meticulous account of their results can researchers offer readers the information necessary to draw their own conclusions about the authenticity, portability, and precision of the findings. Qualitative researchers must provide a 'thick description' of their cases; this is often accomplished through the inclusion of direct quotations and copious footnoting. In addition to statistical tables and data appendices, quantitative analyses must involve 'colour' or 'substance' in their reporting, as well; doing so provides the meaning behind the numbers presented.

Established Techniques

Where possible, political scientists should seek to build on established techniques. In quantitative research, this may mean drawing on existing surveys, interview scripts, or coding manuals. Students using qualitative methods may rely on general methodological guidelines, including the widely accepted three-stage process of 'open', 'axial', and 'selective' coding (discussed in Chapter 19). This does not mean the abandonment of methodological innovation. Far from it. Great strides have been made by testing, challenging, expanding, adapting, and improving popular research designs. Rather, building on tested techniques allows researchers to elude many pitfalls encountered during earlier studies, and avoid a state of methodological anarchism (Budge and Bara 2001).

Report Method

In order to provide readers with the opportunity to assess the authenticity and precision of their analyses, researchers must also report the exact process through which they achieved their results. In quantitative analysis, this is most efficiently accomplished through the publication of the research instrument (questionnaire, coding manual, or other guides). With no standardized instrument, analysts conducting qualitative studies must provide their readers with an '**audit trail**'—a detailed account of the coding 'protocol', including how conclusions were reached (Altheide 1996, 25–33). As Holliday (2007, 7) suggests, all research 'needs to be accompanied by accounts of how it was really done . . . [Analysts must] reveal how they negotiated complex procedures to deal with the "messy" reality of the scenarios being studied.'

Discrepant Evidence

Most practitioners readily acknowledge the limitations of political science when it comes to representing and explaining reality. Rather than absolute 'proof' or 'truth', most analysts aim to establish the persuasiveness of their accounts relative to alternative explanations. Many researchers employing quantitative methods turn to the statistics of 'probability', just as those following the qualitative tradition depend upon 'plausibility arguments' to buttress their claims (Richerson and Boyd 2004, 410–11). In both traditions, researchers are encouraged to seek out and report discrepant evidence to place reasonable boundaries on their conclusions. Becker (1998), Esterberg (2002, 175), and Berg (2004, 184) refer to this as the 'null hypothesis trick': analysts ought to approach the data by assuming that no patterns exist, then provide clear evidence, using concrete examples, to establish their presence. As George (2006, 155) explains, the seasoned researcher

> considers not just one inferential hypothesis when reading and re-reading the original . . . material, but also many alternatives to it. He systematically weighs the evidence available for and against each of these alternative inferences. Thus, the results of his analysis, if fully explicated, state not merely (1) the favored inference and the content 'evidence' for it, but also (2) alternative explanations of that content 'evidence', (3) other content 'evidence' which may support alternative inferences, and (4) reasons for considering one inferential hypothesis more plausible than others.

Without these qualifications and justifications, the analysis may lack validity or credibility (Holliday 2007, 167–81).

Publish Data

To guard against criticisms of inauthenticity, imprecision, and partiality, political scientists should also provide reasonable access to both their data and their raw materials. In qualitative research, coding databases and memos should be made available for verification—privately, if not publicly—as should the original documents. In an electronic age, sharing this information has never been easier, and there are few legitimate excuses to withhold access to such material (beyond important privacy concerns).

Member Checks

Most researchers seasoned in the qualitative tradition are familiar with the notion of '**member checks**'—a process through which their inferences are verified by the subjects of their analysis. Field observations may be referred to some of the participants involved, surveys may be followed by in-depth interviews of the respondents, or focus group data may be shared with members of the study. In content analysis, this means consulting the authors of the source documents. Sometimes this is not desirable, or even possible. (Some documents may not have identifiable authors, or too many to consult, for instance, while others may have no willing or surviving authors with whom to confer.) When completed, however, member checks may alert researchers to inauthentic claims or biased interpretations.

Intense Exposure

Extended, intense contact with source materials is more likely to produce valid or credible interpretations of their contents. To produce authentic results, both qualitative and quantitative researchers must read and re-read these materials, much the same way that field researchers spend prolonged periods with their subjects, or interviewers in close contact with their respondents. Various researchers refer to this process as one of 'immersing', 'marinating', or 'soaking' oneself in the data, in order to 'absorb' their meanings. While no disciplinary standard exists in terms of how long researchers ought to spend with their raw materials, as a general rule, analysts should remain immersed in the data until they are 'saturated'—that is, until no new meanings or interpretations appear evident.

Research Teams

Political analysis is no longer conducted solely by independent researchers toiling by lamplight. The academic community has long since embraced the value of collaboration, be it intra- or interdisciplinary in scope. **Investigator triangulation** refers to the use of research teams, rather than individuals, to study and interpret events or phenomena. The material benefits are obvious: a large group of researchers can collect and process a wider range of materials, generate more data, and produce more analyses than a single individual. More than this, however, a larger working group can help to ensure the precision of the data and impartiality of the analyses. More eyes mean more perspectives, and more minds mean more debate. As we all know, three people observing the same event will have differing reports and interpretations of what actually occurred. Increasing the number of observers helps increase our confidence in the interpretations.

Whether because of their ontological predispositions or lack of experience with collaboration, many analysts conducting qualitative research have been less eager or equipped to adopt the team-based approach. Doing so may lead to an improved sense of dependability and confirmability in their analyses.

Pilot Studies and Training

Conducting a **pilot study** is another important means of improving the precision of political science research. Pretesting allows analysts to hone their research techniques and tools, while submitting their results to critical internal and external review. To be accurate, every scientist requires properly calibrated instruments. In qualitative political analysis—where the researcher, herself, is an important instrument in the process—each analyst must be well-trained prior to engaging her raw materials (Morse and Richards 2002). Options include attending coding workshops held at many universities and conferences, collaboration with experienced researchers as a means of apprenticeship, or intensive study of a variety of methods guidebooks. Above all, practice is the best means of attaining experience, and publication, the best means of attaining credentials. Both help enhance the reliability or dependability of one's work.

Report Biases

To convince readers that a body of research offers an impartial view of the world, analysts ought to recognize, acknowledge, and minimize the amount of personal bias that enters the study. Critical self-reflection and open admission of bias is a key component of qualitative research, particularly for those who engage in field studies and participant observation (Creswell 2003, 182).

Peer Assessment

Ultimately, the trustworthiness of research is judged by its legitimacy in the eyes of the scientific community (Kuhn 1962). Peer assessment is critical to such judgments, whether it takes place near the beginning of the research process, or in its end-stages. Where possible, it is wise to have a diverse group of peers assessing one's work, including experts with the methodology, experts in the subject matter, and outsiders. In the interests of interdisciplinarity, it may be suitable to invite input from peers outside one's home academic community. Doing so often sets high standards of trustworthiness, but there is no better way to test the authenticity, portability, precision, and impartiality of the research. As Merriam (2002a, 26) contends:

> In one sense, all graduate students have a peer review process built into their thesis or dissertation committee—as each member reads and comments on the findings. Peer review or peer examination can be conducted by a colleague either familiar with the research or one new to the topic. There are advantages to both, but either way, a thorough peer examination would involve asking a colleague to assess whether the findings are plausible based on the data.

Even with the inclusion of these various checks, political scientists are still vulnerable to charges that they have been selective in incorporating data to suit their purposes. That is, they may have purposefully misrepresented, omitted, or downplayed evidence in order to bolster their arguments. The qualitative student of rhetoric is not unlike the quantitative survey researcher, in this sense; all face the temptation to massage data or falsify results (King, Keohane, and Verba 1993). In this vein, beyond assurances of academic integrity, both qualitative and quantitative analysts must make every effort to be as transparent as possible to allow for the verification of their method, data, and findings.

SUMMARY

A lot has been made of the differences between quantitative and qualitative research, both in this chapter and historically within the political science discipline. Indeed, previous generations of political scientists would have perceived a deep divide between those studying in the quantitative tradition and those employing qualitative methods. Scholars would have spent their entire careers in one 'camp' or the other. They would have learned and applied one set of methodological tools, with little regard (and, in some cases, respect) for researchers in the other tradition. While the core epistemological and methodological distinctions between quantitative and qualitative research remain, times have changed in that more political scientists see value in approaching politics from a variety of different empirical perspectives.

This need not mean a 'watering down' of disciplinary standards, however. To move beyond cold number-crunching and armchair musings, analysts employing both quantitative and qualitative methods must take numerous steps to ensure the trustworthiness of their research. From triangulation, audit trails, and member checks, to computerized coding, intercoder reliability tests, and peer review, a host of tools exist to protect the authenticity, portability, precision, and impartiality of their work. These four standards may be given different names in each tradition, and researchers pursuing either quantitative or qualitative analysis must approach them in slightly different ways. Nonetheless, as criteria for trustworthiness, scholars in both methodological traditions must pay heed to their principles. Thus, a methodological middle ground exists between the statistical and interpretive approaches, helping practitioners of both camps to work together in furthering our understanding of the political world.

In an age when social scientists must carry complete 'toolboxes' when approaching their research problems, the willingness, ability, and desire to combine various methodological techniques are definite assets. By appreciating the credibility, transferability, dependability, and confirmability of the qualitative method and the validity, reliability, and objectivity of the quantitative approach, political scientists may gain the 'best of both worlds', and get the most out of their research.

WORKING AS A TEAM

1. Discuss with your group the main similarities and differences between the qualitative and quantitative approaches to politics. Identify a research question that is of interest to the group and discuss whether one can explore this question with both qualitative and quantitative approaches.

2. Elaborate on the type of data collection strategy that would be used for either approach.

SELF-STUDY

1. This chapter shows that although qualitative and quantitative approaches can be viewed as mutually exclusive and competing perspectives, it argues that they can (and should) be viewed as complementary. What do you think? Make an argument that these approaches are either contradictory or complementary.

2. Justify your argument by using an example to illustrate.

NOTES

1. Divisions within the American political science community run particularly deep, as evidenced by the recent 'Perestroika' movement. For more information, see Monroe (2005).
2. The following discussion draws upon a wide range of sources (Bryman 2001, 272–6; Creswell 1998, 197–209; George 2006, 155–7; Hodder 1994, 401; Holliday 2007, 167–81; King, Keohane, and Verba 1993; Krippendorff 2004, 212–16, 313–21; 2003, 196; Lewis and Ritchie 2006, 275–6; Marshall and Rossman 1989, 144–9; Merriam 2002, 24–31; Platt 2006, 112–13).
3. Some qualitative scholars disagree with this view, arguing that 'triangulation is not a tool or strategy of validation, but an alternative to validation' (Denzin and Lincoln 1994, 2).

Chapter 7

COMPARATIVE RESEARCH

DESTINATION

By the end of this chapter the reader should

- understand the limitations of making generalizations from single cases;
- be able to explain the difference between most-similar-systems and most-different-systems designs; and
- appreciate the importance of understanding context in comparative research.

An important question in research is whether or not to use a comparative research design. Political science research often focuses on a single jurisdiction (such as Canada, Quebec, or Toronto) or a single institution (such as the Supreme Court or the BC Legislature). When we study Albertans' attitudes toward health care, the process of policymaking in the New Brunswick legislature, or the concentration of power in the Canadian Prime Minister's Office (PMO), we are often interested not only in the specific site (Alberta, New Brunswick, the Canadian Parliament) but also in the broader pattern of behaviour. How do individuals (be they in Alberta or elsewhere) form health-care opinions? What is the policymaking process (be it in New Brunswick or other provinces)? How does power concentrate into the hands of political leaders (be it in Canada or elsewhere)?

In this way, political scientists are more likely than historians to treat individuals and events as examples of some broader phenomenon, as **case studies**, rather than as something unique. For example, a political scientist doing a study of former prime minister Paul Martin would be inclined to treat Mr. Martin as a specific case of a more general class or species—perhaps Canadian prime ministers—and thus to use the Martin experience to shed light on the broader phenomenon, to *generalize* from the specific case to the larger population of Canadian prime ministers. By contrast, a historian would be more inclined to focus on the details of Mr. Martin's own experience and would feel less compelled to speculate on the larger population.

One of the goals of political science is to broaden our understanding of the political world, to be able to make generalizations and increase our predictive accuracy. There is always a broader phenomenon lying at the back of the researcher's mind. This in turn ties into the theoretical nature of political science research.

Describing the case is not enough; something must be done to fit the case into a larger theoretical perspective or framework. Political science, therefore, drives from the specific to the general, from the case or sample to the population within which it is embedded.

The challenge is to create generalizations that cut across systems and societies, that are not bound by time and place. Thus, rather than merely describing Canada or Newfoundland or Winnipeg, we seek to understand society and politics *as a whole,* the dynamics of people living in coordinated commonality. However, problems emerge when we try to take the lessons from one province or country to make generalizations about other provinces and countries. How do we decide which province or country (or other unit of study) should be considered representative? If there is any interest whatsoever on behalf of the researcher in making generalizations from the case to a broader phenomenon, then the selection of the case becomes critically important. Is the case representative of the broader phenomenon? Does it shed useful light on the theoretical questions under examination? With single-site research, such as a study of one province or one country, external validity is dependent upon the appropriateness of the case: if the case is representative, external validity is high, but if the case is poorly chosen, external validity can be very low.

Many experiences are context-specific. For example, if we were to make generalizations about federalism based solely on the Canadian experience, we might conclude that federalism involves never-ending struggles over money and the division of powers. But is this representative of the federal experience in other countries? Only **comparative research** can answer such questions.

There are two chief advantages to comparative research. First, it forces us to realize how many of our conclusions about life and politics are in fact culture-bound (Bahry 1981, 230). Many of our assumptions about politics and society do not hold true in other cultures, and as political scientists we need to distinguish between what is held in common between societies and what is unique to a particular community. Second, comparative research also allows us to move beyond the study of smaller units to consider *system-level* analysis (Bahry 1981, 231): what do particular systems have in common? Thus, we can look at 'democracies' or 'federal systems' or 'developing countries'. From this type of analysis, we can increase our predictive abilities: if we know that qualities A and B usually lead to condition C, and country Z has both A and B, we have a reason to expect C. This can be useful information for the study of subjects such as development, peace efforts, and the global economy. A great deal of political science research is comparative in nature. Indeed, a recent edited volume (White et al. 2008), titled *The Comparative Turn in Canadian Political Science,* argues that research on Canadian politics is increasingly comparative in nature. As Robert Vipond (2008, 4) writes, 'the introspective, insular, and largely atheoretical style than informed Canadian political science for most of the postwar period has given way to a deeper engagement with, and integration into, the field of comparative politics.'

The principal issue when beginning comparative research is, Which units should be included in the comparison? What should be compared with what? Random sampling does not provide an answer to such questions for a number of reasons. First, not all political units are suited for all research questions (Bahry 1981, 232). For example, if we were to study the interplay between electoral law and party systems, we would want to include only those countries with true democratic elections, in other words, those with open, competitive elections. States that hold nondemocratic elections and then use these results to support their authoritarian regimes must be excluded. Of course, we could always take care of this issue with our sampling frame: we could first begin with a list of only countries we consider democratic and then randomly sample. However, the utility of this is questionable. As we will discuss in Chapter 8, sampling error increases in random sampling as the sample size decreases; in other words, when sample sizes are very small, the benefits of random sampling are lost, because we are less certain that our selected cases are truly 'representative'. When comparing political units such as countries rather than individuals within countries, we have a limited number of potential cases; the populations are even smaller when we specify by regime type or legislative systems or some other system-level characteristic. Thus, the second reason that random sampling is not appropriate for comparative research is that the logic behind random sampling does not hold for such small populations. *Purposive sampling* best allows the researcher to use her knowledge of the systems to choose political units that allow for the most fruitful comparisons and in so doing to choose between two main approaches to selecting cases for comparative research: the most-similar-systems design and the most-different-systems design. These approaches were first identified by John Stuart Mill in 1888 (labelled by Mill as the 'Method of Similarity' and the 'Method of Difference') and continue to inform comparative research design.

MOST-SIMILAR-SYSTEMS DESIGN

One approach is to compare very similar systems, seeking to explain differences between them. This **most-similar-systems design** allows researchers to hold constant all shared characteristics between the countries in the attempt to explain variation in the dependent or independent variables. This is perhaps best understood by way of example. Political scientists have noted that the United States is unique from Europe in that it lacks a true socialist ideological voice; although the United States has 'left' and 'right' parties (the Democrats and the Republicans, respectively), these parties both adhere to the tenets of liberalism, which include the principles of individualism, the free market economy, and meritocracy (the idea that hard work should be rewarded). There does not exist in the United States a viable socialist party that recommends significant levels of state ownership and wealth transfer; such ideas conflict with 'the American dream' and are essentially absent from the political psyche. But why does the United States lack a true socialist alternative? In *The Founding of New Societies* (1964), Louis Hartz argues that the American settlement lacked a 'tory fragment'; the settlers who arrived did not create a strict class system as existed in Europe. This feudal background was seen by Hartz to be necessary for the development of socialism, and he concluded that the settlement history of the United States can explain the failure of socialism on American soil.

This is all well and good for students of American politics but should raise some questions in the minds of Canadian students. Canada also has a settlement history and a political culture that is in many ways similar to that of the United States. Yet despite the many similarities between the Canadian and American histories, cultures, and systems (both are democratic federal systems), successful socialist parties have emerged in Canada. Although some may question the true socialist leanings of the current New Democratic Party, the socialist influence on its predecessor, the Co-operative Commonwealth Federation (CCF), is certain. So the question is, Given the similarities between Canada and the United States, why has socialism achieved a degree of success in one country and not the other? This question was taken up by Gad Horowitz in his article, 'Conservatism, Liberalism and Socialism in Canada: An Interpretation' (1966). Horowitz accepts the thesis that the United States lacked a 'tory fragment' but argues that the same was not true for Canada. He asserts that Canada did in fact have a small 'feudal fragment'. In addition to a degree of feudalism in the French settlements (which Hartz acknowledges), Canada was home to the expelled Loyalists after the American War of Independence. The Loyalists were, in essence, a second Tory fragment loyal to British traditions and ideas of hierarchy. The Loyalists' Tory influence was felt in Canada because of the small population. Horowitz thus concludes that the Tory fragment provided by the Loyalists allowed Canadian political culture to be more receptive to socialism:

> In Canada, socialism is British, non-Marxist and worldly; in the United States it is German, Marxist and other-worldly. . . . The socialism of the United States . . . is predominantly Marxist and doctrinaire, because it is European. The socialism of English Canada . . . is predominantly Protestant, labourist and Fabian, because it is British. (1966, 159–60)

By comparing two very similar systems, Horowitz was able to focus all on a single point of variation. All potential explanatory variables, that is, variables that would have been considered in single-state analysis, that the two systems held in common were ruled out, reducing the number of factors that Horowitz needed to explore.

Another example of the most-similar-systems design is Arend Lijphart's (1994) analysis of electoral systems. Lijphart examined the use of 70 different electoral systems in 27 democracies between 1945 and 1990, and uses this analysis to first describe and classify electoral systems, and, second, to consider the effects of electoral systems.

EXPAND YOUR KNOWLEDGE

Using Comparative Research to Study System-level Traits: Testing Smiley's Theory of Executive Federalism

In *Canada in Question*, Donald Smiley (1980) noted that Canadian decision-making had evolved to a system by which provincial and federal elites negotiated behind closed doors. He termed this elite-dominated decision-making process 'executive federalism'. Why did executive federalism exist in Canada, when no parallel system emerged in the United States? Smiley argued that the reason lay in the system of government; while federalism alone does not necessarily lead to elite-driven decision-making, the combination of federalism with parliamentary systems of government inevitably creates executive federalism. Parliamentary systems are cabinet- and therefore elite-dominated, allowing executive federalism to emerge, whereas the American federal system is based on a system of checks and balances, precluding cabinet domination.

In essence, Smiley put forward a rather simple formula: parliamentary systems + federalism = executive federalism. If this formula is valid, then other systems with these two characteristics should also experience executive federalism. Is this the case? Ronald Watts (1989) tested this equation by looking at federal systems in Australia and Germany, and he found that similar elite-dominated politics characterized the two systems. Watts concluded (1989, 455) that 'Donald Smiley has been right to emphasize the extent to which "executive federalism" is a logical dynamic resulting from the combination of federal and parliamentary institutions.'

MOST-DIFFERENT-SYSTEMS DESIGN

Whereas the most-similar-systems design takes alike systems and seeks to explain variation between them, the second comparative approach works in the opposite manner. The **most-different-systems design** involves taking very dissimilar systems and attempting to explain commonalities between them (Bahry 1981, 236). How could two such very different systems produce the same social outcome? As with the previous approach, the most-different-systems design works by allowing the researcher to eliminate possible sources of explanation: any variable that does not exist in all systems under study is eliminated. For example, Theda Skocpol's *States and Social Revolutions* explored what the social revolutions in France, China, and Russia held in common. The three revolutions were very different in many respects—in addition to different political cultures, each occurred in a different time period—but important commonalities emerged nonetheless. In the description of her methodology, Skocpol points out that 'comparative historical analysis works best when applied to a set of a few cases that share certain basic features' (1979, 40). She then goes on to explain how the three social revolutions in her study do, in fact, share such basic features, even though this similarity may not be immediately apparent:

> All of them, for one thing, happened in countries whose state and class structures had not been recently created or basically altered under colonial domination. This consideration eliminates many complexities that would need to be systematically included in any analysis of revolutions in postcolonial or neocolonial settings. . . . it is the premise of this work that France, Russia, and China exhibited important similarities in their Old Regimes and revolutionary processes and outcomes—similarities more than sufficient to warrant their treatment together *as one pattern calling for a coherent causal explanation* [emphasis added]. (1979, 40–1)

Such similarities, however, need not blind the researcher to the unique features of the particular cases. As Skocpol explains (1979, 42):

> For even as we primarily look for and attempt to explain patterns common to France, Russia, and China, we can also attend to the variations that characterize pairs of cases or single cases. These can then be explained as due in part to variations on the shared causal patterns, in part to contrasts among the social structures of France, Russia, and China, and in part to differences in the world-historical timing and succession of the three great Revolutions.

APPLY YOUR UNDERSTANDING

Choosing a Comparative Approach

Consider the following research questions. Which are better suited for a most-similar-systems design? For which would you use a most-different-systems design? For each, suggest countries that you could use for your study, as well as positing hypotheses.

1. What factors influence voter turnout?
2. What is the relationship between socio-economic class and partisanship?
3. Is there a relationship between levels of income inequality within a state and that state's behaviour on the international stage?
4. Does state intervention in the delivery of health care result in better overall levels of health within the community?

Which comparative research design we choose depends in part upon the theory that underlies our study (Bahry 1981, 236). If our theory is such that we are able to identify ahead of time the variables that may be influential, we can then choose countries that match on these variables, rendering the most-similar-systems design appropriate. However, if we have less knowledge of influential factors, or if we are unable to match countries appropriately on particular variables, the most-different-systems design is preferred. Donna Bahry (1981, 236) writes: 'a most-different-systems approach offers us somewhat better control over the factors that might influence or bias what we find, and more assurance that our results are valid.'

CONSIDERATIONS FOR COMPARATIVE RESEARCH

When conducting comparative research, the researcher must be careful about how he operationalizes his variables. A measure that is appropriate in one culture or society may not measure the same concept in another culture or society. Context is very important. In designing a comparative study, a researcher must be highly cognizant of the social and political context. The goal is to have **equivalent measures** and not necessarily identical measures (Bahry 1982, 233). For example, imagine that you are conducting a study of women's political power in communist and democratic regimes. You decide to compare the number of women holding legislative seats in the national Soviet and American legislatures in the 1980–7 period. You find that the Soviet legislature had a high proportion of female representatives, while the American legislature had a small proportion of women. From this you conclude that women have greater political power under communism than under democracy. Would your conclusion be valid? In a word, no. What is missing is attention to context, which results in a variable (proportion of federal representatives) that measures different things in different countries. In the Soviet system, the legislature had little influence, and the women who sat on its seats held very little power or influence despite their numbers. The assumption that legislative presence has the same meaning in two very different cultures is false. Remember that ultimately our goal is to measure a *concept* (in this case, women's political power); a particular indicator is merely a means by which to measure a concept. As researchers, we must ensure that the indicators we choose are actually measuring our concepts. This may mean using different indicators in different countries or working hard to ensure that the indicators chosen do, in fact, measure the same concept in all countries under study. Obviously, both options require a solid understanding of the societies being considered; the importance of context in comparative research cannot be overemphasized.

A second caution for comparative researchers is known as *Galton's problem*: the researcher must ensure that the units under observation are independent of one another. This can be a problem because societies and cultures do not stay fixed within territorial units. Consider this problem of *diffusion* with respect to Canada and the United States. Although technically distinct states and societies, many American influences are felt north of the Canadian–American border. (The influence of Canada on the United States is less clear.) Most of our television programming is American, as are many of the popular music bands, magazines, books, and so forth. Because of this diffusion of cultural norms and experiences, comparisons of popular culture between Canada and the United States are difficult. Neuman (1994, 391) notes that 'cultures rarely have fixed boundaries. It is hard to say where one culture ends and another begins, whether one culture is distinct from another, or whether the features of one culture have diffused to another over time.' In the case mentioned above, comparisons of the American and Canadian cultures must also come to grips with the influence of American culture *in Canada*. As barriers to communication steadily decrease, we can expect diffusion problems to become increasingly problematic for social researchers.

Overall, comparative research is useful for ensuring that our theories are not culture-bound and for allowing us to conduct system-level analysis. In comparative research the researcher must pay particular attention to context and must select his cases carefully.

EXPAND YOUR KNOWLEDGE
Comparative Societal Research: The Civic Culture

What is necessary for a democratic regime to survive? Decolonization of African and Latin American states illustrated that democratic institutions are not sufficient; many societies reverted back to non-democratic practices despite the presence of legislatures and the other paraphernalia of democracy. Some theorists argued that for a democratic regime to survive, the *political culture* must support the principles of democracy; without this societal support, the system is predicted to fail. In their classic *The Civic Culture* (1963), Gabriel Almond and Sidney Verba use comparative analysis of five states (Germany, Italy, Mexico, the United Kingdom, and the United States) to test the relationship between political regime and political culture.

Almond and Verba argued that there are three stages of political culture. The 'parochial' stage is characterized by a disinterest in, and almost unawareness of, the government. Citizens live their lives as if the state did not exist. In the 'subject' culture the citizen is aware of the state and the impact that it has on her life but makes little or no effort to influence the workings or outcomes of the state. The final stage, the 'participant' culture, is defined by both an awareness of the state and a belief that one can and should influence its output and social effects. It is the participant culture that is necessary for a democratic system to survive.

Almond and Verba's analysis has not been free from criticism. Some argue that the measures used to assess public attitudes regarding the system's legitimacy were flawed. Others assert that Almond and Verba failed to note significant variation *within* cultures, for instance, that the working and middle classes exhibit different feelings of 'political efficacy' (feeling that one can influence the political system).

WORKING AS A TEAM

Let's consider how we can differentiate between most-similar and most-different-systems design in political science research. Consider a research question concerning electoral system reform. It is fairly simple to identify the jurisdictions that have similar electoral systems (such as first-past-the-post, or simple member plurality, for example). It may not be so simple, however, for research that examines attitudes toward environmental protection. It may not be so simple, however, to identify similar or different jurisdictions when conducting research that examines attitudes toward environmental protection.

How do you know when cases fit either the most-similar or most-different categories?

SELF-STUDY

This chapter has differentiated between the use of most-similar and most-different-systems designs. Suppose you wished to understand why Canada has the party system it does—in which only two parties have ever formed government federally, and in which there has been a series of 'third' parties. Canada has sometimes been described as a two-plus party system. Consider how either a most-similar or a most-different system design would proceed in a study of the Canadian party system.

What defines a case as 'most-similar' for this research question? Should the set of cases viewed as 'most-similar' change if the research question changes?

Chapter 8
SAMPLING THE POLITICAL WORLD

DESTINATION

By the end of this chapter the reader should

- have a thorough grounding in the theory of sampling in the social sciences;
- understand the logic of drawing representative samples from larger populations;
- have been exposed to a number of practical techniques by which samples are drawn; and
- understand the basics of probability and know how to apply probability theory in simple situations.

As we move through our personal lives, we continually confront situations in which we attempt to generalize from our own experience, or from the experience of friends and family, to the larger world. We note, for example, that our performance on exams seems to be better if we cram the night before and wonder if this is true for all students. We feel embarrassed in certain social situations and wonder if everyone feels the same. We react with anger or dismay to an event and wonder if others share the same reaction. There is, then, a constant curiosity about generalizing or extrapolating from the particular circumstances of our personal lives to the world around us. To what extent, we ask, are our own experiences, emotions, beliefs, and values typical, or to what extent are they idiosyncratic?

This question is fundamental to social science research, where we are always asking whether our knowledge of a particular event, group, or personality sheds useful light on larger phenomena. Thus, if we are studying a set of elected officials, we are seeking to advance our knowledge of all elected officials; if we are studying a set of nation-states, we aim to increase our understanding of all nation-states with roughly similar characteristics. The group that we wish to generalize about is known as a **population** (another term commonly used is 'universe'). Within political science, there are many subjects of interest that involve very large populations. For example, if we wish to discuss the voting behaviour of Canadian females, we are looking at a voting age population of over 10 million individuals. Obviously, we cannot study each member of such a large population, regardless of the research design we select. The solution is to select a **sample** of cases that is *representative* of the population under study and from the study of this sample to make generalizations about the population as a whole. Sampling is an issue of concern for all forms of data collection; whether conducting a content analysis or survey, or conducting interviews or focus groups, the researcher must think through sampling as part of his research design. This chapter will explore the logic of sampling and outline a number of common techniques.

POPULATIONS AND SAMPLES

As noted, a population is any group that we wish to study. The first step in commencing a research project is to clearly identify the population to be considered. When doing so, three factors must be considered: the unit of analysis (for example, individuals, political parties, municipal governments), the geographic location, and the time period to be explored (Neuman 1994, 195). Thus, instead of studying 'Members of Parliament', we might study 'Canadian MPs in the 39th Parliament' (3 April 2006–7 September 2008). If the unit is stated without geographic and temporal qualifications, the population is unclear. Do British MPs count? What about MPs throughout history? By defining our population strictly, it is easy to decide who (or what) should be included in the population and who (or what) should be excluded (Singleton et al. 1988, 134).

When we study a population, the goal is to uncover *characteristics* of the population. How many people vote in municipal elections? What is the preferred taxation policy among Canadian voters? How do feminists feel about neoconservatism? How do neoconservatives feel about feminism? For smaller populations, it is possible to obtain information for every unit. For example, if our population is a single section of a political science research methods course, we can survey or interview all students with relative ease. However, for larger populations, such as 'Canadian citizens in 2010', time and financial constraints as well as practical considerations (it would be impossible to locate *everyone*) make it virtually impossible to include all cases in the study.[1]

The solution to this dilemma is **sampling**: researchers draw information about a characteristic from a sample of the population. Simply put, sampling is the process of drawing a number of cases from a larger population for further study. The advantages of sampling for large populations are many: sampling is efficient and less expensive than a study of the whole population; sampling allows the study to be restricted to a certain time frame; and sampling ensures less data collection and entry needs (Bailey 1978, 72).

Quantitative research seeks to measure population characteristics in numeric terms. When the responses of *each and every* member (or case) of the population are measured, the resultant characteristic is known as a **population parameter**. When the responses of a sample of the population are measured, this information is known as a **statistic**. Sample statistics are used to *estimate* the values of the population parameters (Neuman 1994, 196). It is important to remember that we are ultimately interested in the population and the population parameters; the sample and the sample statistics are merely a means to these ends.

Qualitative research also seeks to use select cases to draw conclusions about a larger population. When designing the research study, the researcher must think through the characteristics of the population that need to be reflected in the sample. As qualitative approaches often have smaller samples, the selection of cases is important.

EXPAND YOUR KNOWLEDGE
Population Research

Most research in the social sciences relies upon sample data and therefore entails inferences back to population parameters. However, ecological analysis—that is, research based on population data—is not unknown. Consider the following examples:

- David Lublin and D. Stephen Voss studied francophone support for Quebec sovereignty in the 1992 and 1995 referenda and the 1993 and 1997 federal elections. Using the 75 Quebec federal electoral districts as their unit of analysis, they considered the relationship between support for sovereignty (drawn from electoral returns data) and a number of demographic factors (drawn from the Census), as well as incumbency. They found that 'francophone support for sovereignty consistently rose with the proportion of francophones' (2002, 96), and that support was lower in ridings with high proportions of government workers and agricultural workers.
- Kenneth Avio's study (1987) of the exercise of the Royal Prerogative in Canada examined the 440 capital cases considered by the federal cabinet between 1926 and 1957. He found, incidentally, that labourers were more likely to be executed than nonlabourers and that nonwhite offenders who killed whites were more likely to be executed than were other offenders.
- Linda M. Gerber examined how demographic features of federal electoral districts related to party voting in the 2004 Canadian federal election. She combined socioeconomic variables drawn from the Census with electoral returns data and concludes that 'riding composition—in terms of ethnic diversity, affluence and education—and region are powerful predictors of voting patterns' (2006, 112).
- Matthew E. Wetstein and C.L. Ostberg's study (2003) of the Canadian Supreme Court examined all written judgments published in the Supreme Court Reports between 1973 and 2002, considering the records of Justices Dickson, Lamer, and McLachlin. Among other findings, they note differences between the two male chief justices (Dickson and Lamer) and the one female chief justice (McLachlin).
- R. Kenneth Carty and Munroe Eagles (2006) use federal electoral district-level data to consider the relationship between federal voting and local party factors, such as organization, local party finance, and local candidates. They argue that local campaigns do make a difference to federal voting.

If we are to use a sample to make generalizations about a population, the sample must be **representative** of the population, 'a microcosm, a smaller but accurate model, of the larger population which it is taken to reflect' (Manheim and Rich 1981, 87). For example, if the population has approximately 30 per cent Asians, 60 per cent Caucasians, and 10 per cent African-Canadians, a representative sample will consist of a similar racial distribution. Keep in mind, however, that we often do not know anything about the population characteristics other than what we can gather from the sample statistics. We would never know, for example, how many Canadians actually support capital punishment or employment equity, for the population will never be asked. As we will see, therefore, population characteristics can be estimated but seldom proved.

Three important factors influence the representativeness of a sample: the accuracy of the sampling frame, the sample size, and the method by which the sample is selected. A **sampling frame** is a list of all the units in the target population. If our target population is students at Canadian universities during the 2010–11 school year, our sampling frame would list all registered students. Ideally, our sampling frame would capture every member of the target population (Singleton et al. 1988, 135), meaning that not a single individual or case would be missing from the list. However, this is rare, particularly for large populations. Records are often incomplete and are subject to change.

Consider the sampling frame for our population of university students. We would begin by obtaining student registration lists from all universities (assuming the universities were all willing to make such lists available), but the lists would not include students who registered late and would include individuals who are no longer members of the target population (due to death or dropout). Another problem is that for many populations, there does not exist any official or even unofficial list that can be used as a sampling frame. For example, what is the sampling frame for a target population of 'Canadians' in 2010? Lacking an official list of Canadians, researchers often turn to indirect lists, such as driver's licences and telephone directories. Of course, these lists are also incomplete, failing to capture (in the case of the former) nondrivers and new drivers and (in the case of the latter) those without land-line telephones, new telephone subscribers, and those with unlisted telephone numbers. These incompletions undermine the representativeness of a sample because 'the excluded persons usually constitute some distinguishable and homogenous group' (Bailey 1978, 73). Those without telephone service, for instance, are most often poor; the use of a telephone directory as a sampling frame thus leads to the underrepresentation of the poor. In addition to exclusion problems, most lists used as sampling frames fail to account for changes to the population caused by birth, death, or migration.[2]

The point to stress is that almost all sampling frames will be to some degree inaccurate (Neuman 1994, 196). The challenge to researchers is to find a sampling frame that minimizes such inaccuracies. For example, one technique popular among telephone survey researchers is the random generation of a list of telephone numbers. This process involves the computer generation of telephone numbers; therefore, the sampling frame is all active telephone numbers. This method is an improvement on the use of telephone directories as a sampling frame, because it includes newly listed and unlisted telephone numbers and eliminates cancelled numbers. However, persons without telephone service remain excluded.

EXPAND YOUR KNOWLEDGE

The Importance of Sampling Frames: The Case of *Literary Digest*

The most notorious and often-cited example of a poor sampling frame involves a mail-back survey conducted by *Literary Digest* in 1936. Seeking to predict the outcome of the 1936 presidential election, a contest between Democrat Franklin D. Roosevelt and Republican Alf Landon, the *Digest* staff sent surveys to 10 million Americans (Neuman 1994, 196). The sampling frame consisted of a number of lists, including automobile registration lists, telephone directories, and the *Digest's* subscription list (Singleton et al. 1988, 133). From the 2 million responses gathered, the *Digest* predicted a landslide election for Landon, when in fact Roosevelt was elected.

Although many flaws have been noted with the *Literary Digest* survey, one of particular interest here is the mismatch between sampling frame and target population.[3] The target population was all eligible American voters, but the sampling frame failed to cast such a broad net. Recall that the election occurred in 1936, a time when many of the American poor and lower-middle class could not afford telephones, automobiles, or subscriptions to magazines such as the *Literary Digest*. Given that support for the Democratic Party in 1936 came largely from the working and lower-middle classes, the failure of the *Literary Digest* to include the poor in their sample led to embarrassing results. The moral of the story? Researchers must think carefully when selecting a sampling frame, considering not only who is included but also who is excluded. Efforts must be made to ensure that as much of the target population as possible is included in the sampling frame. If our sampling frame is inappropriate or biased, we cannot make generalizations to the target population with any degree of confidence.

It should be noted that not all target populations have a listing (be it direct or indirect) to which we can refer. This may be due to an unwillingness on the part of individual members to identify publicly with a given population; homeless persons, drug addicts, and rape victims are all examples of such hard-to-identify populations. In such situations, the researcher has difficulty establishing a truly representative sample. We will return to discussing the study of hard-to-access groups later in the chapter.

The second factor that determines the representativeness of a sample is sample size, and we will turn to this matter shortly. The third factor is the method by which the sample is selected. Sampling techniques can be divided into two categories: those that are based on probability theory and those that are not. Probability sampling allows researchers to use inferential statistics to test the representativeness

EXPAND YOUR KNOWLEDGE

The Hite Reports

A somewhat more contemporary example of problematic sampling frames comes from the work of American sociologist Shere Hite on human sexuality. *The Hite Report: A Nationwide Study of Female Sexuality* was first published in 1976, and *The Hite Report on Male Sexuality* was published next, in 1981. Both books, which contain detailed and often vivid accounts of sexual behaviour, were bestsellers and received extensive media coverage. The two books, and subsequent publications by Hite, helped establish new empirical norms of sexual behaviour in the United States. However, whether the research findings are *representative* of the American public is unclear when one turns to the sampling frames and methodology.

The report on female sexuality was based on slightly over 3,000 replies to more than 100,000 questionnaires which were distributed during the early 1970s. The response rate itself is problematic; are the 3,000 respondents representative of the 100,000 individuals who received copies of the questionnaire? However, what is even more problematic is the sampling frame used for the distribution of the questionnaire. The questionnaire was distributed through the National Organization for Women, abortion rights groups, women's newsletters, and university women's centres (1976, xix). Notices asking readers to write in for copies of the questionnaire were published in *The Village Voice, Mademoiselle, Brides,* and *Ms.* magazines. Just under 10 per cent of the completed questionnaires came from women readers of the men's magazine *Oui*. The question, then, is whether this sampling frame, or assortment of sampling frames, could generate a representative sample, particularly given the added problem of low response rates.

The report on male sexuality was based on 7,239 replies to 119,000 questionnaires (1981, xvii–xix). Here, the sampling frames included men's clubs, church organizations, and male readers of the first *Hite Report, Sexology* magazine, *Penthouse,* and *Sexual Honesty, by Women for Women.*

To be fair, Hite addresses the matter of representativeness with considerable caution and finesse. Indeed, her methodological discussions are well worth reading in and for themselves. However, her publications still speak to the experiences of men and women, broadly defined. The message, inadvertent though it may be, is that this is how American women and men feel, believe, and behave. And yet, unless we have some confidence in the representativeness of the sample, it is difficult to place ourselves against the norms of the Hite reports. Do her respondents in fact reflect the American norm? The norm for men and women in general? Given that we have no independent measure beyond our own limited personal experience regarding what the population norm might be, the question is extremely difficult to answer.

of their sample. Quantitative research typically uses probability sampling, while nonprobability sampling is more commonly used in qualitative research.

The discussion of probability and nonprobability sampling provides much of the content of this chapter. At this point, we only want to stress that all three factors—sampling frame, sample size, and sampling method—are important, and that weakness with respect to one cannot be compensated by strength with respect to another. As we saw in the *Literary Digest* example, a sample drawn from a poor sampling frame does not become better or more accurate by becoming bigger.

Selecting Sampling Frames

For each of the following target populations, identify a list that could serve as a sampling frame. What limitations (potential inaccuracies and omissions) can you identify for each list?

- Toronto small businesses, 2010
- City hospital admissions, January 2010

- Nova Scotia voters, 2010
- Canadian citizens, 2010
- Vancouver heroin addicts, 2010
- Quebec sovereigntists, 2010

PROBABILITY SAMPLING

Sampling based on probability theory allows us to estimate the likelihood that our sample provides a representative picture of the population. Recall that in quantitative research our goal is to use the sample to calculate estimates, known as statistics, of the population parameters. In order for these estimates to be useful, we need to be confident that our sample is an accurate representation of the population. Probability theory allows us to state with a specified degree of confidence that our sample is, in fact, representative.

Probability sampling can be understood as the **random selection** of a sample. To understand probability sampling, we first need a basic understanding of probability theory. After this brief introduction, we will move to discuss the impact of sample size and various techniques of probability sampling.

Introduction to Probability Theory

When we are considering probabilities, we want to estimate the likelihood that a particular outcome will occur. For example, if we roll a die, what is the probability that we will get a 6? If we pull a card from a deck, what is the probability that it will be a diamond? In sampling, we are interested in questions such as, What is the probability that we will select person A for the sample? Or what is the probability that our sample statistic will fall within a given range of values?

Probabilities can range from zero to one. A probability of zero indicates that there is *no* chance of an event occurring. A probability of one indicates that there is a 100 per cent chance of the event occurring; it is certain. To calculate the probability of an event occurring, we divide the number of possible *favourable outcomes* by the total number of *possible outcomes*. For example, if we have 10 students, and 6 are female, our probability of randomly selecting a female student's name from a hat is equal to 6 (number of favourable outcomes) divided by 10 (number of total outcomes), which means that the probability of selecting a female student is .6. Another way of expressing this is to state that there is a 60 per cent chance that a female student will be selected. To calculate the probability of a single event, we use the formula $P(A) = r/n$, where $P(A)$ is the probability of event A, r is the number of favourable outcomes, and n is the number of total outcomes.

Often we are interested in the probability of two or more events occurring together. The joint occurrence of two events is calculated by the formula $P(AB) = P(A)\,P(B|A)$, where $P(AB)$ signifies the probability of the joint occurrence of events A and B, $P(A)$ is the probability of event A, and $P(B|A)$ is the probability of event B *after* event A. When events A and B are *independent*, $P(B|A) = P(B)$. For example, what is the probability of rolling two dice and getting two 6s? Each die is independent of the other, so

$$P(A) = \frac{1}{6} = .17$$

$$P(B|A) = P(B) = \frac{1}{6} = .17$$

$$P(AB) = P(A)\,P(B|A) = (.17)(.17) = .029$$

Therefore, there is a 2.9 per cent chance that rolling two dice will result in two 6s. Note, incidentally, that probability equations use a number of different notations to indicate multiplication: *A times B* may be written as $A \times B$, $(A)(B)$, $A(B)$, or AB.

APPLY YOUR UNDERSTANDING

Calculating Probabilities: Exercise 8.1

Calculate the probabilities of the following events:

1. selecting a face card from a deck of cards;
2. flipping a coin and getting 'heads';
3. rolling a die and getting a 6;
4. buying three home lottery tickets and winning the prize, assuming 200,000 tickets were sold and only one prize is given.

Events A and B are *dependent* when the outcome of A influences the outcome of B. For example, if we are selecting cards from a deck, what is the probability that we will select two diamonds in a row?[4] Note that after we have selected the first diamond, both the number of diamonds (r = favourable outcomes) and the number of cards (n = total outcomes) are reduced:

$$P(A) = \frac{13}{52} = .250$$

$$P(B|A) = \frac{12}{51} = .235$$

$$P(AB) = P(A)\,P(B|A) = .250(.235) = .059$$

There is a 5.9 per cent chance that we will select two consecutive diamonds from a full deck.

APPLY YOUR UNDERSTANDING

Calculating Probabilities: Exercise 8.2

Calculate the probabilities of the following events:

1. You have the names of 16 Liberals, 12 Conservatives, and 5 New Democrats in a hat. What is the probability that, upon selecting three names, you will select all Liberals? All Conservatives? All New Democrats?

2. What are the odds of rolling a single die and getting a 6 five times in a row?

3. You have bought one ticket of 10,000 tickets on a home lottery. The lottery procedure is to return tickets to the draw after each prize is awarded, thus ensuring everyone is eligible for every prize. If there are three prizes, what is the probability that you will win one of them? What is the probability that you will win all three?

Probability Theory and Sampling

Knowledge of probability theory is necessary to understand the principles of random sampling, both how it is conducted and why samples based on probability theory produce accurate estimates of population parameters. The principle of random sampling is rather straightforward and resembles a lottery (Manheim and Rich 1981, 89). Each case has an equal probability of being selected: $1/n$. **Simple random sampling** is the process by which every case in the population is listed, and the sample is selected randomly from this list. For large populations, each case is assigned a number, and then a computer randomly selects numbers that will compose the sample. There are practical limitations to the application of simple random sampling, but the principle underlies all forms of probability sampling.[5]

Probability theory allows us to determine the probability that our calculated sample statistic is a good estimation of the population parameter, because statisticians have found that sample statistics (used to estimate the population parameter) distribute themselves around the population parameter in a normal (bell-shaped) distribution. An example will help clarify this point.[6] You are given the following data set:

Name	Number of Pets
Arnie (A)	3
Beth (B)	1
Cathy (C)	2
Derek (D)	0
Ethel (E)	2
Frank (F)	4

The population size in this example is 6; our universe is restricted to the six individuals. The population parameter we are interested in is the **mean** (or arithmetic average, discussed in Chapter 15), which is equal to the sum of the individual scores (3 + 1 + 2 + 0 + 2 + 4 = 12) divided by the total number of cases (6); thus, in this example, the mean number of pets owned is 2 (12 divided by 6). However, if we take samples from this population, we will find sample means that differ from the population parameter. If our sample size is 2, there are 15 possible samples, each with its own sample mean, as Table 8.1 illustrates.

Taken together, all the possible sample means for a given sample size create a **sampling distribution**. The sampling distribution of means for this two-case

TABLE 8.1 All Possible Samples of Size 2, with Sample Means

Combination*	Mean	Combination	Mean
AB	2.0	CD	1.0
AC	2.5	CE	2.0
AD	1.5	CF	3.0
AE	2.5	DE	1.0
AF	3.5	DF	2.0
BC	1.5	EF	3.0
BD	0.5		
BE	1.5		
BF	2.5		

*AB = the sample composed of Arnie (A) and Beth (B); AC = the sample composed of Arnie (A) and Cathy (C); etc.

TABLE 8.2 Sampling Distributions from the Pet Illustration

Sample Mean	Number of Samples	Probability
0.5	1	.07
1.0	2	.13
1.5	3	.20
2.0	3	.20
2.5	3	.20
3.0	2	.13
3.5	1	.07

sample illustration is presented in Table 8.2 and graphically presented in Figure 8.1. The sampling distribution is created by totalling the number of combinations that present the specified sample mean. For example, in the two-case samples there are two combinations (CD and DE) that have a mean of 1.

We can apply probability theory to determine the probability of selecting any particular mean. For example, in our two-case samples the probability of obtaining a sample mean of 2.5 is equal to .2 (3/15 = .2); there is a 20 per cent chance that we will select a sample mean of 2.5. As Table 8.2 suggests, our probabilities of obtaining a sample mean close to the population parameter (which, as you will re-call, is 2) are higher than our probabilities of obtaining sample means that diverge greatly from the parameter; that is to say, you are more likely to get a sample mean that is close to the parameter than one that is not. In our example, the probability of getting a sample mean that is within 0.5 units of the parameter (between 1.5 and 2.5) is .6 (9/15 = .6). This range is known as a **confidence interval**, a concept to which we will return in Chapter 16.

The difference between the sample statistic and the population parameter is referred to as **sampling error** (Singleton et al. 1988, 143). Thus, a sample mean of 1.5 has a sampling error of 0.5, since it is 0.5 units off the population mean of 2.0.

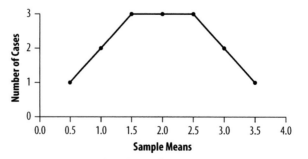

FIGURE 8.1 Sampling Distribution (sample means for *n* = 2)

A large sampling error indicates that the sample statistic deviates greatly from the population parameter, whereas a small sampling error indicates that the sample statistic is close to the population parameter.

SAMPLE SIZE

Statisticians have found that sample statistics are more likely to be closer to the population parameter when the sample size is larger than when the sample is small (Singleton et al. 1988, 143); sampling error is reduced as the sample size increases. Given that our goal is to reduce error, it is not surprising that we prefer large samples over small samples; we desire sample statistics that are as close to the population parameter as possible. However, larger and larger samples are also more and more expensive samples. Since resources are always limited, how large should our sample be? To determine the appropriate sample size, we need to consider a number of factors: the homogeneity of the sample, the number of variables under study, and the desired degree of accuracy.

APPLY YOUR UNDERSTANDING

Calculating Sampling Distributions

Using the 'number of pets' data set from the previous example, calculate a sampling distribution for sample means from samples containing three cases. (There should be a total of 20 combinations.) What is the probability of selecting each of the sample means? What is the probability that a selected sample mean will fall between 1.5 and 2.5? What is the sampling error for the sample ABC? For the sample ABD?

Homogeneity refers to how similar a population is *with respect to the variable of interest* (Manheim and Rich 1981, 96). **Heterogeneity** refers to how *dissimilar* a population is with respect to the variable of interest. The goal of our studies is to explain variation. What we as researchers need to estimate is how homogeneous or heterogeneous our population is: a highly homogeneous population allows us to use a smaller sample, whereas a highly heterogeneous population requires a larger sample. The appropriate sample size increases as we move along the continuum from homogeneity to heterogeneity (see Figure 8.2).

Pure Homogeneity
Sample = One

Sample Size Increases ➤

Pure Heterogeneity
Sample = All

FIGURE 8.2 Continuum of Homogeneity

The number of variables we wish to explore also influences sample size. The more complex our study becomes, the more variables and relationships that we include, the more cases we need in our sample (Singleton et al. 1988, 161). The need for a larger sample stems from the desire to look at subgroups within the sample and to impose statistical controls. A sample of 500 voters, for example, might have only 10 individuals with postgraduate education. If the education variable is necessary to your study, you will need to greatly increase your sample size to *randomly generate* a large enough subgroup to conduct analysis. (Alternative techniques are discussed later in this chapter.)

A third factor that influences sample size is the desired degree of accuracy. Recall that sampling error decreases as sample size increases. Before conducting an analysis, researchers can state the **margin of error** they are willing to accept, or tolerate (expressed as a percentage). Knowing the margin of error allows researchers to state their sample statistics as a confidence interval. For example, a research team may conduct a survey to determine the level of public support for same-sex marriage. If the survey finds that 57 per cent of the respondents support same-sex marriage, and the sampling error is ±5 per cent, then the sponsors of the survey can conclude that between 52 per cent and 62 per cent of Canadians support same-sex marriage. Researchers can preset the margin of error they want and then, using the information illustrated in Table 8.3, determine the *minimum* sample size required to yield such a confidence level. Of course, researchers may have reasons to exceed this minimum level. For example, a major television network may commission a poll immediately prior to a federal election. Because they will be making a very high-profile prediction regarding the election outcome, they may want to minimize the sampling error by using a larger than usual sample (Manheim et al. 2002, 115).

It should be clear from Table 8.3 that the law of diminishing returns applies to sample size: at a certain point, dramatically increasing sample size results in only modest improvements in accuracy. For example, with a large population, moving

TABLE 8.3 Minimum Sample Sizes at a 95 Per Cent Confidence Level

Sampling Error (%)	Minimum Sample Size
±1	10,000
±2	2,500
±3	1,111
±4	625
±5	400
±10	100

Source: Table 6.1, p.121 from *Empirical Political Analysis* by Jarol R. Manheim and Richard C. Rich. Copyright © 1995 by Longman Publishers USA. Reprinted by permission of Pearson Education, Inc.

EXPAND YOUR KNOWLEDGE

Sampling Error in Pre-election Polls

Pre-election polls are now commonly reported in the media with a specified margin of error. For example, an online Angus Reid survey shortly before the 2008 federal election was based on 1,039 interviews, and the margin of error for the total sample was estimated to be 3.0 per cent, with a 95 per cent confidence level (Angus Reid 2008, 1). Put somewhat differently, if the survey found that 40.0 per cent of the sample intended to vote for party X, then we could assume that within the population of all voters there was a 95 per cent chance that between 37.0 per cent (40 per cent − 3.0 per cent) and 43.0 percent (40.0 per cent + 3.0 per cent) would vote for party X. There is also a 5 per cent chance (100 per cent − 95 per cent) that party X would get either less than 37.0 per cent of the vote or more than 43.0 per cent. The odds would be small but not negligible.

Now let's apply this logic to the actual results of the survey described earlier in this chapter. The survey found that 37 per cent of the respondents intended to vote for the Conservatives, 27 per cent for the Liberals, 20 per cent for the BQ, and 7 per cent for the Green Party. Thus there was a 95 per cent chance that the level of support for the Conservatives within the electorate at large was between 34 per cent and 40 per cent (37 per cent ± 3.0 per cent), and that the level of support for the Liberals was between 24.0 per cent and 30 per cent (27 percent ± 3.0 per cent). At one extreme, the Conservatives could end up with 40 per cent of the vote and the Liberals with only 24 per cent. At the other extreme, the Conservatives could end up with only 34 per cent and the Liberals with 30 per cent.

In the actual election, the Conservatives won 37.6 per cent of the vote, compared with 26.2 per cent for the Liberals—outcomes very close to those predicted by the Angus Reid survey.

from a sample of 100 to a sample of 625 takes us from 10 per cent error down to 4 per cent; increasing the sample size by over six times results in a substantial reduction in error. However, increasing the sample size from 2,500 to 10,000—an increase of four times—results in a mere 1 per cent improvement in accuracy. Given the significant financial costs in increasing sample size, researchers are willing to tolerate some error. Note as well that, as population size exceeds 100,000, the size of the population itself does not influence sample size (Manheim and Rich 1981, 99). Thus, a sample size of 2,500 used for both a study of Saskatoon and a study of Canada as a whole would have the same degree of sampling error. This explains why national public opinion polls in the United States are generally of the same size as national polls in Canada, even though the American population is 10 times as large.

In summary, when selecting sample sizes, we need to consider the homogeneity of our population, the complexity of our study, and the degree of accuracy desired. In general, a larger sample is always preferred to a smaller sample, but obtaining large samples is a costly process in terms of both time and money. Bernard Lazerwitz (1968, 278–9) argues that the ideal sample is representative, obtained by probability sampling, and 'as small as precision considerations permit, as economical as possible, and gathered as swiftly as its various measurement techniques permit'. We seek samples that are just large enough to ensure the precision necessary; any larger is a waste of resources.

CONDUCTING PROBABILITY SAMPLES

As we have already noted, the basic procedure of probability sampling is known as simple random sampling. In this procedure, all the cases are listed and assigned numbers 1 . . . N. Through computer selection or by use of a table of random numbers, cases are selected until the desired sample size is met. Thus, if we had a population of 10,000 and a desired sample size of 2,000, we would number the cases individually from 1 to 10,000 and then randomly select 2,000 cases to serve as our sample.

Occasionally, researchers will use a method known as **systematic selection**. In systematic selection, a *selection interval* (1/k) is calculated based on the sample size needed. If, for example, we want 5 per cent of the population to be included in the sample, we need to select one out of every 20 cases (1/20 = 5 per cent), and our selection interval is therefore 20. If we want 1 per cent of the population included in the sample, we need to select one out of every 100 cases (1/100 = 1 per cent), and our selection interval is 100. Once our selection interval is determined, a random number is selected to serve as a starting point; this number is known as a *random start*. For example, if our selection interval is 20, we begin by selecting a random number between 1 and 20; let's use 6. We then add the selection interval until the sample size is reached: cases numbered 6, 26, 46, 66, 86, 106, and so on are selected. Recall that numbers correspond to individual cases; the numbers selected represent the cases that will be included in the sample. Systematic sampling can be more practical and efficient than simple random sampling, but it is less random and thus less accurate than simple random sampling. In addition, it necessitates a random sampling frame; a list of the population that is ordered (for example, alphabetically) may lead to biased results. One solution is to randomize the sampling frame before beginning systematic sampling (Bailey 1978, 78).

Stratified sampling involves breaking the population into mutually exclusive subgroups, or strata, and then randomly sampling each group. For example, if we are interested in differences between undergraduate and graduate students, we could break the population into two groups—undergraduates and graduates—each with its own sampling frame. We would then randomly sample from each list and combine the subsamples together to construct our larger sample. An advantage of stratified sampling is that it increases the homogeneity of the samples and reduces sampling error (Singleton et al. 1988, 145). Another benefit is that it allows us to focus on small subgroups within the population. If a particular group of interest is small, we may choose to sample a larger proportion of that subgroup to ensure numbers large enough to produce significant statistics. For example, if the population of subgroup A is 100, and the population of subgroup B is 1,000, we may choose to include 50 per cent of A in the sample (for a total of 50 cases) but only 10 per cent of B (for a total of 100 cases).

This procedure is known as *disproportionate stratified sampling*, and it is routinely used in Canada to deal with variance in provincial populations. Imagine, for example, that you have the money to do a national survey of 1,500 respondents on a matter of public policy interest. It is important, therefore, that you report not only on Canadians at large but also on provincial differences. Now, in a purely random sample, 585 respondents could be expected from Ontario and 45 from Saskatchewan, because Ontario and Saskatchewan have, respectively, 39 per cent and 3 per cent of the Canadian population (based on the 2008 postcensal population estimate). You would have more than enough respondents to provide a reasonable read on Ontario opinion; you would have 'oversampled', but you would not have enough for Saskatchewan. Therefore, disproportionate stratified sampling could be used to increase the number of Saskatchewan respondents and to decrease the number from Ontario. The catch is that your final sample would no longer be representative of the Canadian population, for you would have too few Ontario respondents and too many Saskatchewan respondents. To reconstruct a representative national sample, it is necessary to assign *weights* to respondents. If, for example, we had sampled 200 individuals each from Ontario and Saskatchewan, we would assign a weight of 2.925 to each Ontario respondent (200 *times* 2.925 = 585) and a weight of 0.225 (200 *times* 0.225 = 45) to each Saskatchewan respondent. Although this procedure makes mathematical sense, it can be difficult to explain in public forums.

Cluster sampling is the process of dividing the population into a number of subgroups, known as clusters, and then randomly selecting clusters within which to

APPLY YOUR UNDERSTANDING

Probability Sampling

Using the local telephone book, list the first 50 names on page 200 (exclude business listings).[7]

1. What is your target population? What is your sampling frame? What are the limitations of the sampling frame?

2. Using a selection interval of 5 and a random start of 2, select a systematic sample.

3. Divide the list into two strata: males and females. (Place all initialized listings, for example, B. Smith, in the female strata.) Using a selection interval of 4 and a random start of 1, select a systematic sample.

randomly sample. This is best understood by considering geographic units. Let's say our population is Canada as a whole, and we are conducting individual interviews that require the researcher to travel to the door of each case. If we were to randomly sample all Canadians, we could end up with cases all over the country, resulting in considerable travel costs. Instead, we could use cluster sampling. First, we need to divide the country into clusters, for example, federal electoral constituencies. There are 308 constituencies, and we could randomly select a number of them, say 2. These constituencies are then further broken down into clusters of similar population size, for example, municipalities, and again a number of them are randomly selected, say 2. We now have 4 municipalities within 2 federal constituencies. We then further subdivide into even smaller areas, such as wards, and then city blocks, and then housing units (houses and apartments), using random selection at each stage (Manheim and Rich 1981, 94). The end result is a list of randomly selected but geographically concentrated housing units that will serve as the sample.

Cluster sampling allows the researcher to greatly reduce costs while using probability sampling for a large population. However, sampling error increases with every sample taken; therefore, the numerous stages of random sampling within the cluster sampling method results in larger sampling errors (Neuman 1994, 208). To address this problem, researchers need to increase their sample sizes. In addition, cluster sampling can appear to produce, indeed it can in fact produce, samples that on face value are not representative. In the preceding example the representative nature of the sample could become suspect in the public's eyes if you had poor luck at the first stage of the sampling procedure. If you drew two constituencies in northern Ontario, would you have a sample that was representative of the Canadian population?

In summary, there are a number of means that researchers can employ to obtain probability samples, and the probability of any individual case in the population being selected into the sample depends on the random sampling method used. In general terms, the advantage of probability sampling is that it allows us to use sample statistics to estimate population parameters. However, not all research problems allow the use of probability sampling, which requires complete sampling frames.

NONPROBABILITY SAMPLING

Nonprobability sampling methods are those that do not employ random selection of cases. The nonrandom selection means that we cannot identify margins of error or confidence intervals, and thus it is more difficult to make generalizations and draw conclusions about the general population. Qualitative research designs often use nonprobability sampling. It should be noted that nonprobability samples usually have smaller sample sizes; for example, researchers using an interview research design would typically conduct fewer than 50 interviews (Ritchie et al. 2003, 84).

Singleton et al. (1988, 152) identify four situations in which nonprobability sampling should be used. The first is exploratory research or pilot studies in which

EXPAND YOUR KNOWLEDGE

The Census Debate

Sampling theory became a national news story in the summer of 2010 because of changes announced to the Canadian Census. The Canadian Census includes both a short and long form. The short form includes questions about the number of household residents and their ages and sexes; this form is sent to all households in Canada. The long form includes questions about language, ethnicity, income, and employment, among other topics; this form is sent to only 20 per cent of Canadian households, with households selected based on probability sampling techniques. Completion of the Census was mandatory for Canadians; individuals failing to return the form(s) faced possible fines or jail time. (In practice, jail time was not used.)

On 29 June 2010 the Harper Conservative government announced that it would be replacing the mandatory long form Census with a voluntary long form. (Completion of the short form Census would remain mandatory.) Industry Minister Tony Clement stated that the government was making the long form voluntary because of privacy concerns. He announced that the 20 per cent mandatory sample would be replaced by a one-third voluntary sample and claimed that the increase in sample size would compensate for the anticipated drop in response rate. This claim drew harsh criticism from Canadian statisticians, who stated that the voluntary long form Census would greatly undermine data quality, because some social groups would be more likely to respond than others.

The National Statistics Council urged the government to reverse its decision; more than two hundred groups (including universities, industry and medical associations, nonprofit organizations, and think-tanks) voiced opposition and more than fifteen thousand Canadians signed a petition opposing the move to the voluntary long form. Most dramatically, Statistic Canada's Chief Statistician, Munir Sheikh, resigned when Minister Clement claimed that Statistics Canada had advised that a voluntary Census would result in reliable data. (Documents revealed in August 2010 demonstrated that Statistics Canada had in fact expressed concerns about the voluntary Census.) When asked by the House of Commons Industry Committee if the voluntary Census could adequately substitute for the mandatory survey, Mr Sheikh replied clearly, 'It cannot.'

the investigator does not seek to make broad generalizations about the population. An exploratory study based on nonprobability sampling might be used to discover trends; the researcher would then follow with a study based on probability sampling to test these trends in the population. Thus, nonprobability sampling can serve as a first research step, followed by probability sampling research. Given that nonprobability sampling can be less expensive and easier to conduct than probability sampling, this process is understandable.

A second use for nonprobability sampling arises when the samples to be drawn are extremely small. This might apply, for example, in a study of MPs who are visible minorities. In such instances, making generalizations from the samples is a matter of judgment on behalf of the researcher. Thus, she may use her advanced knowledge of the subject matter to select the cases in the sample. The third instance in which nonprobability sampling occurs is when sampling frames are unavailable or inadequate; again, the researcher must use judgment in selecting the sample. Finally, nonprobability sampling may be used for studies in which the cases (individuals, organizations, or governments) are likely to refuse to participate. In such instances, the researcher often must make use of the cases available to him or abandon his study.

Nonprobability sampling can be accidental or purposive. In an **accidental sample**, also known as a *sample of convenience* or *haphazard sample,* the researcher gathers data from individuals whom she 'accidentally' encounters or are convenient. An example of this is the 'man on the street' opinion polling, often done by news programs. Designed to tap the 'pulse of the city', such samples are actually quite biased. A poll taken at a weekday noon on a downtown corner is limited to those individuals who tend to be downtown during the week for lunch, typically office workers. Many other individuals in the city, such as students, union workers, homemakers, and the retired, have a very low probability of being included in the sample, and therefore what is stated to be the 'common' opinion is actually the opinion of only a small group. A related, similarly biased form of sampling is any

EXPAND YOUR KNOWLEDGE
University Classes as Samples of Convenience

It is not surprising that many professors turn to their classes as samples of convenience. Students, after all, are close at hand, inexpensive to survey, and generally predisposed or at least resigned to playing the respondent role. In some psychology departments there is a formal expectation that students will act as subjects for faculty, graduate, and undergraduate research as long as that research is conducted according to approved ethical guidelines.

Of course, there are also disadvantages to using student respondents or subjects. The primary drawback is that students are not typical or representative of the general population. Seldom are we interested in making generalizations from student samples to the student population; the population that is of interest is the broader population, but generalizations in this respect are suspect. At times, however, research with students can reveal dynamics and relationships that are at least suggestive of broader population dynamics and relationships. For example, a 1994 study of 2,114 students at l'Université de Montréal (Blais et al. 1995) explored the relationship among concerns about the language situation in Quebec, expectations about the short- and long-term economic costs of separatism, and support for sovereigntist and federalist options. The findings that economic expectations had greater weight than linguistic expectations in explaining support for sovereignty and that long-term economic considerations outweighed short-term economic expectations provide useful insights into the broader dynamics of referendum voting in Quebec.

sample that involves **self-selection**, such as call-in programs on the radio or television or mail-in surveys for magazines and newspapers. The sample is limited to those who are exposed to the relevant form of media and who care about the topic enough to participate in the study (Neuman 1994, 197).

Purposive sampling (also known as *judgmental sampling*) involves researcher selection of specific cases; the researcher uses his judgment to select cases that will provide the greatest amount of information. Cases are selected both 'to ensure that all the key constituencies of relevance to the subject matter are covered' and 'to ensure that, within each of the key criteria, some diversity is included so that the impact of the characteristic concerned can be explored' (Ritchie et al. 2003, 79). Researchers may take different approaches to purposive sampling. For example, a researcher may choose cases that appear to be 'typical' and use the data gathered to make generalizations, or he may choose cases that appear 'extreme' and attempt to understand why they differ from the norm (Singleton et al. 1988, 154).

Researchers will often use purposive sampling for interview or focus group research. For example, the researcher may interview experts on a particular topic, or stakeholders with respect to a specific policy area. Purposive sampling is particularly useful with specialized populations that are difficult to reach (Neuman 1994, 198) or for populations that lack a sampling frame. For example, a researcher exploring eating disorders might select cases from a hospital outpatient treatment program. A researcher studying the homeless might attempt to discover where the homeless spend their time and attempt to identify a sample. Purposive sampling requires a significant knowledge base of the target population (Singleton et al. 1988, 154).

Snowball (or network) **sampling** is often employed to study social networks. Every case in the sample is directly linked to at least one other case in the sample (Neuman 1994, 199). The researcher begins by identifying a few cases and from these cases gets referrals for other cases and continues to branch out. For example, the researcher might interview three self-identified environmentalists and at the conclusion of the interview ask each respondent to suggest three other environmentalists who could be interviewed. The researcher would then interview the suggested nine environmentalists and again ask for further referrals. This process would continue until sampling is completed. Just as a snowball rolled down a hill picks up snow and grows in size, the sample picks up more cases over time and becomes larger and larger until logistical and financial considerations force the researcher to stop.

When purposive or accidental sampling is combined with stratification, the result is known as **quota sampling**. The researcher identifies a number of target groups (strata), for example, men and women, and then sets a quota number that must be met for each group. For instance, the researcher may decide that she needs to sample at least 15 men and 15 women in her study. How the researcher then meets the quota can vary; she may use accidental sampling or use her knowledge to create a purposive sample.

This chapter has explored the need for a representative sample in our research. It was noted that representativeness is determined by three factors: sampling frame, sample size, and the method of sampling. Sampling is an important consideration in data collection. The following chapters will consider a number of different data collection techniques, each with unique sampling considerations.

APPLY YOUR UNDERSTANDING

Choosing a Sampling Approach

For each of the following, select a sampling technique. Explain your choice.[8]

1. Internet survey of Canadian public servants, to discuss career satisfaction.

2. Telephone survey of Canadians, to assess voting intentions.

3. Mail survey of elected officials in your province, to assess the impact of gender on policy preferences.

4. Interviews with members of the gay and lesbian community, to discuss experiences with discrimination.

WORKING AS A TEAM

Imagine that your group has been commissioned to conduct a study of drug use among teenagers aged 14 to 18. The agency that commissioned the study is particularly interested in those individuals who in fact use drugs; issues of concern include frequency and type of use, peer pressure, religious beliefs, and degree of social integration. Up to 200 interviews will be funded, and the results of the study will be used to provide policy recommendations to the provincial government.

Define the population for your study. Is there a sampling frame? What sampling method would you use? What ethical issues might you encounter?

SELF-STUDY

1. You wish to conduct a survey of political science majors on your campus to find out which subject field—Canadian politics, political theory, international relations, or comparative politics—is preferred (adapted from Singleton et al. 1988, 166). The department provides you with a list of all political science majors in the undergraduate and graduate program. This list also differentiates between nonhonours, honours, and graduate students. You will use this list to draw your sample.
    a. Identify your target population and sampling frame. What possible problems can you identify with your sampling frame?
    b. Explain how you would conduct a simple random sample for this study.
    c. Explain how you would conduct a systematic sample for this study.
    d. Explain how you would stratify the study on the basis of position (honours, nonhonours, graduate) in the program. What would be the benefit of doing so?
    e. Which sampling procedure is best for your research question? Explain your reasoning.
2. You now wish to extend your study of political science majors to all Canadian universities.
    a. Identify your target population and sampling frame. What possible problems can you identify with your sampling frame?
    b. How will you obtain a representative sample? Defend your choice of approach, and explain all steps.

NOTES

1. Even the Census, which attempts to contact every Canadian household, is unable to reach all citizens.
2. Singleton et al. (1988, 136) note that lists tend to be most accurate at local levels and least accurate at the federal level.
3. One problem is that of nonresponse bias. Mail-back surveys generate a greater response from the middle class and from those with a greater interest in the study. In this case, both the middle class and Landon supporters (who tended to be more passionate about the election than Roosevelt supporters) were more likely to return the surveys than were other groups, thus biasing the survey results toward Landon (Singleton et al. 1988, 133).
4. Example comes from Hayslett (1968, 38–9).
5. Lazerwitz (1968, 279) notes that the limitations are (1) the need for a complete listing and (2) the assumption that cases are statistically independent of one another.
6. The following example is modelled on an example presented in Singleton et al. (1988, 140–4).
7. Adapted from Singleton et al. (1988, 166).
8. Adapted from Singleton et al. (1988, 166).

Chapter 9

OBSERVING THE POLITICAL WORLD: SURVEY RESEARCH

DESTINATION

By the end of this chapter the reader should

- be aware of the ubiquity of survey research in a variety of settings in Canada—assessing public policy, understanding social trends, and measuring public opinion;
- understand the advantages and disadvantages of using various means of gathering survey research data; and
- appreciate the attentiveness that should be focused on issues such as question wording and question type.

THE UBIQUITY OF SURVEY RESEARCH

Survey research, including telephone, Internet (or web-based) mail, and (less frequently) face-to-face surveys, are an important component of quantitative social research. In addition to providing a great deal of the empirical database for the social sciences, surveys inform political and social commentary in the media. Survey research is a ubiquitous feature of modern life, from massive pre-election polls to the notice that '4 out of 5 dentists surveyed recommend sugarless gum for their patients who chew gum'. It is difficult to read an issue of a major newspaper without running across one or more stories drawing upon survey 'evidence' of some sort or another. Public opinion polls are used for insight into everything from voting and consumer behaviour to public policy preferences and sexual behaviour. They offer important glimpses into how the average Canadian, the mythical 'man in the street', sees the world. In so doing they enable us to compare our own beliefs, values, and preferences to societal norms. Are we typical, different, or even deviant compared with our neighbours, colleagues, and fellow citizens? Polls provide us with a point of comparison, a standard against which we can place our own worldviews. We can judge whether we sleep more, drink less, exercise more frequently, watch more television, or have fewer pets than others around us. We can also compare the values and beliefs of Canadians to those of other nationalities. We assume, and not always correctly, that polls provide us with a broader, less biased insight into the world than we can get by talking to friends, neighbours, and colleagues.

But surveys do more than enable us as survey consumers to compare our beliefs and patterns of behaviour to others. They are used by a diverse set of individuals and organizations to provide insight into the attitudes and behaviour of citizens. For example, governments, at the federal, provincial, and municipal levels, are active consumers of survey research, particularly with respect to identifying the public's policy preferences, and assessments of program initiatives. Generally, the expectation is that there is a distinction between government's polling of attitudes toward policy issues, and the more partisan polling in which political parties may be engaged with respect to assessments of attitudes toward political leaders and the parties. Attitudes of the public toward policy preferences is also of interest to interest groups, nongovernmental organizations, think tanks, and industry, as each is involved at various points in the public policy process. News organizations also are significant consumers of survey research, particularly on matters relating to the 'horse race' character of politics, knowing which party is ahead in public preferences at any given time, which leader is most popular, and the like. Similarly, political parties and individual candidates (either for leadership or in a constituency election) often rely on public opinion polls to measure their relative standing with the electorate. Indeed, contemporary Canadian politics is positively infused with survey research data and analysis.

Ideally, and if ethical guidelines were to permit, the researcher would like to peer inside people's heads without disturbing their thoughts by so doing. In practice, however, this is impossible to do. No matter how skillfully designed questions might be, they do disrupt pre-existing patterns of thought, and clumsy questions cause even more disruption. Respondents can be very sensitive to the research environment and, in the case of in-person or telephone surveys, may react to the physical characteristics and mannerisms of the interviewer, particularly if the interview touches on sensitive topics. In such a context respondents may watch or listen to the interviewer to try to gauge how their answers are received and then tailor later responses to produce a more favourable social response from the interviewer. This general phenomenon is known as the **interviewer effect** and is more problematic than one might expect. There is also a concern that in some cases survey research may create opinion as much as measure it. In an interview situation, as in other social situations, there is an innate desire to please. Because respondents are unwilling to display a lack of knowledge, or simply because they are trying to be helpful, respondents may make up answers to questions about which they have never thought. For example, an informal survey conducted by a colleague in an undergraduate political science course at the University of Calgary in the early 1980s asked for the respondents' opinions on a number of issues ranging from capital punishment and the legalization of marijuana to foreign aid for Peru and the advisability of building a bridge linking Prince Edward Island to the mainland.

The questionnaire was administered well before any serious discussion of a fixed link to PEI, and Peru, much less Canadian aid to Peru, was not in the news. It could readily be assumed, therefore, that although students might well have had pre-existing opinions on capital punishment and marijuana, they would not have pre-existing opinions on the fixed link to PEI or foreign aid to Peru. And yet, more than two-thirds of the students provided an opinion when asked.

Even if we are measuring rather than creating, we are often measuring the *potential* profile of opinion should an issue emerge for public debate. Thus, when you read about a survey that concludes that 48 per cent of Canadians believe *X* or would prefer *Y*, do not assume that some 14,000,000 individuals are carrying those beliefs or preferences in a conscious, active way. A more appropriate interpretation of the poll would be to conclude that *if* all Canadians were in fact confronted with the question posed to the survey respondents, then close to 14,000,000 would likely believe *X* or opt for *Y*. It should be remembered in this context that we should never assume that public opinion is or should be translated in some immediate or automatic fashion into public policy. Public opinion is only one element in a very complex political process; it is sifted and weighed by political actors who must take into account not only the general distribution of opinion but also the intensity with which particular opinions are held and by whom they are held. Governments, moreover, not only are influenced by public opinion but also seek themselves to shape public opinion as it relates to matters of public policy.

Furthermore, when we encounter polls on voting intentions, we must keep in mind that the popular vote is filtered through an electoral system that does not faithfully translate votes into legislative seats. To know, for example, that the Liberal and Conservative parties each have 30 per cent of the national vote in a recent poll tells us little about how well they might do in terms of seats; it all depends on where the respective party support is concentrated. Surveys, therefore, provide a valuable window on the political process, but they provide far less than the complete picture.

This brings to mind an important limitation on quantitative analysis in Canada. The constraints of party discipline in the House of Commons and provincial legislatures mean there is little to be gained by studying the impact of sociodemographic characteristics or ideological beliefs on the voting behaviour of MPs or provincial legislators. Once you know the partisanship of an elected member, you know how he or she will vote, and there is little if any additional predictive power from knowing more about the individual's personal characteristics. (However, a recent study by Soroka, Penner, and Blidook [2009] argued that even in Canada, MPs are influenced not only by their party but also by their constituents.) By contrast, a rich roll-call voting literature has been created in the United States, where elected members are less constrained by party discipline and loyalties and, therefore, have greater freedom of action. In short, there is American variance beyond partisanship, but no Canadian variance, to be explained.

EXPAND YOUR KNOWLEDGE

The Canadian Election Studies

The primary source of survey data for students of Canadian politics is to be found in the **Canadian Election Studies** (CES). This comprehensive set of **cross-sectional studies** began with the 1965 federal election and now encompasses the elections of 1968, 1974, 1979, 1980, 1984, 1988, 1993, 1997, 2000, 2004, 2006, and 2008, along with the 1992 constitutional referendum. The series tracks many variables over time, although the focus and format of the CES have changed with changes in the research teams, in our understanding of electoral dynamics, and in the nature of the political landscape. While the CES surveys concentrate on their respective elections and on explaining the vote, they also pick up a good deal of attitudinal and sociodemographic information, which can be used to address a wide range of other research topics. The data sets are generally available to the political science community at large—including students—within a year of the election. Much of the empirical work on Canadian public opinion and political behaviour published in the *Canadian Journal of Political Science* is rooted in CES data sets. For an historical summary and assessment of the CES, see Elisabeth Gidengil (1992).

QUESTION WORDING

The goal of survey research is to obtain an accurate (valid) and reliable assessment of the attitudes or behaviour of the sample population (for discussion of validity and reliability, see Chapter 4). The responses to the survey questionnaire serve as the data for subsequent analysis, so that quality of the data analysis ultimately is dependent upon having good-quality measures drawn from survey responses. The way in which questions are worded has a significant impact on the quality of data provided by surveys. Poorly worded questions can be worse than having no information at all, since they can lead to the assumption that the data provide a meaningful insight into the values, beliefs, and behaviour of the sample, when in fact they may do nothing but provide a misleading understanding.

One goal in designing survey research questions is that each question is intended to measure one and only one quality, whether that is one attitude, one belief, or one specific behaviour. Where questions have multiple stimuli, for example, in which individuals are asked to respond to more than one attitude, then the interpretation of the answer is **nonsingular**, or is open to different interpretations. For example, an agree/disagree question in which the statement is phrased as follows, Canada's military involvement in Afghanistan should be ended because there has been too much loss of Canadian life and it is time for the Afghanis to take responsibility for their own security, is an example of a question with two separate stimuli. A respondent might believe that there has been too much loss of Canadian life but might also believe that Afghanis are not prepared to assume more responsibility for their security. Therefore, it is not evident how they should answer the question, nor is it obvious how one would interpret an answer of either agree or disagree.

A question that is worded such that only one stimulus is included in the question wording can resolve this dilemma. For example, there may be a number of reasons that a respondent could support Canada's military withdrawal from Afghanistan, and the research may be interested in assessing the relative importance of each reason. One way of doing so is to provide a set of questions that enable the complex reasoning of respondents to be revealed. For example, the sequence of questions may look something like the following:

Question 1. Please indicate which of the following statements comes closest to your personal views of Canada's military involvement in Afghanistan:

> Canada's military involvement should end no later than 2011.
> Canada's military involvement should end at a time when Afghanistan can provide for its own security, which may be later than 2011.

Question 2. Ask if respondent answered (a) to Question 1. Why do you think Canada's military involvement should end no later than 2011 (indicate agree or disagree to as many of the following statements as you wish):

> Canada should not be involved in external military operations.
> We've done our share. It is now time for the Afghanis to provide their domestic security.
> There has been too much loss of Canadian life.
> Our involvement cannot provide long-term security.

And of course, the researcher can increase the list of possible reasons for military withdrawal to include other reasons he or she believes may form the basis of the opinion of respondents in favour of withdrawal. The key is that the questions provide a single stimulus on which the respondent is indicating support or opposition.

A second issue that arises in question wording is the use of **ambiguous questions**. The goal is to use questions that are clear and commonly understood by all respondents (and subsequently by all users of the data). A question can be ambiguous for a number of reasons. For example, a question may use a concept that is not defined in the question itself, and for which respondents may hold different interpretations of its meaning. To illustrate, respondents could be asked, Are you generally satisfied with the way in which democracy works in Canada? Respondents may have different things in mind when they respond to this question, because they may have different interpretations of the meaning of democracy. A respondent might think of democracy as a set of institutional characteristics centred on the right to vote, and given the fact that there are periodic elections and near universal enfranchisement, this is sufficient to satisfy that respondent's expectations for a democracy. Another respondent might be thinking about the decline of voter turnout, and expects that a 'well-functioning' democracy should have higher voter turnout than has been occurring in Canada of late. Therefore, his or her assessment may be negative because of their different understanding of what is implied in the question.

Questions should be worded so as not to 'lead' respondents to answer one way or another. This can be done by ensuring that value statements are not included in the wording of a question either implicitly or explicitly. For example, one might be interested in knowing people's evaluation of the objectivity of newspaper coverage of the military campaign in Afghanistan. A leading, and therefore inappropriate, question would preface the question with a value statement about the media's purported ideological bias. An example of a leading question is the following: Do you think that Canada's liberal-dominated press has provided fair and unbiased reporting of Canada's honourable military campaign in Afghanistan? In this instance, the respondent is cued that there may be a generally liberal orientation among the media, and also that the military campaign has been honourable. Leading questions are likely to **skew the opinion** expressed among survey respondents.

QUESTION TYPE

Is it better to give respondents an **open-ended question** that allows them to provide whatever response they deem appropriate to the question, or to provide a **close-ended** response set that identifies all the responses from which they can choose? The answer is that neither question type is inherently better, and the choice of question type is dependent upon whether the researcher has confidence that he or she knows all of the response sets to include in the close-ended question, or whether there is an interest in obtaining an uncued or unfiltered response from the respondents.

An open-ended question is often used where the question may have a wide variety of responses, and the researcher is interested in having the least amount of influence on the answers provided. For example, the researcher may be interested in obtaining from respondents their assessment of why they voted the way they did in a recent election. The researcher might feel that there are a large number of potentially important factors that explain the voting decision, and probe this issue with an open-ended question such as the following: What (two or three) factors were most important to you in voting for the _____ party in the last election. The researcher could use this question to see what kinds of factors were most important for voters (the impact of party leaders, long-standing party attachments, the issue stances of the parties, media coverage, the role of a local candidate, etc.), and could make this assessment by examining what factors were mentioned by respondents and in what order they were mentioned. Therefore, a strength of open-ended questions is that they provide a very 'raw' form of response, unconditioned by perceptual or analytical frameworks that may be introduced by the researcher.

However, open-ended questions also have a number of analytical challenges. For one thing, they often produce a very long list of response categories when used in survey research. As one can imagine, asking people to tell you why they voted as they did in the election may produce a wide variety of responses, some of which may be subtly different from one another. For example, one respondent may say they voted for the Conservative party in 2008 because they liked the party leader, Stephen Harper; another because they liked the 'leadership' displayed by Harper and Peter McKay when they worked together to create the Conservative Party of Canada; others because of the 'leadership' Harper displayed in Canada–US relations; and others because Harper was perceived as a better 'leader' than Stéphane Dion. While all of these respondents mentioned 'leader', there were subtle differences in the meaning attached to this description. The analytical challenge is to find a way to capture the nuance in these multiple meanings of leadership when analyzing the data on the reason for voting for the Conservative party. As noted in Chapter 2, our goal in empirical political science research is to develop models that simplify the political world, and yet the detailed data available through open-ended questions invites analysis in a more complex manner.

To conduct statistical analysis on the data from open-ended questions, it is often necessary, or at least desirable, to reduce the amount of diversity in responses and to regroup the data into a smaller number of somewhat more generic categories. To continue with the example discussed earlier regarding the reason cited for voting, in addition to those respondents who mentioned some aspect of leadership, other respondents likely would mention factors such as a specific policy put forward by one of the parties, the general economic circumstances in the country or perceptions of the government's performance. Some respondents might make reference to their family voting history—that they come from a tradition of Liberal or Conservative voters, and continued on with the family tradition in this election. Others might mention things that were seemingly trivial—they might not like a certain leader's moustache, or think that one of the leaders looks untrustworthy, or are punishing a party for perceived transgressions of a year, a decade, or a generation ago. In short, there are so many categories of responses with open-ended questions, it may be necessary to collapse all of the respondents who mentioned 'leadership' into a single category, thereby losing the diversity of response that the open-ended question was designed to provide.

Although it may seem a relatively trivial point, it also should be noted that the use of open-ended questions has the added drawback of generally requiring an additional step in recoding the data before they can be used in quantitative analysis. Where the timeliness of data release is important, it is less likely that open-ended questions will be used. For example, commercial public opinion surveys, particularly those that are conducted and published during election campaigns, are less likely to rely extensively on open-ended questions. One of the goals of such surveys is to release the data as quickly as possible, and with as much fanfare as possible, so that the polling company can benefit from the publicity it receives through the publication of the data in high-profile media outlets. Since open-ended questions generally take longer to code, and hence to analyze, they tend not to be featured in such surveys.

Close-ended responses are by far the more popular question type in survey research, both the commercial and academic variety. In a number of instances, the question pertains to a situation in which there is a limited number of responses, and therefore presenting these responses in the question is sensible. Questions such as a person's age, their party identification, their religion, or their education are all generally close-ended questions. In addition, a number of standardized response sets have been developed that enable a number of questions to be asked and the results analyzed from a comparative perspective. For example, the **Likert scale** is a response set that includes (1) strongly agree, (2) agree, (3) neither agree nor disagree, (4) disagree, (5) strongly disagree, and (9) no opinion/don't know. Another example is a 'feeling thermometer', in which respondents indicate their warmth of feeling toward an object using a standard response scale, such as (0) very cold, (25) cool, (50) neutral, (75) warm, and (100) hot. Yet a third type of close-ended question offers respondents statements that are viewed as opposites on an opinion scale, such as, Which of the following statement comes closest to your view: The government's primary job in the economy is to keep inflation under control. OR Government policy should put employment ahead of inflation in its economic policies. In each example of close-ended questions, the result for the analyst is a limited set of common responses that can be used for analysis.

Close-ended questions also can have an influence on the percentage of respondents who answer a question and are perceived as having an opinion based on whether the question provides an option for the respondent to say they 'don't know' or have 'no opinion' on a matter. This issue arose, among other places, in analyses on Canadians' partisan attachments. Prior to the 1988 Canadian Election Study, the question about respondents' partisan identification was asked without including a 'don't know/no opinion' option. From 1988 onward, the question has been asked with this option. When respondents have a chance to indicate a non-committal response—don't know or no opinion—on a matter such as their partisan image, they are more likely to take advantage of this sentiment than when not offered this option. This matter has also arisen when Canadians in the Canadian Election Study have been asked to indicate the income their family earned in the previous year. This question often has indicated that upward of 20 per cent of respondents don't know what their income is. In this instance, the 'don't know' response is likely a euphemism for respondents who actually know their income, but want to convey to the interviewer that it is none of his or her business.

Close-ended questions are not without limitations. Perhaps the most important challenge with close-ended questions is that the researcher is forcing a choice among respondents who may not have had an opinion at all on the topic. Therefore, rather than measuring a pre-existing attitude among respondents, the researcher may be creating the attitude that he or she is measuring. The research finding may be presented as an analysis of the attitudes of the electorate toward some policy or another, when in reality it consists of an analysis of nonattitudes. Second, the use of close-ended questions presupposes that the researcher is aware of and has included in the response set all of the possible and appropriate responses. In instances where the list is incomplete, or incorrect, the findings necessarily will be similarly mistaken.

QUESTION ORDER

If you have ever been a respondent to a significant national or regional survey, you might have answered all the questions without becoming aware that there was a definite order in which the questions, or question types, were asked. Question order is obvious in those instances in which the question design is one of root and branch—that is, where one set of questions logically follows from an answer to an initial question. For example, when asking about a person's party identification, the root question often begins, Do you usually think of yourself as a Conservative, Liberal, NDP, Green, some other party, or none of the above? For those respondents who indicate that they identify with one of the parties, they are then asked which party that is. For those who don't identify with a party, they are asked, Do you usually think of yourself a closer to one of the parties? And if so, which party that is. In this case, the logic of responses to the initial question determine the order of the subsequent question.

More generally, however, there is an order in the presentation of questions in survey questionnaires. Generally, and this is particularly true of many of the commercial surveys, political surveys are short in duration. It is common to include a few questions at the outset of a survey that are fairly innocuous and nonthreatening, such as, Have you noticed that a provincial election campaign is underway? or Do you usually pay much attention to political ads on TV?

Fairly early in the survey, following such questions, it is common to see the placement of the key 'horserace' questions. These questions, the responses to which often lead newscasts, include, If an election were held today, for which party would you vote? On a scale of 1 to 10, how would you rate the leader of the X party? The reason these questions occur early in the order is that they are often the key items for which the survey company is basing its overall assessment of voting intentions. Some respondents, for a variety of reasons, may choose not to complete the full survey, and it is generally preferred that data be gathered on their voting intentions early on. In addition, it is generally desirable to obtain information on such questions before the respondent is asked to provide their assessment of factors that might influence their voting decision or assessment of the leaders. For example, if there were a series of questions about the parties' stands on issues, and a respondent indicated a preference for the position of party Y, then it could create cognitive dissonance for the person to indicate they intended to support party X. To avoid introducing such psychological cross-pressures, asking the vote-intention questions early ensures that voters aren't influenced by their answers to other, related, questions.

Once the vote-intention questions have been asked, questions follow about issue influences and perceptions, the party leaders or their personal characteristics, and general deep-rooted values and beliefs. If the survey is administered during an election campaign, questions about the campaign are asked. These questions can be either open-ended or close-ended, depending upon the needs of the survey's sponsor and the timeliness of their use. Once the full set of attitudinal and behavioural questions are asked, the final section of a survey asks about respondents' personal characteristics—their age, marital status, gender, income, education, and the like. These questions generally are placed at the end of a questionnaire because some respondents don't like to answer them and if asked too soon, could lead people to question whether they are really going to be treated with anonymity. In some instances, respondents terminate interviews when demographic questions are being raised. If a respondent is going to terminate the interview, best that this occur after they have provided much of the attitudinal information that is generally of greatest interest.

PRETESTING QUESTIONNAIRES

Researchers take much care in designing clear questions that have only one stimulus per question and order questions to conform with standards used by other researchers; however, prior to 'going into the field' to administer the survey, it is a good practice to administer the survey to a small number of respondents who are similar to the people in the population frame from which the survey respondents will be drawn. A pretest will assist with a number of administrative matters: How long does it take to administer the questionnaire? How does the survey flow? Do respondents lose interest? It will also help ensure that questions that seemed clear and straightforward when being developed are similarly clear when people hear them 'cold' for the first time. Are there any technical terms that are confusing, for example, the difference between a government 'debt' and a 'deficit'? Are any questions offensive or off-putting to respondents? Do questions that use a close-ended response set include all the responses needed to assist people to convey their sentiments? Considering the time and expense involved in conducting a survey of 1,000 to 4,000 respondents, including the valuable time of the respondents themselves, a pretest of 5 to 10 people is a small price to pay for ensuring that the survey will produce high-quality information.

SOURCES OF DATA COLLECTION

Survey research can take many forms, just as survey samples can be drawn in many different ways. (For a discussion of sampling techniques, see Chapter 8.) The four basic forms are personal interviews, telephone interviews, mail-back surveys, and Internet surveys.

Personal, in-home interviews provide the most versatile methodology because respondents can be presented with a mix of question formats and visual aids. However, these interviews are also very expensive and can be difficult to conduct in a security-conscious environment where people are uneasy about admitting strangers into their homes. In-home interviews have traditionally enjoyed higher response rates than other survey techniques, but this advantage is now less apparent. Where in-home interviews, or, more likely, 'in-office' interviews, have a decided response rate advantage is in elite interviewing. (As discussed in Chapter 13, for research purposes an 'elite' is someone with specialized information relevant to the research.) For elite respondents, telephone interviews can be difficult to arrange and conduct, and mail-back questionnaires seldom enjoy a satisfactory response rate.

Telephone interviews are the most common format for contemporary survey research. They are less expensive than in-home interviews and, when coupled with new computer technologies, provide for question versatility, quick data summaries, and speedy analysis. Telephone interviews also avoid some of the security problems confronted by the in-home format, although answering machines and call-screening are causing new and potentially serious problems for locating respondents.

Mailed surveys provide an even less expensive way of conducting survey research. Mailed questionnaires can be longer, more complex, and more interesting in layout and design than in-home or, in particular, telephone questionnaires, but they tend to suffer from relatively low response rates. This is problematic since it cannot be assumed that those who complete the surveys are necessarily similar to those who do not. In fact, we know they are not. It should also be noted, however, that the response rate is in large part a function of the population from which the sample is drawn. General samples, such as the Canadian electorate, tend to have the lowest response rates, whereas samples of highly specific populations often have quite high response rates. (The more specialized and homogeneous the population, the more likely that its members will be interested enough in the topic of the survey to respond.) The Canadian Election Studies often combine detailed telephone interviews with follow-up, mailed surveys. One advantage of mail-back surveys is that the respondent is more willing to address controversial questions honestly, since there is no interviewer present (in person or in voice) to make judgments. Interviewer effects are therefore eliminated.

Internet surveys (also known as web-based or online surveys) have increased in popularity of use tremendously in the past decade, particularly because survey companies have developed a group of people to serve as members of an ongoing pool of respondents who can be contacted relatively easily and inexpensively. Early trials of Internet surveys in the 1990s tended to produce disappointing results because the portion of the population that had ready access to the Internet was both limited and highly skewed in favour of young people. However, as online access has spread and the user group has become much more diverse, given the potential reach of the Internet and its low cost, survey firms look increasingly to it for survey respondents. The advantages of this survey method are that it is relatively inexpensive to administer and it potentially offers a rapid turnaround between the time that the survey is released and the time that the responses are gathered. In addition, the survey instrument can be designed with fairly complex questions. The most important disadvantage is the challenge associated with securing a representative sample. Not only is there self-selection bias among online survey responders, but also the sampling frame may be sufficiently distorted that the resulting sample is unrepresentative. However, with appropriate weighting of the sample, at least some of the distortion can be mitigated.

EXPAND YOUR KNOWLEDGE
Innovative Methods to Study Bisexuality

In 1996 the National Health Development and Research Program of the federal Department of Health sponsored a $200,000 telephone survey by a University of Toronto team into the prevalence and character of bisexuality in Canada. Because it is difficult to identify and therefore sample the bisexual community, the research team relied on a 1-800 phone number through which potential respondents could contact the team and complete the anonymous, 45-minute interview. The survey also employed an unusual form of bilingualism (Strauss 1996, A6):

> The language of the survey is English with a bilingual sexual twist. Those who want to be spoken to in a clinical language will hear that. Those more comfortable with street argot will be spoken to in that. Previous sexual behavioural studies show that while people start out saying they want clinical terms, it is often unsatisfactory when sexual practices are investigated.

These four survey techniques have been adapted to incorporate commercial research opportunities and limited research budgets. *Piggy-backing* and the use of **omnibus surveys**, provide means by which researchers can add a few questions to a larger survey. Many commercial firms, for example, will conduct regular national surveys with standard demographic questions and some questions of particular interest to the firm. The rest of the questionnaire space is then sold to clients, including private firms, government departments, interest groups, political parties, think tanks, and academics. A single survey may therefore have questions on a wide range of disjointed topics: voting intentions, consumer preferences, reactions to government policy initiatives, lifestyle issues. The disadvantage to the academic researcher is that she does not know the context in which her own questions are being asked; the advantage is a tremendous cost-saving, since the expense of the national survey is spread over a number of clients.

Panel studies (also known as *longitudinal studies*) provide a valuable means by which to study change over time. Most surveys are *cross-sectional* in that the respondents are interviewed only once and all approximately at the same time. Thus, a detailed snapshot is produced of opinion at that particular point in time, but change over time is difficult to assess. Although one can compare snapshots taken at different points in time, it is difficult to decide if the difference between two snapshots is accounted for by change in the composition of the two groups of respondents or by a real change in social and political attitudes. By contrast, panel studies interview the same respondents at different points in time, thereby facilitating the study of change.

For example, the *Bibby Reports* (discussed later in this chapter) include a group of respondents who participated in the 1975, 1980, 1985, 1990, and 1995 surveys. Panel studies can be expensive to mount in that contact with respondents must be maintained or renewed; the longer the time interval between survey waves, the more complicated the task of tracking respondents becomes. Attrition rates are illustrated by a study of job-related educational training that began with 1985 baseline questionnaires completed by 1,000 grade 12 students in six Edmonton high schools and by 600 graduates from the five largest faculties at the University of Alberta. By 1992, 40 per cent of the high school students and 60 per cent of the university graduates remained in the fifth wave of the panel study (Lowe and Krahn 1995, 364). As a consequence of attrition, it is sometimes necessary to replace panel members as the study progresses and early respondents move, die, or lose interest in the project. Recent CES surveys have included panel components and have used a rolling cross-section ('rolling thunder') strategy in which the almost 4,200 interviews are portioned out over the duration of the campaign. With approximately 100 to 120 interviews being conducted each day, it is possible to track campaign effects and changes in voting intentions over the course of the campaign.

EXPAND YOUR KNOWLEDGE
The *Bibby Reports*

One of the most high-profile, mail-based surveys of Canadian public opinion is the *Bibby Report*, published by sociologist Reginald W. Bibby (1995) from the University of Lethbridge. Bibby's first study was conducted in 1975 and was based on a mail survey of 1,917 respondents. The size of the sample, the focus of the study on prominent social issues of the day, and Bibby's energy in publicizing the study's findings quickly established the 1975 Report as a benchmark for Canadian social trends. Bibby repeated the survey in 1980, 1985, 1990, and 1995 and in each survey included a substantial number of respondents from past surveys, thus providing an important panel component. The surveys were all mail surveys, and averaged 1,643 respondents with a very respectable response rate of nearly 60 per cent. The questionnaires were long, detailed, and covered a wide swath of Canadian social and political life. The accumulated *Bibby Reports* provided a useful series of snapshots of Canadian society and demonstrate how much can be done with relatively modest resources.

In all forms of survey research there are tradeoffs among complexity, cost, and response rates. As a consequence, there is no *best* way to do a survey; it all depends on the resources you have and the research questions that need to be addressed. The internal validity of survey research depends upon the questions chosen for the study (see Chapter 4), while external validity depends heavily upon the sample chosen (see Chapter 8). If the sample is large and randomly selected, external validity can be high.

Conducting survey research can be a very complex undertaking. In essence, however, virtually all survey research follows a similar template. We begin with a *population* in which we have some research interest; the population could be Canadian voters, supporters of a particular party, members of an interest group or religious faith, female MPs, holders of a specific ideological orientation, or whatever. We then devise means by which to draw a *sample* from this larger population; Chapter 8 discussed a variety of ways, some good and some bad, in which this

EXPAND YOUR KNOWLEDGE

Surveys on Aboriginal Populations

Although political scientists are often interested in studying the behaviour and attitudes of subpopulations, doing so can be challenging with survey research because of issues of sample size. The study of Aboriginal political participation presents a good example of these challenges. Aboriginal Canadians are a growing population, and in the 2006 Census it was found that over one million Canadians self-identify as Aboriginal (Statistics Canada 2008). However, Aboriginal people remain a relatively small percentage (3.8 per cent) of the overall Canadian population, and in a survey based on random sampling, the number of Aboriginal respondents is typically too low to allow for meaningful analysis. This is particularly true if researchers wish to control for geography (province of residence; urban, rural, and on-reserve populations) and/or population (First Nation, Métis, and Inuit). An additional challenge for research is that Aboriginal Canadians can be harder to access with telephone surveys; this has particularly found to be a challenge with urban Aboriginal populations.

Because of these data limitations, empirical studies of Aboriginal political participation in Canada are limited. However, researchers are increasingly using Aboriginal oversamples and Aboriginal-specific surveys to fill the knowledge gaps. One such example is the *Equality, Security and Community (ESC)* survey, directed by Richard Johnston. This 2004 survey included 608 Aboriginal people living in Alberta, Saskatchewan, and Manitoba. In an analysis of the ESC Aboriginal survey, Allison Harell, Dimitrios Panagos, and J. Scott Matthews (2009) found Aboriginal Canadians are less likely than the general population to report voting; interestingly, they also found that individuals involved in Aboriginal organizations have higher voter turnout than those who are not involved in such organizations. More recently, the Environics Institute conducted the Urban Aboriginal Peoples Study, in which Aboriginal interviewers conducted in-person interviews with 2,614 urban Aboriginal peoples living in large Canadian cities (Environics 2010). Environics reports: 'A significant minority (4 in 10) feel there is no one Aboriginal organization or National political party that best represent them, or cannot say'.

might be done. The next step is to come up with a set of questions to *measure* the underlying concepts, values, or beliefs in which we are interested; this step was discussed in Chapters 3 and 4. We may also want to supplement the empirical information with more *qualitative data*; selected means of doing so are discussed in Chapters 13 and 14. Once the survey data are in hand, they must be tabulated and described. Then we find a way of working back from the sample data to the population in which we are interested. Here, the tools of *descriptive* and *inferential statistics*, discussed in Chapters 15 through 18, are indispensable.

Survey research has become a ubiquitous research methodology in political science and in the social sciences more generally. This is not to say, however, that it is always done well. Nor is it to deny a large number of complex problems that churn around virtually all aspects of survey research. Finally, the pervasive nature of survey research should not blind us to the variety of other research methodologies that are available.

WORKING AS A TEAM

1. Use this group discussion to help explore in more detail issues concerning question wording and question type. The text suggests that questions are most useful if they contain only one stimulus (that is, you are asking people their views about one thing at a time), they are clear and unambiguous, and they are phrased in an unbiased way, without trying to lead the respondent to say one thing or another. The text also differentiates among open-ended and close-ended questions. Now, select a topic or theme you'd like to know about (people's attitudes toward left-right distinctions; as-sessments of the performance of the prime minister; their vote decision, etc.). Using a close-ended format, develop at least three questions that help measure people's attitudes toward this topic. Make sure that your response set is comprehensive and complete.

2. Now, do the same thing, using open-ended questions. Select a small group (such as 10 classmates), and administer these short questionnaires. Compare the results that are obtained by using the different question formats, and discuss the advantages and disadvantages of each.

SELF-STUDY

1. Perhaps the most quickly growing area in survey research is the use of Internet-based surveys to measure the attitudes and behaviour of groups. It is quite likely that as a university or college student who has used the Internet extensively for a number of years, you have received and possibly completed a web-based survey. A number of reputable commercial polling companies use web-based surveys quite extensively. Discuss some of the strengths and limitations to the use of web-based public opinion surveys.

2. What techniques could be used to ensure that the information obtained from such surveys is as free as possible from random and nonrandom errors?

Chapter 10

GOVERNMENT DATA SOURCES

DESTINATION

By the end of this chapter the reader should

- appreciate the diversity of government data available in Canada;
- be familiar with the advantages and limitations of using government data;
- understand the distinction between aggregate and individual data; and
- be familiar with the ethical considerations in the use and interpretation of government data.

Although a good deal of political science research involves the creation of new research materials through primary data collection, political science research also involves the secondary analysis of data collected by others. An important source of **secondary data** is government agencies, such as Statistics Canada and Elections Canada. In Canada, these data sources can be of extremely high quality and are underutilized in political science research.

WHY USE GOVERNMENT DATA SOURCES?

Government data sources provide a wealth of information. Statistics Canada, Canada's leading statistical agency, has created data sets on topics related to the population, society, the economy, the environment, and government. Obesity, crime, urbanization, energy, gambling, climate change, forests, labour, volunteering, religion, transportation . . . the list of topics is considerable. Additional information can be obtained from other government agencies, including Elections Canada and its provincial counterparts, and provincial statistical agencies.

One advantage to using government data is data quality and sample size. Statistics Canada and other Canadian government agencies devote considerable attention to ensuring data quality at all stages, from question wording to sampling to data entry and cleaning to data analysis and presentation. And while survey research is often limited in its ability to draw conclusions about subgroups in the population because of a small number of cases in a particular subgroup, this is often not an issue with government data. Some government data sources, such as the Census and electoral returns data, are based on the full population (or nearly the full population). Other government data sources are based on very large samples;

for example, since 1999 the General Social Surveys (GSS) has had a sample size of 25,000 respondents.

A second advantage is efficiency and cost-savings. By using government data, the researcher saves data collection time: rather than spending months designing and implementing a study, the researcher can access data almost immediately. Government data also saves the researcher the (often considerable) costs associated with data collection. Many government data sources are freely available from public websites; for example, the Elections Canada website includes both web-based summary tables and raw data files for download. Other data sets (or select portions of data sets) can be accessed through university research data libraries. University-based researchers, including undergraduate and graduate students, enjoy free access to many Statistics Canada datasets through the Data Liberation Initiative (DLI).[1]

A third advantage, at least for some government data sources, is the ability to compare data over time. Most surveys collect **cross-sectional data**, or data collected from individuals at one point in time. However, some government surveys provide **longitudinal data** (also known as **panel data**), that is, data collected from the same individuals over time. Longitudinal data allow researchers to consider change over time and to clarify if certain events preceded other events. By allowing consideration of temporal order, longitudinal data enable researchers to better assess causality. Examples of available longitudinal data include the Survey of Labour and Income Dynamics and the National Longitudinal Survey of Children and Youth.

Yet while there are many advantages to using government data, there are, of course, also limitations. The most important to be aware of is that researchers are often limited to **aggregate data**—that is, grouped data for a specified geographic area. In some cases, such as electoral returns data, data are available only in aggregate form. In other cases, such as Statistic Canada surveys, access to nonaggregated **microdata** files is highly restricted because of strict confidentiality rules.[2]

Aggregate data present challenges for analysis. First, aggregate data are not always available in the manner that a particular researcher prefers. As Statistics Canada (2009a) writes:

> Not all aggregate data contain the combination of variables from the microdata that a user may desire. For example, a patron may be looking at whether alcohol use and gambling are correlated and wishes to know if these variables differ between men and women, by age group, and whether the results vary across Canada. Although data in the Canadian Community Health Survey (CCHS) 3.1 are collected about the respondent's geography, gender, age, Canadian Problem Gambling Index, and alcohol use, this combination of variables may not have been used in creating an aggregate data product.

Second, because aggregate data provide group-level (as opposed to individual-level) information, researchers must be careful to ensure that their conclusions do not imply individual-level behaviours. For example, an analysis of aggregate electoral returns data may find that electoral districts with greater proportions of high-income households tend to have greater support for the Conservative party. From this, it is tempting to assume that high-income *individuals* are more likely to vote Conservative. Although it is possible that this is true, the aggregate data do not support this assumption; it may be that lower- and/or middle-income individuals living in higher-income ridings are more likely to vote Conservative, or the relationship between income and vote choice may be spurious. When we assume that group-level patterns imply individual-level patterns, we fall victim to the **ecological fallacy**. To avoid this, researchers must be cautious in their language in describing their results. For example, in their analysis of Alberta electoral returns data, Edward Bell, Harold Jansen, and Lisa Young make clear reference to districts as the unit of analysis. They write, for instance, '[h]aving a higher proportion of immigrants was associated with higher levels of Liberal voting' (2007, 41) but do not imply that immigrant voters were more likely to vote Liberal.[3]

KEY SECONDARY DATA SOURCES IN CANADA

There are a number of high-quality, accessible government data sources available to Canadian political scientists. These include (but are not limited to) the Census, Statistics Canada surveys, and electoral returns data.

Census of Canada

A **Census** is a record of the full population, as opposed to a sample (or subset) of the population. The Census has a long history in Canada; indeed, Canada's Constitution Act, 1867 requires that Census population figures be used to determine the allocation of Members of Parliament (MPs) to provinces and to adjust district boundaries, and the first post-Confederation Census was taken in 1871 (Statistics Canada 2009b). Since 1956, the Canadian Census has been taken every five years; this practice was put into law with the Statistics Act of 1971. Censuses taken at the start of a decade (for example, 1991, 2001, 2011) are referred to as **decennial Censuses**, while Censuses taken mid-decade (for example, 1996, 2006, 2016) are referred to as **quinquennial Censuses** (Statistics Canada 2009b).

Until 1966, Censuses were done by door-to-door interviews; since 1971, Canadian households have completed and returned questionnaires. In 2006, Canadians were given the option to complete their Census form over the Internet. It is important to note that there are two forms of the questionnaire. The short form, mandatory for all households, contained only eight questions in 2006, whereas the long form, mandatory for 20 per cent of households (selected randomly), contained 61 questions. Thus, some Census data tables note that they are based on the 20 per cent sample, rather than the full population. Starting in 2011, the long form of the Census will be voluntary—that is, Canadians who receive the long form will not be legally required to complete the form. This change has prompted concerns about the quality of the resultant data.

Although the Statistics Act legally obligates every Canadian household to participate in the Census, some groups are undercounted. According to Statistics Canada (2009c), in 2001 '[t]hese groups included people who speak neither of the official languages, people with visual disabilities, people with low levels of literacy, seniors, students, the homeless, immigrants, Aboriginal people, young men and, in some areas, young women, between the ages of 18 and 30.' Additionally, in some years some First Nations reserves refused to permit Census enumeration. In the 2001 Census, there were 30 'incompletely enumerated reserves and settlements'; this dropped to 22 reserves for the 2006 Census (Statistics Canada 2009d).

Statistics Canada Surveys

Statistics Canada data are not limited to the Census; indeed, its website (2009e) reports that Statistics Canada has 'about 350 active surveys on virtually all aspects of Canadian life'. Many of these surveys are based on samples of the Canadian population. An important data source is the General Social Survey (GSS), which covers a wide range of topics; for example, the 2009 GSS (Cycle 23) examined criminal victimization and public perceptions of crime and the justice system, while the 2008 GSS (Cycle 22) examined social engagement, including voting and civic participation.

Statistics Canada data are also compiled through mail-back surveys of governments and through government administrative sources. These data sets are Censuses—that is, the federal government and all provincial and territorial governments participate, rather than a sample of these 14 governments. (Some government surveys also include municipal governments and other public service bodies.) In addition to tracking government revenues and expenditures broadly, data are collected on specific policy areas, such as culture (the annual Survey of Federal Government Expenditures on Culture and the annual Survey of Provincial/Territorial Government Expenditures on Culture). It is important to note that revenue and expenditure data are typically presented in consolidated form in order to allow for comparability; the Statistics Canada technical documentation provides considerable detail about the process of consolidation.

Electoral Returns Data

Many political scientists are interested in questions of voting, including voter turnout and vote choice. Electoral returns data, available from Elections Canada for federal elections and from provincial elections organizations (for example, Elections Manitoba, Elections Ontario) for provincial elections, provide population-level data on voting. These data can be used to describe voting in specific geographic units, such as ridings or polling stations.

Canadian researchers have used electoral returns data to analyze on-reserve First Nations voting. Survey research is limited in its ability to explain Aboriginal political behaviour, as the typical random telephone survey includes only a small number of Aboriginal respondents. Because electoral returns data are available at the polling station level, it is possible for researchers to isolate on-reserve polling stations to draw conclusions about on-reserve First Nations voting. Such research has considered on-reserve voter turnout (Bedford 2003; Bedford and Pobihushchy 1995; Guérin 2003) and vote choice (Berdahl et al. 2009; Kinnear 2003; Pitsula 2001); the data suggest that voter turnout is lower at on-reserve polls than at non-reserve polls and that the provincial New Democratic parties typically receive a higher percentage of votes at on-reserve polling stations than they do at non-reserve polling stations. These data tell us something about on-reserve First Nations voting but cannot be used to describe Aboriginal voting more broadly because the data do not include off-reserve First Nations, Métis, Inuit, or non-status Indian persons.

Political scientists have also combined Statistics Canada data with electoral returns data in order to consider the relationship between constituency-level socio-economic variables and voting. Statistics Canada provides Census population data according to Federal Electoral Districts (FEDs). The FED profiles include variables such as age, marital status, median income, immigrant status, and other key socio-demographic variables. Researchers can use FED-level Elections Canada and Census data to look for constituency-level sociodemographic variations in voting. In such analyses, the variables are often univariate descriptive statistics (discussed more in Chapter 15), such as percentages (for example, 'percentage of the district population who report being retired') and medians (for example, median age, median income in district), and not raw count data. For example, Linda Gerber (2006, 108) describes her variables as follows: 'census variables were compiled for each riding, converted to percentages and rates, and merged with the results of the federal election of 2004—as the percentage voting for each party—to provide the database for the following analyses.'

ETHICAL CONSIDERATIONS

Given that government data are already collected, ethical considerations for government data are focused on the use of the data, rather than data collection. When using government data, it is critical that researchers carefully review the technical documentation—referred to as '**metadata**'—associated with the data file. It is very easy to unintentionally misuse or misrepresent government data. Some areas to watch for:

- *Concepts.* Data sets may contain multiple measures of similar concepts, and it is important for the researcher to be clear in reporting the measure used. For example, the 2006 Census included a number of questions on the following topics to identify the Aboriginal population: Aboriginal ancestry, Aboriginal identity, Registered Indian status, and Band or First Nation membership. The different measures provide considerably different counts for the Aboriginal population: in the 2006 Census, 1,678,200 Canadians reported Aboriginal ancestry; 1,172,790 reported Aboriginal identity; 623,780 reported Registered Indian status; and 620,340 reported Band or First Nation membership (Statistics Canada 2009f). It is incumbent on the researcher to select the measure that best fits the research question and to clearly specify the measure in the analysis.

- *Question wording.* When one is comparing data sets (such as different Censuses), it is important to watch for differences in question wording and response categories. Question wording and response categories evolve over time, and these changes can influence the results. Researchers should acknowledge such changes in their analyses.
- *Geographic boundaries.* In addition to watching for changes in question wording, researchers should watch for changes in geographic boundaries. For example, electoral district boundaries change over time, and additional districts are occasionally added. (The 2003 Representation Order includes 308 federal districts, compared with the 301 districts in the 1996 Representation Order.)
- *Population of study.* Data sets differ in who is included in the population of study. Some data sets consider individuals, and may vary in terms of the age parameters (for example, Canadian Community Health Surveys include individuals aged 12 and over, while General Social Surveys include individuals aged 15 and over) or other parameters (for example, the Longitudinal Survey of Immigrants to Canada was limited to immigrants who met particular criteria). Some surveys are based on households rather than individuals (for example, Survey of Household Spending). Researchers should clearly report the population of study in their analysis.
- *Data cautions.* Statistics Canada often provides caveats or cautions about the use of its data in its technical documentation. It is important that researchers respect this advice. For example, the following note is provided with respect to Aboriginal identity data: 'Caution should be exercised in analyzing trends for Aboriginal peoples based on previous census data. Over time, patterns in Aboriginal self-identification have changed. In recent years, a growing number of people who had not previously identified with an Aboriginal group are now doing so. Changes in the participation of First Nations people living on reserve in the census over time also affect historical comparison' (Statistics Canada 2009f). Given this warning, researchers should either not report trends in Aboriginal identity data or report the concerns about the data in their discussion.

Government data sources are accompanied by technical documentation. It is the ethical obligation of the researcher to read this documentation and to report data accurately.

WORKING AS A TEAM

1. The text mentions data available in the Census, collected by Statistics Canada, that are aggregated by Federal Electoral Districts (FED). For your group, identify 15 electoral districts. For each district, use the Census FED data to identify the constituency's characteristics based on average family income, age, educational attainment, and ethnic composition. Discuss any trends that you see in terms of the regional or urban-rural character of the constituencies.

2. Now, using Elections Canada data, insert a new variable in the dataset—percentage vote for the Conservative, Liberal, NDP, Bloc, and 'other' parties in the most recent federal election. Discuss any trends that you now see. (Depending upon the technical expertise of the group, you may wish to import the data for all federal constituencies into a statistical package, such as SPSS, and run similar analyses for the country as a whole.) Discuss the findings among the group.

SELF-STUDY

1. One of the challenges associated with using aggregate data is the risk of committing the ecological fallacy—drawing inferences about units of analysis based on data gathered at a different level of analysis.

Provide an example in which an ecological fallacy may occur.

2. Discuss the strategies that could be used to decrease the likelihood of creating an ecological fallacy.

NOTES

1. Access to Statistics Canada data by individuals outside the academic community can be costly, depending on the data being sought.
2. Statistics Canada (2009a) defines microdata as 'the data directly observed or collected from a specific unit of observation', such as 'an individual, a household or a family'. Researchers can access Statistics Canada microdata through Research Data Centres

after completing a rigorous application process, but this can be a time-consuming process.
3. Researchers who wish to make individual-level inferences from aggregate data can use specific ecological regression analyses; for an example, see Lublin and Voss's (2002) analysis of francophone support for sovereignty.

Chapter 11

EXPERIMENTS

Daniel Rubenson, Ryerson University

DESTINATION

By the end of this chapter the reader should

- understand what randomized experiments are and how they are used in political science;
- be aware of the challenges involved in causal inference and the advantages of randomized experiments; and
- have an understanding of the basic steps and considerations involved in designing and carrying out an experiment.

One of the key tasks of empirical political science is to investigate the causes of political phenomena, that is, to predict the outcomes of interventions in the political world. Does contact by a political campaign increase the vote share of the candidate? Do get-out-the-vote efforts raise turnout? Does public deliberation strengthen good governance? Do news media affect what citizens consider important? Do individuals' policy preferences change when the way those policies are framed changes? Answers to these questions—and many other similar questions in political science—include some implicit statement about causation. If, as the result of some empirical research, we answer 'Yes' (or 'No') to the first question, we are making a statement, an inference, about the causal effect of campaign contact on vote choice.

As discussed later in this chapter, studying causal processes and drawing inferences about causal effects presents researchers with several methodological hurdles. Randomized controlled experiments—where researchers intervene to **randomly assign** subjects to different experimental conditions—offer important advantages over other empirical strategies for overcoming these hurdles. This chapter introduces the basic logic of randomized controlled experiments (sometimes called randomized controlled trials or RCT) as they apply to political science research. The challenges involved in causal inference are described and the chapter lays out why randomized experiments are indispensable when it comes to meeting these challenges. The growth of experimentation in the discipline of political science is described and the chapter discusses different types of experimental designs that have been—and can be—brought to bear on political science questions. The chapter identifies the kinds of research questions that have been studied by using experimental research designs and discusses the potential for experiments to be applied to a broader set of political science questions, drawing examples from both Canadian and comparative political science. The chapter goes through the practical steps involved in conducting an experimental study and concludes with a brief discussion of the challenges and ethical concerns involved.

THE GROWTH OF EXPERIMENTATION IN POLITICAL SCIENCE

Political scientists have, as James Druckman et al. (2006) note, generally been skeptical toward the use of experimentation. This skepticism probably arises, in part, because of practical concerns about the feasibility of experiments in political science and perhaps in part because of ethical concerns about the implementation of experiments. Thus, before discussing the nature of causal inference and describing the logic and process of randomized controlled experiments, it is useful say something about the prevalence of this type of research in political science.

The use of randomized controlled experiments in political science, and social science more generally, is not new. Indeed, the tradition dates to the 1920s and Harold Gosnell's experiments on political behaviour (Gerber and Green 1999, 10939). Gosnell (1927) studied voter registration and turnout in Chicago by randomly assigning households in some city blocks to be mailed reminders to register and to vote and then comparing registration and turnout between those blocks and others that received no reminders. Samuel Eldersveld's (1956) work on the effects of voter mobilization on turnout, in which he randomized direct mail and door-to-door canvassing as well as the mobilization message, represents a breakthrough for the application of experimentation in political science and laid the foundations for the resurgence of the use of randomized experiments half a century later, beginning with the work of Alan Gerber and Donald Green (2000).

Although randomized controlled experiments in political science have a relatively long pedigree, there is no doubt that a marked increase in the application of this method began in the 1990s. Peter Loewen, using data from Krueger and Lewis-Beck, shows that the prevalence of articles published in three leading political science journals—the *American Journal of Political Science* (*AJPS*), the *American Political Science Review* (*APSR*), and the *Journal of Politics* (*JOP*)—has increased significantly since the 1990s. The mean percentage of articles each year applying experiments in these journals during the 1990s is 4.8 per cent, whereas for the period 2000–5 the proportion of experimental articles increased to 6.8 per cent (an increase of close to 30 per cent) (Loewen 2008, 21–2). Moreover, if one analyzes the trends within the subfields of political science, a more dramatic picture of the growth of experimentation is revealed. The use of experiments in the study of political behaviour and political psychology has close to doubled if we compare the mean number of articles published in the *AJPS, APSR,* and *JOP* in the years between 1990 and 1999 (11.7 per cent of all articles) to those for the period 2000–5 (21.6 per cent).

Other scholars looking at publication trends in political science make similar observations about the growth of experimentation (for example, Morton and Williams 2008). Druckman et al. in their analysis of the first hundred years of the *APSR* chronicle the growth in prominence and impact of randomized experiments in political science. Again, it is worth noting that this growth has not been uniform across the subfields of the discipline. Druckman et al. maintain that the bulk of the expansion has involved research addressing questions in 'formal theory, public opinion research, electoral politics, and legislative politics' (Druckman et al. 2006, 633).

Therefore, although it is far from being the case that randomized controlled experiments are commonplace in political science, recent trends in the discipline point to the growing use of such designs. The reasons for this no doubt include the great advantages randomized experiments offer over other empirical strategies when it comes to studying causal processes. In the following sections the fundamental challenge of drawing causal inferences is described and the advantages afforded by randomized controlled experiments in overcoming these issues are outlined.

THE CHALLENGE OF CAUSAL INFERENCE

Causal inference, as David Freedman puts it, is both 'the most interesting and the most slippery' of the purposes to which we apply statistical methods (2009, 1). What makes causal inference 'slippery'—that is, difficult to pin down—is the problem of **confounding**. To invoke an oft-used expression, the problem is that correlation—or association—between variables does not imply causation between these variables. For example, in any election campaign there will be some people who are contacted by a political party and some who are not. If we observe that individuals who are contacted are more likely to vote for that party, we cannot conclude that contact *causes* support for the party to go up. The reason we cannot draw this causal inference is the presence of some difference between the two groups—other than contact by the party—that also affects vote choice. This is what is meant by *confounding*.

Another way to think about this problem is to consider what Paul Holland called the 'Fundamental Problem of Causal Inference' (1986, 947). A causal effect is the difference between two conditions, or states of the world. Formally, we could write these conditions as $Y_t(u)$ and $Y_c(u)$. In this notation, u is the unit of analysis (our subjects), individual voters, students in a school, or MPs, for example. Y is some outcome we are interested in studying. This could be turnout, vote choice for a particular party, whether an MP voted for a bill, and so on. The subscripts t and c denote different *causes*. In the experimental terminology these would be **treatment** and **control**. Thus, there are two *potential* values for the outcome Y for any given unit u: the value of Y when a unit is exposed to one cause (the treatment) and the value of Y when the same unit is exposed to the other cause (the control). The **causal effect** of the treatment is the difference between the two:

$$Y_t(u) - Y_c(u)$$

The 'Fundamental Problem of Causal Inference' is that we can never observe any given subject in both conditions. We cannot observe a subject in both its treated and untreated (control) condition. Therefore, we can never actually observe the causal effect of some variable (t) on a subject (u) (Holland 1986, 946–7). The preceding example of campaign contact is illustrative. Here u could be a particular voter in an election, t would be the situation in which that voter is contacted by the party, c is the situation where the party does not contact the voter, and Y represents whether the voter cast a ballot for that party. It is clearly impossible to observe both $Y_t(u)$ and $Y_c(u)$ in this scenario. We could observe that the party contacts the voter *or* we could observe that the party does not contact the voter. As such, it is impossible to observe the causal effect of party contact on vote choice for that party.

What if we were to simply compare people who were contacted with those who were not? The problem in taking such an approach is that it does not allow the researcher to avoid the issue of confounding. One cannot be certain that the difference in vote choice between the two groups is not caused by some other variable lurking in the background that affects *both* vote choice *and* the likelihood of being contacted by a political party. For example, the competitiveness of the race in the riding a person lives in is likely to be correlated with both vote choice and contact.

Randomized controlled experiments are one way in which researchers have attempted to deal with these problems. In a randomized controlled experiment subjects are assigned to *treatment* and *control* groups in such a way that the only difference between the two groups is the treatment—the variable of interest. By randomly assigning the treatment—in other words, assigning treatment by a lottery or coin toss—a researcher can ensure that, in expectation, the two groups will be identical aside from the presence of the treatment in one group. Any differences in the outcome across the two groups can then be inferred to be the result of the treatment. In this way randomized controlled experiments overcome the issue of confounding and facilitate causal inferences about political phenomena.

DEFINITIONS AND TYPES OF EXPERIMENTS

The term 'experiment' is one that is often found in political science research. It does not always mean 'randomized controlled experiment.' Sometimes researchers use the term simply to denote something new or something innovative (for example, Brown et al., 2006). At the heart of the kinds of experiments discussed here, however, is the random assignment of some **stimulus** to a group within a population. That is, observations are *assigned* to one of two or more conditions.

These conditions are commonly referred to as treatment and control conditions—the **treatment group** would typically be those observations that receive the stimulus and the control group would not receive any stimulus.[1] This is in contrast to 'observational designs' in which the researcher has no control over whether observations receive the stimulus. The researcher simply observes the outcome, ex post, and then analyzes the data in order to draw inferences. In an experiment, the researcher intervenes in the process ex ante by assigning observations to different experimental conditions.

There are several different types of randomized controlled experiments in political science. Generally experiments are divided into three types:

1. experiments embedded in surveys;
2. experiments carried out in a laboratory settings, including those in the context of games; and
3. field experiments.

Survey Experiments

Survey experiments involve researchers assigning survey respondents to different treatments within a survey and then measuring differences in responses. This can be as basic as randomly assigning different question wordings to respondents to test the effects on responses. However, the range of survey experiments is much broader than simply varying question wording or ordering.

One example of an area in which survey experiments have contributed greatly to our understanding of public opinion is the study of party identification. Party identification—the extent to which an individual identifies with a particular political party—has long been measured in surveys. However, the advent of survey embedded experiments allowed for important strides to be made in reconciling theoretical constructs of the term with its empirical measurement. For example, Richard Johnston (1992) showed, through an experiment in a Canadian national survey, how cross-national variation in party identification was largely an artefact of American election surveys prompting respondents for nonpartisanship. Similarly, Barry Burden and Casey Klofstad (2005) make a significant contribution with their survey experiment testing questions about party identification that ask respondents to 'feel' rather than 'think' about their party identification (see also Loewen 2008, 9–10).

Laboratory Experiments

Framing—the idea that an issue can be presented in more than one way and that this variation can affect opinion—is another important domain that has benefited from the employment of randomized controlled experiments, often in a laboratory setting. For example, Dennis Chong and James Druckman (2007) are interested in the effects of political competition on the ability of elites to frame public opinion. In order to test their theory they conducted two separate experiments on two issues: urban growth management and the right of an extremist group to hold a rally. Chong and Druckman randomly assigned participants to one of 17 conditions that varied the number of frames, the strength of the frames, as well as the direction of the frames received, the idea being to test whether opinion was affected by such variation in how issues are presented. The stimulus here was in the form of various 'frames' that were presented by using newspaper editorials that used various arguments. Participants' opinions on the issues were measured before and after receiving the frames. By randomly assigning participants, Chong and Druckman are able to ensure that the type of frame a participant received was not associated with characteristics of the participant that might also be related to their opinion on the issues under investigation, thereby making causal inferences about the effects of framing possible.

Other examples of laboratory experiments dealing with public opinion and voting include ones in which participants are presented with varying levels of information about the quality of candidates in order to study the effects of such information on voters, independent of issue positions (Canache, Mondak, and Cabrera 2000; Kulisheck and Mondak 1996; Mondak and Huckfeldt 2006) and experiments testing the effects of the tone of political discourse on awareness of opposing views (Mutz 2006; 2007).

A growing number of political scientists are joining social scientists from other disciplines, such as economics and psychology, in employing experimental games to study political behaviour. For example, Donna Bahry and Rick Wilson (2006) and James Fowler (2006) have used laboratory experiments to study patterns of altruism, cooperation, and trust (see Camerer 2003 for a recent review). In the Canadian context, Loewen (2009) has used games embedded in online surveys to study altruism, partisanship, and political participation. Scholars are also using laboratory experiments and experimental games to learn about institutions and decision-making (Greig and Bohnet 2006; Henrich et al. 2004).

Field Experiments

Field experiments involve implementing randomized controlled experiments in a natural environment. That is, unlike survey and laboratory experiments that are several steps removed from the arena of actual politics, field experiments take place 'in the real world' and involve interventions in real political events. Field experiments are complex undertakings in that the researcher has limited control over the process aside from the design of the intervention. Nevertheless, when well executed, field experiments offer unparalleled advantages precisely because they occur within real events and measure real behaviour.

As mentioned earlier, some of the earliest experiments in political science were field experiments. More recently, field experimentation has seen a resurgence, first in the area of mobilization and, more recently, in studies designed to answer questions about political persuasion. Alan Gerber and Donald Green's (2000) study of the mobilizing effects of direct mail, door-to-door canvassing, and telephone calls is a landmark in field experimentation and has inspired numerous similar studies.[2] In the experiment, Gerber and Green randomly assigned households in New Haven, Connecticut, to be contacted with get-out-the-vote appeals either by mail, by canvassing, or by telephone. Some households were randomly assigned to receive two of these treatments and some households were assigned to a control group that received no treatment.

The beauty of this experiment is threefold. First, it allowed the researchers to speak to the debate over whether turnout decline was a function of lack of contact or changes in the way citizens are contacted. Second, and more importantly, because this was a randomized controlled experiment, the researchers were on far more solid ground than they would have been after an observational study when it came to drawing conclusions about the results. If Gerber and Green had taken a standard observational approach and conducted a survey during the election, asking respondents whether they were contacted and whether they voted and then carried out a statistical test of the association between contact and turnout, controlling for other factors such as sociodemographics, they would not be able to make strong statements about the effects of contact on turnout. The reason is that contact is not random. It is correlated with factors that also predict turnout. Finally, because this was a *field* experiment, it occurred in the context of a real campaign with real voters (and nonvoters).

While much of the field experimental literature has focused on mobilization, there are several recent examples of field experiments that look at persuasion in politics, usually in elections. Often these experiments are conducted in cooperation between researchers and real campaigns. This is both a challenge and an advantage. It is challenging in that studies of this kind involve managing a relationship with a political campaign.[3] The great advantage is that, in contrast to many other experiments, the treatments in these studies are entirely realistic in that the campaign and not the researchers design them. There are several recent examples from Canadian politics. Loewen and Rubenson's (2010) study of persuasion in the 2006 Liberal Party of Canada leadership race and their experiment on the persuasive effects of two-sided direct mail in the 2007 Ontario referendum on electoral reform (Rubenson and Loewen 2010) represent the first two field experiments in Canadian politics. Brown, Perrella, and Kay (2010) implemented a randomized field experiment during the 2007 Ontario provincial election in which, working with one of the candidates, they randomly assigned some polling divisions in a constituency to receive the candidate's campaign material. They then compared the candidate's vote shares in the treated polling areas with the control areas. Finally, Dewan, Humphreys, and Rubenson (2009) carried out a field experiment during the 2009 British Columbia referendum on electoral reform, designed to distinguish the effects on public opinion of leaders from the messages they convey.

A growing body of literature has begun to apply field experiments to questions of politics in the developing world. Examples include the work of Habyarimana et al. (2007; 2009) on ethnic diversity and public goods; Humphreys, Masters, and Sandbu (2006) on leadership and deliberation; Moehler (2007) and Paluck (2009) on media effects on political knowledge and attitudes; Hyde (forthcoming) on elections and corruption; and Atchade and Wantchekon (2007), Wantchekon and Vermeersch (2005), and Wantchekon (2003; 2008) on information, clientelism, and public goods provision.

THE BASIC STEPS OF CONDUCTING A RANDOMIZED CONTROLLED EXPERIMENT

Experimentation is becoming more common in political science. However, it is still the case that many scholars shy away from designing and implementing randomized controlled experiments because they perceive them to be more complicated and costly than other, observational, designs for empirical political science. For graduate students, in particular, it might appear daunting to have to design a randomized experiment and collect the data. The temptation to use one or another of countless already existing off-the-shelf data sets from surveys and other studies is no doubt large, but students and other scholars should take seriously the possibility of implementing randomized controlled experiments. First, it is not obvious that the cost is higher. Second, while certainly not *easy*, the work going in to designing and carrying out a randomized experiment is not greater than that for a large, well-designed survey, for example. Moreover, randomized controlled experiments offer advantages over observational research that make them more than worth whatever the minor differences in cost and effort.

This section briefly outlines the steps involved in conducting a randomized controlled experiment. Readers should note that these are general remarks and, of course, the precise process of carrying out an experiment in practice may differ from study to study.

Hypotheses before Empirics

The first step in any research project is to generate a question. Conducting a randomized controlled experiment is no exception. Experiments, however, in contrast to observational research designs, have the advantage of forcing us to consider our hypotheses *before* we collect our data. This is so because in an experiment the analyst is intervening in the data-generating process rather than analyzing data ex post. The logic of an experiment is to assess the causal effect of some variable. Therefore, a necessary condition of an **experimental design** is to have a clear idea of what one's dependent and independent variables are before one collects any data. Implicit in the act of selecting some treatment variable is the idea that this variable will have some impact on some phenomenon of interest—the dependent variable. The researcher is forced to work out what are the independent and dependent variables before the data collection can begin. This entails working out hypotheses about the predicted effect of X on Y. In an observational study there is far more risk of sloppy hypothesizing and ex post data fitting. In this way experiments can contribute to more theoretically thoughtful research designs.

Statistical Power

Once one has a research question and a clearly defined set of hypotheses, one can begin to design the practical elements of the experiment. An early step in this is to get a sense of how large a sample one needs in order to be able to detect effects.

Statistical power refers to the ability of a design to detect effects, if such effects really exist. Suppose, for example, that you have an experimental design meant to test whether an appeal to citizens' sense of civic duty increases turnout. Suppose further that the appeal *does* have the effect of raising turnout by, say, two percentage points among those who receive it. If the design does not have enough statistical power, the researcher will not see a significant effect in the results, even though it does in fact exist in the real world. One way to think about this is to consider the crucial difference between concluding there is *no evidence of effects* versus concluding that there is *evidence of no effects*.

In other words, designs have to be sensitive enough to detect effects that exist. Statistical power depends on several factors, including the number of units in treatment and control—sample size. It is highly advisable to conduct a power analysis *before* implementing any experimental design. Many modern statistical computing programs include packages for conducting power analysis.

The Randomization Procedure

A key element to designing a RCT is the level of randomization. That is, the researcher must decide whether to assign the treatment to individuals or groups of one kind or another (for example, households, polling precincts, villages, schools, etc.). This decision is often driven by concerns about both theory and practicality. For example, if one is conducting a field experiment to study turnout in a Canadian election, one might choose to randomize a treatment across polling divisions because this is the lowest level at which official election results are collected. The advantage of this over using households as the unit of randomization is that one could use official election results to measure the dependent variable rather than a survey.

There are several methods for randomly assigning observations to treatment. The important thing to keep in mind is that assignment must be random. Every observation must have the same probability of ending up in the treatment group. Once random assignment has occurred it is important to check the integrity of the process by confirming that treatment is not correlated with observable characteristics of study subjects.

Model Selection

The design of an experiment—the method of random assignment—will determine the structure of the data that results from the study. For example, if you have an experiment in which households within polling precincts are selected for treatment and control, the data will be *clustered* at the polling-precinct level. Ignoring that clustering when analyzing the data will lead to violations of statistical assumptions and result in biased estimates of effects. Therefore, it is important to select a statistical model that is appropriate given one's method of randomization and the unit of analysis (for example, is the data at the level of individuals or some higher level of aggregation?).

A word of caution is warranted here: in analyzing the data, it is important not to include control variables that are themselves determined by the random assignment of treatment. That is, do not include covariates that are endogenous to the treatment. Doing so undoes much of the benefit of an experimental design by essentially turning it into an observational study.

CONCLUDING THOUGHTS, PRACTICAL CHALLENGES, AND ETHICAL CONSIDERATIONS

In conducting experiments of any kind in political science, there are several practical and ethical concerns that need to be kept in mind.

- *Spillovers and crossovers.* The great advantage of randomized controlled experiments is the ability to identify causal effects. As explained earlier in this chapter, this is achieved by randomly assigning some group to a treatment condition and other subjects to a control condition, thereby ensuring that any observed differences across groups is due to the treatment. However, if researchers are unable to ensure that the control group is not contaminated by the treatment, drawing causal inferences will be made more difficult. Suppose some households were treated with political information to encourage them to vote. If they talk to their neighbours who are in the control group, they might pass that information along, making the neighbours more likely to vote as well. This is an example of a spillover whereby the control group no longer represents a good comparison.

  Crossovers present a similar threat to experimental designs. For example, if we are interested in evaluating the effects of access to electricity in rural African villages and we randomly assign solar panel–generated electricity to some households and not others, we must be careful to guard against villagers from control households travelling to treatment households in order to access electricity.

  Should that happen and we ignore these crossovers or spillovers, our comparisons between treated and control groups will be biased. Researchers can try to minimize these problems by adjusting the level of randomization. In this example, the researchers could do this by randomizing at the village level instead of the household level.

- *Political feasibility.*   Often as researchers we want to design ambitious and creative experiments. Sometimes the implementation of these designs is constrained by political realities outside of our control. As an illustration consider the field experiment conducted by Loewen and Rubenson in the 2006 Liberal party of Canada leadership race. The experiment randomized the direct mail from the Michael Ignatieff campaign to delegates pledged to other candidates. In order to obtain agreement from the campaign, the researchers had to limit their study to a sample of delegates rather than all delegates and they had to conduct their study within a certain timeframe during the lead up to the leadership convention. Ideally, the experiment would have been free of these constraints; however, they were a necessary condition of being able to do anything at all. Given the tradeoffs, the researchers felt the benefits outweighed the relatively minor drawbacks imposed. For a fuller discussion of working with political elites in conducting experiments see Loewen, Rubenson, and Wantchekon (2010).

- *Fairness and ethics.*   One concern that is often raised in the context of randomized controlled experiments, in particular, field experiments, is the perceived lack of fairness in allocating to only a subgroup of the population a treatment that might be beneficial to all. Critics argue that if the program being randomized is potentially beneficial then it should be given to everyone. This is an ethical concern that needs to be taken seriously when designing field experiments. There are several solutions. If resources are scarce and it is impossible for the program of treatment to be given to everyone, a random assignment of the treatment is actually *fairer* than the alternatives. Researchers can also sometimes exploit the timing of program implementation by designing an experiment in which randomization is carried out in phases. In this case, a subset of the population would be randomly assigned treatment and analysis would proceed as in any other experiment, the only difference being that everyone would receive the treatment at the end of the study period. Of course, all studies involving human subjects need to be submitted to a Research Ethics Board (REB) for ethics and human subjects approval.

Randomized controlled experiments are increasing in frequency in political science and are used by scholars interested in a wide range of research questions. Experimental designs carry with them great benefits and are the gold standard when it comes to making causal inferences. The reason is that they allow researchers to deal with the ubiquitous problem of confounding far better than observational studies. Randomized controlled experiments make a valuable contribution to the empirically minded political scientist's tool kit.

WORKING AS A TEAM

1. With your group, brainstorm five political science research questions that include questions of causality. Select one question, and discuss how it might be examined by using an experimental research design.

2. What type of experiment (survey, laboratory, field) would you use? How, if at all, would your experiment be limited by political or ethical considerations?

SELF-STUDY

Imagine that you are interested in assessing the influence of civics education initiatives for youth (such as the nonprofit Student Vote program in Canada) on voter turnout. Is this research question well-suited for an experimental design? Explain why or why not.

NOTES

1. Though, as Loewen (2008, 5) correctly points out, experiments need not, strictly speaking, include a 'control' group. There are experiments in which researchers compare across several 'treatment' groups and no group can obviously be referred to as being the control.
2. Examples of mobilization field experiments include Arceneaux and Nickerson (2005); Gerber and Green (1999; 2000a; 2001); Gerber, Green, and Larimer (2008); Gerber, Green, and Kaplan (2004); Gerber, Green, and Green (2003); Gerber, Green, and Shachar (2003); Green, Gerber, and Nickerson (2003); Green and Gerber (2004); Green and Krasno (1988); Nickerson, Friedrichs, and King (2006); Panagopoulos (2009); Rubenson and Loewen (2010).
3. For a discussion on conducting field experiments with political elites, see Loewen, Rubenson, and Wantchekon (2010).

Chapter 12

CONTENT ANALYSIS

Linda Trimble and Natasja Treiberg, University of Alberta

DESTINATION

By the end of this chapter the reader should

- understand what content analysis is and how it is used in political science research;
- explain the strengths and weaknesses of content analysis as a research design; and
- describe the ethical considerations related to content analysis.

WHAT IS CONTENT ANALYSIS?

Content analysis is a systematic quantitative research technique used to analyze the message characteristics in any form of communication. By employing this method of gathering and analyzing information, researchers can methodically account for the content in a text (or texts). **Content** is any message that can be communicated, including words, meanings, symbols, or themes (Neuendorf 2002, 1, 227). A **text** is any form of communication, be it written, visual, spoken, or even sung (Neuman 2007, 227). The conversation you just had with your friends after class constitutes a text; so does a music video. For students of politics, relevant texts include government documents such as press releases, Hansard records of legislative debates, Supreme Court decisions, Royal Commission reports, policy information presented in government advertisements or on government websites, and, of course, actual legislation. But we also find political content in political party election advertisements, talk radio debates, protest signs and slogans, and even in country music lyrics. Mass media texts are ripe for political analysis, as there is a great deal to be learned from examining mainstream media coverage of politics on television, on radio, and in newspapers, and also from looking at web-based texts such as blogs, websites, social networking sites, and Twitter. In short, there is a wealth of political messages out there, ready to be examined with content analysis techniques.

WHY USE CONTENT ANALYSIS?

Political scientists use content analysis because it can help them answer, in a systematic, reliable, and rigorous manner, important and interesting questions about the ways in which political issues and actors are represented, or ideas, assumptions, and norms are conveyed. For example, from reading the newspaper and watching TV news, you might have the impression that media coverage of electoral politics is quite critical of parties and their leaders, but without evidence to back up your observation it is merely an impression. Content analysis provides reliable evidence. Indeed, Stuart Soroka and Blake Andrew used content analysis to analyze news about the 2004 and 2006 national election campaigns printed in seven major daily newspapers across Canada, analyzing 6,694 articles in total (2010, 114). While most coverage was neutral, when evaluations of political parties and their leaders were offered, the assessments were much more likely to be negative than positive. Because Soroka and Andrew examined all of the coverage (a **census**), and tested for **intercoder reliability** (checking to see that different coders came up with the same interpretation), their findings are dependable. In other words, these researchers can say with confidence that newspaper coverage of parties and their leaders in recent Canadian elections is predominantly negative in tone.

Content analysis allows measurement of many features of political communication, including structural and substantive aspects. **Structural features** focus on the structure of the communication or how it is conveyed. For newspaper articles, important structural features are the type of story (for example, hard news, opinion, editorial, feature), its location in the newspaper, its length, and who wrote it. The **substantive features** of a communication can be measured by focusing on what is said—the words, themes, ideas, or symbols in a text. With substantive measures it is important to note the distinction between manifest and latent content in communications. **Manifest content** is the literal, or surface, meaning of the message (Neuman 2007, 229). **Latent content** is the underlying or implied meaning (Sumser 2001, 200). Manifest content is much easier to account for and measure objectively with content analysis, while latent content is trickier because its meanings are often a matter of interpretation. For example, determining whether or not the physical appearance (looks, clothing, hairstyle) of a politician is mentioned in newspaper stories is straightforward; assessing what these representations imply about gender politics requires careful thought and attention to validity in measurement.

Content analysis is a useful methodological tool for many approaches to political science research, including cross-sectional, comparative, case study, and longitudinal research designs. Because content analysis can be used to compare many different types of texts, it lends itself nicely to a cross-sectional analysis. For example, Elizabeth Gidengil and Joanna Everitt (1999; 2000; 2003) carefully analyzed the behaviours of male and female party leaders during televised leaders' debates in the 1993, 1997, and 2000 Canadian national elections, and compared the actual behaviour of the leaders with the reporting of the debates by television news. They found that the aggressive behaviours of female leaders were exaggerated by the news media while the combative performances of male leaders were normalized. Examples of comparative research featuring content analysis include multinational comparisons of political party manifestos (see Burnham et al. 2004, 239–10). Content analysis of political party documents has been used to develop case studies as well, for instance, an examination of publications by the British far-right, anti-immigrant National Front Party (see Burnham et al. 2004, 238). Content analysis also lends itself quite well to longitudinal analysis, allowing the researcher to map changes in communications over time. For example, Trimble (1997; 1998) detailed the amount and type of attention to women's political interests and claims in Alberta legislative debates between 1972 and 1994 and was able to demonstrate shifts over time reflecting the increased representation of women in the Legislative Assembly. Content analysis can even supplement experimental research designs. Iyengar (1996) coupled content analysis with an experiment to investigate how television's reliance on episodic news framing (which focuses on the specific news event and does not explain its history or context) affects the viewing public's understanding of, and attribution of political responsibility for, political issues.

CONTENT ANALYSIS RESEARCH IN CANADA

Content analysis is frequently used to analyze media representations of politics. Canadians don't typically experience political life first-hand, by participating in political parties or interest groups, but rather are spectators to politics. As a result, the mass media, especially news media, play a significant political role because they provide the lenses through which most citizens see the political world. Because media coverage has the potential to shape what we know, and think, about politics (Nesbitt-Larking 2007, 333–7) it is useful for political scientists to know what the media are saying about politics and how they are saying it. A few examples of content analysis of media texts will illustrate the vibrancy of this research trajectory in Canada.

One notable study is Sauvageau, Taras, and Schneiderman's book *Last Word*, which provides a detailed account of media coverage of Supreme Court of Canada decisions in English- and French-language television broadcasts and newspapers (2005). Research on media coverage of Canadian elections has examined the issues that are raised, how elections are framed, and how parties and their leaders are evaluated (see Soroka and Andrew 2010; Trimble and Sampert 2004). Additionally, analysis of media coverage of women politicians reveals differences in reporting of male and female party leaders and leadership candidates (Everitt and Camp 2009; Gidengil and Everitt 1999; 2000; 2003; Trimble 2007; Trimble and Everitt 2010). The adequacy of media reporting of public policy issues has been assessed with content analysis as well; for instance, Pilon (2009) scrutinized Ontario broadsheet newspaper coverage of the province's referendum on electoral reform and Gingras, Sampert, and Gagnon-Pelletier (2010) compared English- and French-language newspaper framing of the Gomery Inquiry into the 'sponsorship scandal'.

Unfortunately, to date, relatively few Canadian political scientists use content analysis to account for the messages in other types of political texts such as government documents. However, some examples do exist, including work by Trimble and Tremblay who have both employed this method very successfully in their analyses of legislative debates (Tremblay 1998; Trimble 1997; 1998). Soroka, Penner, and Blidook (2009) constructed a content analytic database of all oral questions asked during Question Period in the Canadian House of Commons between mid-1983 and 2004 and used it to explore the relationship between constituency interests and the legislative behaviour of MPs. As well, Soroka (2002) mixed content analysis with survey research and other empirical methods to analyze policy agenda setting by policymakers. Small (2007) has also used content analysis to examine the Internet as a party campaign tool during the 2004 Canadian national election. The role of citizens and civil society groups in communicating political ideas, to each other in their newsletters or blogs, and to the public through everything from YouTube to public demonstrations, could also be explored with content analysis techniques.

HOW IS IT DONE?

Content analysis research uses objective and systematic counting and classification procedures to 'produce a quantitative description of the symbolic content in the text' (Neuman 2007, 227). It typically proceeds in a series of steps (some of which are detailed by Manheim et al. 2008, 181–4). The first step is the key to effective content analysis—determining the research question. A clear, concise research question is essential because a vague or imprecise question cannot be operationalized. As discussed in Chapter 4, **operationalization** is the 'process of moving from the conceptual definition of a construct to a set of specific activities or measures that allow a researcher to observe it empirically' (Neuman 2007, 370). A question such as, What do Rick Mercer's rants say about Canadian politics? is difficult to answer because the concepts ('say about' and 'Canadian politics') are too broad. A more precise question might work: Which Canadian political actors or institutions does Rick Mercer criticize in his rants?

The second step is to choose the **population** and **unit of analysis** (Manheim et al. 2008, 181–2). The population is the communications sources most appropriate to answering the research question. Examples include newspaper articles, speeches, legislative debates, newscasts, movies, songs, blogs, political advertisements, and so on. A researcher can also decide to look at more than one form of communication (for example, both newspaper and television coverage of an event). The unit of analysis is the portion of a text that will be coded, and it does not need to be the entire text. In the case of a newspaper article, the researcher could examine the entire article (for example, Soroka and Andrew 2010) or focus on the headline (for example, Trimble and Sampert 2004) or compare the content of the headline with the article (for example, Andrew 2007). With the Rick Mercer example, the unit of analysis is one segment of the weekly *Rick Mercer Report* program, the short spots identified as 'Rick's Rant', in which Rick delivers biting commentary on some aspect of Canadian politics or culture.

Once the texts have been selected and the unit of analysis determined, the researcher establishes which cases will be included in the analysis. This is often referred to as a sample of the cases, though sometimes it is appropriate to look at all the cases (a census). The census approach worked for Abu-Laban and Trimble's (2010) analysis of Canadian newspaper coverage of Muslim-Canadians during the 2000, 2004, and 2006 Canadian federal elections because even though they searched 8 newspapers, only 67 news stories met the search criteria. But if the **universe** (all the texts available) is large, it must be narrowed to a manageable number. The decision about the size of the population depends on the research question as well as available resources, including time. One option is to carry out a nonrandom sample based on certain criteria that are logical and clearly related to the research problem, for instance by reducing the number of sources or reducing the timeframe. With the *Rick Mercer Report* example, to determine whether Rick is more critical of the Conservatives than the Liberals, it makes sense to compare Rick's rants before and after the election of the Conservative government in 2006. Another option is to carry out a random sample of the texts, thus eliminating sampling bias. (Random [probability] sampling was discussed in Chapter 8.)

The fourth step is to determine the appropriate **measures**. What are the particular elements or characteristics in the text that you will account for in your study? Content analysis is used to systematically categorize different aspects of a communication. This process is called **coding**, and it can identify several types of characteristics of a text: idea, frequency, direction, intensity, prominence, and size. **Idea** refers to the issue or message being communicated. (For instance, do speeches by the minister of the environment make reference to the concept of climate change?) **Frequency** means whether or not something occurs in a text, and if it does, how often. (How often does the minister of the environment mention climate change in her speeches?) **Direction** means identifying the type of message by situating it along some sort of continuum or classification scheme. (When the minister mentions climate change, is she accepting the phenomenon as a fact, expressing skepticism about its very existence, or denying the phenomenon outright?) Content analysis can be used to measure the **intensity** of a message. (Is climate change emphasized through the minister's commanding rhetoric or with strong, emotive images?) **Prominence** can be important, too. (Is climate change the first issue mentioned in the minister's speeches?) An additional measure is the **size** of a message, that is, how much space or time it takes within the text. (What proportion of each speech is devoted to the topic of climate change?)

The fifth step is to develop a **codebook** that lists the items you plan to code (**variables**), and how you plan to count them (**values**). Values must be mutually exclusive (that is, they must not overlap) and collectively exhaustive (include all the possible answers to the question). In the *Rick Mercer Report* example, for instance, one variable could be 'Which political actor or institution is criticized?' In this case, the researcher might want to employ open coding before settling on a concrete list of values. Open coding requires listing, for each case, all the possible answers that appear in the texts. These can then be categorized for closed coding—coding each case based on a specific list of values. The codebook should outline consistent rules for coding the texts so that all coders are provided clear criteria for judgment. These coding notes may include observations about items you have decided to include or exclude as you go along, or detailed instructions for coding latent content. It is very important to test and retest the coding frame on a sample of the cases to resolve any coding issues. For example, if the testing shows that classifying the main focus of a news story is difficult, as many stories cover several issues or themes, this problem will need to be resolved before coding begins.

When the coding frame is completed, and fully tested, the researcher creates a **coding sheet** on which coders can record the values for each case. (A sample codebook and coding sheet are presented at the end of this chapter.) Coding all the cases in the sample is the penultimate step in the content analysis process. This means using the coding frame to answer the questions posed on each variable and writing the corresponding value onto the coding sheet for each case. As well, each case is assigned a **case identification** number as a way of locating it in the database. The final step is data entry and analysis. Typically researchers create SPSS or Excel files featuring a variable ID for each variable and the corresponding values for these variables. Data are entered from the coding sheets into the database. Once all the data are entered it is advisable to run frequencies on each variable to identify and correct any errors in data entry. From this point the quantitative data analysis can be conducted, including means (see Chapter 15), cross-tabulations (see Chapters 16 and 17), and regression analyses (see Chapter 18). Finally, the researcher analyzes the findings, determining how well the research question was answered and possibly deciding to test alternative hypotheses.

STRENGTHS AND WEAKNESSES

As with all research methods, content analysis has both strengths and weaknesses. When carefully designed and carried out, content analysis yields valid, rigorous, reliable, and replicable results. In other words, the study measures what it intends to measure, categories of measurement are precisely defined and consistently applied, and if the project were to be conducted by someone else, it would produce the same or very similar results. As well, content analysis facilitates examination of large volumes of text, and allows comparisons within and between texts, as well as over time. As an example, Linda Trimble (1997) wanted to know if electing more women to the Alberta legislature generated more legislative debate about women's experiences, issues, and policy demands. This meant looking at a large timeframe—1972 to 1994 (22 years)—to include periods when there were few women in the legislature to periods when the percentage of female MLAs met or exceeded 15 per cent of the total number of elected legislators. Trimble compared the amount of attention to women's issues by different legislative actors (cabinet ministers, backbenchers, government members, or opposition members) and by discrete time periods based on the number of women in the legislature. She demonstrated that electing more women did generate more attention to women's concerns, though typically female opposition MLAs were at the forefront of this discussion.

These important virtues of content analysis manifest two equally vexing drawbacks. First, content analysis is time-consuming and labour-intensive. Large volume studies require multiple coders, and the coding process itself can take a great deal of time, especially when coding latent content, as coders need to discuss possible interpretations and resolve coding differences. Second, the emphasis on **rigour** in measurement may mean that important messages are not captured by the analysis. For example, Trimble's data on legislative speeches about women measured the topics addressed by legislators but did not reveal whether the speakers or the speeches were sympathetic or hostile to women's policy needs and claims. (Trimble used discourse analysis—a qualitative research methodology—to identify the tone and direction of the comments, with feminist theory as a conceptual framework for analyzing the meanings conveyed by the Alberta MLAs in their discussion of women.) Also, as mentioned earlier, content analysis is much better at measuring manifest content than latent content. While it is easy to code the overt references within a text, it takes some ingenuity to identify the messages that are excluded or marginalized.

Trimble (1998) realized there were many 'missing women' in her first analysis of Alberta legislative debates, so she further developed the variable list to identify which groups of women were referenced. She found that Aboriginal women, women with disabilities, and lesbians were rarely if ever mentioned. As this example shows, content analysis can be reductionist and therefore can miss the most important meanings in the text. Sometimes the meaning structures of a text cannot be reduced to words or phrases or images. Visual communications are difficult to assess by using content analysis; for instance, the overall gist of an advertisement is not easily disaggregated.

Researchers using content analysis need to be particularly careful to take the validity of the data source and the context of the communication into account when designing their research projects. Who produces the text, and under what circumstances and conditions? What is the intended purpose of, and audience for, the communication? What are the biases of the data source? For instance, a study of the prime minister's statements to the press could take note of what he says to the media in press conferences, but it would be remiss if it did not also account for the gatekeeping function played by his communications staff, who determine which journalists are allowed to ask questions during scheduled interactions with the news media. As this example illustrates, all texts reflect 'antecedent choices, conditions or processes' (Riffe et al., 2005, 10). Texts are produced with particular audiences in mind, under particular rules and conditions, and through particular routines. These factors must be addressed when analyzing the content of a text or texts; after all, a Rick Mercer rant has a very different purpose, audience, and style of delivery than does the federal government's Speech from the Throne.

There is considerable potential for bias when accounting for latent messages in texts. The objectivity of this methodology cannot be assumed, and it is important to carefully examine the assumptions underlying the research design as well as the rigour with which the research was carried out (Hackett, Gilsdorf, and Savage 1992). Finally, content analysis cannot measure the impact of communications on their intended audiences, thus it cannot get at media effects or the impact of other types of political communications on citizen attitudes, opinions, and behaviours. For these reasons, content analysis can and often should be supplemented with additional data gathered through other research methods such as interviews, discourse analysis, and surveys (Neuendorf 2002, 69).

ETHICAL CONSIDERATIONS

One of the most important strengths of content analysis is that it is unobtrusive and nonreactive (Krippendorff 2004, 40; Riffe et al. 2005, 38). The texts have already been produced, so analyzing them doesn't have an impact on the time or convenience of others. As well, there is no danger of the texts being affected or influenced by the research process. Most texts analyzed by political scientists are in the public domain, and analyzing them does not raise ethical issues such as requiring the informed consent of the subject, or the need to guarantee subject confidentiality. However, if the researcher wishes to analyze communications that are considered personal or private, ethical concerns are raised, and both consent and confidentiality must be considered in the research design.

SAMPLE CODEBOOK AND CODING SHEET

Following is an excerpt from the codebook used by Linda Trimble, Laura Way, and Shannon Sampert to analyze election-related editorial cartoons printed by the *Globe and Mail* and the *National Post* during the 2004, 2006, and 2008 national elections (see Trimble, Way, and Sampert 2010). Note that this example does not replicate all the variables included in the study.

Codebook for Cartoons, 2004, 2006, and 2008 Elections

General Coding Notes: For editorial cartoons to be selected for coding, their focus must be the federal election.

Variable #	Variable Name	Values and Value labels
Structural Variables		
1	case id	Coding Notes: Case identification number begins with a C (for Cartoon), then the initials of the paper being coded, followed by the sequential number; Cnp1, Cnp2; Cgm1, Cgm2, etc.
2	election	1 = 2004 2 = 2006 3 = 2008
3	paper	1. *National Post* 2. *Globe and Mail*
Substantive Variables		
4	frame	What is the main frame of the cartoon? 1 = Game frame 2 = Issue frame 3 = Other (specify in variable 34) Coding Notes: Determine which is the dominant frame of the cartoon. *Game frame*: reflects a preoccupation with winners and losers, conflict, strategy and personalities. Words like winning, ahead, beats, etc. will be prominent in the cartoon *Issue frame*: refers to the focus on campaign issues, party platforms, party ideologies, or the government record on particular issues
5	liberal	Is the Liberal Party depicted in the cartoon? 1 = Yes 2 = No Coding Note: Code as yes <u>only</u> if the party is named (there is a separate measure for the party leader, below) *If the party's symbol is included, code as yes.*
6	conserv	Is the Conservative Party depicted in the cartoon? 1 = Yes 2 = No
7	ndp	Is the NDP depicted in the cartoon? 1 = Yes 2 = No
8	bq	Is the Bloc Québécois depicted in the cartoon? 1 = Yes 2 = No

Sample Coding Sheet

Case id	election	paper	frame	liberal	conserv	ndp	bq	othparty
CNP1	1	1	1	2	1	2	2	2
CGM1	1	2	2	1	2	2	2	2
CGM2								
CNP2								

WORKING AS A TEAM

1. Your team plans to do a content analysis of provincial Throne Speeches given since 2005 to explore the evolving issue priorities of your provincial government. (For an example of a content analysis of Speeches from the Throne, see Stuart Soroka, *Agenda-Setting Dynamics in Canada*, Vancouver: UBC Press, 2002, pp. 64-6.) Would your project involve a census or a sample of the Throne Speeches? What measures would you consider?

2. Develop a codebook and coding sheet for your study. Print a copy of the most recent provincial Speech from the Throne, and complete the sheet. Does your completed coding sheet match the results of your team members?

SELF-STUDY

1. You are curious about the gender of journalism, specifically whether the authoritative voices of television news are more likely to be male than female. Your project contrasts the presence of women as anchors, reporters, and experts on the CBC National News broadcast with the equivalent national news broadcast of a private broadcaster (CTV or Global National). Choose one weekday for your study and watch the CBC and CTV (or Global) broadcast: both are available online. Using the coding sheet on page 222, record the number of males and females in each category for the top five stories in each broadcast.

2. Record the topic for each story in exercise 1. It may be the case, for instance, that male reporters and experts are more likely to report on so-called hard news stories such as economic issues, politics, or conflict whereas women are assigned to soft news stories (human interest, good news, lifestyle, entertainment). Tabulate and analyze your results. Is TV news a level playing field for women and men, or does it continue to illustrate a gendered division of labour?

CBC	Topic	Anchor(s)		Reporter(s)		Experts	
		Male	Female	Male	Female	Male	Female
Story #1							
Story #2							
Story #3							
Story #4							
Story #5							

CTV or Global	Topic	Anchor		Reporter(s)		Experts	
		Male	Female	Male	Female	Male	Female
Story #1							
Story #2							
Story #3							
Story #4							
Story #5							

Chapter 13

ELITE INTERVIEWS

DESTINATION

By the end of this chapter the reader should

- understand the types of research questions suited to elite interview research;
- appreciate the ethical issues that must be considered when conducting elite interview research; and
- know the basic steps of conducting elite interviews for political research.

Many research questions that political scientists encounter require specialized or 'inside' information. For example, to study the dynamics of a party caucus, we can interview members of that caucus. To create a leadership profile of a provincial premier, we can discuss his or her style with top aides or with other elected representatives. To describe how a particular public policy decision was made, we can interview elected officials, public servants, and key stakeholders who are involved in that policy field.

Elite interviews are an important tool for political science research. An 'elite' in this sense is an individual or a group with access to the specialized information we need. Thus, the term 'elite' is not used in the conventional sense, which suggests privileged political or economic elites (although they may in fact be the group you are studying).

Elite interviews take on the tone of a conversation, but some important differences exist. In interviews, one person asks questions and the other answers. In a 'normal' conversation, each individual contributes equally, and there is an exchange of ideas. (Of course, we have all had conversations in which the level of contribution is unbalanced; when it is the other person, rather than ourselves, who is dominating the discussion, we often consider the speaker to be a bit of a bore!) In ordinary conversation, if we do not wish to answer a question, we have the option of changing the subject or making a joke. Usually, the other person picks up on such cues and lets the issue pass. In an interview, however, the interviewer is likely to return to these 'dismissed' questions in her efforts to obtain the necessary data.

QUESTIONS SUITED TO INTERVIEW RESEARCH

Interviews are particularly valuable for **exploratory research** or **inductive research**. Recall from Chapter 2 that, unlike deductive hypothesis-testing, inductive research seeks broad information to aid in the formulation of new theories and hypotheses. Elite interviewing can be very useful in this process. When little knowledge exists about a subject or when researchers wish to go beyond existing theories and approaches, interview research can help to establish a rich understanding of the topic. For example, Christopher Alcantara (2007) interviewed 28 individuals, including federal and provincial officials and Innu and Inuit respondents, to assess comprehensive land claim negotiation outcomes in Labrador. In particular, he was interested in explaining why the Labrador Inuit Land Claims Agreement was successfully signed, while the Innu were unable to complete their agreement. Going beyond previous research that focused on the roles of federal and provincial governments, he argues that First Nations also play an important role in negotiation outcomes. One advantage of interview research is that it allows the researcher to 'learn from respondents and acquire unexpected information that can lead to truly new ways of understanding the events being studied' (Manheim and Rich 1981, 134). With more structured forms of research (such as survey research), the relevance of particular issues has been predetermined: only issues that are addressed in the questionnaire are included in the study. In an interview, by contrast, the respondent is able to indicate what *she* feels to be important. By indicating her own priorities and concerns, the respondent may suggest to the researcher a new way of approaching the research question or new avenues to be explored in the research.

Interview research can be particularly useful for research questions that lack sufficient available data. **Policy analysis** often relies heavily on interview research. As Patton and Sawicki (1993, 98) explain, 'Often the analyst must quickly obtain data that have never been organized or tabulated. Experts in the area may be the best source of such information; they will often know where to locate unpublished material or who else to contact.' In many cases, the interview respondent wishes to be of maximum assistance to the researcher and makes valuable suggestions for the research study. For example, a respondent may direct the researcher to contacts for additional interviews, or may suggest to the researcher particular documents, records, or sources that will further the research study.

Explanatory research is also well served by interviews. Why was a particular decision made? Who were the key actors? What are the organizational procedures? What were the circumstances surrounding a particular event? Answers to such questions often cannot be found in written documents, and the questions may not be well suited to a survey. For example, Leo and Enns (2009) used unstructured interviews in their analysis of the implementation of a federal-provincial immigration agreement in Vancouver. By interviewing BC provincial and municipal government officials and community representatives, they were able to clarify the provincial government's perspectives on the agreement and identify community concerns about the agreement. An advantage of elite interviewing is that researchers can access very detailed, directed, and often private, otherwise inaccessible information. Information and opinions that a respondent would feel uncomfortable describing in an email or writing on a mail-back survey can often be addressed in an intensive interview. The personal contact that occurs during an interview allows for a sense of rapport to develop between the interviewer and the respondent; over the course of the interview trust develops, and the interviewee is more likely to discuss the issues of interest. In addition, the respondent sets aside a greater amount of time for a personal interview than for telephone or mail-back surveys, or for email communications. This allows for more detailed data than can be accessed by other means.

Many political and policy research questions require an understanding of context or political processes. Research on political or policymaking processes often requires interviewing. As Putt and Springer (1989, 144) explain, 'Organizations rarely run completely by stated procedures. Program processes and procedures are shaped and reshaped as the program evolves. Intensive interviewing of program managers and staff is an important means of documenting current procedures used in organizational processes. Interviews also provide insight into the conditions that affect these procedures and the ways in which they have evolved.' In his research on economic union reform in Canada and Australia, Canadian political scientist Douglas Brown (2002) used elite interviewing to understand the intergovernmental policymaking process in each country, conducting approximately 70 interviews with key actors. As he explains, '[T]he interviews covered considerable ground, including such topics as: the rationale for reform; assessment of the federal system; specific reform objectives of governments; the nature of representations and pressures from social groups (including business); the intergovernmental negotiation process; and an assessment of the policy outcomes' (2002, 14). Such information could be accessed only through elite interviews.

Finally, research on **small** or **hard-to-reach populations** is also well suited to interviews. For many research questions the size of the elite or group under study is very small and/or is difficult to access. Certain individuals, including politicians, deputy ministers, and business elites, are less likely to respond to a survey than to an interview. Paul Thomas (2008), for example, interviewed six politicians and public servants in his analysis of Manitoba intergovernmental relations. Brown's research, noted earlier in this chapter, included interviews with deputy ministers and assistant deputy ministers. For some elites, being selected for an interview presents a welcome opportunity to talk at length, explaining personal and political choices. Such interviews can give the researcher a rich understanding of historical background.

Interviews are not appropriate for all research questions. Obviously, the process is very time-consuming. In addition to the time spent on the interview itself, the researcher needs to factor in the possibility that respondents will have difficulties fitting the interview into their busy schedules. This can lead to delays in data-gathering. Given the demands placed on both the researcher's time and the respondents' time, interviews should not be used when the necessary information can be more efficiently obtained through other means.

The ability to test hypotheses is limited with interview research, because there can be difficulties in processing and comparing data. Unlike standardized surveys, each interview is unique. The researcher usually has a set of central questions to address in the interview, but he may choose to add additional questions in the course of the interview. The conversational style of interviews can lead respondents in different directions, depending upon their personal interests and experiences. Thus, while some 'core' data can be compared across respondents, other data may not be amenable to comparisons. Overall, 'interviews are likely to be most useful for facts, history, and projections. . . . they are likely to be less useful for either a theoretical explanation of what is going on (that is, a model) or a clear and reasoned delineation of goals. These must usually come from your own familiarity with theory and your literature review' (Weimer and Vining 2005, 320).

It is important to always keep in mind that interviewing is *reactive*: the respondents are aware that their answers will be used in a research study, and this may lead them to alter the information given. Thus the survey research problems with interviewer effects and 'created opinion' discussed in Chapter 9 are by no means absent in interviewing. People do not wish to look unknowledgeable and prefer to be seen in the best possible light. The desires for self-promotion and self-protection can lead people to embellish or downplay certain issues; the temptation to act as one's own 'spin doctor' is great. In addition, interviewees may present you with information that, although they believe it to be true, is in fact erroneous. (They may also mislead or lie.) Thus, the possibility exists that a researcher will collect data that are either partially or completely false. For this reason, researchers must remember to 'never treat what interviewees say as factual data, but rather *treat the fact that they said it as data*' (Manheim and Rich 1981, 134). If, for example, a respondent reports that the majority of Canadians support a carbon tax, we treat the *belief* as data. Beliefs and perceptions strongly influence individual actions and are interesting in their own right. However, if we are interested in a particular 'fact' put forth by a respondent, the onus is on the researcher to verify the fact, in this case, by exploring opinion poll data.

ETHICS AND INTERVIEW RESEARCH

As noted in Chapter 5, it is important to ensure that research participants are not harmed as a result of your research. This may include protecting the participant's identity. With elite interviewing, the researcher must clarify to informants *prior to the interview* if data collected during the interview will be attributed to the individual, or if the interview will be treated as confidential or anonymous. Protection of identities for individuals holding public office is not required *if* the individual agrees to an on-the-record interview and *if* that agreement is conveyed through signed consent that explicitly waives anonymity.

It is also important to be clear and honest about the purpose of your research. This not only ensures more ethical research, but also facilitates your current and future research. Bardach (2009, 77) writes, 'Your informants will often be acquainted with one another and will occasionally talk among themselves about you and your work. Since you want such discussions to serve your interests rather than to work against them, you should try to develop a reputation as a competent, knowledgeable, and energetic researcher who is likely to produce something of intellectual or political significance. The best way to develop such a reputation is to actually be such a person.'

INTERVIEW PROCEDURES

The first step in interview research is to figure out who you want to interview. Which individuals have the information necessary to answer your research questions? You may generate this list based on job descriptions (for example, public managers, Members of Parliament, leaders of nonprofit organization), memberships (for example, members of political parties or interest groups), social groups, or other criteria suited to your research question. Interview research is almost always based on nonprobability sampling, with a relatively small number of cases selected. Because of the limited number of cases, researchers typically use purposive sampling, carefully selecting individuals to interview.

Your next task is to contact potential respondents and request an interview. One strategy that can be effective is to first contact the individual in writing and then follow up by telephone. It may be easier to get a response from potential respondents if you are able to mention an individual whom they know, mention an organizational affiliation, and/or write the letter on organizational letterhead. (However, you must be certain that you have clear permission from the noted individual and organization before you do so!) In your written communication, be certain to clarify the purpose of the discussion and the anticipated length of the interview. It should be noted that it may require a number of attempts before you are able to schedule an interview with a respondent. If, after you follow up by telephone, a potential respondent fails to respond to your request for an interview, Pierce (2008, 121) suggests that you 'write again. Attach a copy of your earlier letter. Be gently persistent.' In following up in such cases, it is important to be cautious not to badger or annoy the individual or his staff. Similarly, if a potential respondent declines your request for an interview, accept this gracefully and do not attempt to convince her.

Bardach (2009, 92–3) suggests that researchers be strategic in when they schedule interviews over the research process. Individuals who are likely to be helpful or particularly knowledgeable should be interviewed in the early stages of your research, because they can direct you to additional sources and may provide access to both information and people. Individuals who are likely to be very busy or potentially hostile should be interviewed at a later stage, allowing you to go into the interview as informed as possible. Bardach (2009, 79) writes, 'When you suspect that access to an informant may be exhausted relatively quickly, defer interviewing her until later in the research process, principally because your accumulated knowledge will then support a more productive interview.'

Before conducting the interview, it is important for the researcher to be clear on the data he is seeking. Interview time can pass quickly, and many respondents are fascinating people; it is very possible for the interview time to expire before the researcher has obtained all the necessary information. Note, too, that time is scarce for many people, researcher and respondent alike. For these reasons, it is advisable to have an **interview framework** before entering an interview. The framework is merely a set of questions to be asked of the respondent. Using a framework keeps the researcher on track during the interview and ensures that important, core questions are asked in each interview. This allows the researcher to compare answers provided by different respondents. The researcher still retains flexibility during the interview: inserting questions as they fit naturally into the discussion (rather than necessarily sticking to a preset ordering) and inserting additional questions when necessary. The framework is only a guide to aid the interview, rather than a strict outline that must be followed absolutely. It also provides a useful cue to the interviewee that her time is not being wasted by inadequate preparation, and that the interviewer is not making it up as he goes along.

How does one create a framework? The researcher starts by asking himself, What do I want to know? What topics need to be addressed? What issues are of less importance? In essence, one must distinguish between what knowledge is wanted and what knowledge is needed, ensuring that the questions tapping 'needs' are given higher priority than the questions addressing 'wants'.

In order to ask productive questions, you will need to have a basic familiarity with the subject matter and context. You should learn as much as possible on your own prior to the interview, and incorporate this learning into your interview framework. Doing so creates personal credibility and demonstrates respect for your respondent's time. It may also make you aware of major controversies or sensitivities, and thus allow you to avoid missteps or gaffes during the interview. An additional advantage of doing background research is that it allows you to 'learn the language' relevant to your research question. Understanding and using the appropriate terminology establishes rapport and removes 'interviewer as outsider' tone (Putt and Springer 1989, 148).

Question ordering is important. The initial questions should lead into the subject area without threatening the respondent in any way; you may opt to start with simple, factual questions that the respondent can answer with relative ease.

Difficult, controversial or sensitive questions should be left for later in the interview, after a sense of rapport and comfort has had a chance to build. Always aim to end the interview on a positive, or at least neutral, note; to achieve this, end with more neutral questions (Patton and Sawicki 1993, 102). Woliver (2002, 677) recommends ending interviews with very open questions, such as, Is there anything you would like to tell me about which I haven't thought to ask you? This allows the respondent to bring unexpected information to your attention.

As with formulating survey questions, one needs to ensure that the questions are clear and not phrased in ways that 'lead' the respondent. In general, **close-ended questions** (such as questions that can be answered in a 'yes–no' manner) should be avoided; the goal is to promote discussion. You should also plan segues between discussion topics and *probes* (follow-up questions) to provide direction and encourage more comments. Probes are used for clarification (when details provided are vague or overly brief) and for elaboration (when details provided are vague or overly brief) (Putt and Springer 1989, 155).

In addition to drawing up an interview framework, the researcher can prepare by investigating the background of the interviewee. The purpose of this is twofold. First, it gives the researcher insights into the personality and style of the interviewee. Rapport is built most easily when we confront people who are similar to us in dress and energy; if you are aware that your interviewee is very formal in speech and dress, for example, matching her on these details can help build the initial comfort level of the interview. Background research also helps prevent the wasting of interview time on information that can be found elsewhere; for example, the interviewee's position in the government and the duties associated with that position might be found in public records. The interviewee has every reason to assume that a researcher has done her homework before conducting the interview; a researcher who devotes considerable interview time to information that can be easily found elsewhere may annoy individuals who see their time as scarce.

Elite interviews should be prescheduled to ensure that the interviewee has sufficient time to spend with the researcher. At the beginning of the interview the researcher should briefly explain the purpose of the meeting, and care must be taken to ensure that the information provided does not reveal your specific hypotheses. Recall that one problem with interviewing is that the process is subject to reaction: respondents consciously or unconsciously alter their behaviour and responses to fit the researcher's expectations, resulting in biased data. During the interview itself, the researcher should avoid 'leading' the interviewee with body language or facial expressions. If, for example, the researcher shows disapproval at certain types of statements, the interviewee may begin to guard her statements.

Meticulous notes should be taken throughout the interview, regardless of whether one makes an electronic recording. Recorders may have technical or sound problems (for example, some statements are inaudible), and recordings cannot capture nonverbal communication such as body language. The body language and voice intonation of the interviewee can prove as interesting as the statements themselves; it is useful to note if the respondent became nervous when a particular topic was broached or scowled when a certain name was mentioned. If a recorder is used, the researcher must first secure the consent of the interviewee. When taking notes, be as clear and thorough as possible; if a statement is particularly important, record it word by word so you can quote verbatim. After the interview, the researcher should write up the notes and transcribe the recording as quickly as possible. It takes very little time for the memory of the interview to fade, particularly if one is interviewing more than one person.

SUMMARY

Manheim and Rich (1981, 128) write, 'The personal interview is simultaneously one of the worst and one of the best data collection tools available to political scientists.' Done correctly, the elite interview can lead to new research insights and a richer understanding of the subject area. Done incorrectly, the data risk bias and are difficult to interpret, and the final results are of limited use. Interviewing skills take time and practice to develop. Although interviewing may appear simple in theory, in practice interview research can be challenging. That being said, interview research skills are a valuable skill set for political scientists, and it is worth taking the time to learn how to conduct interviews effectively.

APPLY YOUR UNDERSTANDING

Constructing an Interview Framework

You are investigating if male and female candidates enter politics for similar reasons. As part of your research design, you have decided that interviews are essential. But whom would you interview and why? Outline the topics you would wish to explore in the interview. What questions could be used to get the information you need? Draft an interview framework.

WORKING AS A TEAM

1. With a partner, conduct a mock 10-minute interview. (Yes, you will feel ridiculous doing so, but push through this!). One partner will assume the role of a provincial deputy minister of health, and the other partner will assume the role of the researcher who is interested in knowing why the government has not committed to building a new Children's Hospital in your city, despite public pressure to do so.

2. After the interview, share your thoughts on the following:

a. Interviewer: How difficult was it to take notes and conduct the interview at the same time? What note-taking strategies would you adopt in the future?

b. Interviewee: Where there any questions that you felt unable or unwilling to answer as a senior public servant? If so, why? How might the interviewer have reworded the question to get the information she or he needed?

SELF-STUDY

1. Your research project is to explore the leadership style of a prominent young politician with a reputation for his or her consensual approach to politics. How could you use elite interviewing to gain insights into this style?

2. Whom would you interview? What questions would you ask?

Chapter 14

OBSERVATION AND FOCUS GROUP RESEARCH

DESTINATION

By the end of this chapter the reader should

- know the distinction between obtrusive and unobtrusive observation research, and how they can inform political analysis; and
- understand what focus groups are, how they inform research, and why they are often used in triangulated research designs.

Surveys, interviews, content analysis, and, increasingly, experiments are commonly used data-collection techniques for political science research. But there are other options for data collection that are available. Two of these are observation research and focus groups.

OBSERVATION RESEARCH

One problem with research instruments such as surveys and interviews is that they leave the researcher dependent upon *reported* behaviours. At times, there can be significant disjunctures between reported and actual behaviour, in part because many things have normative social value. Because voting, for example, is seen as a social responsibility, many people claim to have voted when in fact they did not. Often the respondent truly believes he engaged in a particular action—for example, voting for the popular winning party rather than the 'losers'—that in fact he did not do. The possibility of faulty recall is particularly high for events that occurred in the past; as the months and years go by, we can forget whom we voted for, how many news programs we watched, and even what organizations we supported financially. This is an example of the background noise that is common to empirical research in political science and that can lessen the power of statistical analyses.

In addition to problems of reporting false behaviour, there is a tendency to over- and underestimate certain behaviours. For example, let's say you ask Nathan how many hours he studies every day. He reports four hours of concentrated study per day, yet his grades are much lower than classmates who study for the same amount of time. You are wondering what is going on, so you decide to watch Nathan study. Something interesting emerges: although he does indeed spend four hours in the library as he claims, much of that time is spent doing activities other than studying. Nathan spends 10 minutes arranging his papers, goes on three 20-minute coffee breaks, and devotes almost a full hour to rewriting his class notes (a very inefficient study technique). When all these factors are considered, he has actually devoted less than two hours to effective studying and has exaggerated his study time by 100 per cent. When we observe actual behaviour, rather than relying solely on reported behaviour, we are conducting **observation research**.

Observation research (also known as 'field research' and 'ethnography') has the advantage that events occur in natural circumstances, which means that the external validity of our study can be quite high. We engage in observation research on a casual basis in our everyday lives; 'people-watching' can be an enjoyable pastime. Observation allows us to explore interpersonal dynamics, and it is therefore useful for studying group dynamics and political processes. In such research we pay particular attention to context; cultural settings and power relations figure prominently. In fact, ethnography is the process of 'describing a culture and understanding another way of life from the native point of view' (Neuman 1994, 333).

Observation research can be obtrusive or unobtrusive (Manheim et al. 2002, 332). **Obtrusive observation** occurs when the subjects are aware that they are being observed. In private forums or small group settings where the researcher's presence is sure to be noticed, research must be *overt*: the researcher informs the subjects that they are being observed as part of a research project. For example, a researcher may receive permission to sit in on a committee session and watch the dynamics: who speaks and for how long, what are the responses, what is the mood, and so on. Of course, there exists the possibility again for reaction problems: if the subjects know they are being watched, they may begin to alter their behaviour. This phenomenon—altering one's behaviour when under observation—is known as the *Hawthorne effect*. To minimize this, the researcher must take care not to reveal his hypotheses and does *not* take extensive notes. The goal is for the group or individual to proceed with their activities *as if the researcher were not there*, which requires the researcher to be as inconspicuous as possible. If the researcher is taking detailed notes, his presence is felt more readily. For this reason, the researcher should develop extensive notes immediately after the observations have been completed for the day.

Unobtrusive observation occurs when the subjects are unaware of the researcher; they do not know about the research study and proceed with their activities in a normal manner. For example, a researcher might sit in Parliament and observe MPs' behaviour without informing the members. When the forum is public, this can be the best way to conduct observation research.

One particular type of unobtrusive observation research is **participant observation**. In this strategy, the researcher becomes part of the community that she is observing. For example, to study the dynamics among political campaign staff, she may volunteer for a campaign. One advantage of participant observation is that it

EXPAND YOUR KNOWLEDGE
The Hawthorne Effect

Earle Babbie (1989, 215–16) provides us with the following summary of the Hawthorne effect:

The need for control groups in social research became clear in connection with a series of studies of employee satisfaction conducted by F.J. Roethlisberger and W.J. Dickson (1939) in the late 1920s and 1930s. These two researchers studied working conditions in the telephone 'bank wiring room' [at the Hawthorne plant] of the Western Electric Works in Chicago, attempting to discover what changes in working conditions would improve employee satisfaction and productivity.

To the researchers' great satisfaction, they discovered that making working conditions better consistently increased satisfaction and productivity. As the workroom was brightened up by better lighting, for example, productivity went up. Lighting was further improved, and productivity went up again. To further substantiate their scientific conclusion, the researchers then dimmed the lights: Productivity again improved!

It became evident that the wiring room workers were responding more to the attention given them by researchers than to improved working conditions. As a result of this phenomenon, often called the **Hawthorne effect**, social researchers have become more sensitive to and cautious about the possible effects of experiments themselves. The use of a proper control group—studied intensively without any of the working conditions changed otherwise—would have pointed to the existence of this effect in the wiring room study.

Source: Babbie, E. *The Basics of Social Research*, 5e. © 2011 Wadsworth, a part of Cengage Learning, Inc. Reproduced by permission. www.cengage.com/permissions

allows for greater understanding of context: by becoming a member of the group, one has maximum access to that group's beliefs and world paradigm. An action may have significantly different meaning in a particular group context than in the world at large, and in some cases being a member of the group is the only way that a researcher can access this information. Finally, there are some subgroups that can be accessed only through covert participant observation. Consider a sociologist exploring a particular religious cult or a police officer investigating drug smuggling. Neither group could be penetrated unless the researcher assumed the identity of a group member.

Participant observation is very context-driven and less structured than other forms of observation research, rendering it particularly useful for descriptive and exploratory research (Brown 1981, 173). As with other forms of observation research, note-taking should be kept to a minimum in the presence of the research subjects; in the case of covert observation, note-taking might be restricted to times when the researcher is completely removed from the subjects.

For participant observation to work effectively, the researcher must be accepted into the group. The process of building trust and rapport can be time-consuming, but is necessary for valid data. W. Lawrence Neuman (1994, 339) notes that 'Entry [to a group] is more analogous to peeling the layers of an onion than to opening a door.' To access very sensitive information, the researcher must obtain high levels of trust and respect in the group. This can involve adopting the dress, speech patterns, social interests, and personal style of group members; the researcher needs to not only 'talk the talk' but also 'walk the walk' if he is to be trusted with group secrets and viewpoints. In some cases, assuming the status as a group member can be a difficult task. In the late 1950s, John Griffin sought to study the black community of New Orleans. A white man, he used drugs prescribed by a dermatologist to darken his skin and shaved his head to conceal his straight hair. He then experienced life as a black man and recounted his experiences in the classic *Black Like Me* (1960).

Participant observation carries a number of risks. First, certain forms of participant observation may put the researcher at physical risk should his purposes be discovered. After the publication of his study, Griffin was hanged in effigy and his family harassed. A second risk comes from the association with the group. Let's imagine that a researcher, studying neo-Nazism in Canada, joins a neo-Nazi group. After the researcher has completed her study, she will always be plagued by that association; taken out of context, she may be seen as a true supporter of the group. Some affiliations can be difficult to shake and may be used to damage the researcher's credibility. For example, in 1963 Gloria Steinem took a job as a Playboy Bunny (a waitress position, not a 'Playmate', which is a nude model) to investigate how women were treated in the Playboy clubs. Later, Steinem became a leader in the mainstream feminist movement, and the former Bunny association, taken out of context, proved at times a liability. She reports '[c]ontinuing publishing by *Playboy* magazine of my employee photograph as a Bunny amid ever more pornographic photos of other Bunnies. The 1983 version [of the Steinem photo] insists in a caption that my article 'boosted Bunny recruiting' (1983, 69).

A third potential problem with participant observation involves exiting the group. It is possible that one can do such a good job convincing others of group status that disengagement is problematic. Also, the researcher may have developed friendships that are difficult to leave. Finally, the researcher faces the risk of becoming so entrenched in a group and so identified with its positions that objectivity is lost (Chadwick et al. 1984, 214). A researcher's sympathy for the group and its causes may lead her to forget why she is there, and rather than providing a balanced analysis of the group, she may turn into an apologist. This problem of bias may lead all her conclusions to be suspect.

Observation research, be it obtrusive or unobtrusive, can vary in the degree to which it is structured or unstructured. When observation is unstructured, the researcher typically is not looking for any particular patterns; the research is mostly inductive and exploratory. Here, the researcher can consider both the specific behaviours of the subjects and the subjective values attached to those actions (Brown 1981, 169). However, even with unstructured research, the observer should develop a number of issue areas that he wishes to explore that will help direct his study by

EXPAND YOUR KNOWLEDGE
Participant Observation with the Reform, Canadian Alliance, and Conservative Parties

It should come as no surprise that many political scientists move back and forth between the study and practice of politics. Indeed, much of the richness and excitement of the social sciences in general comes from this interplay. Political scientists have a wide array of applied skills and knowledge: they have substantive expertise, an ability to write and to think analytically, often a detailed understanding of the public policy process, and, in many cases, a comprehensive grasp of empirical research methodologies. In this last case, they know how to collect data, orchestrate surveys, design questionnaires, and make complex data stand up and sing for diverse sets of clients.

However, participant observation means more than applying or marketing one's analytical skills. It entails working for governments, parties, interest groups, social movements, or community associations with the objective of improving one's understanding of the political process. Participant observation, therefore, goes well beyond providing a source of anecdotes and illustrations to use in class.

Tom Flanagan, a professor from the Department of Political Science at the University of Calgary, has considerable experience working with political parties. In 1991 he was hired as the director of policy, strategy, and communications for the Reform Party of Canada, a position he held until the end of 1992. Flanagan's experiences were woven into his 1995 book *Waiting for the Wave: The Reform Party and Preston Manning*. (A second edition was released in 2009.) The book draws on Flanagan's participant observation and goes well beyond his direct experience in providing a detailed historical account of the party and a theoretical treatment of the Reform party's place on the Canadian political landscape.

Flanagan also worked with Stephen Harper for a number of years, first with Canadian Alliance and then with the Conservative party. He retired from the Conservative party after the 2006 election, when Harper became prime minister. He has written about his experiences with these parties in *Harper's Team: Behind the Scenes in the Conservative Rise to Power* (2007; updated in 2009).

leading him to pay greater attention to particular issues and dynamics. The data collected in unstructured observations are collected as **fieldnotes**, detailed descriptions of events and their subjective meanings. The researcher later takes these fieldnotes and looks for emerging groupings, categories, or patterns (Brown 1981, 177).

More structured (and thus more quantitative) research is necessary for hypothesis-testing. In this research, the observer considers only the actions that occur. Prior to the observations, she draws up an **observation schedule**, which is essentially a checklist for recording behaviour (Brown 1981, 178). For example, in our study of parliamentary behaviour, we might create a checklist to tick off who spoke and for how long. Our prior research has suggested to us ways by which to classify behaviours; all we do during the observation research is note frequencies of behaviour. After the session, we examine the data to see if the results fit our hypotheses.

When creating the observation schedule, we must ensure that our indicators are clear; if we leave categories broadly defined, we may have trouble deciding if a given behaviour fits into a particular category. For example, imagine that you are observing a city council session to see if female politicians are more consensual than their male colleagues. How are you going to determine what counts as 'consensual' behaviour? Will voice tone be included? Efforts to compromise? An explicit desire to avoid arguments? Clearly, observing 'consensual behaviour' can be quite subjective if specific indicators of such behaviour are not included. In addition, if we do not have clearly defined ideas of what a given behaviour is, we may be inconsistent between observations. At one council meeting we may be in a good mood and see everything as efforts to compromise. At a meeting later in the week, after a long day that included a minor car accident and getting yelled at by a co-worker, the world may not seem so rosy, and very little is seen as 'consensual'. Using specific indicators of behaviour can help overcome such problems. A number of the rules from survey research also apply to the creation of observation indicators: researchers should first operationalize their key concepts to develop valid measures and should ensure that the categories available are mutually exhaustive (that all possible categories are included in the schedule) (Brown 1981, 179).

Overall, observation strategies are an important means by which researchers can explore what *really* happens in groups. They give the role of context its due and provide a richer understanding of social dynamics. However, the method requires a great deal of the researcher's time: it is not a method for the uncommitted! Also, in the realm of politics, there are a number of areas that are not open to observation, such as cabinet dynamics. In such cases, researchers must rely on first-hand accounts through elite interviewing or written documentation.

APPLY YOUR UNDERSTANDING

Constructing an Observation Schedule

Your task is to explore the interpersonal dynamics of political science professors at the annual faculty retreat. You suspect that as seniority increases, faculty members are more likely to raise 'thorny' issues and vigorously defend their positions. In other words, you suspect that a sessional instructor will not raise such issues, while an associate professor will, and that the assistant professor is more likely to back down on her position than is the full professor. Develop your schedule, and identify your key concepts. How will you define 'thorny' issues? How will you categorize the faculty? What will constitute 'raising' and/or 'supporting' an issue?

FOCUS GROUPS

When hearing the term 'focus group', many people immediately think of market research, in which a small group sits in a room and discusses the pros and cons of a product. Is it too harsh? Too bright? Too expensive? Focus groups are also important research tools for policy research, political parties, and campaign organizers. They enable researchers to probe beneath the surface of public opinion, to explore what people *really* like or dislike about political parties, leaders, policies, or advertisements.

While a questionnaire in a survey research project may get hundreds and perhaps thousands of individuals to address a topic for a few minutes, a focus group will pull a small handful of people together to discuss the same topic for an extended period. Focus groups are not designed to be representative; they are simply designed to bring together a group of individuals to discuss a specific product or issue at length and in depth. For example, in her study of rural women's political participation, Louise Carbert (2006) conducted 14 focus groups with a total of 126 women in Atlantic Canada. The focus group approach allowed for a more fulsome understanding of women's political engagement.

Focus groups can provide a useful complement to conventional survey research. They allow the researcher to dig beneath the surface opinion captured by the larger survey, to probe for details and nuance. Gupta (2001) writes, 'Focus groups can shed light on complex areas of public policies and other important issues that might be missed by a survey, which can be too structured.' Luntz (1994) presents a similar argument: 'Unlike traditional quantitative research, focus groups are centrally concerned with *understanding* attitudes rather than *measuring* them.'

Running a focus group effectively is not something that just anyone can do. Managing the interpersonal dynamics and drawing out opinions without imposing the researcher's own biases are art forms in themselves. Questions are open-ended, and the facilitator must guide the group discussion to remain focused on the topic. To do so, the facilitator must be clear about the goals of the focus group; she will have a number of scripted questions and prompts but will be flexible in moving between these as the conversation naturally unfolds. The facilitator also must be flexible in allowing the discussion to veer off-course on occasion, as this may allow for unanticipated but valuable information.

The composition of the focus group can be key to its success. Homogenous groups often work best. Luntz (1994) writes, 'Human behavioral studies have consistently proven that people will reveal their innermost thoughts only to those they believe share a common bond. For example, if your goal is to study the real, in-depth *feelings* of whites and blacks toward affirmative action, welfare, or crime, you cannot have an integrated focus group. Similarly, women will not talk freely and emotionally about abortion if men (including a male moderator) are present. This is just a fact of life.' It is also important to remember that, although the researcher should be certain to do his best to ensure confidentiality, he is not able to *promise* the participants the same degree of confidentiality as one would expect with an interview, given that focus groups involve multiple people. For this reason, focus groups are often not appropriate for the discussion of sensitive information.

Focus groups are weak with respect to external validity, as the nonrandom selection of focus group participants makes generalizations to larger populations hazardous at best. Focus groups are often combined (or 'triangulated') with other methodologies, such as surveys. Focus group research is also used to provide context and community perspective around a broader issue. For example, in their assessment of the Vancouver food system, Barbolet et al. (2005) conducted focus groups with 'workers in and clients of the City's charitable food resources,' analyzed municipal and provincial food security documents, and developed and mapped a database of food resources.

Copsey (2008, 9) acknowledges: 'There will always be political scientists whose epistemological standpoint encourages them to scoff at focus group findings.' However, he argues that 'those who dismiss focus groups as too "soft" and unrepresentative to be of use misunderstand their purpose. Focus groups . . . complement quantitative data and must be employed as part of a properly triangulated research methodology.'

WORKING AS A TEAM

1. With your group, brainstorm five political science research questions that could be examined by using observation research. Select one question, and discuss how you would design your observational study.

What type of observation research (obtrusive or unobtrusive) would you use?

2. Discuss the extent to which your study would be limited by political, practical, or ethical considerations.

SELF-STUDY

1. Imagine that you are considering how environmental and business interests in your province perceive current water protection policies. You are planning to use focus groups to inform your research. How many focus groups would you hold? Would you distinguish among types of business interests (for example, agricultural, energy, manufacturing)?

2. What types of questions would you ask? Would the questions differ across the focus groups? Why or why not?

PART III
DATA ANALYSIS

Once the researcher has collected and cleaned the data, she then turns to data analysis. Chapters 15 through 18 focus on quantitative data analysis and introduce readers to introductory-level statistics. Chapter 15 examines univariate statistics, or statistics used to describe a single variable. Such descriptive statistics are of interest not only in their own right, but also as a foundation for statistics used in later chapters. Chapter 16 introduces inferential statistics, which are the statistical tests we use to assess if the sample statistics are reasonable estimates of the population parameters. (Recall that we are interested in the population itself, and not just the sample!) Chapter 17 considers relationships between two (bivariate) or more (multivariate) nominal and ordinal level variables, and Chapter 18 introduces the more advanced statistical technique of regression analysis. Chapter 19 focuses on qualitative data analysis, and introduces qualitative data-coding techniques.

It should be noted that throughout the quantitative analysis chapters, we provide an overview to the step-by-step hand calculation of key statistics used in political science research. Understanding the mechanics of the statistics better equips political scientists to use the statistics appropriately. In real life, one rarely calculates such statistics by hand; instead, computer software programs, such as SPSS, Stata, SAS, and R, are used to quickly conduct the sometimes cumbersome calculations. However, it is the researcher who decides which statistics to run in the computer program, who must ensure that the statistical assumptions are met, and who must interpret the statistical results. For this reason, we suggest that students familiarize themselves with the individual statistics.

The chapters in this section introduce readers to the basics of quantitative and qualitative data analysis. In doing so, they aim to provide readers with a general level of 'research literacy': on completing the chapters, students should be able to read and understand political science research that presents data analyses. Students should also be able to conduct their own basic analyses and should have a general foundation for pursuing more advanced study of data analysis techniques.

Chapter 15

DESCRIBING THE POLITICAL WORLD: UNIVARIATE STATISTICS

DESTINATION

By the end of this chapter the reader should

- understand and be able to construct frequency distributions;
- understand and be able to compute the descriptive statistics used to measure the *central tendency* of and *variance* within data sets; and
- know the properties and characteristics of the *normal curve*.

We are all used to describing the world in terms loosely based on statistical concepts. Think, for example, how often you use such phrases as 'typical', 'representative', or 'on average'. The goal of this chapter is to sharpen your conceptual language by introducing a number of specific terms used to measure both the average or 'central tendency' of data sets and the manner in which individual cases are dispersed around the average. When we calculate measures of central tendency or dispersion, we are looking at just one variable at a time, hence the expression 'univariate analysis'. As we will see, however, **univariate** analysis provides the foundation for the more complex forms of statistical analysis to come.

Before the chapter begins to unfold, you should refresh your memory with respect to nominal, ordinal, and interval levels of measurement. Many of the distinctions between the various measures of central tendency will refer to these different levels of measurement. It should also be kept in mind that this chapter is initially concerned with the statistics used to describe sample data. However, as we move through the chapter, the focus will shift toward inferential statistics and the estimation of population parameters. The transition between *descriptive* and *inferential* statistics will come through the discussion of the normal curve. For now, we begin with measures of central tendency, which provide the foundation for descriptive analysis.

MEASURES OF CENTRAL TENDENCY

The description of virtually any data set in the social sciences, and particularly data sets drawn from survey research, begins with the identification of **central tendencies**, or, in more common usage, averages. For example, survey findings in the press frequently start with phrases like 'a majority of Canadians believe that . . .' or even 'Canadians believe that. . .'. There is no assumption that *all* Canadians believe this, and the article will likely go on to point out specific levels of agreement and disagreement. We begin, though, with the *average*, or *typical*, response and then fine-tune the analysis. However, determining this **central value** is not as straightforward as you might expect, for we have three different measures at our disposal. Furthermore, there is no correct measure for all situations, although there are more or less useful measures. Often, our choice depends upon the level of measurement used; interval-level variables provide more options than do nominal-level variables.

Our assessment of the central tendency of variables in a data set usually begins with the visual inspection of **frequency distributions**, which record the possible values of the variable under discussion along with the number of cases associated with each value. Table 15.1 provides an illustration of a frequency distribution. There we find a hypothetical distribution of the number of political science courses taken by graduating majors in political science and the number of graduating students associated with each value. For example, 14 graduating majors had completed 16 courses, and 7 had completed 22 courses. No students completed 26 courses, although it would be possible to do so. Most frequency distributions report not only the number of cases but also the percentage of cases associated with each value of the variable. In Table 15.1, then, we find that 11.3 per cent of the students (13 out of 115) had completed 19 courses. Finally, frequency distributions sometimes report cumulative percentages. In the example provided by Table 15.1, 68.7 per cent of the students (79 out of 115) had completed 20 courses or fewer. Cumulative percentages build from lower variable values to higher values; the cumulative percentage for a given score is the proportion of cases with that score *or lower*.

A close visual inspection of a frequency distribution can tell us a good deal. We can see, for example, where the majority of scores fall and whether scores tend to cluster toward high or low variable values. However, it is very difficult to articulate visual impressions for others, or at least to do so with any numerical precision. It is even more difficult to compare such impressions. Hence the need for simple summary measures of central tendency, and here we have three options.

The **mode** refers to the most frequently occurring value in a distribution of scores. For example, in the 2008 online Angus Reid survey mentioned in Chapter 8, 37 per cent of the respondents said they would vote Conservative, 27 per cent Liberal, 20 per cent NDP, 9 per cent BQ, and 7 per cent intended to vote for the Green party in the 2008 election. Therefore, the modal value is 'Conservative' or, more precisely, the intention to vote Conservative. In Table 15.1, the mode would be 18 courses; more graduating students have taken 18 courses than any other number.

The mode is the least useful of the three available measures of central tendency, in large part because it incorporates only one value—the most frequently occurring

TABLE 15.1 Number of Political Science Courses Taken by Graduating Political Science Majors

Number of Courses Taken	Number of Students	Percentage of Students	Cumulative Percentage
15	10	8.7	8.7
16	14	12.2	20.9
17	15	13.0	33.9
18	16	13.9	47.8
19	13	11.3	59.1
20	11	9.6	68.7
21	9	7.8	76.5
22	7	6.1	82.6
23	9	7.8	90.4
24	5	4.3	94.8
25	3	2.6	97.4
26	0	0.0	97.4
27	0	0.0	97.4
28	2	1.7	99.1
29	0	0.0	99.1
30	1	0.9	100.0
Total	**115**	**100.0%**	**100.0%**

value—in a range of values. It therefore fails to make use of much of the data. Also, the mode is not a particularly stable measure, since it can change if only a few cases change. In Table 15.1, for instance, the mode would change from 18 to 17 if just one student taking 18 political science courses had dropped a course. Finally, the mode is highly sensitive to how measurement categories are constructed. If, in the Angus Reid survey described above, we grouped voters into just two categories, those who intended to vote Conservative and those who intended to vote for a different party, then the mode would no longer be a Conservative voting intention, since 63 per cent of the respondents indicated that they would not vote Conservative.

Nevertheless, the mode is not without some utility. First, it is the only measure of central tendency available for nominal data (such as sex, party identification, and religious affiliation), although it can also be used for ordinal and interval data.

EXPAND YOUR KNOWLEDGE
Practical Usage of the Mode: Anthony Downs and Party Competition

In his 1957 publication *An Economic Theory of Democracy*, Anthony Downs used unimodal, bimodal, and polymodal images of the electorate to develop some remarkably useful models of party competition. As noted in Chapter 2, Downs's models assumed that all voters could be placed along a single left-right continuum and that their placement would determine the nature of party competition and the number of parties likely to enter the competition.

For example, if the electorate is distributed in a unimodal fashion, as in Figure 15.1 b), then party platforms are likely to converge on the mode as parties compete for the greatest concentration of voters. In this situation party platforms will be similar and only two primary competitors will survive, one placed slightly to the left of the mode and one slightly to the right, with the parties competing for the same modal voters. Minor parties may exist at the tails of the distribution, but there will not be enough voters at the extremes to propel such parties into office.

If the distribution of the electorate is bimodal, as in Figure 15.1 c), then the major parties will locate themselves at the two modes. In this case there will be no convergence in party platforms; parties will appeal to their own constituencies and will not attempt to poach upon the turf of other parties. A polymodal environment (Figure 15.1 d) will promote a multiparty system, again marked by the absence of convergence among party platforms. Parties will concentrate on mobilizing voters at their own modes and will not venture off in pursuit of the small number of voters to be found in the troughs between modes.

Downs's work shows both the power of economic models and the utility of simple distributional diagrams in illustrating some of the important dynamics of party formation and electoral competition.

Second, it is an appropriate measure of central tendency for J-shaped distributions, illustrated in Figure 15.1 a). In such cases, the frequency distribution would be highly *skewed* (discussed later in this chapter) toward one side of the measure, and the mode would aptly describe where the bulk of cases fell. Third, the mode can be of considerable descriptive utility if we expand the definition from *the* most frequently occurring value to the most frequently occurring values. If we describe a distribution as unimodal, bimodal, or polymodal, as illustrated by Figures 15.1 b) to d), the description immediately conveys useful images. Finally, it should be noted that finding the mode does not require any calculation; visual inspection of frequency distributions will alone suffice.

The **median**, a measure of central tendency that can be used with both ordinal and interval data, refers to the value above which and below which 50 per cent of the cases fall. It is the midpoint in the *distribution of cases*; it is *not* the midpoint of the *scale* upon which those cases are distributed. To find the median, we order the cases from low to high—hence the need for ordinal or interval data—and then find the middle observation if the number of cases is odd or the midpoint between the two middle observations if the number of cases is even. In Table 15.1, for instance,

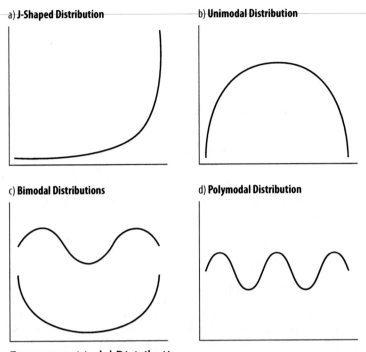

a) **J-Shaped Distribution**

b) **Unimodal Distribution**

c) **Bimodal Distributions**

d) **Polymodal Distribution**

FIGURE 15.1 Modal Distributions

the median for the distribution of scores is 19. (Note that the midpoint of the *scale* running from 15 to 30 courses would be 22.5.) The precise calculation of the median can be difficult if it falls within an interval. In the Table 15.1 illustration, the median of 19 courses is not an interval because a student cannot take partial credits. The median, therefore, cannot be 19.1 courses. Formulas do exist for calculating medians for such interval data, but this is unlikely to be something that you would be required to do.

The most common, useful, and stable measure of central tendency is the arithmetic **mean** ($\overline{X}$), which is calculated by adding together all scores in a distribution and dividing by the total number of cases. (*Sample* means are designated by $\overline{X}$; *population* means are designated by σ.) In Table 15.1 this would be done by multiplying each value by the number of cases, summing the scores,[1] and dividing by the total number of cases; the mean works out to be 19.3. (Try the calculations yourself!) The mean can be thought of as the 'centre of gravity' for a distribution of scores (Elifson et al. 1990, 105). Unlike the mode, but like the median, each and every value is included in the calculation of the mean. However, the calculation of the mean uses precise scores, whereas the calculation of the median uses only the order in which scores fall. *When most people talk about averages, they are talking about means.*

$$\text{Mean} = \overline{X} = \frac{\Sigma X_i}{N}$$

Mean scores should be calculated only if we have interval data. Thus, for example, you can compute your GPA, which is a mean score, because the precise distance between the various grades is known. An A grade is not 'somewhat better' than an A– grade; it is exactly 0.3 better on a 4-point scale ranging from 0.0 (F) to 4.0 (A). Yet in practice, means are often calculated for ordinal data. This commonly occurs with Likert scales measuring public opinion or political attitudes, scales that may range from strongly agree to agree, disagree, and strongly disagree. It is not

EXPAND YOUR KNOWLEDGE
The Use of Mean Scores with Ordinal Data

Given that the mean score provides a concise summary of central tendency and that the mean corresponds more closely to common understandings of 'average' than does the median, it is not surprising that means are often calculated in circumstances where a different measure of central tendency might be technically correct. In a 2007 report, André Turcotte reports on young adults' attitudes regarding different citizen-oriented behaviours. He uses 2005 International Social Survey Programme data, in which respondents were asked to 'Rate the importance of each of the following on a scale of 1 to 7 where 1 is "not at all important" and 7 is "very important"' (Turcotte 2007, 13). For such data, we cannot be sure that in respondents' minds the distance from 2 to 3 on this scale was the same as the distance between say 3 and 4 or between 6 and 7, and for this reason the mean is often not the most appropriate measure of central tendency. However, in this case the mean scores reported by the author do make intuitive sense and therefore provide useful insight into the thinking of young Canadians.

Behaviour	Mean Score for 18- to 30-Year-Olds
Serve in the military	3.55
Always vote in elections	5.62
Keep watch on government	5.73
Never try to evade taxes	5.88
Always obey laws	6.07

Source: Adapted from International Social Survey Programme 2005 as presented in Turcotte 2007, p. 13.

How do these perceptions of relative importance of civic behaviours square with your own perceptions?

unusual to see numerical values attached to these values (strongly disagree = 1; somewhat disagree = 2; somewhat agree = 3; strongly agree = 4) and then to have mean scores computed. The problem is that we cannot assume that the distance, for instance, between 'agree' and 'agree strongly' is the same as the distance between 'agree' and 'disagree'. However, and notwithstanding this problem, means are frequently used with ordinal measures such as Likert scales.

The values of the various measures of central tendency for a given distribution of scores are seldom identical. To illustrate why this is the case, refer again to Table 15.1. Imagine a political science department where students require 15 courses for a degree with a major in political science but where most students take the minimal number of political science courses needed for their major and degree. In this case, the mode could well be 15 while the mean would be higher, inflated by the smaller number of students who take more than 15 courses *en route* to their degree. The general rule is that the mean, as an arithmetic average, is affected by or is sensitive to extreme scores. Therefore, it is less useful as a measure of central tendency than is the median when distributions are skewed or asymmetrical, with extreme values falling to only one side of the distribution. Measures of average income, for example, can be significantly affected by relatively few individuals with very high incomes; therefore, the mean can give a distorted impression of central tendency. The advantage of the median in such cases is that it is insensitive to extreme scores.

Imagine, for example, a professional basketball team of 10 players whose salaries range from a 'mere' $1 million to a high of $4 million. Imagine further that the mean and median salaries are both $2 million and that the distribution of player salaries is symmetrical about the mean. If the team then releases a $3-million-dollar player and hires a superstar with an annual salary of $10 million, the median salary for the team will be unchanged. However, the salary distribution is now skewed toward the high end of the scale, and the mean salary will increase from $2 million to $2.7 million. (Go ahead: work out the math!) If the superstar demanded and received a salary increase to $20 million,[2] the mean salary for the team would increase but the median salary would not. In summary, 'when the score distribution is symmetrical, the median has a value equal to the mean. If the distribution is skewed, the median usually lies closer to the bulk of the scores than the mean does' (Wright 1976, 93). In this case, 'skewed' refers to the mean being pulled in the direction of extreme scores. Thus, the mean would be greater than the median. The difference between the mean and the median provides a rough measure of how skewed a distribution of scores might be; the greater the difference in the two measures of central tendency, the greater the skew.

Measures of central tendency are used all the time to compare individuals or groups. We talk, for example, about how the average doctor makes more than the average welder or how the average professional basketball player makes *many* times the income of the average political science graduate (assuming, alas, that the two are mutually exclusive categories!).[3] We compare GPAs, batting averages, average

EXPAND YOUR KNOWLEDGE

Median Measures of Average Income

Because the median is unaffected by extreme scores, it is the preferred measure of central tendency for income distributions. In 2007, for example, Statistics Canada reported that the median after-tax income for families of two persons or more was $61,800. Median after-tax incomes varied by place of residence:

Alberta	$75,300
Ontario	65,900
British Columbia	63,300
Canada	**61,800**
Saskatchewan	59,900
Manitoba	58,300
Quebec	54,500
Nova Scotia	54,200
Prince Edward Island	52,600
Newfoundland and Labrador	50,900
New Brunswick	50,600

Source: 'Median Measures of Average Income, 2007', adapted from Statistics Canada publication, *Income in Canada, 2007*, Catalogue no. 75-202-X, http://www.statcan.gc.ca/bsolc/olc-cel/olc-cel?catno=75-202-x&lang=eng.

APPLY YOUR UNDERSTANDING

Selecting a Measure of Central Tendency

For each of the following, which measure of central tendency would be best for expressing the 'average': the mode, median, or mean? Why would you make these choices?

- the average salary paid to all actors in a blockbuster movie
- the average salary of public servants
- the average (or typical) supporter of the Liberal Party of Canada
- the average age of undergraduate students in political science
- the average age of first-time voters in federal elections
- your GPA at college or university

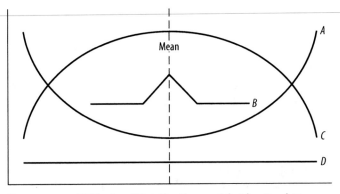

FIGURE 15.2 Differing Distributions with Identical Means

heights, average weights, average election turnouts, and average votes received by different political parties. However, comparing groups by looking at differences in central tendencies alone can be a risky endeavour. Figure 15.2, for example, displays a number of possible distributions that all have the same mean score but that differ dramatically in other respects. Thus, for a more useful and meaningful group comparison, we also need to know something about the distribution of scores around the measure of central tendency.

TABLE 15.2 Summary of the Three Measures of Central Tendency

Measure	Level of Data	'How to'	Pros	Cons
Mode	Nominal Ordinal Interval	Use the frequency distribution to find the most frequent value.	Only measure for nominal data; apt for J-shaped distributions	Fails to use all information; varies with category construction; unstable
Median	Ordinal Interval	Place all cases in order, and then find the middle value.	Stable; not affected by extreme scores; uses all cases	Does not use precise values
Mean	Interval	Sum all scores and divide by the total number of scores.	Most reliable; uses all information, including precise values	Affected by extreme scores

MEASURES OF VARIATION

Statistical measures for the dispersion of scores around the central tendency are termed **measures of variation**. Just as there are a number of ways in which we can measure central tendency, there are a number of descriptive statistics that can be used to measure the *dispersion* or *variation* within a set of scores. As with measures of central tendency, our choice is determined in large part by the level of measurement.

For nominal data, the only available measure of variation is the **variation ratio**. The variation ratio is simply the number of cases that are not in the modal category. A high variation ratio indicates that the data are more dispersed, while a low variation ratio indicates that the data are more concentrated. To calculate the variation ratio, we use the following formula:

variation ratio = 1 − (number of cases in modal category/number of total cases)

Thus, if there are 25 cases in the modal category and there are 100 cases in the full sample, the variation ratio equals .75 [1 − (25/100)]. This ratio suggests that the data are more dispersed. Given that there is a high variation ratio, it is possible that the mode is not very representative of the data taken as a whole.

For ordinal and interval level data, researchers have additional measures of variation to consider. The simplest but least useful measure of variation is the **range**, which is the difference between the lowest and highest values in a distribution of scores. If we found, for example, that among the 23,000 medical doctors in Ontario the highest annual income was $1,200,000 and the lowest was $30,000, the income range would be $1,170,000 (the highest value minus the lowest value). However, the range would tell us something about only two of the 23,000 physicians, and we would have no idea if most doctors were near the bottom, top, or middle of the range. The range ignores all information but the two most extreme scores. Sometimes the range is calculated by taking the difference between the highest and lowest scores and then adding 1. To illustrate why this is the case, imagine a set of scores ranging from 1 to 5. If we subtract the lowest score from the highest score (5 − 1), the range is 4. In fact, five scores are possible: 1, 2, 3, 4, and 5. Therefore, adding 1 gives us a more precise estimate of the range:

range = highest score − smallest score + 1

While we can easily calculate how much any particular score deviates from the mean, it is not as easy to put that deviation into perspective. Is the deviation *relatively* small? *Relatively* large? To answer such questions, we need a measure of the *average* deviation from the mean, while at the same time locating individual scores with respect to both the mean and the other scores in the data set. The catch, however, is that deviations about the mean will always sum to zero. If we have 10 scores, subtract the mean from each score, and sum the deviations, the total will always be zero. Given, then, that *mean deviation* does not provide a useful measure of variation about the mean, we need to turn to a more complex measure.

The **standard deviation** provides the most common measure of average deviation from the mean. Although the standard deviation may be initially difficult to grasp conceptually, its properties become more readily apparent if we work through the calculations. The standard deviation for a set of scores is calculated by the following steps: (1) find the mean for the set of scores; (2) subtract the mean from each individual score; (3) square each difference, that is to say, each $X_i - \overline{X}$; (4) find the sum of these squared differences; (5) divide that sum by the number of cases; and (6) find the square root for the result of step (5). The fourth step produces the **sum of squares**. If we were to stop at the fifth step, we would have the **variance**, which can be defined as the sum of the squared deviations from the mean, divided by the number of cases. The standard deviation is the square root of the variance:

$$\text{variance} = S^2 = \frac{\Sigma(X_i - \overline{X})^2}{N}$$

$$\text{standard deviation} = \sqrt{S^2} = S = \sqrt{\frac{\Sigma(X_i - \overline{X})^2}{N}}$$

To illustrate the calculation of both the standard deviation and the variance—if you can calculate one, then you can do the other—imagine a set of five scores: 4, 4, 4, 4, and 9. The calculations steps are as follows:

1. Find the mean:

$$\text{mean} = \overline{X} = \frac{\Sigma X}{N} = \frac{25}{5} = 5$$

2. Subtract the mean from each score: $X - \overline{X}$ in the table that follows.
3. Square the difference between the mean and each score: $(X - \overline{X})^2$ in the table that follows.
4. Total the sum of the squared differences (sum of squares):

$$\Sigma(X_i - \overline{X})^2 = 20$$

5. Divide the sum of the squares by the number of cases:

$$\frac{20}{N} = \frac{20}{5} = 4 = \text{variance}$$

6. Take the square root of the variance: $\sqrt{4} = 2$

Score (X)	$X - \overline{X}$	$(X - \overline{X})^2$
4	−1	1
4	−1	1
4	−1	1
4	−1	1
9	4	16

Fortunately, this calculation is routinely done by computer-based statistical packages; therefore, you will not need to do it by hand for large data sets.

The larger the standard deviation (or variance), the greater the variability in scores. When variability is low, the mean is more representative of the bulk of the scores than

APPLY YOUR UNDERSTANDING

Calculating the Variance and Standard Deviation

You have been asked to calculate the 'average age' of a group of Bloc Québécois voters. You have also been asked how typical the average is. To this end, calculate the mean age, variance, and standard deviation for the following set of respondents. Round all calculations to the nearest decimal point. If, for example, the mean age is 34.567 years, round to 34.6 years.

A = 21 years
B = 27 years
C = 46 years
D = 65 years
E = 23 years
F = 37 years

G = 83 years
H = 22 years
I = 29 years
J = 47 years
K = 41 years
L = 56 years
M = 62 years
N = 19 years
O = 47 years
P = 58 years
Q = 51 years
R = 45 years
S = 72 years
T = 18 years
U = 40 years

it is when variability is high. Put somewhat differently, the mean is a better predictor of individual scores when the standard deviation is low than when it is high. It should also be noted, however, that the absolute values of the mean and standard deviation are independent of each other. A large mean in absolute terms (say 200 rather than 20) does not necessarily generate a large standard deviation; the size of the standard deviation depends on how tightly the scores are clustered around the mean rather than on the value of the mean itself. Like the mean, the standard deviation incorporates each and every case in the distribution of scores. Also like the mean, and the variance upon which it is based, the standard deviation is sensitive to extreme scores. Therefore, if outliers exist, the standard deviation will not accurately reflect variability among the bulk of the scores.

To demonstrate this sensitivity to extreme scores, turn again to the simple illustration in the preceding calculations. Most of the 'variance' in that case came from a single score (9). As the calculations show, it is because the deviations from the mean are squared that extreme scores have such a disproportionate effect on the calculation of the variance. That effect is moderated in the calculation of the standard deviation in that by taking the square root, the impact of squaring deviations from the mean is reduced. Note also that the values for the standard deviation (or variance) are always positive; it is impossible to have a negative standard deviation.

EXPAND YOUR KNOWLEDGE

Means and Standard Deviations

The utility of having measures of both central tendency and variation is demonstrated in an analysis by Michael A. Goldberg and Maurice D. Levi, which considered annual growth rates in provincial economies over the 1962-91 period. As the mean scores in the table that follows show, the Canadian provinces have differed considerably in their annual growth rates. This, however, is only half the picture. They also differ in variability; Alberta and Saskatchewan, for example, have had much more volatile economies—reflected in the larger standard deviations—than has Ontario or Quebec. Clearly, if we want to make sense out of the relative economic performance of provincial economies, we need to take both average growth and volatility into account. The variability of the resource-based Alberta economy, for example, was also seen in the province's economic downturn in 2008-9.

	Mean Growth Rate	Standard Deviation of Growth
Yukon and Northwest Territories	6.84	8.14
British Columbia	4.87	3.52
Alberta	5.25	6.39
Saskatchewan	3.37	8.24
Manitoba	3.15	3.16
Ontario	4.09	3.30
Quebec	3.67	2.65
New Brunswick	4.29	4.76
Nova Scotia	4.09	3.41
Prince Edward Island	4.46	4.95
Newfoundland	4.39	3.45
Canada	**4.06**	**2.55**

Source: Michael A. Goldberg and Maurice D. Levi, 'Growing Together or Apart: The Risks and Returns of Alternative Constitutions of Canada', *Canadian Public Policy* 20, 4 (December 1994): 343.

When you think of it, how could there be less than zero variance? If all scores are identical, then each score would equal the mean, there would be no deviation from the mean, and both the variance and the standard deviation would equal zero.

We can use the standard deviation to describe how far an individual case is from the mean. We often hear references to cases being '2 standard deviations from the mean' or '0.5 standard deviation from the mean'. Another way to express this is with **standardized scores** (also known as **z-scores**), which are scores expressed in terms of the number of standard deviations they fall from the mean of the total distribution of scores. If, for example, the mean of a distribution was 150 and the

TABLE 15.3 Summary of the Measures of Variation

Measures of Variation	Levels of Measurement		
	Nominal	Ordinal	Interval
Variation ratio	✓	✓	✓
Range	✗	✓	✓
Standard deviation	✗	✗	✓
Variance	✗	✗	✓

standard deviation was 20, then a score of 120 would be −1.5 standard deviations from the mean. Therefore, the score of 120 expressed as a standardized score, or z-score, would be −1.5. Unlike the standard deviation, standardized scores can be positive or negative. Scores greater than the mean yield positive standardized scores, and scores falling below the mean yield negative standardized scores. In either case they allow us to compare scores in terms of their relative distance from the mean.

Standardized scores enable the comparison of an individual score relative to the scores of a group as a whole. Standardized scores also enable a comparison of scores across different populations. For example, in surveys such as the Canadian National Election Studies, respondents are often asked to indicate their feelings toward the party leaders by using a 100-point feeling thermometer. Let's focus for a moment on assessments of Prime Minister Stephen Harper and Official Opposition leader Michael Ignatieff in a hypothetical 2010 study. Let us assume that the average rating of Harper was 55 on the 100-point scale, with a standard deviation of 15, and the mean for Ignatieff was 48, with a standard deviation of 18 units. We could draw two conclusions from these data: Canadians felt more positively toward Harper than Ignatieff ($\overline{X} = 55$ versus 48), and they were somewhat more consensual in their attitudes toward Harper than Ignatieff ($S = 15$ versus 18).

We can extend the analysis from the aggregate data (mean and standard deviation) to the individual level of analysis by comparing raw scores and standardized scores. Assume that one respondent (Jane Porter from Halifax) rated both Harper and Ignatieff 60 on the 100-point thermometer. By examining the raw score, we might conclude that the party leaders had no effect on her vote, since both were assigned the same score. However, by using standardized scores, a different portrait, and a different conclusion, emerges. Jane's rating of 60 for Harper is slightly above the average ($\overline{X} = 55$) and well within the standard deviation ($S = 15$). Using the formula for z-scores, we would calculate her z-score for Harper as $(60 - 55)/15 = 0.33$. The conclusion would be that Jane's feelings toward Harper were 0.33 standard units above the mean. For Ignatieff, however, the calculation is as follows: $(60 - 48)/18 = 0.67$. In this instance, Jane's evaluation of Ignatieff was 0.67 standard units above the mean. Therefore, in comparison with other voters, Jane rated Ignatieff more positively than Harper. We could hypothesize that this more positive evaluation had an impact on her voting behaviour.

Let's take another illustration of the use of z-scores, one that is closer to home for many university students, particularly those wishing to be admitted to graduate or professional schools. Let's assume that your major is political science and that your GPA is 3.2 on a 4-point scale. Let's also assume that the GPA of political science majors as a whole is 2.4, and the standard deviation is 0.6. Let's also assume that your friend, and potential competitor for a valued place in the admission to law school, is a psychology major. We'll assume that her GPA is 3.4, and the GPA for psychology majors is 2.8 with a standard deviation of 0.6.

Which of the two should be admitted to law school? Her higher GPA (3.4 versus 3.2) suggests she might be the one most likely admitted. Let's compare performance by using z-scores. Your score, which would be called your standardized GPA, is $(3.2 - 2.4)/0.6 = 1.33$. Your friend's standardized GPA is $(3.4 - 2.8)/0.6 = 1.0$. Thus, your standardized score, in relation to all political science majors, is higher than your friend's, in relation to all psychology majors. Leaving aside arguments about the potential superiority of psychology students in relation to political science students overall (i.e., they did attain higher GPAs), the z-scores might lead one to conclude that you should be offered admission to law school ahead of your friend. Thus, the purpose of z-scores is to try to standardize the base of comparison between groups. Standardized scores also provide a conceptual bridge to the discussion of the normal curve.

Computing Standardized Scores

$$\text{Standardized score} = Z = \frac{X_i - \overline{X}}{S}$$

If $X_i = 20$, $\overline{X} = 17$, and $S = 1.4$, then

$$Z = \frac{X_i - \overline{X}}{S}$$
$$= \frac{20 - 17}{1.4}$$
$$= \frac{3}{1.4} = 2.14$$

If $X_i = 50$, $\overline{X} = 55$, and $S = 7$, then

$$Z = \frac{X_i - \overline{X}}{S}$$
$$= \frac{50 - 55}{7}$$
$$= \frac{-5}{7} = -0.71$$

APPLY YOUR UNDERSTANDING

Calculating Z-Scores

You have been told that the average GPA for political science majors is 2.7 and the standard deviation is 0.8. Given this information, convert the following GPAs to z-scores. How would you verbally express such z-scores to someone without a statistics background?

Schulmit:	GPA = 3.41
Andrew:	GPA = 2.76
Christine:	GPA = 3.01
Malinda:	GPA = 3.17
Scott:	GPA = 3.56

NORMAL CURVE

The **normal curve**, or what is often known as the 'bell-shaped curve', is a particularly useful statistical concept. Normal curves need not have identical shapes; the example in Figure 15.4 later in this chapter is perhaps the most typical shape, but other normal curves could be more or less peaked than our illustration. However, all normal curves and the **normal distributions** that they contain share a number of characteristics:

- The normal curve is bilaterally symmetrical; its shape is identical to the left and right of the mean.
- As a consequence, the mode = the mean = the median of the normal curve.
- The tails of the normal curve are *asymptotic*; they approach but never quite meet the horizontal axis. As a consequence, *any* value can be placed under a normal curve; the tails stretch to infinity.
- The total area under the normal curve = 1.
- 68.3 per cent of the area under the normal curve falls within ±1 standard deviation of the mean.
- 95.4 per cent of the area under the normal curve falls within ±2 standard deviations of the mean.
- 99.7 per cent of the area under the normal curve falls within ±3 standard deviations of the mean. The importance of the normal curve does not arise because real data are distributed in a normal fashion; 'the normal distribution is a mathematical distribution that is not found in the real world' (Elifson et al. 1990, 149). Real-world distributions, which we often think of as normally distributed, do not actually fit the conditions stated above. For example, we may think of IQ, or weight or height, as being normally distributed. However, if they were normally distributed, *any* score would be

possible, no matter how unlikely. We could have, for instance, adults who were 20 metres or 20 centimetres tall. The real world, then, is not normal, *but large parts of the statistical and mathematical worlds are.* This fact is of considerable importance in the chapters to come.

EXPAND YOUR KNOWLEDGE

The Central-limit Theorem

Although no real-world data are normally distributed, many statistics are. If we take repeated samples of the same population, a given statistic (for example, the mean) will follow a normal distribution. Indeed, this is the case even if the data upon which those statistics are based are not themselves normally distributed. As Allen Edwards (1969, 123) points out, 'The fact is, that regardless of the shape or form of a population distribution, the distributions of both the sum and the mean of random samples [taken from that population] approach that of a normal distribution as the sample size is increased. This statement is based on an important theorem known as the *central-limit theorem.*' Note the role that sample size plays in this theorem; statistics generated by large samples are more normally distributed than are statistics generated by small samples.

One way to think about how the normal curve is derived, and in particular the importance of the central-limit theorem in survey research, is to consider what happens when we toss coins. Assume that we have an unbiased coin, that is, a coin that is equally likely to land on heads or tails. If we tossed the coin 10 times, we would expect to produce 5 heads and 5 tails. In doing this, however, we find that we don't always produce 5 heads and 5 tails. Sometimes we get 4 heads and 6 tails or 6 heads and 4 tails. Or we could get 3 heads and 7 tails or 7 heads and 3 tails. There might even be rare occasions when we get 10 heads and no tails. If we flipped a coin 100 times, we would find the distribution of samples would approximate a normal curve as shown in Figure 15.3 a) on page 260.

If the 'true' result of tossing coins is an equal number of heads and tails, the samples will be normally distributed around this value. The distribution in Figure 15.3 a) indicates that while not all samples will exactly produce the 'true' value, they are likely to approximate it. Furthermore, as is discussed later in this chapter, we know what proportion of the cases falls within given standard deviations of the mean under the normal curve, a fact that proves to be very useful when testing hypotheses about the statistical significance of findings.

The other significant implication of the central-limit theorem is that as sample size increases, the distribution of cases more closely approximates a normal curve. Let's assume that instead of tossing a coin 10 times over 100 samples, you tossed a coin 100 times over 1,000 samples. (This assumes, of course, that you have a lot of time on your hands!) The larger sample size will ensure that more

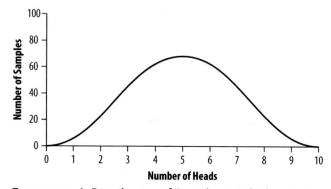

FIGURE 15.3 a) Distribution of Samples in Which 10 Coins Were Tossed 100 Times

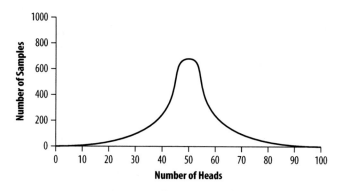

FIGURE 15.3 b) Distribution of Samples in Which 100 Coins Were Tossed 1,000 Times

of the samples will approximate 50 heads and would produce a distribution as shown in Figure 15.3 b).

As the sample size increases, the distribution of samples collapses more tightly around the 'true' population value. As a result, with large populations the likelihood of producing results that deviate substantially from the true value is very small. We can use the idea embodied in the central-limit theorem when we are testing hypotheses. In survey research we draw samples to test hypotheses about the causal relationship between variables. Of course, we're never sure if our particular sample measures the 'true' value of a variable and of the relationship between variables. We do know, however, that samples are normally distributed around the true value, and the larger the sample size, the more closely the samples approximate the 'true' values.

You will note from Figure 15.4 that 95.4 per cent of the total area of the normal curve falls within ±2 standard deviations of the mean, and 99.7 per cent of the

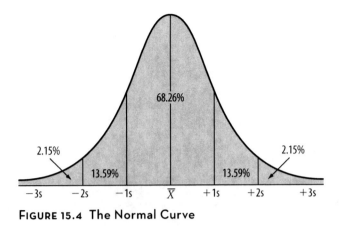

FIGURE 15.4 The Normal Curve

area falls within ±3 standard deviations. You should also note that the area of the normal curve encompassed within ±1.96 standard deviations from the mean includes 95 per cent of the cases, and the area encompassed within ±2.57 standard deviations from the mean includes 99 per cent of the cases. These latter percentage distributions come into play when we take up tests of statistical significance and confidence intervals, which we will explore in the next chapter.

COMPARING UNIVARIATE STATISTICS BETWEEN TWO SUBGROUPS

The discussion to this point has stressed that measures of central tendency and dispersion are closely connected, not only in their calculation (as in the case of the mean and standard deviation) but also in the role they play in interpreting empirical data. To illustrate the interplay between measures of central tendency and measures of dispersion, turn to Figures 15.5 a) and b) on the next page, which present two quite different comparisons of the relative physical strengths of men and women. The two figures show *hypothetical* distributions of two subgroups, men and women, across a scale measuring physical strength; the higher the score on the horizontal axis, the stronger the individual. The means for women are identical in both figures, as are the means for men. In both figures, the mean score for men is higher than the mean score for women; men, on average, are stronger than women. The difference between the two figures comes from the dispersion of scores around the means; in Figure 15.5 a) the scores are tightly bunched around the mean, whereas in Figure 15.5 b) the dispersion is much looser.

   Now suppose a fire department is hiring new staff and decides that a minimum strength of 150 is needed to perform satisfactorily as a firefighter. Suppose further, and as was often done in the past, that sex is used as a proxy for strength. Instead of actually measuring the physical strength of individual applicants, the fire

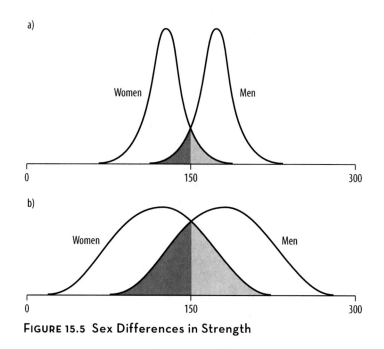

FIGURE 15.5 Sex Differences in Strength

department decides that any man who applies is strong enough (he is, after all, a man) and that any woman who applies is not (she is, after all, a woman). What errors would be made? In Figure 15.5 a) the lighter shaded section shows the women who might be strong enough to do the job yet who would not be hired, and the darker shaded section shows the men who might be hired even though they would not have sufficient strength to do the job. In both cases, the errors that would be made by using sex as a proxy measure of strength would be quite small; most men are strong enough to do the job and most women are not. But if we turn to Figure 15.5 b), the potential for error increases dramatically. There are now many more men who might be hired even though they lack sufficient strength, and many more women who would be denied employment even though they have the necessary strength. Sex, therefore, serves as a poor proxy of strength in this case, and a fire department that relied upon it rather than on individual measures of strength would end up with suboptimal firefighters. (And, in a modern context, a host of legal challenges!) Figure 15.5 b), we would suggest, illustrates the job discrimination women faced in the past when sex was used indiscriminately as a proxy of strength.[4]

Figures 15.5 a) and b) can also be used to illustrate some of the complexities in the long-standing debate about sex differences in mathematical ability. Let's suppose hypothetically that *on average* men do have a greater aptitude for math than do women, that men have a higher mean score on some measure of mathematical ability. As we have seen from the firefighter example, the relevance of this difference depends upon the dispersion of male and female scores around their respective means. If the distribution resembles Figure 15.5 a), then we could use sex as a proxy of mathematical ability and assume that, *as a rule,* men are better at math than women. However, if the distribution resembles Figure 15.5 b), then sex cannot be used as a proxy for mathematical ability. In this latter case, *there is no rule;* knowing an individual's sex provides little assistance in predicting his or her ability in math. The sex difference in mean scores is irrelevant. In all likelihood, Figure 15.5 b) more closely approximates social reality in this case than does Figure 15.5 a), if indeed there is *any* sex difference in mathematical ability. Therefore, a female student in a political science research methods course cannot assume that she is labouring under some disadvantage because of her sex!

The point to emphasize is that the contrast between Figures 15.5 a) and b) stems not from differences in mean scores but rather from differences in the dispersion of scores around the means. Thus to make sensible intergroup comparisons, and indeed to provide a complete descriptive profile of data sets, we need information on both central tendency and the manner in which scores are distributed about those measures of central tendency. We also need a statistical measure of differences in mean scores to which we can attach levels of confidence. Is the difference in mean scores significant? Or did it occur by chance? We will look at how to assess these questions in the next chapter.

The above discussion of hypothetical sex differences in strength and mathematical ability illustrates the conceptual underpinnings for the **analysis of variance**, or ANOVA, one of the most useful statistical techniques in the social sciences. In one form or another, social scientists are often interested in subgroup differences—between men and women, liberals and conservatives, Canadians and Americans, Quebeckers and western Canadians—that are conceptually analogous to the differences in group means discussed above. However, and as we have seen, the difference between groups is only half the story; we also need to know about the dispersion or *variance* of scores within groups. Analysis of variance provides a systematic method for comparing the relative strength of *between-group* and *within-group* differences. Simply put, and as illustrated by the examples discussed above, between-group variance takes on greater importance as within-group variance declines. In other words, small differences between relatively homogeneous groups can be significant, whereas large differences between relatively heterogeneous groups may not be.

WORKING AS A TEAM

1. Return to Figures 15.5 a) and b). Assume first that your group has conducted a survey of racial differences between two groups in math ability and came up with a pattern similar to Figure 15.5 b): a significant inter-group difference combined with substantial intragroup variability. How would you report these results to the public? How would you counter the likely charge that you were providing empirical support for racism?

2. What would be the ethical considerations with respect to publishing or suppressing the findings?

SELF-STUDY

1. As a class project you have asked 22 of your fellow students to locate themselves on a 7-point left–right scale with values ranging from 1 (far left) to 7 (far right). In order to protect the respondents' anonymity, a letter of the alphabet rather than a name has been assigned to each of the 22 responses. The left–right scale locations were as follows:

    A = 6   B = 1   C = 3   D = 7   E = 6
    F = 4   G = 4   H = 2   I = 7   J = 5
    K = 3   L = 1   M = 6   N = 6   O = 2
    P = 1   Q = 3   R = 4   S = 5   T = 2
    U = 6   V = 1

    a. Construct a frequency distribution for the set of scores.
    b. Calculate the cumulative percentages for the frequency distribution.
    c. Find the mode, median, and mean for the distribution of scores.
    d. Calculate the standard deviation and variance for the distribution of scores.

NOTES

1. The symbol for 'sum of' is Σ.
2. In 2008–9, the highest paid NBA player, according to insidehoops.com, was Kevin Garnett (Boston), who earned $24,751,934.
3. Note, however, Wright's caution (1976, 97): 'the concept of "average" *is applicable only to scores,* not to the people who provide those scores. Being of average *height* doesn't make you an average *person*'.
4. There were, of course, other reasons for discriminating against women, and strength criteria were often used to mask sex discrimination.

Chapter 16

ASSESSING THE POLITICAL WORLD: INFERENTIAL STATISTICS

DESTINATION

By the end of this chapter the reader should

- understand the conceptual nature of tests of significance and the roles that inferential statistics play in hypothesis-testing;
- be familiar with various types of data distributions;
- be able to distinguish between Type I and Type II errors and appreciate the factors to consider in choosing between the two types;
- understand the difference between parametric and nonparametric statistics; and
- be able to select and calculate appropriate tests of significance.

We conduct research on *samples* in an effort to gain knowledge about *populations*. The descriptive statistics that we calculate—be they the univariate statistics of Chapter 15, the bivariate statistics of Chapter 17, or the multivariate statistics of Chapter 18—provide us with concrete information about the sample. We can calculate sample means or uncover relationships between two or more variables within the sample, but these are of theoretical interest only to the degree that we can use them to make inferences about the population from which the sample was drawn. This chapter will explore **inferential statistics**, which test the probability that sample statistics are reasonable estimates of population parameters. Inferential statistics provide the bridge between what we know about samples and what we would like to know about populations.

Recall that the principles of random sampling are based on probability theory. Inferential statistics address the question, What is the probability that the relationship we found occurred by chance in the sample? Was the sample finding a fluke, or was it reflective of a relationship in the population? Essentially, inferential statistics are used to determine if sample statistics are *representative* of population parameters. If the sample statistic is found to be representative, we say that it is 'statistically significant'.

Inferential statistics are a crucial step in hypothesis-testing. Hypotheses, which have been discussed in a number of previous chapters, are operationalized statements of propositions; they assert the existence of a relationship between two or more variables. When we gain support for our hypothesis, we gain support for the proposition and the underlying theory. In order to support our hypothesis, we must first reject the null hypothesis, or the supposition that no relationship exists between the variables in the general population. We ask whether there is sufficient evidence to reject the null hypothesis, to conclude that the relationship observed in the data reflects a similar relationship in the larger population. In other words, is the observed relationship *significant*? Or is it *insignificant*? Do we conclude that the sample relationship is not sufficiently robust to provide compelling evidence for a similar relationship in the population from which the sample was drawn? It is only once we have rejected the null hypothesis that we can begin to argue in favour of our alternative hypothesis and the theory from which it is drawn. Therefore, a lot is at stake with tests of significance.

The five basic steps of hypothesis-testing are as follows:[1]

1. Formulate the null and alternative hypotheses.
2. Select a confidence level.
3. Calculate the appropriate inferential statistic.
4. Using the table for the test statistic, find the critical value (expected value) at the selected confidence level.
5. If the calculated statistic equals or exceeds the critical value, reject the null hypothesis.[2]

The first of these steps was addressed in Chapter 2; this chapter will explore the remaining steps. Before we begin, however, two important points must be addressed.

First, when we discuss 'significance' in this chapter, we are focusing on *statistical significance*, on tests that allow us to assess whether sample statistics are acceptable estimates of population parameters. However, there are some instances where rather weak relationships are found to be statistically significant. Significance tests are affected by sample size; the larger the sample, the more likely it is that a relationship of a given strength will be significant. Therefore, some trivial relationships from large samples will be 'statistically significant', and other potentially interesting relationships from very small samples will be 'insignificant'. The point to stress is that statistical significance does not always entail *substantive significance*. A relationship or a statistic is substantively significant if it is theoretically important, if it plays a role in elaborating, modifying, or rejecting your theory. The need for substantive significance as well as statistical significance requires that the researcher rely not only on inferential statistics but also on an assessment of the supporting descriptive statistics and contingency tables. We need to look at all parts of the data analysis, rather than relying on summary statistics alone.

Second, inferential statistics are either statistically significant or they are not. Some relationships are not 'more significant' than others. The desire to make such statements arises from confusion between substantive and statistical significance.

If we wish to argue that one relationship is *stronger* than another, and *not more significant*, we need measures of association (discussed in Chapter 17) rather than inferential statistics. Statistical significance is a statement about the correspondence between the sample and the population and cannot be used to draw conclusions about the relative importance of variables. Students must be clear about this distinction.

EXPAND YOUR KNOWLEDGE
Pre-election Surveys and the Margin of Error

In most forms of survey research, and virtually all forms of attitudinal research, we never know what the population parameters are. Surveys provide the best estimate we have of those parameters, but there is nothing against which we can place the survey results to see if they are accurate or correct. We do not know, for example, what proportion of Canadians might support a more liberalized immigration policy; we only know the survey proportions that do so. However, pre-election surveys are an important exception to this rule.

It is common for the media to conduct polls shortly before elections are held and use the survey results to predict the election outcome. But in this case, the actual election outcome—the population parameters—will shortly be known, and therefore error on the part of the media outlet will be apparent to all. In short, it is possible to be shown to be wrong in this case. Polling organizations and their media clients try to avoid such embarrassment by using unusually large samples in the last pre-election poll. This reduces the margin of error and provides greater confidence in the survey results. It is money worth spending if the media outlet wants to protect its credibility.

SELECTING CONFIDENCE LEVELS

Deciding whether or not a relationship exists in the population, whether the co-variance found in the data is significant, is by no means a straightforward process. How do we distinguish between random variation in the sample and evidence of a 'real' relationship in the population? What standard of proof do we employ? If it were left to each researcher to determine the standards by which the null hypothesis would be rejected, there would be little consistency within or across the social sciences disciplines. When confronted with the same empirical evidence, two researchers could come to very different conclusions. One could decide that the relationship was significant, the other, that it was not. What has evolved, therefore, is a set of norms by which null hypotheses are accepted or rejected. These norms are based on probabilities. The question we ask is, If *no* relationship exists between two variables in the population from which the sample was drawn, what is the probability that by chance alone we would observe a relationship in the sample data? If the chances are pretty good that the observed relationship could have emerged by chance alone, we tend to discount it and conclude that it is the product of sampling error or random variation. However, if the odds are remote that by chance alone we would have observed a relationship in the sample data, then we tend to reject the null hypothesis, concluding instead that the best explanation for the sample finding is that a relationship indeed exists within the larger population from which the sample was drawn.

But how do we operationalize 'pretty good' or 'remote'? The scientific norms provide two primary standards, known as **confidence levels** or **alpha (α) levels**. The first is the 5 per cent ($p < .05$) confidence level: we *reject the null hypothesis* if the probability of finding the observed relationship *by chance alone* is less than 5 per cent, or less than five chances in a hundred. The second standard is similar but more rigorous: *we reject the null hypothesis* at the 1 per cent ($p < .01$) confidence level if the probability of finding the observed relationship *by chance alone* is less than 1 per cent, or less than one chance in a hundred. Very occasionally you will encounter published research in which a 10 per cent ($p < .10$) confidence level is used. Because this is a more lenient test, it tends to be employed only with pretest data or where sample sizes are very small.

Regardless of which standard we use, if we reject the null hypothesis, we conclude that a significant relationship exists. Hence the term 'tests' of significance. A significant relationship is one that, within specified limits, we are confident exists in the population from which the sample was randomly drawn. We never reject the null hypothesis with total certainty, for there is always the possibility, no matter how remote, that the observed relationship was the product of chance alone. We can only reject the null hypothesis with varying degrees of confidence; therefore, confidence levels are always specified when tests of significance are reported.

Keep in mind that researchers will use different language to describe the same thing. A 95 per cent confidence level and a 5 per cent confidence level ($p < .05$) both mean that the chances of having made an error in rejecting the null hypothesis are less than 5 per cent; a 99 per cent confidence level and a 1 per cent confidence level ($p < .01$) both mean that the chances of having made an error in rejecting the null hypothesis are less than 1 per cent. The first approach (95 per cent or 99 per cent) expresses the probability of *not* making an error by incorrectly rejecting the null hypothesis; the second approach (5 per cent or 1 per cent) expresses the probability of making such an error.

The question remains regarding which confidence level to adopt. The answer is by no means clear-cut and depends, in part, on the quality of the data and the consequences of making a mistake. When psychologists work within an experimental setting where measurements of the dependent and independent variables are precise and tightly controlled, they are prone to adopt the more stringent test. They want compelling evidence before rejecting the null hypothesis and will therefore employ the .01 confidence level or even a .001 level, refusing in the latter case to reject the null hypothesis unless the chances of being wrong in so doing are less than one in a thousand. Political scientists often work with less robust data and confront greater measurement noise and subject variability, particularly in survey research. As a consequence, they may adopt a less stringent test and reject the null hypothesis at the .05 confidence level. As suggested above, sample size also influences the confidence level chosen: researchers with large samples generally employ more stringent significance tests than do researchers with smaller samples. Finally, exploratory studies where the researcher is looking for suggestive findings rather than ironclad results may employ lower levels of confidence, perhaps even the .10 confidence level.

No golden rule exists for the choice of confidence levels; therefore, the possibility arises that two researchers could look at the same empirical results with one rejecting the null hypothesis at the .05 confidence level and the other failing to do so at the .01 confidence level. What is essential is that the researcher makes the decision regarding what level of confidence to use *before looking at the empirical results*. This will reduce the temptation of changing confidence levels in midstream in order to convert insignificant relationships ($p > .01$) into significant relationships ($p > .05$).

You might assume that social scientists would do everything possible to minimize the probability of error by using the most stringent significance tests. However, there are two different types of errors that can be made, and by minimizing the probability of one we increase the probability of the other. A **Type I error**, or 'false positive', is made when the null hypothesis is incorrectly rejected; we conclude on the basis of sample results that a relationship exists in the population when in fact it does not. Type I errors are more likely if we adopt a .05 confidence level, making it relatively easy to reject the null hypothesis, than if we adopt a .01 confidence level. A **Type II error**, or 'false negative', is made when we incorrectly fail to reject the null hypothesis; we conclude on the basis of the sample evidence that a relationship does not exist in the population when in fact it does. Type II errors are more likely to be made if we adopt a .01 confidence level than if we adopt a .05 confidence level. The distinction between Type I and Type II errors is expressed in Figure 16.1.

Unfortunately, there is no strategy that minimizes the probability of both Type I and Type II errors. We have to choose, and the choice will hinge upon a number of factors, including the risks associated with either type of error and perhaps

		Reality	
		No Relationship	Relationship
Researcher's Conclusion	Relationship	**Type I Error**	Correct Conclusion
	No Relationship	Correct Conclusion	**Type II Error**

FIGURE 16.1 Type I and Type II Errors

even the personality of the researcher (some people are naturally more cautious than others). The best illustration of the stakes involved comes from medical research. Suppose, for instance, that a new drug has been developed that appears to offer a promising treatment for a particular form of cancer. However, before the company that developed the drug can release it for general use, clinical trials must be conducted to see if there are dangerous side effects. The null hypothesis is that there are no side effects. The question is, What standard should be employed to accept or reject the null hypothesis? If the researchers conducting the clinical trials make a Type I error, concluding that there are dangerous side effects when in fact there are not, then the opportunity for a promising drug treatment would be missed. If the researchers make a Type II error, concluding that there are no side effects when there are, then a dangerous drug could be unleashed on unsuspecting patients and their physicians. As you can imagine, the company that developed the drug, the researchers conducting the clinical trials, public health officials, insurance firms, patients, and physicians may have quite different views over whether a Type I or Type II error would be more problematic.

APPLY YOUR UNDERSTANDING

Choosing between False Positives and False Negatives

Imagine you are in a situation where you are trying to decide between two home pregnancy test kits. The box for one promises that the risk of a false positive is only 1 in 100, but the risk of a false negative is 5 in 100. The second kit promises that the risk of a false negative is only 1 in 100, but the risk of a false positive is 5 in 100. Which kit would you choose, and why? If you had to make the same choice with respect to tests for breast cancer or AIDS, would your choice change? If so, why? What factors might lead you to prefer the risk of a false positive to a false negative, or the reverse?

In drawing this discussion to a close, we should note that confidence levels can also be established for a range of scores. For example, a polling organization may report that 45 per cent of respondents support the government of the day, and that the poll findings are accurate within ±3 per cent, 19 times out of 20. In effect, the polling organization has established a **confidence interval** and has concluded there is a 95 per cent probability that the percentage of the *population* (in this case, the electorate) supporting the government lies between 42 per cent (45 per cent – 3 per cent) and 48 per cent (45 per cent + 3 per cent). If the polling organization wanted to be even more confident that its poll result fell within population parameters, if it wanted to establish a 99 per cent confidence interval, then the interval would have to be larger. Hence the tradeoff: a small confidence interval provides greater precision but less confidence, while a large confidence interval provides less precision but more confidence. The norm among commercial pollsters is the 95 per cent confidence interval, or '19 times out of 20'. This means, incidentally, that one poll in 20 will be a 'rogue' poll with results that are not as close to the population mean as the polling organization might suggest. Unfortunately, because population parameters are estimated rather than known, it can never be determined which is the rogue poll and which are the 19 out of 20.

Although there is no magic rule for selecting a confidence level, a choice must be made.[3] Once the confidence level has been established, an inferential statistic must be selected and calculated.

SELECTING INFERENTIAL STATISTICS

How one selects the appropriate inferential statistic depends upon the assumptions underlying the statistic itself. **Nonparametric statistics** are those that are not contingent on particular assumptions (or parameters) about data distribution (Bailey 1978, 332). **Parametric statistics**, in contrast, have built-in assumptions about the distribution parameters. For *inferential statistics*, readers should note that only interval-level variables are able to meet the distribution assumptions of the parametric tests; thus, to use a parametric test, one of the variables must be interval-level. In addition, not even all interval-level variables meet the distribution

EXPAND YOUR KNOWLEDGE
The Debate over Significance Tests

There is a methodological debate over the use (and misuse) of significance tests. As Christopher Shea (1996) writes, the critics of significance tests 'point out that decisions about whether something is due to chance are based on a sliding scale of probability. Therefore, dividing research findings into two categories—significant and not significant—is a gross oversimplification'. Gill (1999, 669) writes, 'The basic problem with the null hypothesis significance test in political science is that it often does not tell political scientists what they think it is telling them . . . it is very easy to confuse statistical significance with theoretical or substantive importance. It is also possible to have data which tells us something about an important political question, but which does not pass an arbitrary significance level threshold'.

Part of the reaction to significance tests is manifest in the increased use of *meta-analysis*. This approach pulls together large sets of studies done over the years on particular research questions. Patterns are sought that run through the various studies, patterns that may be statistically significant in some, not in others, but nonetheless are pronounced when the various studies are pooled. In this manner, meta-analysis gets around the problems associated with small samples and is able to bring into play studies that were insignificant in themselves but that give added weight to general patterns of research findings.

requirements of the parametric tests.[4] A 'rule of thumb' chart for selecting inferential statistics is presented in summary in Table 16.7 at the conclusion to this chapter. Please note, however, that there are always exceptions to such guidelines and that because of space limitations, not all possible significance tests have been included in the table or in the chapter.

We will look in turn at the chi-square, the t-test for differences between means, the Mann-Whitney U-test, and F-ratios. In each case we will calculate the test statistic, compare this statistic with the critical value, and, using this comparison, decide whether or not to reject the null hypothesis.

CHI-SQUARE

Chi-square is a test of the independence of two variables. The null hypothesis states that the two variables are independent or unrelated to one another in the population from which the sample was drawn. The chi-square test assesses the likelihood that the relationship observed in the sample is due to chance; in other words, what is the probability that the relationship does *not* exist in the population? As a nonparametric statistic, chi-square lacks the power of the other significance tests. However, its lack of parameters makes it the only test statistic available when we look at relationships among nominal- and ordinal-level variables. (Nominal variables require nonparametric tests because the values of the variable—1, 2, 3, 4—refer to differences in kind, not differences in degree; ordinal variables because there is not a standard unit difference between numerical values.) Chi-square has the distinct advantage, as we will see, of being a highly stable measure, one based on a cell-by-cell comparison of the observed relationship and the expected relationship under the null hypothesis.

We can state the null and alternative hypotheses of chi-square as follows:

$$H_0 : f_O = f_e$$
$$H_a : f_O \neq f_e$$

where f_O is observed frequencies, and f_e is expected frequencies.

Before calculating chi-square, we must construct a **contingency table** (also referred to as a cross-tabulation table). To create a contingency table, we first need to identify the two variables under question and the number of categories, or values, within each variable. Let's say that our variables are age and support for conservatism. The variable 'age' in this example is divided into three categories: young (18–30 years), middle (31–50 years), and old (51+ years). The variable 'support for conservatism' is also divided into three categories: low, moderate, and high. To create our table, we place one variable across the top of the table, being certain to place the categories in order (low to high) if the variable is ordinal rather than nominal and to label the variable as well as all categories. We then place the second variable on the left-hand side of the table, again paying attention to ordering and labelling. The result is the table presented in Figure 16.2.

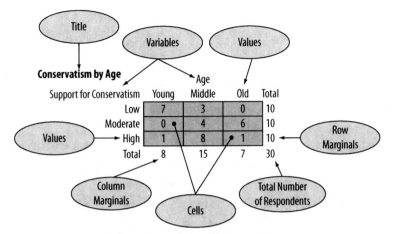

FIGURE 16.2 Creating a Contingency Table

Our next step is to take individual cases and locate them in the cells of the table. In a contingency table, the location of a particular case is *contingent* upon its values for each of the two variables. Robert is 20 years old and ranks low on conservatism. To locate Robert on the table in Figure 16.2, we first find his location on the age variable. Because Robert is 20 years old, he will be placed in the 'young' category, which is the first *column* of the contingency table. We then need to place Robert according to the second variable. Robert is located in the 'low' category of conservatism, which is the first *row* of the table. Thus, we place Robert in the cell where young intersects with 'low conservatism,' in this case, in row 1, column 1. Looking at the table, where would you place someone who is 58 years old and moderately conservative? Someone who is 31 years old and highly conservative? To create a contingency table, we must locate each individual case in its appropriate cell. We then total the number of cases in each cell; for example, if the old, moderate conservatism cell (row 2, column 3) has a total of six cases, we place the number 6 in that cell.

Our final step is to total the numbers in each row and column. These totals are known as **marginals**. To find row marginals, we add *across* the cells for each row. The row marginals provide the frequency distribution for 'support for conservatism'. To find column marginals, we add *down* the cells for each column. The column marginals provide the frequency distribution for age. The total number of cases in the data set (identified as *N*) is designated outside the lower right-hand corner of the table. Obviously, the row marginals summed together should be equal to *N*, as should the column marginals. If they are not, some sort of summation error has occurred. Be sure to double-check your numbers!

Once the contingency table is constructed, we are able to use chi-square to test our hypothesis. The independence of the two variables is assessed by comparing the *observed frequencies* in a bivariate relationship with the *expected frequencies* that would occur if perfect independence existed. How many cases would we expect in each cell of our contingency table if the variables are independent? We calculate the expected frequencies for each cell of the contingency table, and then calculate chi-square by the following formula:

$$\chi^2 = \frac{\Sigma(O - E)^2}{E}$$

where E is the expected frequency for a given cell, and O is the observed frequency for the same cell.[5]

For each cell in the contingency table we subtract the expected frequency from the observed value to find the difference between the two frequencies. This value must be squared because of the fact that we are summing variation: if we fail to do so, the deviations total to zero.

Table 16.1 provides an opportunity to work through the chi-square calculations. The table presents the observed values for 100 respondents, categorized by both their sex and support for a hypothetical policy. The question being asked in this analysis is, Does an individual's sex have an impact on attitudes toward this policy among the population as a whole? We don't know the answer with certainty, because the population as a whole has not been asked their views on this policy issue. Instead, we have (hypothetical) data from 100 people. Therefore, a more refined question is, How likely is it that we would find a relationship of the strength observed in Table 16.1 in a sample of this size *if* there was no relationship between these variables in the population? Thus, we wish to compare the number of respondents in each cell (the observed frequency) with the number of people we would expect to find under the null hypothesis (the expected cell frequency) if the two variables were unrelated.

The data in Table 16.1 present the observed cell frequencies. The upper left cell, for example, shows that 15 of the respondents were women who registered a low level of support for the policy in question. The first step in computing the chi-square is to calculate the expected frequencies for every cell of the contingency table. Thus, for example, we wish to know how many women and how many men would have a low level of support for this policy if sex did not affect support. To answer this question, assume the *marginals* of the table do not change; there are

TABLE 16.1 Support for Policy X by Sex (Observed Values)

	Female	Male	Total
Low support	15	5	20
Medium support	15	15	30
High support	25	25	50
Total	55	45	100

always 55 females and 45 males, and 20 people with low support, 30 with medium support, and 50 with high support. But the numbers *within the cells* can change to reflect the null hypothesis.

One way of thinking about this is to ask what percentage of the total sample population has low support. In this example, it is 20 out of 100 cases, or 20 per cent. If sex does not affect attitudes toward the policy in question, then 20 per cent of women and 20 per cent of men should have low support. How *many* women and men should have low support depends upon the number of men and women in the sample. Since there are 55 women, we can calculate that 55 × 20 per cent = 11, for an expected cell frequency of 11 women. The expected cell frequency for men is 45 × 20 per cent = 9. Notice that to calculate the expected cell frequencies for women we divided the row marginal (20) by the total marginal (100) and multiplied this by the column marginal (55). By changing the order of operations, we derive the following general formula:

$$E = \frac{(\text{row marginal})(\text{column marginal})}{N}$$

Thus, for the low-support, female cell, our expected frequency is 11:

$$E = \frac{(\text{row marginal})(\text{column marginal})}{N} = \frac{20 \times 55}{100} = 11$$

If sex and support for policy X are independent, we would expect 11 women to support policy X.

The same calculation is used to determine the expected frequency for all other cells. Thus, for the low-support, male cell, the expected frequency is 20 (row marginal) multiplied by 45 (column marginal) divided by 100, which equals 9. The expected frequency for the medium-support, female cell is 16.5 (30 × 55, divided by 100); the expected frequency for the medium-support, male cell is 13.5 (30 × 45, divided by 100); and so on. We continue calculating expected frequencies until we have completed the expected frequencies table, shown in Table 16.2. Try calculating the last two expected frequencies on your own.

TABLE 16.2 Support for Policy X by Sex (Expected Frequencies)

	Female	Male	Total
Low support	11	9	20
Medium support	16.5	13.5	30
High support	27.5	22.5	50
Total	55	45	100

The next step is to calculate chi-square itself. The chi-square compares the observed frequencies (Table 16.1) with the expected frequencies (Table 16.2). Recall that the formula for chi-square is as follows:

$$\chi^2 = \frac{\Sigma(O - E)^2}{E}$$

We need to square the difference between the observed and expected frequencies, and then divide that figure by the expected frequencies. This step must be undertaken for *each cell*. For the low-support, female cell we get the following:

$$\frac{(O - E)^2}{E} = \frac{(15 - 11)^2}{11} = \frac{16}{11} = 1.45$$

For the low-support, male cell we have

$$\frac{(O - E)^2}{E} = \frac{(5 - 9)^2}{9} = \frac{16}{9} = 1.78$$

This process is repeated for each cell until all values are calculated. The results are shown in Table 16.3.

We next need to take all of the resultant figures and sum them together:

$$1.45 + 1.78 + 0.14 + 0.17 + 0.23 + 0.28 = 4.05$$

TABLE 16.3 Observed and Expected Frequencies

	Female	Male
Low support	Cell 1	Cell 2
Medium support	Cell 3	Cell 4
High support	Cell 5	Cell 6

Cell	Observed	Expected	$O - E$	$(O - E)^2$	$\dfrac{(O - E)^2}{E}$
1	15	11	4	16	1.45
2	5	9	−4	16	1.78
3	15	16.5	−1.5	2.25	0.14
4	15	13.5	1.5	2.25	0.17
5	25	27.5	−2.5	6.25	0.23
6	25	22.5	2.5	6.25	0.28

This final number is chi-square. We can now use chi-square to determine whether we should accept or reject the null hypothesis. Before doing so, however, we need to calculate the degrees of freedom for our contingency table, using the following formula:

$$d.f. = (r - 1)(c - 1)$$

where r is the number of rows, and c is the number of columns. In our example, we are using a 3 × 2 table; thus, $d.f. = (3 - 1)(2 - 1) = 2 \times 1 = 2$. Degrees of freedom are important when we look at the chi-square table. (An excerpt from the table has been presented in Table 16.4.)

TABLE 16.4 Critical Values for Chi-square

d.f.	p = .05	p = .01
1	3.841	6.635
2	5.991	9.210
3	7.815	11.341
4	9.488	13.277
5	11.070	15.086

Source: Adapted from Elazar J. Pedhazer, *Multiple Regression in Behavioral Research*, 2d ed. (Fort Worth, TX: Harcourt Brace, 1982), p. 792.

In the chi-square table we find our critical value. Note that we look down the rows to find the degrees of freedom, and across the columns to find our confidence level. Each cell contains the **critical value** for the given degrees of freedom and confidence level. This is the number that the calculated chi-square must meet or exceed if we are to reject the null hypothesis. Thus, for a 5 *d.f.* table and 99 per cent confidence level, our calculated chi-square would need to meet or exceed the critical value 15.086. For a 1 *d.f.* table and 95 per cent confidence, our critical value is 3.841. Let's return once again to our example. We had a 2 *d.f.* table, and we will assume that we are using a 95 per cent confidence level (used most commonly in political science research). Our critical value is 5.991. How does this compare with our calculated chi-square value? We found chi-square to equal 4.05. Our calculated value does *not* meet or exceed the critical value; therefore, we must conclude that there is a high probability that the sample relationship occurred by chance. The null hypothesis, which stated that the two variables are independent ($H_0: f_o = f_e$), cannot be rejected. In other words, we *fail to reject the null hypothesis*. The relationship has been found to be statistically insignificant. If our calculated value had met or exceeded the critical value, we would have concluded that the relationship was, in fact, statistically significant and rejected the null hypothesis. The conclusion, then, is that in the population as a whole, the sex of individuals has no significant impact on attitudes toward this policy question.

Summary: Using Chi-square

1. Calculate the expected frequencies table.
2. Calculate chi-square.
3. Determine the degrees of freedom.
4. Find the critical value on the chi-square table.
5. Compare the critical value and the calculated chi-square to draw a conclusion about the null hypothesis.

Chi-square tests are commonly used nonparametric tests for nominal- and ordinal-level relationships. There are, however, a few problems with the chi-square test that should be noted. First, it lacks the power of many of the parametric tests. Second, chi-square values reflect not only independence but also sample size. As our sample size increases, so too do our calculated chi-square values, making it easy to use chi-square to reject the null hypothesis. Thus, the chi-square test can deem extremely weak and substantively insignificant relationships found in large samples 'statistically significant'. Researchers should keep this limitation of chi-square in mind when interpreting their data. On the other hand, large samples are

APPLY YOUR UNDERSTANDING

Calculating Chi-square

A researcher is interested in the extent to which Quebec emerges as a 'distinct society' on public policy issues having no immediate connection to constitutional policy. To this end he collects survey data on public opinion toward tobacco advertising. Eleven hundred respondents were asked if they favoured a complete ban on tobacco advertising, a partial ban, or no restrictions whatsoever. The pattern of response for Quebec respondents and respondents in the rest of Canada was as follows:

Opinion toward Tobacco Advertising	Quebec	Rest of Canada	Total
Complete ban	110	450	560
Partial ban	145	280	425
No restrictions	45	70	115
Total	300	800	1,100

Calculate the chi-square for this table. Does the evidence support the conclusion that Quebec is indeed a distinct society?

often used precisely because we wish to have small margins of error and high levels of statistical significance. The key point to remember is not to confuse statistical significance with a strong relationship (substantive significance).

When we have a nominal- or an ordinal-level variable in relationship with a normally distributed interval-level variable, we can use the difference of means *t*-test, rather than chi-square. It is to this test that we will now turn.

T-TESTS FOR DIFFERENCES BETWEEN MEANS

One way to look for relationships between two variables is to divide the entire sample into subsamples based on the categories of one variable and then look for differences in univariate statistics (measures of central tendency or variation) between the subsamples. (An example of this was presented at the end of Chapter 15.) This approach allows us to look at relationships between nominal-/ordinal-level variables and interval-level variables. We use the category of a nominal- or ordinal-level variable to subdivide; for example, we might divide our sample into two subsamples based on sex (men and women) or into three subsamples based on support for policy X (low support, medium support, and high support). This chapter will focus on difference of means tests for two samples. Having subdivided our sample, we then consider the univariate statistics of the *interval-level* variable within each subsample; most commonly, we look to the mean. Are the mean scores for the subsamples similar, or do they differ? This is known as comparing the **difference of means**. If the means are significantly different, this suggests a relationship between the interval-level variable and the nominal-/ordinal-level variable that the subsamples are based on. Thus, our null hypothesis is that the subsamples are the same; there is no difference between the samples and thus no relationship between the two variables. Our alternative hypothesis is that the difference of means is statistically significant, and there is a relationship between the two variables in question. These hypotheses can be stated as follows:

$$H_0: \mu_1 = \mu_2$$
$$H_a: \mu_1 \neq \mu_2$$

where μ_1 designates the *population* mean of sample 1, and μ_2 designates the *population* mean of sample 2. (Recall that we are always interested in parameters, rather than the statistics themselves. Thus, our hypotheses are always statements about the populations, rather than about the samples.)

One of the most common significance tests for differences in mean scores is the *t*-test. This is a parametric test; thus, the researcher must ensure that both samples are normally distributed. In order to understand the conceptual architecture of this test, imagine drawing a series of samples from the same population. If you were to calculate the sample means for this series, you would expect the means to be similar but not identical; random variation would preclude identical means.

(The larger the samples, the closer the means would be to one another.) Now, suppose you were to draw a sample of men and a sample of women and were to compare the mean mathematical abilities of the two samples. The null hypothesis would be that the two samples were drawn from the same population, which is to assume that there is no difference in math ability between men and women in the population at large. The question, then, is whether the observed difference in math ability between the two sample means is small enough to be attributed to chance alone (the null hypothesis is accepted) or whether it is large enough to suggest that the two samples were drawn from populations that differ in their math ability (the null hypothesis is rejected). To make this choice, we need a measure that takes into account the difference in sample means and the dispersion of scores about the two means.

The *t*-test provides just such a measure. It is based on the null hypothesis that the samples being compared are drawn from the same population and, therefore, that any observed difference in sample means can be attributed to chance alone. In order to apply the *t*-test to a difference in mean scores, we need to know the size, mean, and variance for each of the two samples. The formula for the two-sample *t*-ratio, assuming that the samples are approximately the same size, is

$$t = \frac{\overline{X}_1 - \overline{X}_2}{\sqrt{\dfrac{S_1^2}{N_1} + \dfrac{S_2^2}{N_2}}}$$

where $\overline{X}_1$ is the mean of the first sample, S_1^2 is the variance of the first sample, and N_1 is the size of the first sample; similarly, $\overline{X}_2$ is the mean of the second sample, S_2^2 is the variance of the second sample, and N_2 is the size of the second sample. Imagine two samples, with statistics as follows:

Sample 1: mean = $\overline{X}$ = 8; variance = S^2 = 1.6; sample size = N = 30
Sample 2: mean = $\overline{X}$ = 5; variance = S^2 = 2.1; sample size = N = 43

The *t*-ratio for these samples would be:

$$t = \frac{\overline{X}_1 - \overline{X}_2}{\sqrt{\dfrac{S_1^2}{N_1} + \dfrac{S_2^2}{N_2}}}$$

$$= \frac{8 - 5}{\sqrt{\dfrac{1.6}{30} + \dfrac{2.1}{43}}}$$

$$= \frac{3}{\sqrt{0.053 + 0.049}}$$

$$= \frac{3}{\sqrt{0.102}}$$

$$= \frac{3}{0.32} = 9.38$$

Once the *t*-ratio has been found, it must be compared with the critical value found in the table of *t*-values, an excerpt of which is presented in Table 16.5. The formula for calculating the degrees of freedom for difference of means tests is

$$d.f. = N - k$$

where *N* is the *total* sample size ($N_1 + N_2 + \ldots$), and *k* is the number of samples. In our example, *d.f.* equals 71 (73 − 2).

TABLE 16.5 Abbreviated Distribution of *t*

d.f.	One-tailed Two-tailed	.05 .10	.025 .05	.01 .02	.005 .01
40		1.684	2.021	2.423	2.704
60		1.671	2.000	2.390	2.660
120		1.658	1.980	2.358	2.617

You will notice on the *t*-table a distinction between one-tailed and two-tailed tests. If the direction of difference is not important to us, we use a **two-tailed test**. Thus, if we are not interested in whether men or women are better at math, but rather are just concerned whether *any* sex difference exists, we would use the two-tailed test. If the direction of difference does matter to our theory—if, for example, we are testing the hypothesis that men have greater math ability—then we use a **one-tailed test**. Marija J. Norusis (1990, 156) explains the distinction between the two tests: 'The procedure [for the one-tailed test] is the same as for the two-tailed test, but the resulting probability value is divided by 2, adjusting for the fact that the equality hypothesis is rejected only when the difference be-tween the two means is sufficiently large and in the direction of interest. In the two-tailed test, the equality hypothesis is rejected for large positive or negative values of the statistic.' If we have theoretical justification for using the one-tailed test, it is preferred.

Let's return to our example. We have a *t*-ratio of 9.38 and 71 degrees of freedom. We will use the 95 per cent confidence level and a two-tailed test. Looking at the table, we find that the closest critical value is 2.000. Our calculated value exceeds this critical value, allowing us to *reject the null hypothesis* (H_0: $\mu_1 = \mu_2$) and support the alternative hypothesis (H_a: $\mu_1 \neq \mu_2$). In experimental research, the results suggest that samples were, in fact, drawn from different populations, indicating a statis-tically significant relationship between the two variables. In survey research, the results suggest a significant difference between categories of the independent variable (for example, males and females), leading to the conclusion that the relationship did not occur by chance.

APPLY YOUR UNDERSTANDING

Using the *t*-Test

A university decides to generate empirical data showing what a university education pays with respect to personal income. To this end, a survey of 500 respondents from the local community is commissioned, of whom 150 have a university degree and 350 do not. The mean annual income for those respondents with a university degree is $66,000, and the standard deviation is $7,000. The mean annual income for those without a university degree is $61,000, and the standard deviation is $5,000. (Recall from Chapter 15 that the standard deviation is the square root of the variance; thus, to calculate the variance, you must square the standard deviation.) Calculate a *t*-test to determine if the survey evidence supports the proposition that 'a university education pays'.

An alternative method for looking at the significance of relationships between ordinal- and interval-level variables, or between interval-level variables with non-normal data distributions, is the Mann-Whitney *U* rank-order test.

MANN-WHITNEY *U*-TEST

The Mann-Whitney *U*-test is based on the ranking of cases and can therefore be used for relationships where one or both of the variables are ordinal- or interval-level. Like the chi-square test, it is a nonparametric test and is therefore useful when we wish to test relationships in which the interval-level variables do not meet the normal distribution requirements of the parametric tests. Of course, like all other nonparametric tests, the Mann-Whitney *U*-test does not provide as much information as would a parametric statistic. Thus, if the researcher can use parametric tests, it is usually advised that she do so. The tradeoff, then, is between a less informative, nonparametric statistic that does not introduce important assumptions about the distribution of the data (such as a normal distribution or a linear relationship) versus a parametric statistic that provides more information but that may also have assumptions (normality, linearity) that are not met by the data.

The logic of the Mann-Whitney *U*-test resembles that of the difference of means test: we compare two subsamples on a particular characteristic and determine if the populations are significantly different. If they are, we conclude that the bivari-ate relationship is significant. But where the difference of means test compares means, the Mann-Whitney U-test compares rankings. The test works as follows: we combine the two subsamples into a single sample (being certain to remember which case belongs to which sample); we then rank each case, from high to low, according to its score on the variable; and finally, we again subdivide the two samples and total the rankings, comparing the totalled rankings of each subsample. Why would the rankings within the different subsamples matter? Logically, '[i]f the groups have the same distribution, their sample distribution of ranks should be similar. If one of the groups has more than its share of small or large ranks, there is reason to suspect that the two underlying distributions are different' (Norusis 1990, 226). The rankings are summarized into the Mann-Whitney U-statistic, and the significance of the U-statistic is tested with the z-test statistic. The null hypothesis states that the populations will have equal rankings, whereas the alternative hypoth-esis states that the rankings will differ. These hypotheses can be stated as follows:

$$H_0: R_1 = R_2$$
$$H_a: R_1 \neq R_2$$

where R_1 is the ranking in population 1, and R_2 is the ranking in population 2.

We will demonstrate the Mann-Whitney U-test with the nominal-interval re-lationship we considered in the previous section: gender and math performance. We are looking at the final grades of the students in a rather small section of a university math course. Of course, to select the Mann-Whitney U-test over the more powerful differences of means test, we obviously have reason to assume that the math scores in one sample are not normally distributed; in this case, the men's sample has a few 'geniuses' who skew the distribution.

Men		Women	
Case	Score	Case	Score
1	98	6	82
2	99	7	72
3	56	8	70
4	64	9	90
5	72	10	78

The first step is to look at the two samples as a single sample, and assign ranks. For tied cases, they are 'averaged' between the two ranks that they 'share'. For this sample, case 2 is highest and therefore gets the highest ranking; case 1 is ranked second; case 9 is ranked third; and so on. Note that cases 5 and 7 are tied and are therefore ranked at 6.5 ((6 + 7)/2).

	Men			Women	
Case	Score	Rank	Case	Score	Rank
1	98	2	6	82	4
2	99	1	7	72	6.5
3	56	10	8	70	8
4	64	9	9	90	3
5	72	6.5	10	78	5

The next step is to sum the ranks of each sample. For the men, the rankings sum to 28.5 (2 + 1 + 10 + 9 + 6.5); for women, the rankings sum to 26.5 (4 + 6.5 + 8 + 3 + 5). We then calculate Mann-Whitney U, using the formula

$$U = N_1N_2 + \frac{N_1(N_1 + 1)}{2} - \Sigma R_1$$

where N_1 is the sample size of sample 1, N_2 is the sample size of sample 2, and ΣR_1 is the summed rankings of group 1.

Calculating U for this sample, we get

$$U = N_1N_2 + \frac{N_1(N_1 + 1)}{2} - \Sigma R_1$$
$$= 5(5) + \frac{5(5 + 1)}{2} - 28.5$$
$$= 25 + 15 - 28.5$$
$$= 11.5$$

We then need to determine if this U-value is statistically significant. To do so, we calculate a z-value,[6] using the formula

$$Z = \frac{U - \frac{N_1N_2}{2}}{\sqrt{\frac{N_1N_2(N_1 + N_2 + 1)}{12}}}$$

For this example,

$$Z = \frac{11.5 - \frac{5(5)}{2}}{\sqrt{\frac{5(5)(5 + 5 + 1)}{12}}}$$
$$= \frac{-1}{\sqrt{22.92}} = \frac{-1}{4.78} = -0.209$$

This calculated z-value is compared to the charted critical value. Recall that for z-scores, our critical values are constant: at the 95 per cent confidence level, the critical value is $z = \pm1.96$, and at the 99 per cent confidence level, the critical value is $z = \pm2.58$. As we have learned, if the calculated score meets or exceeds the critical value, we can reject the null hypothesis. Clearly, we fail to reject the null hypothesis in this example: our calculated value of -0.209 falls short of the 95 per cent confidence critical value of ±1.96.

On the basis of this analysis, we would conclude that sex has no significant impact on math performance. Looking back at the data, we realize that this conclusion could probably also be reached by 'eyeballing' the data. For example, although two of the males scored very high on the math test (99 and 98) and were ranked 1 and 2, two other males performed quite poorly (scores of 56 and 64), and ranked 9 and 10 out of 10. In this instance, the wide discrepancy in the performance of the males meant that they performed neither consistently higher nor lower than the women. However, these two groups did have different patterns of performance; the women as a group performed more consistently near the middle of the range; the men were more likely to be high or low. These differences, though, did not register with the Mann-Whitney U-statistic. This serves as an important reminder: whenever possible, look closely at the data as well as at the summary statistic.

Although the Mann-Whitney U-test is useful for all ordinal-level relationships, its use with interval-level variables should be limited to those cases where the interval-level variable fails to meet the normal distribution requirements of the parametric tests. If a normal distribution exists, the researcher should use the difference of means (for relationships with ordinal- and nominal-level variables) or the t-test and F-ratio (for relationships with other normally distributed interval-level variables), which we will now examine.

T-TESTS AND *F*-RATIOS FOR INTERVAL-LEVEL RELATIONSHIPS

In Chapter 18 we will introduce the basic linear model used to depict relationships between normally distributed interval-level variables. A line is drawn to 'best fit' the graphical placement of the data. This regression line has a slope (designated by b), which signifies the unit change in one variable for every unit change in the other variable. When the rate of change is more dramatic, the line is relatively steep; when the rate of change is lower, the line is less steep. We can test the 'goodness of fit' of the regression line with a statistic known as R^2. Inferential statistics are used to assess whether the slope of the regression line is significant and whether the R^2 value is significant. This section will introduce the steps necessary to calculate inferential statistics for linear regression analysis but will leave all discussion of the linear model for Chapter 18. It should be noted that the t-tests and F-ratios described in this section are also used to test significance in multiple regression analyses, which will also be explored in Chapter 18.

The test of R^2 is a test of the bivariate linear relationship. The null hypothesis states that a relationship does not exist in the population, whereas the alternative hypothesis states that a relationship does exist. Stated in proper form, this is

$$H_0: R^2 = 0$$
$$H_a: R^2 \neq 0$$

To test the R^2 value, we use the F-ratio, which is calculated with the formula

$$F = \frac{\dfrac{R^2}{k}}{(1 - R^2)/(N - k - 1)}$$

where k is the number of independent variables. For bivariate regression, $k = 1$. Once we calculate the F-statistic, we compare this value to the appropriate critical value (derived from a table of critical values of F) to decide whether to accept or reject the null hypothesis.

Imagine that a regression run between two interval-level, normally distributed variables from a sample of 50 cases produces an R^2 value of 0.30. Is this sample statistic representative of a relationship in the population? To test this, we calculate F:

$$F = \frac{\dfrac{R^2}{k}}{(1 - R^2)/(N - k - 1)}$$
$$= \frac{\dfrac{0.30}{1}}{(1 - 0.30)/(50 - 1 - 1)}$$
$$= \frac{0.30}{(0.70)/(48)}$$
$$= \frac{0.30}{0.015}$$
$$= 20$$

We now need to look up the critical value on the F-distribution table, presented in abbreviated form in Table 16.6. Notice that the table requires two different degrees of freedom values. The formulas for these are as follows:

$$d.f.\ 1 = k, \ d.f.\ 2 = N - k - 1$$

TABLE 16.6 Abbreviated F-Table at the 95 Per Cent Confidence Level

d.f. 1	1	2	3
d.f. 2			
46	4.05	3.20	2.81
48	4.04	3.19	2.80
50	4.03	3.18	2.79

For this example, *d.f.* 1 equals 1, and *d.f.* 2 equals 48 (50 − 1 − 1). Looking at the table, we can see that the appropriate critical value is 4.04. Our calculated *F*-value exceeds the critical value, and we therefore can reject the null hypothesis. The relationship has been found to be statistically significant.

When we test the slope of the regression line, our null hypothesis is that the population slope equals zero; in other words, changes in one variable are not associated with changes in the other. Thus,

$$H_0: \beta = 0$$
$$H_a: \beta \neq 0$$

where beta is the population slope. To test the significance of our slope, we use a *t*-test. Here, *t* is calculated with the formula

$$t = \frac{b}{s_b}$$

where s_b is the standard error of *b*.[7] (An alternative method of finding *t* for bivariate relationships is to take the square root of the *F*-score.) As with the *t*-test for differences of means, we compare the calculated value to the critical value found in the *t*-test. Degrees of freedom are equal to $N - k - 1$.

Overall, we have seen that inferential statistics play a central role in hypothesis-testing. But after we have rejected the null hypothesis, we still need to find substantive support for our alternative hypotheses. It is by this means that we are able to advance our theories. This subject will be addressed in Chapters 17 and 18.

TABLE 16.7 Summary Suggestions for Selecting Inferential Statistics

Variables in Correlation	Suggested Statistic(s)
Nominal-nominal	Chi-square
Ordinal-nominal	Chi-square, Mann-Whitney *U*
Ordinal-ordinal	Chi-square, Mann-Whitney *U*
Interval*-nominal	Difference of means
Interval*-ordinal	Difference of means
Interval*-interval*	*t*-test, *F*-test
Interval**-nominal	Mann-Whitney *U*
Interval**-ordinal	Mann-Whitney *U*
Interval**-interval*/**	Mann-Whitney *U*

*Normal distribution of cases
**Nonnormal distribution of cases

WORKING AS A TEAM

1. Your group has been hired to determine if high school students who have been exposed to educational material on the dangers of smoking are less likely to smoke than students who have not been exposed to such material. By mistake, the data analysis is conducted before a decision has been made on the appropriate level of significance. You now know that there is a difference between the two groups, that students who have been exposed are less likely to smoke, and that the probability of this difference being attributed to chance alone is .02, or 2 chances in 100. You now have to decide whether to employ a .01 or .05 confidence level for the test of significance. What would you recommend? What are the policy implications of your choice? What are the arguments for erring on the side of Type I or Type II error?

2. What are the ethical issues that come into play?

SELF-STUDY

1. Calculate the chi-square for the following table, which looks at the (hypothetical) relationship between partisanship and support for gun control. Would you accept or reject H_o? What critical value would you use, and why?

	Liberal	BQ	Conservative	NDP	Total
Support stronger gun control measures	70	15	12	20	117
Oppose stronger gun control measures	50	10	30	20	110
Total	120	25	42	40	227

2. A (hypothetical) study has been done to examine whether individuals born in Canada have significantly different annual incomes than individuals born outside the country but now living in Canada. The study included 500 respondents in each category. The mean annual income for those born in Canada was $64,000, with a standard deviation of $6,500. The mean annual income for those born outside the country is $59,000, with a standard deviation of $5,500. Construct a one-tailed and a two-tailed t-test. Which would be the most appropriate? Would you use a .01 or .05 test of significance? What would you conclude about the difference in annual income between those born inside and outside Canada?

NOTES

1. Adapted from Norusis (1990, 159).
2. Readers with access to data analysis programs such as SPSS, SAS, Stata, or R should note that the programs will calculate test statistics automatically and compare those statistics with the critical values. Thus, for many, the exercises in this chapter will be more pedagogical than practical.
3. In journal articles, political scientists often select a .05 confidence level, but also distinguish higher confidence levels ($p > .01$, $p > .001$) in the tables. This allows the reader to make her own assessment about confidence levels.
4. To test for the normal distributions required for parametric tests, researchers should examine the data with a diagnostics test such as SPSS's EXAMINE or by using histograms and box plots.
5. Some texts use the symbols f_e and f_o to designate 'frequencies expected' and 'frequencies observed'.
6. For small sample sizes of the kind seldom encountered in survey research, z-scores may not be appropriate. For an alternative interpretive table, see Gibbons (1976, 409–16).
7. To calculate the standard error of b, use the formula $S_b = \sqrt{\text{variance/sum of squares}}$.

Chapter 17

EXPLAINING THE POLITICAL WORLD: NOMINAL AND ORDINAL DATA

DESTINATION

By the end of this chapter the reader should

- be able to construct and read contingency tables;
- understand the use of measures of association to measure the strength of relationships;
- be able to choose from among a variety of measures of association;
- be able to calculate and interpret those measures of association; and
- be able to control for a third variable.

Explanatory research is the means by which political scientists explore questions of cause and effect. We know from descriptive research that there is variation within political phenomena of interest, and our goal is to identify the major causes of such variation. For example, people differ in their party support: some people support the Liberal party, others the Conservative, New Democratic, Bloc Québécois, and Green parties. How can we explain these differences? Are there particular factors that predict the party affiliation of given individuals and help explain why others lack any affiliation?

One assumption of the scientific method is that there is order to the universe; people, for instance, do not randomly adopt party affiliations. Rather, it is assumed that specific factors—variables—influence the choice of party affiliation. There is no assumption, however, that any *single* variable determines party affiliation. In social research, we know that there are no perfect correlations in the real world; it is rare that we can explain even most of the variation in the dependent variable by one external cause. For social researchers, this means that in addition to discovering that a relationship exists between the dependent variable and a particular independent variable, we also need to measure and assess the *strength* of that relationship. How much of the variation in the dependent variable is caused by a given independent variable? We can measure the strength of a bivariate relationship with **measures of association**.

When conducting bivariate research, the political scientist needs to address four questions:

1. Is there a relationship?
2. What is the direction of the relationship?
3. What is the strength of the relationship?
4. Is the relationship statistically significant?

The final question was addressed in Chapter 16, where different tests of significance were introduced. This chapter will address the first three questions for nominal- and ordinal-level data. Chapter 18 will consider interval-level data.

IS THERE A RELATIONSHIP? IF SO, WHAT IS THE DIRECTION OF THE RELATIONSHIP?

To look at a relationship between two variables, we need to arrange them in a way that will allow us to identify patterns. One way to do so is to use contingency tables, introduced in Chapter 16. When reading a contingency table, we are looking for a patterned relationship or correlation. A **perfect correlation** exists when knowing the value on one variable *always* lets us know the value on the other. In Figure 17.1 a) on page 292, we see that there is a perfect relationship between age and support for conservatism: *all* young people show low support, *all* middle-aged people show moderate support, and *all* older people show high support. Under these circumstances, if asked to guess the conservatism of a stranger, we would be able to guess correctly 100 per cent of the time as soon as we discovered her age. If she is 22 years old, she will display low support for conservatism. Note, however, that if even one case deviated from this pattern, we would not have a perfect relationship. Figure 17.1 b) represents a **moderate relationship**: *most* young people show low support, *most* middle-aged people show moderate support, and *most* older people show high support. Under these circumstances, if asked to guess the conservatism of a stranger, knowing her age would improve our guessing ability, but we would not have certainty. Thus, if she is 22 years old, there is a good chance that she will display low support (that is our best prediction), but there is also the possibility that she will display moderate or high support. Moderate relationships, of course, will vary in strength; the second half of this chapter provides a number of techniques through which the precise strength of the relationship can be specified. Figure 17.1 c) displays **no relationship**: there is no discernible pattern between age and support for conservatism. Thus, knowing a stranger's age gives us no clue whatsoever as to her conservative views.

If we find a moderate or perfect relationship, we also want to consider the direction of the relationship. Figures 17.1 a) and 17.2 b) represent a positive relationship: as age increases, support for conservatism increases. Recall that direction applies only to variables that can be ordered.

a) Perfect Correlation

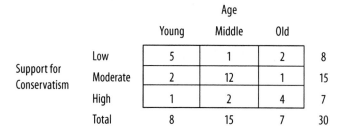

		Age			
		Young	Middle	Old	
Support for Conservatism	Low	8	0	0	8
	Moderate	0	15	0	15
	High	0	0	7	7
	Total	8	15	7	30

b) Moderate Correlation

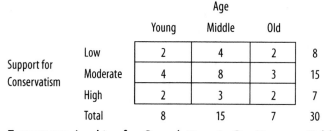

		Age			
		Young	Middle	Old	
Support for Conservatism	Low	5	1	2	8
	Moderate	2	12	1	15
	High	1	2	4	7
	Total	8	15	7	30

c) No Correlation

		Age			
		Young	Middle	Old	
Support for Conservatism	Low	2	4	2	8
	Moderate	4	8	3	15
	High	2	3	2	7
	Total	8	15	7	30

FIGURE 17.1 Looking for Correlations in Contingency Tables

Contingency tables allow us to visually detect correlations for nominal- and original-level data. For interval-level data, correlations can be visually detected in scatter plots or scatter diagrams. Figure 17.2, for example, presents the hypothetical distribution of individuals according to their height (vertical axis) and weight (horizontal axis). Each dot on the diagram represents one individual or case. Figure 17.2 a) shows a perfect correlation; for every increase in height, there is an equivalent increase in weight. (We assume that height drives weight, rather than weight driving height!) The relationship is positive in that an increase in one variable (height) corresponds to an increase in the other variable (weight); this is seen by the scatter-plot line rising as one looks left to right. (For a negative relationship, in contrast, the scatter-plot line would fall as one looks left to right.) Figure 17.2 b) shows a positive but less than perfect correlation; the taller people are, the more

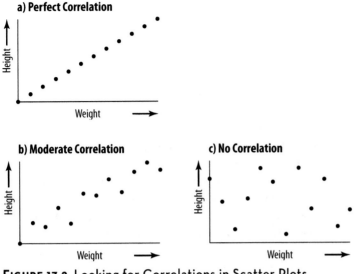

FIGURE 17.2 Looking for Correlations in Scatter Plots

they tend to weigh, but a person's height does not allow us to perfectly predict his or her weight. In Figure 17.2 c), the scatter plot suggests no relationship between height and weight. Having visually established that there is a relationship between two variables, and having determined (for ordinal and interval level variables) the direction of the relationship, our next question is, how strong is this relationship?

WHAT IS THE STRENGTH OF THE RELATIONSHIP?

Most social and political events have multiple causes and influencing factors; indeed, it would be impossible to isolate every single influential factor for such dependent events as 'political partisanship', 'attitudes toward environmentalism', or 'political efficacy'. Given that impossibility, the goal of social science research is to identify the most important explanatory variables. What independent events have the most influence on the dependent event? Ultimately, the objective is to increase our *predictive accuracy*; just as the medical researcher wishes to predict the effect of drug A on a patient's health, we wish to predict the impact of independent variable A on a citizen's partisanship or public policy attitudes. And just as the medical researcher is not dealing with absolutes—there will always be some people for whom drug A has a different effect than clinical trials would suggest—so too must social researchers deal with variations and partial relationships. If we find, for example, that 75 per cent of women vote Liberal, we cannot state with certainty that Tanya will vote Liberal. However, we can state with confidence that, given no information other than gender, Liberal is the *best prediction* for Tanya's vote.

Thus, the overall goal is to identify the independent variable or set of independent variables that allow(s) us to make the best prediction about dependent variables, such as an individual's social and political attitudes. By measuring the strength of a relationship between an independent and a dependent variable, we are measuring *the confidence we can place in our predictions*. The strength of the relationship between two variables is measured with measures of association, also known as 'coefficients of association' or 'relationship measures'. Measures of association condense the patterns in a contingency table or scatter plot into a single numerical value. When we 'eyeball' data, we may fail to notice certain patterns because of inexperience or bias in favour of our hypotheses. Similarly, we sometimes 'see' stronger relationships than actually exist. The measure of association minimizes such problems by providing a numerical check on our perceptions. (On the other hand, eyeballing the data can provide a useful check of the interpretation of summary statistics!) In addition, measures of association provide a standardized and compact way to convey relationship information to others; they are much easier to report and compare across studies than are complex contingency tables.

A number of measures of association are available, and the appropriate selection depends upon (1) the technical limitations of the coefficients and (2) the level of measurement of the variables. As noted in Chapter 16, some statistics, known as **parametric statistics**, have assumptions that must be met if they are to be used and interpreted correctly. Less stringent, and thus more widely available, tests are referred to as **nonparametric statistics**. Parametric tests are used more often than nonparametric tests in published research and tend to be preferred for a number of reasons: they are more robust (less subject to fluctuations), more powerful, and can at times provide a greater amount of information than nonparametric tests (McCall 1986, 317). At the same time, it is often difficult to meet the many stringent assumptions of parametric tests. In addition, many of the variables we consider in political science—race, gender, vote choice, religion, party affiliation—are nominal-level measures. For these reasons, political scientists often select nonparametric statistics.

The second factor to be considered when selecting a correlation measure is the level of data measurement. As we have seen, there are three levels of measurement that political scientists are concerned with: nominal, ordinal, and interval. The measure of association one selects depends upon the *lowest level of measurement in the bivariate relationship*, for we always use the measure of association that is most appropriate for the lowest level of measurement. Thus, if we have a bivariate relationship between a nominal-level variable and an ordinal-level variable, we select a measure of association appropriate for nominal-level variables. If we have an ordinal-level and an interval-level variable, we can use ordinal-level measures. And so on. Clearly, to use interval-level measures, we need to have only interval-level variables. (We will explore exceptions to this rule in Chapter 18.) When interval-level variables are used with nominal- or ordinal-level variables, the interval-level data are often grouped; for example, age (in years) might be grouped into 'young (under 35)', 'middle (35–64)', and 'old (65 and over)'. This makes the contingency tables that accompany the measure of association easier to read.

Measures of association at the nominal level typically range from 0 to 1, while at the ordinal and interval levels the typical range is from −1 to +1. (Interval-level measures will be addressed in the following chapter.) For both nominal- and ordinal-level measures, 0 signifies no relationship (perfect independence): change in the independent variable is not correlated or associated with change in the dependent variable. The closer the coefficient is to 0, the weaker is the relationship. For nominal-level measures, 1 indicates a perfect relationship: change in the independent variable is always and systematically correlated with change in the dependent variable. The closer the coefficient is to 1, the stronger is the relationship. The same principle holds for ordinal- and interval-level measures, with the addition of direction. (Recall that nominal-level variables cannot be ordered and therefore cannot have direction.) For ordinal- and interval-level measures, the coefficient can be either positive or negative. A positive coefficient indicates a positive relationship: as the value of the independent variable increases, the value of the dependent variable also increases. A negative coefficient indicates a negative relationship: as values of the independent variable increase, values of the dependent variable decrease, and vice versa. Thus, the ± signification indicates *direction* rather than strength. As with nominal-level measures, we judge strength in ordinal- and interval-level relationships according to how close the coefficient is to 0 or ±1. If the coefficient is near 0, the relationship is very weak. If it is near ±1, the relationship is very strong.

APPLY YOUR UNDERSTANDING

Selecting Measures of Association

For each of the following bivariate relationships, identify (1) the level of measurement of each variable (nominal, ordinal, interval) and (2) the appropriate level of measure of association (assume all distribution assumptions are met):

1. age (in years) and support for environmentalism (ranges from strong support to strong opposition);

2 gender and ideological position (left–centre–right);

3. party affiliation and level of education (number of years completed);

4. union membership and social class (working–lower middle–upper middle–upper);

5. religion and religiosity (church attendance: daily–weekly–monthly–annually–never).

For a number of reasons, the strength of a relationship is relative; in other words, coefficients of 0.5 do not always indicate relationships of the same strength. First, and as we will see, some measures of association are relatively more conservative or stringent, while others tend to inflate the strength of the relationship and therefore may be less robust. Second, research design has an impact on the strength of measures of association. Experimental research has the greatest ability to control outside influences and therefore tends to generate relatively strong measures of association. Survey research, on the other hand, is subject to greater amounts of 'noise' and measurement error and therefore generates smaller measures of association. Thus, a measure of association of 0.5 might be seen as 'moderate' in experimental research, but 'strong' in survey research. (It is for this reason that political scientists may be very impressed by correlations that leave their psychology colleagues cold.) Finally, we need to keep in mind the context of our study. The goal is to identify the best predictors of a given dependent event. For some situations, the predictors of a dependent event tend to be so weak that even a rather low coefficient may actually be our best known predictor. For this reason, it is always important to keep the hypotheses in mind. If we expect a strong relationship, we will have higher standards and will read the coefficients with a less generous eye, and vice versa (Baxter-Moore 1994, 323).

We should also call attention to a special class of measures of association, the **proportional reduction in error** (PRE) measures. A PRE measure is basically a ratio of errors (Norusis 1990, 121): we compare the amount of error we have without knowing the independent variable with the amount of remaining error after knowledge about the independent variable is taken into account. In other words, to what degree does knowledge about the independent variable reduce our error in predicting values of the dependent variable? The meaning of a PRE measure is best illustrated with an example.[1] Imagine we have 100 people, whose party affiliations are as follows:

Liberal   60
Conservative 30
NDP   10

If one of these individuals were to walk into the room and the preceding distribution was the only information we had, our best guess about the individual's party affiliation would be Liberal; this would ensure that we were right 60 times out of 100 and wrong 40 times out of 100. Not great odds, but as you will recall from Chapter 15, with nominal-level variables such as these, the mode (the most frequently occurring category) is the best predictive option available.

Now imagine that we find out a second piece of information, the region in which respondents live. Given that regional residence may influence party affiliation, we construct a contingency table—party affiliation by region—and get the distributions in Table 17.1.

TABLE 17.1 Party Affiliation by Region (PRE Example)

Party	Region West	Central	Atlantic	Total
Liberal	10	25	25	60
Conservative	20	5	5	30
NDP	0	10	0	10
Total	30	40	30	100

How does this affect our guessing abilities? Let's say we need to guess the party affiliation of one of the respondents from the West. What is our best guess? Clearly, the answer is Conservative; if we guess Conservative, we will be correct 20 times out of 30. What if the individual is from Central Canada? Here, our best guess is Liberal, and we will be correct 25 times out of 40. Finally, for Atlantic Canadian respondents we will guess Liberal, and we will be correct 25 times out of 30. When we combine the results, we find that by using the knowledge provided by the independent variable (region), we are correct a total of 70 times (20 + 25 + 25) and incorrect a total of 30 times (10 + 15 + 5). Thus, our guessing abilities have been improved by adding the knowledge about the independent variable: we have decreased the errors from 40 to 30. What is the *proportionate* reduction of error? To find this, we can use a basic ratio formula:

$$PRE = \frac{\text{error without IV} - \text{error with IV}}{\text{error without IV}}$$

where IV = independent variable. In this example,

$$PRE = \frac{40 - 30}{40} = 0.25$$

The PRE coefficients can be expressed as a percentage; in this case, knowledge about the respondent's region of residence allowed us to improve our guessing by approximately 25 per cent.

This logic is seen in all PRE measures, lambda, gamma, and tau-b being those considered in this chapter, but there are two caveats. First, the formula given above explains the logic of the measures but is not actually the formula used to calculate lambda, gamma, and tau-b. Thus, the formula is provided for illustrative purposes only. Second, only PRE measures can be expressed as a percentage reduction of error. Other measures—such as Cramer's V—can be identified only in terms of strength and, occasionally, direction. With all measures of association, be they PRE or not, we need to note the strength of the relationship and, for ordinal-level measures, the direction of the relationship.

Having looked at the commonalties between measures of association, we can now turn to the various measures. As we do so, the reader should be aware that some students will find the statistical calculations below to be complex and detailed. Thus, it is recommended that you follow each step carefully, and ensure that each aspect of the calculation is clear before carrying on. You will find that calculating the formulas for yourself on paper or with a calculator will help you to better appreciate and interpret computer-generated statistics. The difference is profound, similar to the distinction between visiting a foreign country with a working knowledge of the language and visiting a foreign country with nothing more than a guidebook of common phrases.

MEASURES FOR NOMINAL-LEVEL DATA

Nominal-level measures of strength will be used whenever one of the variables in the bivariate relationship is a categorical variable; thus, we may have nominal-nominal, nominal-ordinal, or nominal-interval relationships (interval-level data in such cases are typically grouped). Also, nonparametric nominal-level measures are used when our data fail to meet the requirements of the parametric tests. Recall that nominal-level measures have no direction and vary from 0 (perfect independence) to 1 (perfect correlation). We will look at two measures for nominal-level data: lambda and Cramer's V. Lambda is a PRE measure that is simple to calculate. Cramer's V is a chi-square-based measure; thus, we must first calculate the chi-square statistic before we can calculate Cramer's V. Although lambda is a more robust measure than Cramer's V and easier to calculate, there are instances in which the use of lambda is not advised. Thus, it is important that students be able to calculate and interpret both measures.

Lambda uses the mode to make predictions. Recall from Chapter 15 that the mode (the most frequently occurring value) is the only measure of central tendency available for nominal-level data. The PRE example presented in the previous section illustrates lambda: both variables (party affiliation and region) were nominal-level, and the mode was used as the best predictor of party affiliation. However, we can calculate lambda in a less involved manner by using the following formula:

$$\lambda = \frac{\Sigma(f_i) - F_d}{N - F_d}$$

where f_i designates the mode (maximum frequency) in each category of the independent variable, F_d is the mode of the marginal totals of the dependent variable (that is, the largest of the row marginals), and N is the total number of cases.

Return to Table 17.1. To calculate lambda, we need to first find the mode for each category of the independent variable. We find that for the West, the mode value is 20, for Central Canada it is 25, and for the Atlantic region it is 25. Summed together, the modes total 70; thus, $\Sigma(f_i) = 70$. The second value we need is the largest row marginal. Quick examination reveals that $F_d = 60$. Finally, we need to know the total number of cases: $N = 100$. Having gathered together the necessary numbers, we are now ready to plug them into the formula:

$$\lambda = \frac{\Sigma(f_i) - F_d}{N - F_d}$$

$$= \frac{70 - 60}{100 - 60} = \frac{10}{40} = 0.25$$

Because this is a PRE measure, we can state that knowledge of the respondent's region improved our prediction ability by 25 per cent. The relationship is of moderate strength.

There are two limitations to lambda. First, because of the formulation, the value that lambda takes will vary according to which variable is designated independent. Thus, the researcher must be clear in her theory (and table construction) regarding which variable is dependent. A second limitation is mathematical: if significantly more cases are grouped in one category of the dependent variable (that is, one row marginal is much larger than the others), lambda will approximate zero. This does not mean that perfect independence exists between the variables – it is simply a mathematical result. (Hence the need to look at both contingency tables and summary statistics!)

Table 17.2 presents a relatively modest adjustment to Table 17.1. In particular, it has an additional 10 respondents who are Liberals from the West. All other aspects of the table remain the same.

In looking at Table 17.2, we ask whether region affects voting. The data in the table appear to indicate that it does. For example, half the voters in the West supported the Conservative Party, whereas only 5 of 40 (12.5 per cent) in Central Canada and 5 of 30 (16.7 per cent) in Atlantic Canada supported the Conservatives. If one were a Conservative candidate, the chances of success would be much higher in the

TABLE 17.2 Party Affiliation by Region

Party	Region			
	West	Central	Atlantic	Total
Liberal	20	25	25	70
Conservative	20	5	5	30
NDP	0	10	0	10
Total	40	40	30	110

West than elsewhere in the country. In addition, New Democrats received 10 of 40 (25 per cent) votes from Central respondents, but none from Westerners or those from the Atlantic region in these hypothetical data. Overall, it would appear that regional residence has an impact on voting.

Let's confirm this observation with λ, which as we said is a measure of association for nominal data. The calculations for λ are as follows:

$$\lambda = \frac{\Sigma(f_i) - F_d}{N - F_d}$$

$$= \frac{70 - 70}{110 - 70} = \frac{0}{40} = 0.0$$

In this case, a λ of 0.0 suggests that the errors in predicting the dependent variable have not been reduced at all by adding information about the independent variable. But eyeballing the table clearly shows there is a relationship. What's going on? The answer lies in the distribution of data in the dependent variable. Notice in Table 17.2 that in a total sample size of 110, fully 70 cases (63.6 per cent) are in the Liberal category. Furthermore, as we read across columns of the independent variable, we find the Liberals are the largest group in each category of the independent variable. Therefore, there were 70 correct predictions before knowing the independent variable, and 70 correct predictions after knowing it, for no net improvement. In short, there is a relationship between region and party in Table 17.2, but this relationship is not captured by λ. Furthermore, this is a more general limitation of λ: it often *underestimates* the strength of the relationship between two variables when there is an unequal distribution among categories of the dependent variable. As a consequence, always look at the table when using λ to confirm that it is not underestimating the strength of the relationship. It is also a good idea to run a second measure of association for nominal data, such as Cramer's V, as a check on the robustness of λ.

Cramer's V is based on the test statistic chi-square. Recall that chi-square compares the observed frequencies in a bivariate relationship with the frequencies that would be expected if perfect independence existed. The steps for calculating Cramer's V are as follows:

1. Create an expected frequencies table.
2. Using the expected and observed frequencies, calculate chi-square.
3. Using chi-square, calculate Cramer's V.

Let's work through the steps by using the data in Table 17.1. How many cases could we expect in the Liberal–West cell if party affiliation and region are independent of each other? How many cases could we expect in the Conservative–Atlantic cell? Our first step in calculating Cramer's V is to calculate the expected frequencies for *every cell* of the contingency table. To do so, we take the row marginal for the cell, multiply it by the column marginal for the cell, and divide by the total number of cases:

$$E = \frac{\text{(row marginal)(column marginal)}}{N}$$

Thus, for the Liberal–West cell, the expected frequency is

$$E = \frac{\text{(row marginal)(column marginal)}}{N} = \frac{60 \times 30}{100} = 18$$

If region and party affiliation are independent, we expect 18 Westerners to be Liberals. We use the same calculation to determine the expected frequencies for all other cells (try the calculations yourself for practice) and thereby produce the expected frequencies in Table 17.3.

TABLE 17.3 Party Affiliation by Region (Expected Frequencies)

Party	Region			
	West	Central	Atlantic	Total
Liberal	18	24	18	60
Conservative	9	12	9	30
NDP	3	4	3	10
Total	30	40	30	100

Our next step is to calculate chi-square itself. The formula for chi-square is

$$\chi^2 = \frac{\Sigma(O - E)^2}{E}$$

Using this formula, we can calculate χ^2 as follows:

Observed	Expected	O – E	(O – E)²	(O – E)²/E
10	18	−8	64	3.56
25	24	1	1	0.04
25	18	7	49	2.72
20	9	11	121	13.44
5	12	−7	49	4.08
5	9	−4	16	1.78
0	3	−3	9	3
10	4	6	36	9
0	3	−3	9	3

$$\chi^2 = \frac{\Sigma(O - E)^2}{E}$$

$$= 40.62$$

For this example, we find that chi-square = 40.62. Having calculated chi-square, we come to our last step: calculate our measure of association, Cramer's V. The formula for Cramer's V is

$$V = \sqrt{\frac{\chi^2}{N(k-1)}}$$

where k is the minimum number of rows or columns (if the number of rows is smaller, we use rows; if the number of columns is smaller, we use columns).

For a 4 × 3 table, $k = 3$. For a 2 × 3 table, $k = 2$. In this example, we have a 3 × 3 table, so $k = 3$, and $k - 1 = 2$. We know already that $N = 100$ and chi-square = 40.62, so we can put all of these numbers into the formula to get our coefficient:

$$V = \sqrt{\frac{\chi^2}{N(k-1)}}$$

$$= \sqrt{\frac{40.62}{200}} = \sqrt{0.203} = 0.45$$

We can interpret this coefficient as indicating that there is a moderately strong relationship between party affiliation and region of residence. Cramer's V is *not* a PRE measure, so we cannot make statements about improvements in predictive accuracy.

APPLY YOUR UNDERSTANDING

Calculating Lambda and Cramer's V

For the following table, calculate and interpret both lambda and Cramer's V.

Support for Social Welfare by Gender

	Female	Male	Total
Low support	5	10	15
Moderate support	15	15	30
High support	20	5	25
Total	40	30	70

Now, as the astute reader has probably noted, the Cramer's V coefficient ($V = 0.45$) suggested a much stronger relationship than did the lambda coefficient ($\lambda = 0.25$). It is not uncommon for two summary statistics calculated on the same table to yield different results, although the difference in this case between $V = 0.45$ and $\lambda = 0.25$ seems especially large. In general, because λ is based on a proportional reduction in error interpretation, it is often preferable to V. If the two statistics yielded similar results, then λ would be the reported statistic. When the two statistics diverge, as they do in this instance, we would ask why they diverge. The answer seems to lie in the distribution of the dependent variable. We showed that by adding another 10 cases to the dependent variable, λ was reduced to 0. That suggests that the present distribution probably underestimates the strength of the relationship. And since λ appears to do this, V would be the preferred statistic. But notice that we lose a bit in interpretive power, since V is not based on a proportionate reduction in error. (A V of 0.45 is larger than a V of 0.225, but it is not twice as large.) In conclusion, there is a moderately strong effect of region on voting ($V = 0.45$).

MEASURES FOR ORDINAL-LEVEL DATA

When we have either two ordinal-level variables or an ordinal-level variable and an interval-level variable, we can use ordinal-level measures of association. The ordinal-level tests are parametric tests: before using an ordinal-level measure of strength, we must first ensure that the relationship between the variables is *linear*. Both positive and negative relationships are examples of linear relationships and could be depicted by a straight line (moving up and to the right in the former, down and to the right in the latter). If our relationship is not linear, for example, a curvilinear relationship, we should use the nonparametric, nominal-level measures. To discover if our bivariate relationship fits the parameters for ordinal-level measures, we need to look at our contingency tables carefully. Does the relationship appear positive at some points and then negative (or nonexistent) at others? Pattern inconsistencies in the data suggest a nonlinear relationship. Tables 17.4 a) to 17.4 d) on page 304 illustrate linear and curvilinear relationships.

The ordinal-level measures of strength considered here are gamma, **tau-b**, and **tau-c**. Gamma and tau-b are both PRE measures and can be interpreted in terms of percentage reduction of error; tau-c is not a PRE measure. Recall that, when interpreting ordinal-level coefficients, we need to consider not just strength but also direction. A negative number indicates a negative relationship, whereas a positive coefficient indicates a positive relationship. Finally, it must be noted that it is extremely important that we ensure that our tables are properly constructed before we begin the calculations. In each description in this section, we will assume that contingency tables are constructed with the independent variable across the top and the dependent variable down the left side; we will also assume that both the

TABLE 17.4 a) Contingency Table Showing a Positive Relationship

	Low	Medium	High	Total
Low	20	10	0	30
Medium	10	10	10	30
High	0	10	30	40
Total	30	30	40	100

TABLE 17.4 b) Contingency Table Showing No Relationship

	Low	Medium	High	Total
Low	10	10	10	30
Medium	10	10	10	30
High	10	10	20	40
Total	30	30	40	100

TABLE 17.4 c) Contingency Table Showing a Negative Relationship

	Low	Medium	High	Total
Low	0	0	30	30
Medium	10	10	10	30
High	20	20	0	40
Total	30	30	40	100

TABLE 17.4 d) Contingency Table Showing a Curvilinear Relationship

	Low	Medium	High	Total
Low	0	30	0	30
Medium	10	0	20	30
High	20	0	20	40
Total	30	30	40	100

independent and dependent variables are ordered from low to high. Thus, before calculating the ordinal-level statistics, our first step is to *check the table construction*. If you are presented with a table that is ordered differently, you will need to reconstruct the table before you can begin your calculations.

Gamma and tau-b are measures that consider ordered pairs of observations. We look at two individual cases, for example, Harry and Sally, and ask how they compare on their rankings for both the independent and dependent variables.[2] Recall that our correlations can be either positive or negative. If we have a positive relationship, an increase in the independent variable will be accompanied by an increase in the dependent variable. When we consider pairs of cases, positive relationships are seen in **concordant pairs**: they exhibit *similar* ordering on the independent and dependent variables. If we have a negative relationship, an increase in the independent variable is accompanied by a decrease in the dependent variable. Negative relationships are seen in **discordant pairs** that exhibit *dissimilar* ordering of the independent and dependent variables.

Consider Table 17.5. Here we are examining the relationship between appreciation for political science and number of years in university. Sally is ranked above Harry on both the independent and the dependent variables. Judging from this pair alone, we would believe that appreciation of political science increases the longer a student is in university. Harry and Sally are an example of a concordant pair. The relationship between time in university and appreciation is positive: as time increases, appreciation increases. Harry and Mike are also an example of a concordant pair: Mike is ranked above Harry on both variables. Similarly, Harry and Troy are a concordant pair. Now consider the pairing of Sally and Sue. Sue ranks above Sally on the independent variable, yet below Sally on the dependent variable. Judging from this pair alone, we would believe that appreciation of political science decreases the longer a student is in university. The pair Sue and Sally is an example of a discordant pair. The relationship between time in university and appreciation is negative: as time increases, appreciation decreases. The pair Troy and Sue and the pair Troy and Mike are further examples of discordant pairs.

TABLE 17.5 Appreciation by Years of Undergraduate Study (Concordant and Discordant Pairs)

	2 years	3 years	4 years
Low appreciation	Harry		Sue
Medium appreciation		Sally	Mike
High appreciation		Troy	

If our tables are constructed properly, we can find concordant pairs by looking *down and to the right* of any given cell. The cells in Table 17.6 have been labelled to make this point more clearly. Start in the upper-left-hand corner cell, cell *a*, and look down and to the right. For cell *a*, concordant pairs can be found in cells *e*, *f*, *h*, and *i*. For cell *b*, concordant pairs can be found in cells *f* and *i*. What are the concordant pairs for cell *c*? Clearly, for this cell, we cannot move both down and to the right; therefore, cell *c* does not have any concordant pairs. For cell *d*, the concordant pairs are found in cells *h* and *i*; concordant pairs for cell *e* are limited to cell *i*. For cells *f*, *g*, *h*, and *i*, there are no cells that are both down and to the right, and these cells have no concordant pairs.

We use a similar process to find discordant pairs, moving *up and to the right* of any given cell. Here, we will start in the lower-left-hand corner, cell *g*, and work up. For cell *g*, the discordant pairs will be found in cells *b*, *c*, *e*, and *f*. For cell *h*, discordant pairs are located in cells *c* and *f*. There are no cells up and to the right of cell *i*; thus, cell *i* does not have any discordant pairs. For cell *d*, discordant pairs are found in cells *b* and *c*; for cell *e*, discordant pairs are found in cell *c*. And what of cells *f*, *a*, *b*, and *c*? If you said that these cells do not have any discordant pairs because of the absence of cells above and to the right, you are correct.

In summary, concordant pairs are found down and to the right on our tables and reflect positive relationships; discordant pairs are found up and to the right on the same tables and reflect negative relationships. Gamma, the measure of association to which we will turn shortly, looks only at concordant and discordant pairs, comparing the number of concordant pairs with the number of discordant pairs. You will notice, however, that looking at the concordant and discordant pairs does not exhaust all possible pairings. Return to Table 17.5. Notice that there are also a number of **ties**, pairs of cases that differ on one variable but are tied on the other. Sue and Harry differ on the independent variable (Sue has 4 years of university education, while Harry has only 2) yet are tied on the dependent variable (low appreciation of political science). Sally and Mike are also tied on the dependent variable. Notice that we look *across the row* for ties on the dependent variable. Troy and Sally are an example of a tie on the independent variable: both have 3 years of

TABLE 17.6 Finding Ordinal Pairs

	2 years	3 years	4 years
Low appreciation	*a*	*b*	*c*
Medium appreciation	*d*	*e*	*f*
High appreciation	*g*	*h*	*i*

university education, although they differ in their appreciation scores. A second example of a tie on the independent variable is the Sue–Mike pairing. For ties on the independent variable, we look *down the column*. Tau-b considers ties, including both independent variable ties and dependent variable ties. We will now look at how to calculate the coefficients, beginning with gamma.

Gamma is calculated by the following formula:

$$\gamma = \frac{N_s - N_d}{N_s + N_d}$$

where N_s designates the number of similar (concordant) pairs, and N_d designates the number of dissimilar (discordant) pairs. To find N_s, we multiply each cell frequency by the sum of the frequencies of the cells below and to the right, and sum these products. To find N_d, we multiply each cell frequency by the sum of the frequencies of the cells above and to the right, and sum these products.

This is best illustrated by the example in Table 17.7. Notice that the cells have been labelled to make the steps clearer.

To calculate N_s, we multiply down and to the right and then sum the products:

$$N_s = a(e + f + h + i) + b(f + i) + d(h + i) + e(i)$$
$$= 0(30 + 5 + 5 + 5) + 10(5 + 5) + 5(5 + 5) + 30(5)$$
$$= 0(45) + 10(10) + 5(10) + 30(5)$$
$$= 0 + 100 + 50 + 150$$
$$= 300$$

TABLE 17.7 Ideological Position by Income

Ideology	Income			Total
	Low	Middle	High	
Left	0	10	5	15
	a	*b*	*c*	
Centre	5	30	5	40
	d	*e*	*f*	
Right	15	5	5	25
	g	*h*	*i*	
Total	20	45	15	80

To calculate N_d, we multiply up and to the right and then sum the products:

$$N_d = g(b + c + e + f) + h(c + f) + d(b + c) + e(c)$$
$$= 15(10 + 5 + 30 + 5) + 5(5 + 5) + 5(10 + 5) + 30(5)$$
$$= 15(50) + 5(10) + 5(15) + 30(5)$$
$$= 750 + 50 + 75 + 150$$
$$= 1{,}025$$

To calculate gamma, we insert these figures into the following formula:

$$\gamma = \frac{N_s - N_d}{N_s + N_d}$$
$$= \frac{300 - 1{,}025}{300 + 1{,}025} = \frac{-725}{1{,}325} = -0.55$$

To interpret gamma, we need to keep in mind strength, direction, and the fact that gamma is a PRE measure. Thus, we can interpret this gamma value of −0.55 as indicating a *negative* and strong relationship: as income increases, support for the 'right-wing' ideology decreases. Knowledge of the independent variable increased our predictive accuracy by approximately 55 per cent.

Tau-b is also a PRE measure, but unlike gamma it includes ties. It is important to note that tau-b requires *square tables*, that is, 2 × 2, 3 × 3, 4 × 4, and so on. If the independent and dependent variables differ in the number of categories available, tau-b cannot be used. Tau-b is often favoured over gamma because it is a more conservative measure. Gamma can inflate the strength of relationships; tau-b, by including a calculation for ties, is less likely to do so. The formula for tau-b is:

$$\text{tau-b} = \frac{N_s - N_d}{\sqrt{(N_s + N_d + T_x)(N_s + N_d + T_y)}}$$

where T_x designates ties on the independent variable, and T_y designates ties on the dependent variable.

To find ties on the independent variable, we remain within the column and move down; to find ties on the dependent variable, we remain within the row and move across. To find T_x, we multiply each cell frequency by the sum of the frequencies of the cells below and sum these products. To find T_y, we multiply each cell frequency by the sum of the frequencies of the cells to the right and sum these products. Let's return to the example in Table 17.7.

To calculate T_x, we multiply down in each column and then sum the products:

$$
\begin{aligned}
T_x &= a(d + g) + d(g) + b(e + h) + e(h) + c(f + i) + f(i) \\
&= 0(5 + 15) + 5(15) + 10(30 + 5) + 30(5) + 5(5 + 5) + 5(5) \\
&= 0(20) + 5(15) + 10(35) + 30(5) + 5(10) + 5(5) \\
&= 0 + 75 + 350 + 150 + 50 + 25 \\
&= 650
\end{aligned}
$$

To calculate T_y, we multiply across in each row and then sum the products:

$$
\begin{aligned}
T_y &= a(b + c) + b(c) + d(e + f) + e(f) + g(h + i) + h(i) \\
&= 0(10 + 5) + 10(5) + 5(30 + 5) + 30(5) + 15(5 + 5) + 5(5) \\
&= 0(15) + 10(5) + 5(35) + 30(5) + 15(10) + 5(5) \\
&= 0 + 50 + 175 + 150 + 150 + 25 \\
&= 550
\end{aligned}
$$

To calculate tau-b, we insert these figures into the formula (we already calculated N_s and N_d for Table 17.7 when we calculated gamma):

$$
\begin{aligned}
\text{tau-b} &= \frac{N_s - N_d}{\sqrt{(N_s + N_d + T_x)(N_s + N_d + T_y)}} \\[2mm]
&= \frac{300 - 1{,}025}{\sqrt{(300 + 1{,}025 + 650)(300 + 1{,}025 + 550)}} \\[2mm]
&= \frac{-725}{\sqrt{(1{,}975)(1{,}875)}} \\[2mm]
&= \frac{-725}{\sqrt{(3{,}703{,}125)}} \\[2mm]
&= \frac{-725}{1{,}924.35} \\[2mm]
&= -0.38
\end{aligned}
$$

We can interpret this tau-b value of -0.38 as indicating a *negative* and moderately strong relationship: as income increases, support for the right moderately decreases. Knowledge of the independent variable increased our predictive accuracy by approximately 38 per cent. Note that the tau-b value suggests a weaker relationship than does the gamma value (-0.55); because tau-b includes information on the number of ties, it tends to be more conservative.

Tau-b is limited to square tables. For nonsquare tables, we can use tau-c. Like tau-b, tau-c is more conservative than gamma. However, tau-c is not a PRE measure, so we must be careful with the interpretation. The formula for tau-c is

$$\text{tau-c} = (N_s - N_d)*[2m/(n^2(m-1))]$$

where m is the smaller of the number of columns or rows (that is, for a 2 $\times$ 3 table, $m = 2$), and n is the sample size. Consider the example in Table 17.8.

To calculate N_s, we multiply down and to the right and then sum the products:

$$\begin{aligned} N_s &= a(d+f) + c(f) \\ &= 5(30+10) + 10(10) \\ &= 5(40) + 10(10) \\ &= 200 + 100 \\ &= 300 \end{aligned}$$

To calculate N_d, we multiply up and to the right and then sum the products:

$$\begin{aligned} N_d &= e(b+d) + c(b) \\ &= 15(30+10) + 10(10) \\ &= 15(40) + 10(10) \\ &= 600 + 100 \\ &= 700 \end{aligned}$$

TABLE 17.8 Ideological Position by Income

Ideology	Low		High		Total
Left	5		10		15
		a		b	
Centre	10		30		40
		c		d	
Right	15		10		25
		e		f	
Total	30		50		80

The sample size (n) is 80, and m is equal to 2 (the lesser of the number of rows and the number of column). Thus, tau-c is

$$\text{tau-c} = (N_s - N_d)^*[2m/(n^2(m-1))]$$
$$= (300 - 700)^*[2(2)/(80^2(2-1))]$$
$$= -400^*[4/(6400(1))]$$
$$= -400^*[4/6400]$$
$$= -400^*0.000625$$
$$= -0.25$$

Compare this to gamma for the same table:

$$\gamma = \frac{N_s - N_d}{N_s + N_d}$$
$$= \frac{300 - 700}{300 + 700}$$
$$= -400/1000$$
$$= -0.40$$

In summary, three measures of strength have been considered for ordinal-level variables. Tau-b and gamma can be used for square tables, while tau-c and gamma

APPLY YOUR UNDERSTANDING

Calculating Gamma and Tau

For the following table, calculate and interpret gamma and, depending on table dimensions, either tau-b or tau-c.

Support for Social Welfare by Ideological Position

	Left	Centre	Right	Total
Low support	0	5	20	25
Moderate support	5	15	5	25
High support	15	10	0	25
Total	20	30	25	75

can be used for nonsquare tables. The tau measures are less likely to inflate strength and are therefore preferred. However, if your analysis includes tables of different sizes, you may wish to report both gamma and the appropriate tau statistic to facilitate comparisons across tables.

APPLY YOUR UNDERSTANDING

Interpreting Lambda, Cramer's V, Gamma, Tau-b, and Tau-c

Interpret the following measures of association in sentence form. Be certain to note strength, direction (where relevant), and PRE (where relevant). Briefly explain why you interpreted strength as you did.

1. gamma $= -0.02$
2. Cramer's V $= 0.4$
3. lambda $= 0.15$
4. tau-b $= 0.6$
5. tau-c $= -0.35$

MEASURES FOR INTERVAL-LEVEL DATA

When we have two interval-level variables, we can use interval-level measures of association. The most commonly used is Pearson's R, which measures the linear relationship between an independent and a dependent variable. Like ordinal measures of association, Pearson's R varies between -1 and $+1$. Pearson's R assumes a *linear* relationship between the two variables. If the relationship is not linear (for example, if the scatter plot suggests a curvilinear relationship), the nonparametric test Spearman's rho is used. Spearman's rho converts numbers into ranks, and then uses the Pearson's R formula. The formula to calculate Pearson's R is presented in Chapter 18.

SUMMARY: BIVARIATE RELATIONSHIPS

As you will recall from the start of the chapter, when we consider the relationship between two variables, we ask four questions:

1. Is there a relationship?
2. What is the direction of the relationship (ordinal- and interval-level variables only)?
3. What is the strength of the relationship?
4. Is the relationship statistically significant?

We determine the existence of a relationship and its direction by looking at the data itself, either in the form of a contingency table or a scatter plot. We determine the strength of a relationship by considering the appropriate measure of association. And as explained in Chapter 16, we determine statistical significance by considering the appropriate inferential statistic.

These principles that we use to consider bivariate relationships are also used to consider multivariate relationships. The next section of this chapter will consider nominal- and ordinal-level multivariate relationships; multivariate relationships among interval-level variables are considered in Chapter 18.

ADDING A THIRD VARIABLE TO THE BIVARIATE RELATIONSHIP

In Chapter 2 we discussed the modelling of a simple bivariate relationship in which a single independent variable is hypothesized to affect a single dependent variable. This takes the form illustrated in Figure 17.3.

In this type of analysis, we isolate these two variables from the complex interplay of social life and test empirically whether *A* has a discernible effect on *B*. Now we'd like to remove the condition of isolation that we imposed and ask whether a true causal relationship exists between these two variables when taking other factors into account. These 'other factors' can affect either the independent or dependent variables separately or the relationship between the independent and dependent variables in a variety of ways. It is up to you as a researcher to model the relationship between the variables in your study and then to conduct an appropriate empirical examination of that model.

To consider the effects of a third variable, we must *control* for that variable. What this means is that we consider the relationship between our independent variable *A* and our dependent variable *B* while holding constant values of our control variable *C*. For example, if we are controlling for sex, we would consider the relationship between *A* and *B* for men only, and for women only. To do so, we would create separate contingency tables and calculate separate measures of association for men and women, and then consider if the relationship between *A* and *B* is similar between men and women.

When we control for variable *C*, there may be a number of outcomes. First, we may see the relationship between *A* and *B* hold constant—the measure of association retains its relative level of strength and the relationship remains statistically significant for all values of control variable *C*. If this is the case, we have greater confidence in our conclusion that *A* influences *B*.

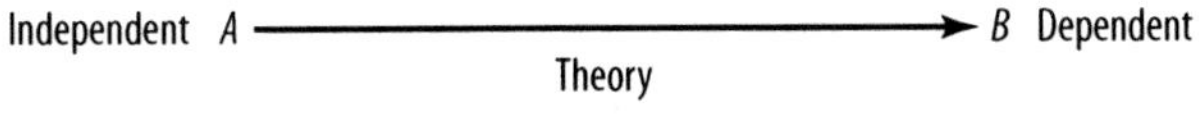

Independent *A* ——————————————→ *B* Dependent

Theory

FIGURE 17.3 A Bivariate Causal Relationship

Second, the relationship between *A* and *B* may strengthen for all values of control variable *C*, as evidenced by an increase in the measure of association. If this is the case, we suspect that variable *C* is a reinforcing variable. A reinforcing variable is one that can strengthen and magnify the relationship between an independent and a dependent variable.

Third, the relationship between *A* and *B* may weaken for all values of control variable *C*, and the relationship may fail to achieve statistical significance. In this situation, we suspect that either the relationship between *A* and *B* is spurious, or that variable *C* is an intervening variable. (As discussed in Chapter 2, a spurious relationship occurs when a relationship between two variables can be accounted for by a third variable. An intervening variable is one that comes between an independent and a dependent variable, but the direction of causality flows from the independent variable to the intervening variable to the dependent variable.) How do we know the difference? Here we must consider temporal order. If variable *C* comes before our independent variable *A*, we suspect that *C* causes both *A* and *B*, and that the relationship between *A* and *B* is spurious. If variable *C* comes after independent variable *A*, we suspect that *C* is an intervening variable.

Finally, the relationship between *A* and *B* may vary between values of control variable *C*: the relationship between *A* and *B* may be strong and statistically significant for women, for example, but weak and statistically insignificant for men. This tells us that we need to consider the influence of the control variable if we are to truly understand the relationship between *A* and *B*.

CONTINGENCY TABLES WITH CONTROL VARIABLES

When beginning an analysis, it is always useful to map the relationship you wish to examine; this will help you in establishing the direction of causality you are hypothesizing and also will help in identifying the role of each variable: which are the independent and dependent variables, and what is the hypothesized impact of the third variable.

The Effect of Age on Political Interest, Controlling for Education

For the current example, we will assume that the initial hypothesis is as shown in Figure 17.4. The initial bivariate relationship is between age and political interest,

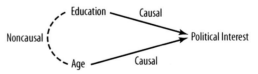

FIGURE 17.4 Hypothesized Impact of Age on Political Interest, Controlling for Education as a Reinforcing Variable

and the hypothesis is that as age increases, so too does political interest. The multivariate model then suggests that education acts to reinforce the relationship between age and political interest. An analysis of this model includes an examination of the following relationships: (1) age and political interest; (2) education and political interest; (3) age and education; and (4) age and political interest, controlling for education.

The data used to test this model are from the 2006 Canadian Election Study (CES).[3] Our dependent variable, general political interest, was coded into a three-point measure ranging from low to high. (Original CES data were grouped for this demonstration.) Our independent variables are age and education. The age variable was coded into four categories (18–34, 35–49, 50–64, and 65 and over). The education variable has three categories (less than completed high school, completed high school and/or attended technical college, and completed college and/or attended or completed university).

Table 17.9 shows the effect of age on level of political interest. Notice that this relationship is between two ordinal-level variables; therefore, we are anticipating a linear relationship between the variables. The data conform to this expectation and also reveal a moderate, positive relationship between the variables. Since these are ordinal data and the table is nonsquare, the gamma and tau-c statistics are appropriate. A gamma of 0.234 and a tau-c of 0.173 indicates a relationship of weak to moderate strength; therefore, we would conclude that age has a weak to moderate effect on level of political interest. The p-value ($p = .000$) indicates that that relationship is statistically significant.

The effect of education on political interest is shown in Table 17.10 on page 316. Since education was measured with three categories, we produce a 3 × 3 table,

TABLE 17.9 The Effect of Age on Political Interest

| Political Interest | Age | | | | |
	18–34	35–49	50–64	65+	Total
Low	336 (40.3%)	390 (30.3%)	262 (21.9%)	174 (18.9%)	1,162 (27.4%)
Moderate	261 (31.3%)	440 (34.2%)	407 (33.9%)	278 (30.3%)	1,386 (32.7%)
High	237 (28.4%)	456 (35.5%)	530 (44.2%)	467 (50.8%)	1,690 (39.9%)
Total	834 (100%)	1,286 (100%)	1,199 (100%)	919 (100%)	4,238 (100%)

Gamma = 0.234
Tau-c = 0.173
$p = .000$

TABLE 17.10 The Effect of Education on Political Interest

Political Interest	Education			
	Less Than Completed High School	High School- Technical College	Postsecondary	Total
Low	280 (37.2%)	710 (30.2%)	157 (15.4%)	1,147 (22.3 %)
Moderate	238 (31.6%)	801 (34.1%)	306 (30.0%)	1,345 (32.6%)
High	234 (31.1%)	840 (35.7%)	556 (54.6%)	1,630 (47.8%)
Total	752 (100%)	2,351 (100%)	1,014 (100%)	4,122 (100%)

Gamma = 0.277
Tau-b = 0.173
p = .000

allowing us to use tau-b. Once again, we find a linear relationship of weak to moderate strength. The effect of education on political interest (gamma = 0.277) is stronger than age on interest (gamma = 0.234). This relationship is also statistically significant.

Table 17.11 shows the effect of age on level of education. Note that these two variables are related but that the relationship is negative: as age increases, level

TABLE 17.11 The Effect of Age on Education

Education	Age				
	18-34	35-49	50-64	65+	Total
Less than completed high school	69 (8.5%)	140 (11.2%)	191 (16.6%)	355 (39.8%)	755 (18.4%)
High school- technical college	549 (67.4%)	738 (59.0 %)	638 (55.3%)	421 (47.1%)	2,346 (57.1%)
Postsecondary	197 (24.2%)	372 (29.8%)	325 (28.2%)	117 (13.1%)	1,011 (24.6%)
Total	815 (100%)	1,250 (100%)	1,154 (100%)	893 (100%)	4,112 (100%)

Gamma = −0.272
Tau-c = −0.178
p = .000

of education decreases. For example, among those aged 18–34 and 35–49, only 8.5 per cent and 11.2 per cent, respectively, had less than high school education, compared with 39.8 per cent for those aged 65 and over. In addition, only 13.1 per cent of those aged 65 and over have a postsecondary education, compared with more than 24 per cent for the other age cohorts. In short, the youngest segments of the population have the highest levels of education, a finding that is very consistent with the rapid expansion in the postsecondary education system that occurred in Canada beginning in the early 1960s. Once again, the relationship is statistically significant.

What impact does a negative association between age and education have on the relationship between age and political interest? To obtain an answer, we can rerun the analysis of the effect of age on political interest, controlling for level of education. To control for education means to hold education constant. We do this by running separate analyses, and producing separate contingency tables, for each category of education. In other words, we ask, What is the impact of age on political interest among those with a low level of education? What is the impact among those with a moderate and a high level of education? Thus, with a three-category control variable, the analysis produces three separate tables, which are labelled Tables 17.12 a) to 17.12 c) on pages 218 and 219.

Table 17.12 a) examines the effect of age on political interest among those with a low level of education. Notice once again that the relationship is statistically significant and linear: as age increases, the likelihood of having a high level of political interest increases as well. Note also that the strength of the relationship has increased, from a tau-c for the population as a whole of 0.173 to a tau-c of 0.222 among those with a low level of education. It is this latter finding in which we are most interested: a stronger impact of age on political interest among those with a low level of education suggests that education intervened in the relationship between age and interest in a negatively reinforcing manner. A similar finding follows from an analysis of Tables 17.12 b) and 17.12 c). Among those with a moderate level of education, the effect of age on political interest is given by a tau-c statistic of 0.203, well above the original tau-c of 0.173. Among those with a high level of education, tau-c remains strong at 0.199. Thus, among each of the three educational groups, the relationship between age and political interest is higher than among the population as a whole. This indicates that the effect of age on political interest is negatively reinforced by level of education. To put this another way, at present there is a relationship between age and interest that is somewhat offset by the negative effect of age on education. This is due to the significant increase in the availability of postsecondary education during the 1960s, an increase that has led to important differences in educational attainment between younger and older Canadians. Over time, as the level of education among all age groups becomes more common, we would expect the effect of age on political interest to strengthen.

TABLE 17.12 a) The Effect of Age on Political Interest, Controlling for Education (Low Education)

Political Interest	Age				
	18–34	35–49	50–64	65+	Total
Low	36 (52.2%)	74 (52.9%)	75 (39.5%)	92 (26.8%)	277 (37.3%)
Moderate	22 (31.9%)	38 (27.1%)	66 (34.7%)	109 (31.8%)	235 (31.7%)
High	11 (15.9%)	28 (20.0%)	49 (25.8%)	142 (41.4%)	230 (31.0%)
Total	69 (100%)	140 (100%)	190 (100%)	343 (100%)	742 (100%)

Gamma = 0.326
Tau-c = 0.222
p = .000

TABLE 17.12 b) The Effect of Age on Political Interest, Controlling for Education (Moderate Education)

Political Interest	Age				
	18–34	35–49	50–64	65+	Total
Low	239 (43.6%)	247 (33.6%)	150 (23.7%)	71 (17.1%)	707 (30.3%)
Moderate	167 (30.5%)	264 (35.9%)	232 (36.6%)	131 (31.6%)	794 (34.0%)
High	142 (25.9%)	225 (30.6%)	252 (39.7%)	213 (51.3%)	832 (35.7%)
Total	548 (100%)	736 (100%)	634 (100%)	415 (100%)	2,333 (100%)

Gamma = 0.272
Tau-c = 0.203
p = .000

TABLE 17.12 c) The Effect of Age on Political Interest, Controlling for Education (High Education)

Political Interest	Age				Total
	18-34	**35-49**	**50-64**	**65+**	
Low	51	67	33	5	156
	(25.9%)	(18.0%)	(10.2%)	(4.3%)	(15.5%)
Moderate	66	125	88	26	305
	(33.5%)	(33.6%)	(27.2%)	(22.6%)	(30.3%)
High	80	180	203	84	547
	(40.6%)	(48.4%)	(62.7%)	(73.0%)	(54.3%)
Total	197	372	324	115	1,008
	(100%)	(100%)	(100%)	(100%)	(100%)

Gamma = 0.315
Tau-c = 0.199
p = .000

WORKING AS A TEAM

1. A common notion in political science is that of the left–right spectrum, with the left representing support for a more interventionist government and the right representing support for minimal government. In surveys, respondents are often asked to locate themselves along this left–right spectrum. You are studying support for the political 'right'. Your theory is that two factors, family income and age, influence self-placement on the spectrum; more specifically, you believe that as each of these two variables increases, support for the 'right' increases. (You also assume that age and family income are not correlated.) You conduct a survey to test your theory. You ask respondents to locate themselves on a 6-point left–right scale, with 1 representing the extreme left and 6 representing the extreme right. Thus, a respondent who identifies herself as a 5 considers herself to be right-wing, whereas a respondent who identifies himself as a 4 considers himself to be politically moderate, or centre-right in orientation.

Left - Right

| 1 | 2 | 3 | 4 | 5 | 6 |

Your survey work provides the following data.

Case	Age	Income ($)	Left–Right Placement
1	42	65,000	5
2	36	28,000	3
3	55	58,000	4
4	19	15,000	2
5	56	45,000	6
6	25	29,000	6
7	31	50,000	2
8	65	90,000	3
9	23	31,000	1
10	47	70,000	5
11	39	10,000	1
12	50	35,000	2
13	28	45,000	4
14	26	34,000	3
15	49	58,000	5
16	63	90,000	5
17	60	67,000	6
18	38	39,000	4
19	30	18,000	1
20	61	40,000	3

a. State your null and alternative hypotheses for each possible relationship.

b. Draw the causal model for your theory. Identify the dependent and independent variables.

c. Create two bivariate tables (spectrum by age, spectrum by income), classifying the data as follows:
age: young = 18–30, middle = 31–49, old = 50+;

income: low = $0–$35,000, middle = $36,000–$59,000, high = $60,000+;
spectrum: left = 1–2, centre = 3–4, right = 5–6.

d. As a group, decide if the tables allow you to reject your null hypothesis. Is there support for your alternative hypothesis? Explain your reasoning.

SELF-STUDY

1. For each of the following tables and data sets, calculate and interpret the stated measure of association. Which would you choose to report in your final write-up? For parametric statistics, indicate how you determined linearity.

a) Opinion on Issue X by Religious Affiliation

	Catholic	Protestant	Jewish	Total
Support X	20	10	0	30
Oppose X	0	10	20	30
Total	20	20	20	60

Compute lambda and Cramer's V. Use inferential statistics to test statistical significance.

b) Support for Issue X by Level of Political Activity

	Low Activity	Moderate Activity	High Activity	Total
Low support	5	9	9	23
Moderate support	9	10	9	28
High support	11	6	7	24
Total	25	25	25	75

Compute gamma and tau-b. Use inferential statistics to test statistical significance.

2. For each of the following, interpret in sentence form:

a. gamma = −0.02

b. lambda = 0.7

c. Cramer's V = 0.12

d. tau-b = 0.3

e. tau-c = −0.42

NOTES

1. Adapted from Manheim and Rich (1982, 284–6).
2. Example adapted from White (1994, 318–19).
3. The principal co-investigators of the 2006 Canadian Election Study (CES) are André Blais, Joanna Everitt, Patrick Fournier, Elisabeth Gidengil, and Neil Nevitte. The CES 2006 survey can be found at: http://ces-eec.mcgill.ca/ces.html.

Chapter 18

MULTIVARIATE ANALYSIS: AN INTRODUCTION TO THE DEEP END OF THE POOL

DESTINATION

By the end of this chapter the reader should

- understand the use of scatter plots for examining the relationship between interval data;
- be familiar with the assumptions underlying ordinary least squares regression techniques;
- understand the relationship between regression coefficients (the slope) and the standard error;
- be able to interpret a regression analysis table that includes the regression coefficients and standard errors for each of the independent variables, together with the intercept and the value of R^2; and
- understand the use of dummy variables in regression analysis.

MEASURES FOR INTERVAL-LEVEL DATA

Recall that interval-level measures of association are parametric tests and as such assume the relationship to be linear; in fact, the most common interval-level statistical technique is known as basic **linear regression**. Almost all advanced statistical techniques follow a logic similar to that of basic linear regression; thus, it is an important technique to understand. Our first step prior to beginning basic linear regression is to test for linearity.[1] Recall that we used a contingency table to look for linearity in ordinal-level variables. However, to do so with interval-level variables would require the creation of an unmanageable table and one that is difficult to interpret. Instead, we use a **scatter plot** to look for linearity in interval-level relationships. A scatter plot is a simple graphic display of the cases. We set up a graph, with the dependent variable along the Y-axis (vertical) and the independent variable along the X-axis (horizontal), and locate each case according to its position on both the X- and Y-axes. We then look at the pattern among the data: does it suggest a linear relationship? A curvilinear relationship? No relationship at all? If we find a pattern that could have a straight line drawn through it, this indicates a linear relationship. Figure 18.1 shows the scatter plot for the very simple data set depicted in the following table.

	X	Y
Case 1	2	8
Case 2	3	5
Case 3	1	4
Case 4	6	9
Case 5	4	7

When using real data in the social sciences, it is rare that we will have a line that perfectly fits, in other words, a line upon which all cases fall exactly. Instead, we seek to find the line that *best fits* the data. This line is known as the **regression line.** The regression line is essentially a line of prediction and is conceptually similar to the PRE (proportional reduction in error) measures. We ask ourselves, without knowledge of the independent variable, what is our best prediction of the value of the dependent variable for any particular case? Given that the dependent variable is measured at the interval level, our best prediction would be the mean. What the regression line provides is a best prediction of dependent variable scores for any given independent variable score. In order to do so, however, the regression line must be calculated according to the **ordinary least squares** (OLS) method.

The OLS method places the regression line in such a way as to minimize the squared deviations between the observed and predicted values. This is analogous to the mean as a predictor of values on a single variable; the mean is the value that minimizes the error in predicting scores on an interval variable. Any other predicted value produces more errors (that is, larger squared deviations) than the mean. Likewise, the OLS regression line minimizes the errors (squared deviations)

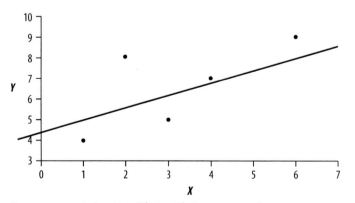

FIGURE 18.1 A Scatter Plot with Regression Line

in predicting the values on an interval-level dependent variable for any given value on the independent variable. The OLS formula is used to determine the position of the regression line. It is stated as

$$Y' = a + bX$$

where Y' is the predicted value of the dependent variable, X is the value of the independent variable, a is the **intercept**, and b is the **slope**.

Notice that Y' (the predicted value of the dependent variable) is understood to be a linear function of X (the value of the independent variable); Y' changes only when X changes (see Figure 18.2). The intercept, symbolized by a, is the value of Y' when X is equal to 0. The intercept is a constant and tells us the position of Y' on our graph where the regression line crosses the Y-axis. The slope, symbolized by b, represents the unit change in Y' for every unit increase in X. We have said that the dependent variable varies with the independent variable, but by how much? The slope tells us the unit change and in doing so indicates the angle that the regression line should take on the graph. The slope also indicates the direction of the relationship: a slope upward and to the right indicates a positive relationship, and a slope downward and to the right a negative relationship.

Let's say that the dependent variable is weekly income (measured in dollars) and the independent variable is university education (measured in years) (Figure 18.3 on page 326). It is hypothesized that income varies positively with university education. The data collected and assessed reveal the following regression formula:

$$Y' = 200 + 100X$$

This formula tells us two things. First, we can see that with no university education ($X = 0$), predicted weekly income (Y') is equal to \$200. We know this because the intercept (a) is equal to \$200. Second, we can see that for every one-year increase in university education (X), we have a \$100 increase in weekly income.

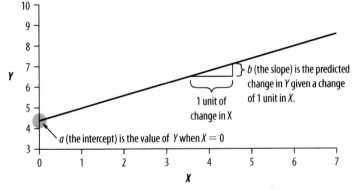

FIGURE 18.2 The Intercept (a) and Slope (b) of a Regression Line

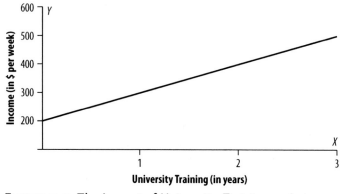

FIGURE 18.3 The Impact of University Training on Income

We know this because the slope (b) is equal to 100. We can see from the slope that the relationship between weekly income and university education is positive: as university education increases, weekly income increases.

Let's try another example (Figure 18.4). The dependent variable is 'total fine due on speeding ticket' (measured in dollars), and the independent variable is 'kilometres over speed limit' (measured in kilometres). Take the time to interpret the following regression formula in writing:

$$Y' = 5 + 0.8X$$

Hopefully, you came to the following interpretations: (1) with no kilometres over the speed limit, the predicted speeding ticket total is \$5; and (2) for every one-kilometre increase in speed above the speed limit, there is an \$0.80 increase in the cost of the ticket. Now, you may be saying to yourself, that does not make sense. How can I get a speeding ticket when I have not exceeded the speed limit? Assuming you are living in an area where police are honest, this is clearly not possible. What this illustration shows, therefore, is that the intercept of the regression line

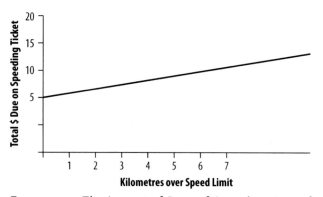

FIGURE 18.4 The Impact of Rate of Speed on Size of Speeding Ticket

can at times be *substantively meaningless,* serving more to help us position the regression line than to accurately predict the values of Y' when X equals zero.

How do we calculate the intercept and the slope? There are specific OLS formulas to determine each. We begin with the slope:

$$b = \frac{\text{sum of products}}{\text{sum of squares}} = \frac{\Sigma(x_i - \bar{x})(y_i - \bar{y})}{\Sigma(x_i - \bar{x})^2}$$

We calculate the slope in a series of steps: (1) find the means of both x and y; (2) from each individual case, subtract the mean; (3) calculate the products $(x_i - \bar{x})$ $(y_i - \bar{y})$; (4) calculate the sum of the products; (5) calculate the squares $(x_i - \bar{x})^2$; (6) calculate the sum of the squares; and (7) calculate the slope. Let's use these steps to calculate the slope for our Figure 18.1 data (the first calculations of each step have been demonstrated for further clarity).

X	Y	$\bar{x}$	$\bar{y}$	$(y_i - \bar{y})$	$(x_i - \bar{x})$	$(y_i - \bar{y})(x_i - \bar{x})$	$(x_i - \bar{x})^2$
2	8	3.2	6.6	$8 - 6.6 = 1.4$	$2 - 3.2 = -1.2$	$1.4 \times -1.2 = -1.68$	$(-1.2)^2 = 1.44$
3	5	3.2	6.6	-1.6	-0.2	0.32	0.04
1	4	3.2	6.6	-2.6	-2.2	5.72	4.84
6	9	3.2	6.6	2.4	2.8	6.72	7.84
4	7	3.2	6.6	0.4	0.8	0.32	0.64
						$\Sigma = 11.4$	$\Sigma = 14.8$

$$\bar{y} = \frac{(8 + 5 + 4 + 9 + 7)}{5} = 6.6$$

$$\bar{x} = \frac{(2 + 3 + 1 + 6 + 4)}{5} = 3.2$$

$$b = \frac{\text{sum of products}}{\text{sum of squares}} = \frac{\Sigma(x_i - \bar{x})(y_i - \bar{y})}{\Sigma(x_i - \bar{x})^2}$$

$$= \frac{11.4}{14.8} = 0.77$$

The slope is 0.77; for every 1-unit increase in X, there is a 0.77-unit increase in Y. The calculations for the intercept are much less involved. The OLS formula is

$$a = \bar{y} - b\bar{x}.$$

After calculating the slope, we have all of these numbers available and can calculate the intercept:

$$a = 6.6 - 0.77(3.2) = 6.6 - 2.46 = 4.14$$

The intercept is 4.14; this tells us that when X is equal to 0, the predicted value of Y is 4.14.

We now know how to calculate the regression line. But how does any of this fit with correlation coefficients? What do regression lines have to do with measures of strength in bivariate relationships? Recall that the regression line is a prediction line: it states what the value of Y is predicted to be at any given value of X. However, the line does not tell us how close the individual cases are to the line, in other words, how good our predictions are. Note that the same OLS equation—identical intercepts and slopes—can represent two very different data sets. Figure 18.5 shows a relatively weak relationship, and Figure 18.6 shows a relatively strong relationship; both have the same slope and Y intercept.

To measure the strength of the linear interval-level relationship, we ask, 'How well does the regression line fit the data?' We are assessing 'goodness of fit'. If there were a perfect bivariate relationship, all of the variation in Y could be explained by X, and all of our cases would line up on the regression line. When we have cases that deviate from the regression line, we have an **unexplained variance**, variation in Y that is not explained by the value of X. If the total squared deviations from the regression line are relatively large, this means that X does not explain a lot of the variation in Y, and we have a weak relationship. If the total squared deviations

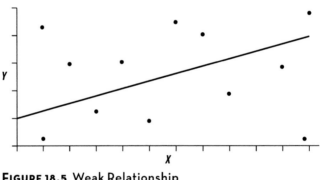

FIGURE 18.5 Weak Relationship

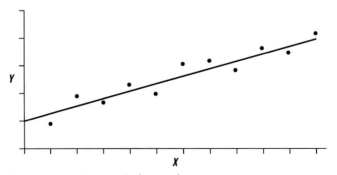

FIGURE 18.6 Strong Relationship

from the regression line are relatively small, this means that X captures much of the variation in Y, and we have a strong relationship.

THE STANDARD ERROR OF THE ESTIMATE

Figures 18.5 and 18.6 provide a graphic illustration of the goodness of fit of the regression line for the two sets of data, illustrating a much better fit (and thus a stronger relationship) in Figure 18.6. A statistic used to calculate the goodness of fit of the regression line is the standard error of estimate. As the regression line is analogous to the mean as the 'best' prediction of the dependent variable (the mean is the best predictor without the independent variable; the regression line (slope) is the best predictor with the independent variable), the standard error of estimate is analogous to the standard deviation of a mean. That is, the smaller the standard error of estimate, the smaller the error in predicting the dependent variable on the basis of the independent variable.

The identification of the standard error of estimate can be seen in Figure 18.7 on page 330. The three panels present the same data and illustrate three types of variation. In Figure 18.7 a), the comparison is between the observed Y values and the mean of Y ($\bar{Y}$). This panel shows the error in predicting the Y value without knowledge of X; we indicated previously that the mean would be the best predictor, since we would minimize the errors of predicting Y via the mean. Figure 18.7 b) compares the mean value of Y (that is, the prediction before knowing the X value) with the predicted value of Y after knowing the X value (that is, Y'). It is labelled 'explained variation' because this is the amount of variation in Y that is accounted for by the X value. Figure 18.7 c) compares the observed values of Y with the predicted values of Y and is labelled the 'unexplained variation', or sometimes called the 'residual variation'. It is the amount of variation in Y that exists after knowing the X values. Notice that the total variation is a sum of the explained and unexplained variations. The unexplained or residual variation is what is used in computing the standard error of estimate. The standard error is given by the following formula:

$$se = \sqrt{\frac{\Sigma(Y - Y')^2}{N - 2}}$$

where se is the standard error, Y is the observed value of Y, Y' is the predicted value of Y, and N is the number of cases.

Continuing with the example from Figure 18.1, we compute the standard error of estimate by first calculating the predicted value of Y' as follows:

$$Y' = a + bX$$
$$= 4.14 + 0.77X$$

Using this formula for each value of X, we find Y'.

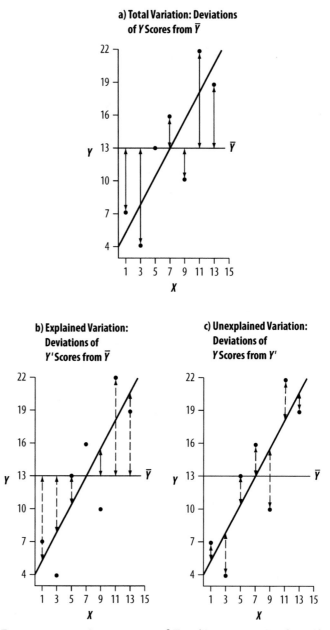

FIGURE 18.7 A Comparison of Total Variation, Explained Variation, and Unexplained Variation in Regressive Analysis

Source: Adapted from Kirk W. Elifson, Richard P. Runyon, and Audrey Haber, *Fundamentals of Social Statistics,* 2d ed. (New York: McGraw-Hill, 1990), p. 238.

X	Y	$Y' = 4.14 + 0.77X$	Y'	$(Y - Y')$	$(Y - Y')^2$
2	8	$Y' = 4.14 + 0.77(2)$	5.68	2.32	5.38
3	5	$Y' = 4.14 + 0.77(3)$	6.45	−1.45	2.10
1	4	$Y' = 4.14 + 0.77(1)$	4.91	−0.91	0.83
6	9	$Y' = 4.14 + 0.77(6)$	8.76	0.24	0.06
4	7	$Y' = 4.14 + 0.77(4)$	7.22	−0.22	0.05

$$\Sigma = 8.42$$

Using this calculation of the unexplained variation, we can complete the calculation of the standard error of estimate:

$$se = \sqrt{\frac{\Sigma(Y - Y')^2}{N - 2}}$$
$$= \sqrt{\frac{8.42}{5 - 2}}$$
$$= \sqrt{\frac{8.42}{3}}$$
$$= \sqrt{2.81}$$
$$= 1.68$$

Figures 18.5 and 18.6 illustrated that a common slope and intercept can represent relationships of very different strength. Thus, it is always useful to evaluate the slope (or the regression coefficient) relative to the standard error. In the present example, the regression coefficient is 0.77 and the standard error is 1.68. This suggests that for each time the value of X increases by one unit, Y increases by 0.77 units. However, on average, we still 'misplace' the values of Y by 1.68 units. The obvious question is, 'Is the new predicted value of Y a good predictor or a bad predictor?' Or, alternatively, is a standard error of 1.68 large relative to the regression coefficient of 0.77, or is it small?

There are two ways of answering these questions, either by using an inferential statistic and asking how likely this result would occur by chance alone, or by using a summary descriptive statistic, which measures the strength of association. The appropriate statistics—and the ones generated by most of the popular computerized statistics packages—are the t-statistic for statistical inference and r^2 as a measure of the strength of relationship.

Student's t was introduced in Chapter 16 and was given by the formula

$$t = \frac{b}{S_b}$$

where b is the regression coefficient, and S_b is the standard error of estimate. In the present example, we calculate t as

$$t = \frac{b}{S_b}$$

$$= \frac{0.77}{1.68}$$

$$= 0.46$$

The degrees of freedom for this example, which has 5 cases and 2 variables, is given by

$$d.f. = N - k - 1$$

$$= 5 - 2 - 1$$

$$= 2$$

Referring to a table of critical values of Student's t, the inclusion of a two-tailed significance test at the .05 confidence level, we find the significant value of t is 4.303. The observed value of t in our example is 0.46, which is well short of the critical value required for statistical significance. Therefore, with this very small sample of five cases, we would conclude that the amount of error was such that we have little confidence the relationship did not occur by chance. Therefore, we would not reject the null hypothesis.

To test for strength of relationships in the regression model, we use a correlation coefficient known as **Pearson's r.** In the OLS method, as we have seen, the total squared distances from the regression line should be less than the total squared distances from the mean (also known as the sum of squares, or the **total variance**). Pearson's r asks if this is in fact the case by comparing the **explained variance** in y (that is, the variance that can be attributed to variation in x) with the total variance:

$$\text{total variance} = \text{explained variance} + \text{unexplained variance}$$

$$\text{Pearson's } r = \frac{\text{explained variance}}{\text{total variance}}$$

Unfortunately, Pearson's r on its own can be difficult to interpret. However, by squaring Pearson's r, we are able to obtain a better elaboration of its meaning. The result, known as r^2, indicates the proportion of y that can be explained by x and can be read as a percentage. Any value of r^2 tells us the percentage of the variation in y that can be explained by some predictor variable x. Using the regression line, we are able to reduce our prediction errors by the percentage given by the value of r^2. Thus,

r^2 is similar (but not identical) in interpretation to PRE measures. We can calculate Pearson's r with the formula

$$r^2 = \frac{\Sigma(xy)^2}{\Sigma x^2 \Sigma y^2}$$

As with calculating the slope, r^2 requires a series of steps: (1) multiply individual x and y scores; (2) square the products of x and y; (3) sum the squared products; (4) square individual x scores; (5) sum the squared x scores; (6) square the individual y scores; (7) sum the squared y scores; and (8) solve for r^2. In the table that follows we have worked through our example data set, showing all calculations for the first case.

x	y	(xy)	(xy)²	x²	y²
2	8	$2 \times 8 = 16$	$16 \times 16 = 256$	$2 \times 2 = 4$	$8 \times 8 = 64$
3	5	15	225	9	25
1	4	4	16	1	16
6	9	54	2,916	36	81
4	7	28	784	16	49
			$\Sigma = 4{,}197$	$\Sigma = 66$	$\Sigma = 235$

$$r^2 = \frac{\Sigma(xy)^2}{\Sigma x^2 \Sigma y^2}$$

$$= \frac{4{,}197}{(66)(235)}$$

$$= \frac{4{,}197}{15{,}510} = 0.27$$

In this data set, 27 per cent of the variation in y can be explained by x, and therefore 73 per cent of the variation in y remains unexplained. Note that the r^2 value does not tell you the unit change in y for every unit change in x, nor does it tell you the direction of change. For this information, we need to look at the slope. Also, notice that the r is lower case. This is used to signify a simple linear regression; only one independent variable is included in the model. When we look at **multiple regression** (multivariate linear models), an upper case R is used. Multiple regression will be explored in more detail later in this chapter.

In summary, when using simple linear regression, we take four steps: (1) construct a scatter plot to ensure linearity; (2) calculate the slope and intercept; (3) calculate the standard error of estimate; and (4) calculate r^2 and interpret. Some additional comments should be made about the first step. Readers of academic literature will often find that, after scatter-plotting the variables, the researcher finds that the relationship is not, in fact, linear. However, he or she may wish to use the regression model in the testing because of the power and accuracy advantages of this technique. To overcome this problem of nonlinearity, the researcher will *transform* the variables, for example, using the logarithm of the variable or the cosine and so forth. Various power transformations for variables have been found by statisticians to transform nonlinear relationships into linear relationships. The important thing to remember here is that we are no longer working with the original variables, but rather a transformed variable. For example, we would be looking at the relationship between level of education and the *log* of income. This requires that we state our interpretations in this form. While this is an advanced technique and therefore beyond the scope of this text, readers can expect to encounter such statistics in the academic literature.

Another technique seen in the literature that is worth noting is the use of **dummy variables**. This technique allows the researcher to use nominal- and ordinal-level variables in the linear model. A dummy variable is one in which a nominal or ordinal variable is transformed into one or more variables that have the presence or absence of a quality or character. For example, to create a set of dummy variables from the nominal variable of region of residence in Canada (assuming four regions of Atlantic, Quebec, Ontario, and the West), one could create three dummy variables (number of categories minus 1: in this example, 4 − 1). One of the categories must be 'suppressed', which means that no variable is created for it, and it becomes the referent or comparison category. So, for example, there could be the variables 'Atlantic', 'Quebec', and 'West', and in each instance, a person is scored '1' if he or she lives in that region, and '0' if he or she does not. The resulting 'dummy' variable coefficients would be interpreted as the effect of living in that

APPLY YOUR UNDERSTANDING

Calculating and Interpreting OLS Equations and Coefficients

For the following data set, (1) test for linearity, (2) calculate and interpret the slope, (3) calculate and interpret the intercept, and (4) calculate and interpret r^2.

Case	Age (years)	Monthly Volunteer Service (hours)
1	18	4
2	63	12
3	47	8
4	56	9
5	36	6
6	42	7

region compared with the suppressed category, in this case to those living in Ontario. In other words, do people in Atlantic Canada, Quebec, or the West think or behave differently from people who live in Ontario? Therefore, although region of residence is a nominal-level variable, by creating a set of dummy variables, region can be used in a regression equation. A second method of exploring the relationships between nominal- or ordinal-level variables and interval-level variables is the **analysis of variance**. A final option, noted earlier in the chapter, is to group the interval-level variable and use nominal- or ordinal-level correlation coefficients.

MULTIPLE REGRESSION ANALYSIS

The simple regression model, using a single independent variable to predict a single dependent variable, can be extended through multiple regression analysis to include additional independent variables. Indeed, one of the most notable advantages of regression analysis is that it enables the simultaneous analysis of multiple predictors in a single equation. This contrasts sharply with the previous discussion of contingency table analysis using nominal or ordinal variables. In the latter instances, the inclusion of additional 'control' variables produced a growing number of tables with decreasing cases. For example, we might wish to examine the effect of attitudes of alienation toward the federal government on voting in the 2008 Canadian federal election. The hypothesis may be that those with higher levels of alienation were less likely to vote Conservative (that is, for the government) than those with lower alienation. Assuming this analysis was conducted on a large sample of 3,000 Canadians, we should be able to examine the impact of alienation with a high level of confidence. Now imagine that we wish to complicate the analysis by examining whether the relationship varies by province of residence; there is good reason to believe that province may influence the level of alienation and party supported in the election. Using the standard five-region categorization (Atlantic, Quebec, Ontario, Prairies, British Columbia), the inclusion of this single control variable would result in the initial table being broken down into five separate tables, with an average sample size of 600 each (the exact number, of course, would depend upon the number of interviews conducted in each province). We might also expect that voting and level of alienation are influenced by feelings toward the prime minister. If we assume that these feelings are measured on a 3-point scale (positive, neutral, negative), the inclusion of the second control variable would produce 3 additional tables for each region, for a total of 15 tables with an average table size of 200 cases. If we assume also that alienation is measured on a 3-point scale, and vote has 6 categories (Liberal, Conservative, New Democrat, Bloc Québécois, Green, and other), each of the 15 tables would have up to 18 cells. Thus, it can be seen that contingency table analysis, with as few as two control variables, can easily produce a table with too few cases in the cells for meaningful analysis.

Yet the point was made earlier that a characteristic feature of the social sciences, generally, and political science, in particular, is that the world we wish to examine and explain is highly complex, and multiple independent variables may affect any given dependent variable. We often wish to model this complexity into our analysis. Multiple regression analysis is a very useful statistical technique because of its ability to examine simultaneously the effects of multiple independent variables on a dependent variable. The number of independent variables included in multiple regression must be no greater than $N - 1$. When the analysis is based on several thousand cases (Ns), as often happens with survey research, the number of independent variables that could be included is well beyond the limit of what one might wish to use.

In view of this feature, it is apparent why political scientists may wish to use multiple regression analysis. However, this approach should be used with considerable caution because of the strong assumptions that underlie it. One key assumption is that the independent variables are independent of one another. When this assumption is violated, the analysis suffers from **multicollinearity**, and the coefficients become less robust. A second key assumption is that the regression line exhibits a constant error term across the values of the independent variables. When this assumption holds, the error is referred to as **homoskedastic**, and when the assumption is violated, the error is called **heteroskedastic**. Once again, heteroskedasticity produces less robust regression coefficients. One of the causes of heteroskedasticity is that the relationship between the independent and dependent variables may be nonlinear, as, for example, where Y' may be a logarithmic function of X. In such instances, one may wish to transform the data to more clearly approximate linearity. More generally, though, it is worth noting that the issues of multicollinearity and heteroskedasticity provide significant challenges to the assumptions of multiple regression analysis. Although a more complete discussion of the problems and possible solutions associated with each is beyond the scope of this book, those wishing to apply this statistical technique should consult more advanced materials on the subject.

A third major assumption of multiple regression analysis and, once again, a possible limitation on its use, is the fact that it assumes that the data are measured at the interval level. We suggested in Chapter 2 that few variables in the social sciences meet the rigorous assumption of interval data: the assumption that increases across the values of a variable are characterized by a constant unit. Consider, for example, the 100-point feeling thermometer used in much public opinion and voting research. Respondents are presented with a 100-point thermometer and asked to state their feelings about some political object, for example, Canada or the prime minister. Such measures are often interpreted as interval data. However, if we consider this further, is it reasonable to expect that all voters mean the same thing by the rating of, for example, 65 on such a scale? Does 65 represent considerable 'warmth' toward that political object, since it is above the midpoint of 50, or does it suggest considerable dissatisfaction, or 'coolness', since it is a full 35 points from 100? Such differences of interpretation speak to the difficulty of assigning an interval category to social data. However, despite such difficulties, many analysts are prepared to accept the conceptual ambiguity in exchange for the more powerful statistical technique available through multiple regression.

With simple regression we examine the effect of a single independent variable on a single dependent variable. We noted that this equation takes the form

$$Y' = a + bX$$

With multiple regression, we can examine the impact of several independent variables by extending the above equation as

$$Y' = a + b_1X_1 + b_2X_2 + b_3X_3 + \cdots + b_iX_i$$

The slope (b) of the regression line for each independent variable represents the amount of change in the Y variable for each unit change in X, controlling for (that is, holding constant) the effects of the other independent variables. It should be borne in mind, though, that the variance within the dependent variable can only be explained once. (Think of the explained variance as a whole pie. When a part of the pie is eaten by one person, it is no longer available for others to eat. So, too, with explained variance of a dependent variable. Once it has been accounted for by one variable, it is not available for the others.) As additional independent variables are brought into the equation, they can account only for unexplained or residual variance. There are a number of procedures available for specifying the order in which independent variables enter a regression equation, so the effect of this can vary in an equation depending upon which procedure is used. Nonetheless, the general point remains. And it suggests the potential problems that can emerge when independent variables are highly correlated. The effect of two independent variables that have much common explanatory power will show more of the effect attributed to one and less to the other. Thus, it is important to be on the lookout for high levels of correlation among the independent variables.

It should also be noted that the simplified model of the multiple regression equation presented earlier in this chapter does not include two different estimates of error. There is error associated with each of the independent variables, and there is error associated with the equation as a whole. Both of these types of error enable us to assess the 'goodness of fit' of the model. The error associated with each regression coefficient (that is, with each b) is called the standard error of estimate (se) and is usually reported along with the regression coefficient. The error associated with the entire equation is referred to as the residual variance. It normally is not reported directly but can be inferred from its opposite, the explained variance (R^2) of the model, which is normally presented.

When conducting a multiple regression analysis, it is often useful to begin by generating a correlation matrix to examine the relationship between the independent and dependent variables, on the one hand, and among the independent variables.

This will enable an initial test of the assumption of independence among the independent variables. Since we discussed previously in the section on simple regression the computation of correlation coefficients, regression coefficients, and standard errors, we will not repeat the computational details for multiple regression. Instead, we will use examples of printed output that one would obtain from a standard statistical package, in this instance, SPSS.

PREDICTING ATTITUDES TOWARD PARTY LEADERS: ASSESSMENTS OF BRIAN MULRONEY

We will use for illustration a model that predicts attitudes toward Brian Mulroney in the 1988 Canadian federal election. You may recall that the 1988 federal election was the second time Canadians went to the polls with Brian Mulroney as Conservative party leader; the Tories had won a landslide victory under Mulroney in 1984. By 1988, Mulroney's leadership had lost some of its lustre; nonetheless, Mulroney enjoyed leadership ratings as high as or higher than the other national party leaders. Because of the assumption that attitudes toward party leaders are important in Canadians' voting decisions (note the use of attitudes toward party leaders as an *independent variable* in the preceding statement), it is useful to try to account for or to explain attitudes toward the leaders (note the switch to viewing this as a *dependent variable*). Based on a reading of previous studies of this topic in the literature in political science, together with extrapolation from some reading you've done in economics and sociology, you might hypothesize the model in Figure 18.8 of the determinants of attitudes toward Mulroney.

Your research design, of course, would provide the rationale for hypothesizing that each of these independent variables affects attitudes toward Mulroney. For example, with the variable 'age' you may be testing the theory that voters become more conservative as they age, which leads to the hypothesis that older voters have more positive assessments of Mulroney, the Conservative leader, than do their

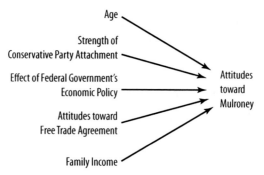

FIGURE 18.8 A Model of Determinants of Attitudes toward Brian Mulroney

younger counterparts. Similarly, you might hypothesize that party identification influences attitudes toward party leaders by 'colouring' one's view of the political world; Conservatives are more likely than Liberals to view Mulroney through rose-coloured lenses. For the variable examining the impact of the federal government's economic policies, you might be testing the theory that voters are self-interested utility maximizers and so support the government because they find it in their self-interest to do so. Similarly, you would want to provide a theoretical justification for the inclusion of other independent variables. You are then able to assess the usefulness and accuracy of the competing theories through the simultaneous inclusion of these variables in the model, which would take the following form:

$$\text{Mulroney} = a + b_1(\text{age}) + b_2(\text{partyid}) + b_3(\text{econpol}) + b_4(\text{freetrad}) + b_5(\text{income})$$

The correlation matrix for these six variables (that is, the single dependent variable and five independent variables) is shown in Table 18.1.

The correlation matrix shows that three of the five independent variables are at least moderately related to attitudes toward Mulroney, and two are very weakly correlated, if at all. It also shows that two of the independent variables—party identification and attitudes toward the Free Trade Agreement—are moderately related ($r = 0.37$). In the context of the 1988 federal election campaign, this latter finding is not surprising, since the Liberal and Conservative parties in particular took such divergent positions on this issue. Although the two independent variables are related, the strength of relationship is not such to suggest that they are measuring the same underlying concept. On the contrary, they clearly seem to be asking quite different things. However, the strength of the correlation is sufficiently large that we need be mindful of possible problems of multicollinearity.

After examining the correlation matrix, we can turn to the multiple regression table. The regression table provides a regression coefficient for each of the

TABLE 18.1 Correlation Matrix of the Determinants of Attitudes toward Brian Mulroney

	Mulroney	Age	Partyid	Econpol	Freetrad
Mulroney	1.000				
Age	0.002	1.000			
Partyid	0.360	0.056	1.000		
Econpol	0.341	−0.001	0.228	1.000	
Freetrad	0.507	0.035	0.372	0.221	1.000
Income	0.050	−0.098	0.067	0.039	0.172

independent variables as well as for the constant (that is, the point of intersection of the Y-axis). In addition, it presents a standard error for each coefficient (printed in parentheses). Normally we are looking for the regression coefficient to be twice the size of the standard error in order that the finding can be said to be 'statistically significant'. Table 18.2 represents statistical significance with an asterisk (*) at the .05 level of significance and two asterisks (**) at the .01 level of significance. In addition, a regression table normally presents the R^2 value, indicating the amount of variance in the dependent variable that is accounted for by the dependent variables.

The table shows that three of the five independent variables are very strong and significant predictors of attitudes toward Mulroney, whereas two others are much weaker, and one lacks statistical significance altogether. Regression coefficients should always be interpreted relative to the size of the standard error: the larger the regression coefficient relative to the standard error, the stronger is the effect of the variable. In this example, the strongest predictor of attitudes toward Mulroney is the respondent's position on the Free Trade Agreement issue. The second most important predictor is the perception that the federal government's economic policies have been of benefit to the respondent. Those who felt this way were much more likely to rate Mulroney positively than those who did not. In addition, the strength of Conservative attachment impacted on attitudes toward Mulroney. Each step up the strength of partisanship measure (from non-Conservatives (0) to weak (1), moderate (2), and strong (3) Conservatives) resulted in a 5-point increase in the 100-point feeling thermometer ratings of Mulroney, other

TABLE 18.2 The Determinants of Attitudes toward Brian Mulroney in 1988

Independent Variables	Dependent Variable	
	Attitudes toward Mulroney	
	b	*se*
Age	−0.04	(0.03)
Partyid	4.99**	(0.61)
Econpol	9.24**	(0.81)
Freetrad	10.32**	(0.51)
Income	−0.45*	(0.20)
Intercept	14.26**	(2.30)

$R^2 = 0.34$
*$p < .05$
**$p < .01$.

things being equal. Income had a weak negative impact on Mulroney ratings; the wealthiest respondents felt less positively toward Mulroney, on average, than their less affluent counterparts. However, the standard error was quite large relative to the regression coefficient, and the relationship barely achieved statistical significance. Finally, the age variable did not achieve statistical significance at all; we would conclude that age does not influence attitudes toward Mulroney, other things being equal.

Thus, the model enabled a fuller comparison of the relative impact of the five independent variables than would have been possible by using a series of contingency tables. It also provides an overall assessment of the importance of these five variables in explaining attitudes toward Mulroney. In this instance, we found that the five independent variables explained 34 per cent of the variance in attitudes toward Mulroney. We might be led to ask what variables could help explain this residual variance. One alternative that has been examined in the political science literature is attitudes toward the personal characteristics of the party leader. Note that in the example just completed, none of the independent variables related to Mulroney's personal characteristics. Instead, we tried to explain attitudes toward Mulroney by reference to respondents' age and income (neither of which was very useful) and by reference to party identifications, perceptions of the government's economic performance, and attitudes toward the Free Trade Agreement, one of the major initiatives of the government. But what about my perceptions of Mulroney's competence or character? Might these also influence my overall assessment of him? The answer, of course, is yes, assessment of Mulroney might very well be influenced by respondents' perception of his personal characteristics. And so, the analysis could continue, with some variables being dropped, such as age and income, and others being added, such as perceptions of Mulroney's character and competence (see Johnston et al. 1992 for a fuller discussion of character and competence as key indicators of leader assessment).

BLOCK RECURSIVE MODELS OF VOTING BEHAVIOUR

In addition to providing the ability to examine the impact of a number of independent variables simultaneously, regression analysis also provides the analyst with control over other elements of the analytical procedure. One such area of control that has become popular in analyses of voting in Canada is specifying the order in which variables are entered into the equation. For example, one can specify a model with the assumption that certain factors arise relatively 'early' in the decision process, and other factors occur 'later', or closer to the actual decision. A block recursive model enables the researcher to specify the order of entry of each variable into the equation so that their inclusion corresponds to the causal sequence of each variable's effect. The term 'block recursive' refers to the fact that each variable that reflects an analytical concept is entered simultaneously. Thus, for example, if there are four questions measuring attitudes to enduring political beliefs, then this group of variables is entered together, as a block. In their use of the block recursive model to explain voting choice in the 2000 federal election in Canada, Blais et al. (2002, 83) describe the model as follows:

> We use a multi-stage explanatory model. The basic idea is that some of the factors that affect vote choice, such as how people feel about the party leaders, are closer in time to the vote decision, while others, such as their ideological orientations, are more distant from actual vote choice. These longer-term predispositions can affect the vote directly, but they can also affect the vote indirectly by influencing more proximate factors, like leader evaluations and issue positions.

The model, therefore, enables the analyst to include a wide range in factors that can affect the voting decision and also to 'stage' the analysis such that each factor is entered sequentially according to the theoretical assumptions the researcher brings to the analysis. In the case of the analysis of Blais and colleagues, the model includes eight blocks of independent variables that are used to explain vote choice. These blocks of variables, in the order of their inclusion in the model, are as follows: sociodemographic characteristics, underlying beliefs and values, party identification, economic perceptions, issue opinions, evaluations of government performance, leader evaluations, and strategic considerations (Blais et al. 2002, 84). The logic of the model is such that the variables entered early in the analysis can affect the vote directly and also can affect the factors that enter the model later. So, for example, the sociodemographic characteristics include things such as the respondents' age, income, religion, marital status, ethnicity, region of residence, and the like. The model suggests that these characteristics can affect the vote directly, or can do so indirectly, by affecting factors entered later, such as a person's underlying beliefs and values. Beliefs and values include such things as attitudes toward social conservatism, free enterprise, feminism, and the like. A recursive model is one in which there is the assumption of one-way causality. In this instance, the block recursive model assumes that sociodemographic characteristics can affect beliefs and values but that the relationship is not reversed, in that beliefs and values cannot affect sociodemographic characteristics.

In a block recursive analysis, the data analysis proceeds by entering each block of independent variables sequentially and assessing the relative impact of variables, as well as the overall goodness of fit of the model, after each set of variables is included. In the case of Blais et al.'s analysis, the situation is somewhat more complicated by the fact that the dependent variable they use is not a continuous variable (as is assumed with ordinary least squares regression), but instead is a dichotomous variable. They wish to explain vote choice in the election and of course cannot use ordinary least squares regression on a variable that includes categories such as (1) Liberal, (2) Canadian Alliance, (3) Progressive Conservative, etc. Instead, Blais et al. conducted separate analyses on pairs of voting options, for example, among respondents who voted Liberal versus Canadian Alliance, or Liberal and Progressive Conservative, or Liberals and New Democrat. Furthermore, they believed that vote choice was significantly different in and outside Quebec in view of the fact that the Bloc Québécois contested elections only in Quebec, and therefore the researchers conducted separate analyses among Quebec voters and non-Quebec voters. The result is a fairly complex analysis of pairs of comparisons for different specifications of the dependent variable.

The other complication of this method is that by specifying the dependent variable as a set of dichotomous choices, the estimation technique used by Blais et al. was multinomial logit rather than ordinary least squares. It is beyond the scope of this book to examine multinomial logit and other variations on the basic theme of regression analysis. But for the purposes of following this example, readers should note that multinomial logit may be used when the dependent variable is dichotomous and there is no rank ordering among the two categories. The resulting outcome from the multinomial logistic regression is a regression coefficient and standard error for each of the independent variables, as well as a measure of the goodness of fit of the model overall (R^2). Table 18.3 shows the results of the analysis presented by Blais et al. (2002), conducted on Canadians living outside Quebec, where the choice of vote was either Canadian Alliance or Liberal. In this specific instance, Canadian Alliance voters were coded as (1), and Liberal voters as (0).

Table 18.3   Multinomial Estimation of Alliance versus Liberal Vote Choice outside Quebec

	1	1-2	1-3	1-4	1-5	1-6	1-7
1. Sociodemographics							
Atlantic	−0.74[b]	−0.99[a]	−0.94[b]	−0.95[b]	−1.09[a]	−0.98[b]	−1.08
West	1.27[a]	0.84[a]	0.38	0.37	0.25	0.26	0.36
Catholic	−0.78[a]	−0.83[a]	−0.69[a]	0.67[a]	−0.58[b]	−0.46	−0.39
Non-religious	−0.63[a]	−0.39	−0.47	−0.44	−0.36	−0.18	−0.74
North European	0.54[a]	0.41	0.52	0.57	0.56	0.61	0.53
Non-European	−1.67[a]	−1.62[a]	−1.16[b]	−1.13[b]	−1.04[b]	−0.99[b]	−0.72
Male	0.54[a]	0.37[b]	0.10	0.12	0.08	0.01	−0.20
Other language	−0.60[a]	−0.81[a]	−0.63	−0.63	−0.58	−0.54	−0.74
Married	0.36[b]	0.17	0.21	0.22	0.17	0.02	0.25
Below high school	−0.04	−0.30	−0.04	−0.09	−0.09	−0.01	−0.47
Rural	0.61[a]	0.51[b]	0.29	0.28	0.29	0.22	0.79[b]

(continued)

	1	1-2	1-3	1-4	1-5	1-6	1-7
2. Values and beliefs							
Social conservatism		0.67[a]	0.37[b]	0.32	0.21	0.17	0.10
Free enterprise		0.91[a]	0.59	0.65[b]	0.61	0.71[b]	−0.44
Racial minorities		−0.53[a]	−0.58[b]	−0.53[b]	−0.49[b]	−0.49[b]	−2.4
Feminism		−0.64[a]	−0.46[a]	−0.48[a]	−0.47[a]	−0.48[b]	−0.43
Religiosity		0.06	0.12	0.12	0.19	0.19	−0.04
Regional alienation		0.69[a]	0.46	0.42	0.41	0.10	0.18
Cynicism		0.89[a]	0.53	0.53	0.43	10.00	0.37
3. Party identification							
Liberal			−2.18[a]	−2.18[a]	−2.09[a]	−2.13[a]	−1.55[a]
Alliance			26.52[a]	26.52[a]	26.31[a]	26.18[a]	26.39[a]
Conservative			1.25[a]	1.26[a]	1.20[a]	1.12[a]	1.70[a]
New Democrat			−1.52[b]	−1.56[b]	−1.51[b]	−1.56[b]	−1.46
4. Economic Perceptions							
Personal past				−0.31[b]	−0.25	−0.14	−0.23
5. Issues							
Federal powers					−0.48[a]	−0.37[b]	−0.16
Public health					−0.42[a]	−0.48[a]	−0.38
Gun control					−0.08	−0.06	0.04
Direct democracy					0.24	0.30	0.20
6. Liberal performance							
Environment						0.12	0.44
Health						−0.38	−0.43
Taxes						−0.73[a]	−0.38
Corruption						−0.46[b]	0.00
Early call						1.31[a]	0.76
7. Leader evaluation							
Chrétien							−3.77
Day							6.43
Clark							−0.60
McDonough							−0.11
Constant	−0.93[a]	−0.61[b]	−0.17	−0.15	−0.11	−0.57	−0.27
Pseudo R^2	0.12	0.22	0.46	0.46	0.48	0.50	0.65
Log likelihood	−1,412.54	−1,189.37	−819.43	−813.90	−790.54	−745.12	−516.86
N	1,280	1,221	1,217	1,215	1,202	1,193	1,181

Source: Andre Blais, Elisabeth Gidengil, Richard Nadeau, and Neil Nevitte, *Anatomy of a Liberal Victory: Making Sense of the Vote in the 2000 Canadian Election.* University of Toronto Press Inc. p. 207. Reprinted with permission of the publisher.

The regression coefficient using multinomial logit analysis is not as readily interpretable as a regression coefficient generated from ordinary least squares regressions. In examining the results presented in Table 18.3, it is useful to focus on the relative effects of each block of variables across the seven stages of the analysis.

In stage 1, only the sociodemographic characteristics are entered. In most instances, the variable is statistically significant at either the .05 or .01 level. The data show, for example, that people from the Atlantic region were more likely to vote Liberal than Alliance, that those in the West were more likely to vote Alliance, and so on. Overall, the model had a relatively modest effect in explaining the vote ($R^2 = .12$). Once values and beliefs were entered, the relative effect of sociodemographic characteristics began to diminish, and partly were supplanted in importance by values and beliefs. Together, beliefs and values along with sociodemographic characteristics increased the overall impact of the model to an R^2 of .22, a substantial improvement over sociodemographic characteristics on their own.

The analyst can proceed through each stage of the analysis as above, examining the changes in the model as each of the blocks of factors is added. In the case of the present example, the largest changes occurred after the introduction of party identification and leader evaluations. Once party identification was added, much of the impact of sociodemographic characteristics and values and beliefs became subsumed within the party identification effect, and the effect even appeared to overwhelm factors such as perceptions of economic performance and a number of political issues. Once leader evaluations were included in the model, little of statistical significance remained, aside from party identification and leader evaluations. Thus, in short, the sequencing of the variables for inclusion in the model enabled the researchers using the block recursive model to more clearly specify the effect each variable had on the analysis.

Most readers of this book will be students who, once equipped with the various analytical techniques introduced in the text, will conduct their own analysis, perhaps even using data from the Canadian Election Study series. When confronted with the results of analyses, such as Blais et al.'s reported above, students might wonder what else is there to study about the voting decision. If Blais et al. conducted the survey for the 2000 federal election, and they have already conducted an analysis to explain the voting decision, is there really any point in doing further work that examines impacts on the vote? The response is that Blais et al.'s analysis was the first word on this matter following the 2000 election, not the last word. For example, subsequent analysis can challenge their conceptual definitions (see our discussion of party identification in Chapter 3) or their operational definitions (for example, have they defined 'social conservatism' to include all of its key dimensions?). In addition, this modelling of the vote decision can be questioned. The block recursive model assumes one-way causality, and for example, party identification was seen to precede leader evaluations. But can the relationship also go the other way—can some respondents change their partisan self-image when parties change their leaders? Changing the specification of the model provides opportunities to look at the reality of the determinants of voting from an entirely different perspective, and may reveal different explanatory values. In short, the research process provides an ongoing method of questioning the findings that have been presented by other researchers, subjecting those findings to rigorous scrutiny, and assessing the extent to which the original conclusions continue to hold under that scrutiny. The contribution of multiple regression analysis to this process is significant in providing the opportunity to model the impact of many potentially important independent variables.

Thus, multiple regression analysis provides considerable analytical advantages. By including a large number of independent variables, we can more accurately map the complex reality of social relations. In addition, the relative impact of variables can be examined directly. It is also worth noting that the logic underlying multiple regression analysis serves in many ways as a gateway to other more complex statistical techniques. Analysis of variance, logistic analysis, path analysis, factor analysis, and LISREL are but a few of the more advanced techniques that are used for quantitative analysis in political science. Once the material from this text has been mastered, you will be prepared to begin exploring these more complex models. In all instances, though, your decision of what statistical technique to employ should be guided by a desire to provide greater insight and understanding of our political world.

WORKING AS A TEAM

1. Conduct a regression analysis of three competing independent variables on a dependent variable by using data from a recent Canadian Election Study data set (you can obtain these publicly available data sets by typing 'Canadian Election Study' into a search engine, and downloading a copy). The dependent variable is political interest. The independent variables are age, family income, and strength of partisan identification. Develop measures of each of these concepts at the interval (or at least the ordinal) level. Briefly review the distribution of each variable. Enter the dependent variable and the three independent variables into the SPSS regression procedure, selecting the STEPWISE selection method. Using the output generated by SPSS, construct a table that presents the results, including the intercept, the regression coefficients, and standard errors for each of the independent variables, and the R^2 value for the full equation. On the basis of the table, discuss the determinants of political interest in Canadian politics.

SELF-STUDY

1. For the following data set, (1) test for linearity, (2) calculate and interpret the slope, (3) calculate and interpret the intercept, and (4) calculate and interpret r^2.

Case	Age (years)	Job Satisfaction (units)
1	25	8
2	63	2
3	47	4
4	50	3
5	36	5
6	42	4

2. Interpret the following simple regression equations:
    a. political interest (in units) = 18 + 2 age (in years)
    b. final grade (in points) = 75 − 4 skipped lectures
3. Describe and assess the assumptions of regression analysis.
4. Obtain a copy of a machine-readable data set and statistical software such as SPSS. Identify a dependent variable and a set of independent variables. Compute a correlation matrix and discuss. Run a simple regression analysis with one of the independent variables. Now include a second independent variable in the analysis and repeat. Note the differences in the regression coefficient and the standard errors of the variable that initially had been used for the simple regression analysis. Interpret the differences in findings. Now add a third independent variable to the analysis. Repeat the steps from above for both of the first two independent variables.

NOTES

1. There are a number of other assumptions that must be met before using linear regression techniques; see, for example, William D. Berry, *Understanding Regression Assumptions* (Newbury Park, CA: Sage, 1993). This material, however, is beyond the reach of this text.

Chapter 19

ANALYZING QUALITATIVE DATA

Jared J. Wesley, University of Manitoba

DESTINATION

By the end of this chapter the reader should

- understand the three-step process of qualitative data coding;
- be aware of coding techniques that can increase trustworthiness; and
- understand how to present qualitative data in written analyses.

Quantitative analysis cannot respond to every research question. Although many things in politics may be measured according to their frequency, salience, or intensity, some phenomena are more difficult to 'count'. Imagine quantifying a concept like 'national identity', for instance, or reducing the entire meaning of the Charter of Rights and Freedoms to a series of numbers. Even if such numbers were attainable—through opinion polling or content analysis—the authenticity of the findings would remain in question. In short, as Albert Einstein famously suggested, '[N]ot everything that counts can be counted, and not everything that can be counted counts.'

This maxim challenges students to learn nonquantitative ways of studying political life. Whether applied to surveys, interviews, content analysis, or any other methodology discussed in this textbook, these *qualitative approaches* involve unique strategies and techniques for dealing with data. To be sure, these involve distinct styles and standards of measurement compared with those applied in quantitative political science. Yet there are obvious bridges between the two traditions. As discussed in Chapter 6, quantitative and qualitative approaches share common allegiance to certain norms about data collection, analysis, and reporting. To advance beyond casual, 'armchair' interpretations, disciplinary standards require all political scientists to adhere to certain rules. The 'raw materials' of politics become scientific 'evidence' only when when treated systematically, and certain standards apply to scholars employing quantitative and qualitative methods alike.

CODING QUALITATIVE DATA

Qualitative research may be conducted on a variety of different raw materials, ranging from documentary sources and oral histories to fieldnotes and interview transcripts. In order to treat qualitative evidence systematically, researchers must code and then analyze their data. Some analysts refer to the qualitative data analysis as a process of 'soaking and poking'—a choice of words that implies less rigour than is actually involved (King, Keohane, and Verba 1993, 36–43; Putnam 1993, 12). Although it is true that qualitative analysts must immerse themselves in their data for an extended period of time, the picture of a researcher casually bathing in a sea of texts, images, or sounds understates the amount of systematic analysis required. Indeed, over time, the social science community has developed a widely accepted, three-step procedure for coding qualitative data (see Biber and Leavy 2006, 279–91; Boyatzis 1998; Creswell 1998, 139–46; Hesse-Marshall and Rossman 2006, 151–76; Neuman and Robson 2007, 336–40; Richards 2005, 85–103).

As displayed in Figure 19.1, the first stage of the process involves '**open coding**'. As part of the initial review of the raw material, the researcher obtains a general sense of its major themes. Whether reviewing fieldnotes, reading through party platforms, listening to speeches, viewing debate footage, or analyzing interview transcripts, the student records any noticeable patterns. Do certain parties emphasize comparable policies? Do certain politicians speak with the same sort of rhetoric? Do certain leaders employ similar hand gestures? Do certain respondents fit into identifiable 'schools of thought'? Depending on his preferences, the researcher stores these conceptual categories in a series of index cards, a notebook, or an electronic journal, or by using computer-assisted qualitative data analysis software (CAQDAS). Because it involves writing a series of memos about these emergent themes, open coding is also referred to as '**memoing**' or 'themeing'.

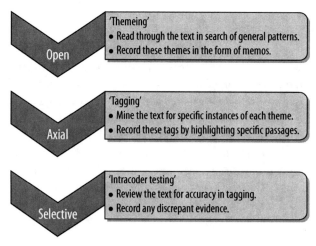

FIGURE 19.1 The Qualitative Coding Process

Depending on their familiarity with the subject matter and research topic, analysts may bring a range of prior knowledge to the open coding stage. Sometimes, there is little existing research upon which to rely. Under these circumstances, the researcher's approach is primarily inductive, as he searches for meaning in the interview scripts, documentary sources, or other bodies of data. Other times, a researcher may enter the coding process with a higher level of knowledge about the subject area, whether rooted in personal experience or grounded in the existing literature. Here, she may approach the data with a preconceived set of codes or categories, which she then seeks to test and fill.

Once this first stage is complete, many qualitative analysts pause for reflection. What do these themes mean, and how do they relate to each other? Why do right-wing parties emphasize policies on crime and punishment in their manifestos, whereas left-wing parties are virtually silent on the issue? Why do conservative politicians speak with a greater sense of urgency and gesture with more aggressive motions, while liberals project certainty and a calmer demeanour? Why do rural interviewees of various backgrounds tend to agree on most issues of public policy? In search of answers, the analyst will typically turn to existing research, conducting a thorough literature review to provide theoretical support for any hypotheses that may have arisen during the open coding stage.

With this backing, the researcher re-engages the data, this time with a more refined sense of purpose and a set of coding categories. During this second stage of 'axial coding', the analyst takes more detailed notes about the content found in the raw materials, categorizing specific phrases, events, or **passages** as belonging under the broad themes identified in stage one. This part of the process is referred to as 'tagging,' with the analyst highlighting important sections of a party platform, transcribing important portions of a speech, splicing together pivotal moments in a televised debate, or copying-and-pasting key responses offered during an interview. These elements (also known as 'bits' or '**chunks**') are then labelled according to one or several of the emergent themes. Once again, depending upon the format of the original materials and the researcher's preferences, this process may be conducted by hand or electronically.

For researchers new to the qualitative tradition, this second stage of the coding process can be the most daunting. Many struggle to identify relevant 'chunks,' and worry whether their choice of categories is appropriate. Given the idiosyncratic, interpretivist nature of qualitative inquiry (discussed in Chapter 6), there are no predefined answers to these questions. Rather, researchers are best advised to treat the qualitative coding process as a creative, interpretive one. They should scour the source material for evidence supporting, and disconfirming, the themes identified in the 'open coding' stage. Tags should be treated more as (re)movable labels based on the researcher's own interpretation at this stage in the process, rather than as permanent markers of some fixed characteristic of the source material. The objective of this second stage is to identify specific evidence of a more general theme—to identify specific elements of more general sets of patterns.

During the third stage of qualitative analysis, the researcher mines the raw materials a final time, examining the data for additional and discrepant evidence. Jones and McEwen (2002, 167) describe this '**selective coding**' process as one in which the researcher seeks 'saturation of categories . . . which means that further analysis produces no new information or need for additional categories. In short, all the data are captured and described by key categories, and a core category emerges that tells the central story'. In other words, the researcher must ask if all the excerpts drawn from the platforms, speeches, debates, or interview transcripts really fit under the themes identified. Do more passages need to be added to substantiate the argument? Are there any passages that appear to contradict the general theme? If so, how do you explain these discrepancies? In this sense, selective coding is a form of intracoder reliability testing and data cleaning, ensuring that all the data fit into the assigned categories, adding, modifying, or deleting tags as necessary.

Throughout this three-stage process, the researcher remains open to revising or refining any of these categories, collapsing some under broader headings, or adding or deleting any as necessary. Any additional notes may be recorded in the margins of the documents themselves, or added to any existing index cards, notebooks, or electronic journals.

A pair of examples may be helpful in understanding this three-stage coding process, one hypothetical and one drawn from a recent research project.

Hypothetical Example of Qualitative Coding: Political Culture and Identity

Imagine analyzing transcripts derived from a series of focus group sessions aimed at understanding political culture and identity in Canada. The moderator has asked each group a series of questions like, What does it mean to be 'Canadian'? and Are there any particular values that appear to unite us as Canadians? Not surprisingly, participants have offered a wide variety of responses. One focus group member stated that Canada is a 'mosaic' of different cultures, while another felt it was more of a 'melting pot'. In another group, one participant suggested Canada is defined by 'not being American', while another added that the country has strong ties to its British heritage. Still others highlighted the existence of unique political cultures in Quebec, the West, and Atlantic Canada, as opposed to a single pan-Canadian identity. How is the researcher to analyze these raw materials (transcripts) and transform them into data?

During the 'open coding' stage, she reviews all the transcripts, making notes about how different statements (or respondents) appear to 'fit together' under different categories. Comments like 'mosaic' and 'melting pot' may be grouped under the heading of 'multiculturalism', for instance; whereas those concerning the role of geography in defining separate subcultures may be considered evidence of 'regionalism'. Other comments may not fit easily into categories at this point in the analysis, forcing the researcher to leave the coding for later stages.

In stage two, any identified themes are used to 'tag' specific statements during the second 'read-through' of the transcripts. This 'axial coding' process consists of labelling various passages as belonging to one of the various categories identified during the 'open coding' stage. This tagging may be done by hand (underlining or highlighting segments of text on paper) or electronically (using the 'comments' or 'captioning' functions found in many word processing or CAQDAS software packages). Once this stage is complete, the researcher proceeds with 'selective coding', reviewing the transcripts again in search of improperly tagged segments or any excerpts that may have been missed.

Real-world Example of Qualitative Coding: Provincial Political Party Platforms

As a second example, consider the coding process employed during a recent qualitative analysis of provincial party campaign literature (Wesley 2011). Here, the researcher was guided by the question, 'Have dominant political parties in Alberta, Saskatchewan, and Manitoba helped to cultivate the three distinct political cultures found on the Canadian Prairies?' In other words, can we find evidence of Alberta's conservative ethos in the campaign rhetoric of its most successful parties and premiers? By the same token, have Saskatchewan's social democratic traditions resonated in the rhetoric of its dominant leaders, and have Manitoba's political parties promoted the province's image of modesty?

An initial review of several hundred pamphlets, speeches, brochures, party platforms, and other election documents revealed stark differences among the campaign discourses in each province. During this 'open coding' stage, the analyst identified a series of distinct rhetorical themes. In Alberta, parties tended to campaign on notions of liberty and anti-conformity, for example, whereas parties in Saskatchewan tended to emphasize the importance of community and solidarity. The researcher recorded these observations as 'memos' to himself, using a combination of traditional notebooks and an electronic journal created by using a standard word processor. These notes proved useful when operationalizing the codes employed in subsequent stages of analysis, and for creating an 'audit trail' for the final report.

A second round of 'axial coding' helped to refine these themes, as the analyst highlighted and tagged key passages as belonging to the unique 'code' of that particular province. Because the documents had been scanned and stored in Portable Document Format (.pdf), this tagging could be done electronically, using the comment and markup tools found in Adobe Acrobat. By highlighting a passage of text and attaching a comment box, the researcher was able to take and store notes about various segments of text. For example, drawing on the rhetoric of prominent Social Credit leaders, such as William Aberhart and Ernest Manning, and successful Conservatives, such as Peter Lougheed and Ralph Klein, campaign literature in Alberta was littered with tags relating to 'freedom', including references to 'individualism', 'populism', and 'provincial autonomy'. By contrast, axial coding of Saskatchewan platforms involved tagging passages relating to 'security', with prominent leaders such as Tommy Douglas, Allan Blakeney, and Roy Romanow emphasizing the importance of 'collectivism', 'strong government', and 'polarization'. A similar, systematic review of campaign literature in Manitoba revealed a provincial code grounded in 'moderation'—a discourse combining more progressivism, pragmatism, and a looser conception of partisanship than those found elsewhere on the Prairies. The names of these various themes were derived in two ways. Given that the terms were used repeatedly in the source documents, some themes (such as 'freedom', 'security', and 'progress') were drawn directly from the raw materials, themselves. This is referred to as *in vivo* coding. In other instances, the researcher imposed his own *conceptual* codes, in effect paraphrasing the nature of the discourse in his own words.

To complete the process, a third round of 'selective coding' was conducted to verify these findings. In some instances, certain passages were reclassified as belonging under a different coding category. A promise to 'preserve the power of the Saskatchewan state against the ill-wishes of the business elite' could be tagged as being evidence of a party's 'strong government' rhetoric, for instance. Alternatively, it could be interpreted as an attempt to 'polarize' the discourse between the forces of left and right. In such cases, a third and closer reading is necessary to uncover the deeper context, and ultimate meaning, of each coded statement.

At the same time, the researcher was on constant alert for discrepant evidence. The active search for data to disconfirm one's hypothesis is a crucial component of the positivist approach to political inquiry (see Chapter 1). In this vein, the researcher reported several competing interpretations of the data. While Alberta party platforms were dominated by references to 'freedom', Saskatchewan, by the notion of 'security', and Manitoba, by 'progress', for instance, the researcher noted that all three terms were found in campaign discourse throughout the region. All Alberta premiers acknowledged the importance of a strong provincial government, just as all Saskatchewan leaders recognized the importance of preserving individual rights. The difference, he argued, lay in the differing levels of emphasis granted by each group of politicians. Whereas Alberta politicians contended 'there could be no security without freedom', Saskatchewan leaders maintained 'there could be no freedom without security'. Caveats and nuances such as these are critical elements of any trustworthy qualitative analysis, because they place reasonable boundaries on the researcher's interpretations.

In sum, the three-part coding process involves a combination of inductive inquiry (stage 1), data mining (stage 2), data cleaning, and intracoder reliability testing (stage 3). Each stage of the procedure may be conducted manually or electronically, depending upon the nature of the raw materials and the proclivities, skills, and resources of the researcher.

Computer-assisted Qualitative Data Analysis

The relationship between the technological advancements of the late-twentieth century and the growth of quantitative analysis is obvious. Regression analyses that once took days by hand or hours by punch-card readers now take fractions of a second thanks to the advent of the personal computer and statistical software packages. Large-*N* survey analysts, in particular, have benefited most from these advances. By the same token, the quest for precision and impartiality has led many researchers in the qualitative tradition to develop automated means of coding their data. Today, many documents can be fed into **optical character recognition** (**OCR**) scanners designed to convert the text into digital/electronic format. With future advances in voice-recognition software, it may be possible to convert orally delivered speeches electronically, as well. This makes the materials conveniently searchable, using keyword or Boolean techniques. Once in electronic format, this data can then be analyzed using any number of programs that help researchers record, file, organize, store, and retrieve their notes.

For the electronically inclined, developments in **Computer Assisted Qualitative Data Analysis Software** (**CAQDAS**) have rendered index cards, notebooks, and sticky notes obsolete. Rather than filing their documents in hard-copy form, recording their notes in handwritten memos, repeatedly transcribing text segments, or tagging passages in the margins of a written page, researchers can use CAQDAS to store, code, search, retrieve, endlessly manipulate, report, and build theories directly from their data. Most programs feature a combination of quantitative and qualitative tools, with many offering the researcher the option of automatically coding data by using a series of predefined and user-defined dictionaries and thesauruses. In addition, memoing, tagging, and themeing can be conducted on-screen, with codes and information stored in a convenient, linkable, fully searchable collection of databases.

Just as earlier discussions in this book did not offer tutorials or weigh the merits of different quantitative software packages such as Stata and SPSS, this is not the place to compare qualitative programs such as ATLAS.ti or NVivo. Each has its own tools, drawbacks, and benefits; choices between them depend upon the skills of the researcher and the nature of the inquiry itself. Suffice it to say that, just as automated quantitative analysis offers certain advantages over manual analysis, so, too, does computer-assisted analysis offer a more reliable and systematic approach to qualitative inquiry. At the same time, researchers must be wary of sacrificing validity, especially when turning to purely automated forms of coding.

REPORTING QUALITATIVE DATA

Just as it takes talent to summarize quantitative findings effectively in the form of tables, charts, graphs, or other figures, qualitative scholars must hone their skills to provide convincing, yet concise, reports of their research findings. However, the latter face unique challenges in presenting their data. On one hand, they are expected to provide sufficient support for their arguments. In most cases, this means including lengthy excerpts from interview transcripts or direct quotations from source documents—both of which consume a great deal of space. On the other hand, qualitative scholarship is expected to conform to the same, tight word limits imposed by publishers, editors, and instructors.

This forces analysts in the qualitative tradition to strike a delicate balance between presenting data and providing analysis. If the researcher presents too much direct evidence, she is criticized for simply transcribing the raw materials. The result is a collection of quotations, rather than an academic analysis (Morse and Richards 2002, 188). On the other hand, if she focuses too heavily on her own interpretation of the data, the researcher is criticized for failing to provide enough evidence. As Platt (2006, 111–12) puts it, '[T]he problem is how to show that the data do indeed support the interpretations made without presenting the reader with all of it.'

But how much evidence is enough, and how much data is too much? How many quotations do researchers need to provide to substantiate their arguments? The answers to these questions will differ from instructor to instructor and reviewer to reviewer. In general, however, a safe rule of thumb is to include a broad cross-section of at least three (3) pieces of evidence to support each interpretation (Berg 2004, 270). For instance, to establish that multiculturalism is a key component of Canadian political culture, the researcher should provide at least three 'chunks' of data, drawn from disparate sources, to substantiate this interpretation. Quotations could be taken from younger and older members of the focus group, and paraphrases could be provided to offer a general overview of the data.

SUMMARY

The political world may be counted or rendered, with each approach requiring its own set of tools and skills. Qualitative research may be less structured than quantitative analysis, but—to be considered empirical—it must be equally rigorous. The qualitative coding process may be more interpretive, and the reporting of qualitative findings, more impressionistic. Yet, just as with quantitative research, all stages of qualitative analysis must be conducted systematically in order to be considered a legitimate element of political science. As a series of guidelines, this chapter has outlined a proven three-step coding process, designed to ensure the soundness of any interpretations drawn from qualitative data. Conducted as part of the initial read-through of the raw materials (be they interview transcripts, political documents, or in any other form), stage one of the process involves 'open coding' the data to identify general themes. A second, more refined round of 'axial coding' is then conducted to 'tag' specific elements of the data as evidence of these various themes. A third stage ('selective coding') involves a combination of intra-coder testing and data cleaning, to verify the accuracy of the interpretations. This three-step process imparts the same level of precision involved in quantitative coding, while maintaining the flexibility necessary to make sense of qualitative data. Einstein was correct: 'Not all that counts can be counted.' But make no mistake: rigour counts, whether counting or not.

WORKING AS A TEAM

Researchers with the Poltext Project have assembled an online collection of party platforms, Throne Speeches, and Budget Speeches from all Canadian jurisdictions, dating back to the 1960s. Visit the Poltext website (www.poltext.org) to view these documents.

1. Divide your members into three subgroups: one in charge of researching Liberal parties, a second responsible for New Democratic parties, and a third, Progressive Conservative parties. Using the three-step coding process outlined in this chapter, have each subgroup analyze the most recent party platforms from the following three provinces: Nova Scotia, Prince Edward Island, and New Brunswick. (The first subgroup will read the Liberal party platforms in all three provinces; the second subgroup will read ndp platforms, and so on.)
   a. Which 'themes' emerged from each group's 'open coding' analysis?

   b. Did these 'themes' change during the process of 'axial coding'?
   c. What types of discrepant evidence emerged during the 'selective coding' stage?
   d. How did these themes differ from party to party? Was there any overlap?

2. Redivide your members, this time assigning each subgroup a different province. The first subgroup will analyze all three parties' platforms in Nova Scotia, for instance, while the other two subgroups study platforms in PEI and New Brunswick, respectively.
   a. Which 'themes' were identified during *this* three-stage coding analysis?
   b. What type of evidence was marshalled to support these interpretations?
   c. Did this second qualitative analysis affect your perception of the trustworthiness of your findings in Question 1?

SELF-STUDY

1. The Financial Crisis (or 'Great Recession') of 2007–10 had a large, but uneven, impact on political systems across the globe. Using the Poltext Project website (www.poltext.org), locate 2009 Budget Speeches for any four Canadian jurisdictions. Conduct a systematic qualitative analysis of these speeches.

   a. How did the style of rhetoric differ in these four jurisdictions? How was it similar?
   b. How did each government's response to the recession differ? Were there any common solutions?
   c. How would you explain these differences and similarities?

Chapter 20

WRITING THE REPORT

DESTINATION

By the end of this chapter the reader should

- have a sound understanding of the strategic considerations in writing a research report;
- understand the components of a research report; and
- appreciate the different elements and formats that can be used to convey research findings.

To this point in the book we have discussed a variety of qualitative and quantitative tools for conducting empirical research in political science. In the vast majority of research projects, we are interested in conveying the findings to an external audience; research is seldom done for personal edification alone, although this may be a motivation lying behind the larger research agenda of many scholars. It is through the research report that we convey our findings to an external audience: a course instructor, fellow students, colleagues in a research project, the sponsors of a particular piece of research, the readers of an academic journal, a government department, or members of a community association or an interest group. The report, then, is the capstone rather than an incidental stage in the research enterprise. It distills, presents, explains, and defends a complex empirical investigation in a format appropriate to its intended audience.

The research report brings together existing knowledge in the field, new data and information generated by the research project, and the expertise and insights of the author(s). Moreover, it does this in a document designed for a particular audience. In these respects, therefore, the research report is an interactive document. The emphasis is not simply on *presenting* one's research findings; it is on *communicating* those findings to an audience.

In this chapter we will explore the interactive nature of the research report by looking first at audience considerations and then at various components of the report.

THE AUDIENCE

A well-written research report is tailored to a specific audience. Because audiences differ in many respects, there is no single, generic format that can be used across all situations. Audiences, for example, will vary in their methodological

Figure 20.1 The Research Report

sophistication. What you might present for the instructor in your course or the assessors for a scholarly journal could be quite different than what you might present in a research report written for a community group. The former will understand quantitative measures of association, such as correlation coefficients, whereas the latter might be best served by a more qualitative discussion of association. It would not be enough, and perhaps would not even be appropriate, to present correlation coefficients; the meaning of covariance must be described in qualitative terms and illustrated. Matters such as tests of significance may be readily understood by one audience, but require detailed explanation for another. Audiences will also differ in the extent to which they are interested in how your research findings fit into the established literature in the field. Your instructor, for example, might be very interested in how you have managed to locate your findings within established disciplinary knowledge, whereas a community group may only want to know the specific results in their case.

All of this means that you must write with a particular audience in mind, remembering their level of sophistication and particular research interests. This does not imply 'dumbing down' the analysis for some audiences. It simply means that effective communication entails knowing one's audience and writing to that audience in a way that clearly transmits the material. Of course, this imperative becomes more difficult to handle if you are writing the same research report for more than one audience. In this case, appendices and footnotes can often be used to convey the detail and complexity required by one audience but not another. Keep in mind that statistical or theoretical 'jargon' is not necessarily bad; the issue is whether the vocabulary you are using is appropriate for your target audience.

It is useful to remember that research reports will often have secondary audiences that may play an important role in the dissemination of research findings. In this respect, the media are an audience to keep in mind. Research reports are seldom written explicitly for media outlets, and when they are, they convey only a fraction of the information contained in the sample research report to be discussed in this chapter. However, reports written for other audiences often find their way into the media and through the media into broader dissemination. You would be well advised, therefore, to keep the potential *public use* of research reports in mind. Off-the-cuff comments, or humour directed at a specific audience, may provide unfortunate grist for editorial comment or news coverage. Pleading that you were misquoted or that the comment was taken out of context will not get you off the hook. It makes sense, then, to keep the potential public audience in mind, even if it is not the primary or intended audience. Thus, before finishing the final draft of the research report, give it a last read as if you were encountering your comments in the *Toronto Star* or *Vancouver Sun*. Would you be pleased with the reporting?

CONSTRUCTING AN ARGUMENT

A good research report is more than a collection of findings; it presents a coherent, well-structured, and thoughtful argument. The report is not only addressed to an audience; it also tells a story. Thus, like a well-told story, it must set the stage, provide some context, move coherently from step to step, follow a consistent story line or plot, and reach a conclusion. Thinking of the research report in this manner is a good way to keep your specific audience in mind. It also helps you keep to the golden rule of storytelling: don't put your audience to sleep! (Even small children will not be amused if you try to put them to sleep by reading dull political science research reports.) Although at times you may find it difficult to write up quantitative research in a lively and engaging fashion, it can be done.

Of course, the analogy between a well-crafted story and the research report should not be overstated, for the two differ in some important respects. The report is theory-driven, or at least reflects theory-driven research, whereas the story sets out to entertain (and perhaps to convey a moral rather than theoretical message). The research report has an explicit thesis statement and employs explicit evidence;

EXPAND YOUR KNOWLEDGE
The Legal Analogue

The components of a good research report are analogous to the components of a good case in a court of law. A lawyer must be aware of legal precedence, just as a scholar must be aware of the existing literature in the field. The lawyer should use her opening statement to capture the interest and attention of the judge and jury. A systematic and solid argument must be developed, one that draws from the facts of the case. While the lawyer is clearly an advocate, it is important not to ignore contrary evidence and soft spots in one's own case. A good argument brings *all* the evidence into play while at the same time emphasizing the most important bits. Ignoring opposing arguments is a poor strategy in court, and ignoring inconvenient or theoretically inconsistent evidence is a poor strategy in the social sciences. A successful lawyer is also attentive to the particular features of the judge and jury, just as the successful research report is crafted with a specific audience in mind. Finally, there must be a strong closing argument; the *facts* cannot be left to speak for themselves. Neither the lawyer nor the social scientist simply reports the facts; it is their expertise that weaves facts into a coherent and compelling argument.

the underlying 'thesis' of a good story is generally implicit, where it exists at all. The report builds directly and explicitly from the data, and the data analysis is linked back to guiding hypotheses and the literature foundation. Perhaps the most important difference is that the research report is held together by a logical argument, whereas the storyteller can draw from a wider range of integrative techniques including imagery, tone, and metaphor.

It is in the construction of the argument that the expertise of the author comes most clearly into play. The research report should be seen as a creative document, not in the sense of inventing information, but rather in the sense of using language to its fullest extent. It is the creative ability of the author that makes data stand up and jump through hoops.

COMPONENTS OF THE RESEARCH REPORT

As we noted earlier in this chapter, there is no generic model of the research report that can be used across all cases and for all audiences. However, there are a number of report *components* that should be addressed in most cases, even though the method by which they are addressed and even the order in which they are addressed will vary according to the report's audience. It is to a discussion of these components that we now turn.

The Abstract or Executive Summary

No matter how brief your report might be, no matter how concise your writing and data presentation, some people will not want to read the entire report, or at least will not want to do so on their first encounter. As a consequence, virtually all publications in scholarly journals include an **abstract** for readers who want to cut to the bottom line, perhaps to determine if the entire report is worth reading in the context of their immediate research interests. Abstracts are particularly useful for readers whose first language is not that in which the report is written; they provide brief overviews that can be digested with minimal effort devoted to translation. For similar reasons of economy, political leaders are notorious for wanting brief **executive summaries**; their days are simply too full to digest more than a page or two. A research study that cannot be summarized on a page, maybe even on a 3 × 5 card, may never be read, much less digested. Therefore, most reports prepared for public consumption, including those prepared for government departments and interest groups, include executive summaries.

It is excellent practice to prepare an abstract or executive summary for writing projects such as term papers. Think of the exercise as similar to a chance encounter at a party, where someone to whom you are attracted asks you to describe your thesis or current work interests. You have a very limited amount of time in which to make your pitch; if you are too long-winded, too boring, your audience will drift away in pursuit of livelier fare. Thus, you need to present the main findings, and the

APPLY YOUR UNDERSTANDING

Writing an Abstract

Find a research report of some reasonable length that does not have an abstract or executive summary attached. You might, for example, use an article in a magazine like *Atlantic Monthly* or *Alberta Views*. Once you have located the article, prepare an abstract of no more than 150 words. Did you find that you were able to capture the major points, findings, and arguments? What kinds of material did you have to set aside? Given your abstract, would there be any need for most readers to read the entire article? What does the article have to offer beyond the information contained in the abstract? Sometimes the answer to this question can be a depressing 'very little'.

principal theoretical hooks upon which those findings are hung, in a concise and interesting fashion. A well-written abstract or executive summary does more than describe; it engages and entices the reader. If you find yourself 'alone at the party', you know that your executive summary needs more work.

The utility of this writing exercise goes beyond the convenience of busy or lazy readers. It forces you to describe your findings and their significance in a precise, interesting fashion. Writing an abstract or executive summary makes you come to grips with the essential core of your research project. As you will discover, it can often be more difficult to 'write short' than to 'write long'. Preparing the abstract or executive summary could be the most difficult writing assignment in the entire report!

Introduction

The primary objective of the introduction is to capture the reader's interest. The introduction should explain both the research topic and its relevance. It should also present the basic research question or thesis statement, sketch in briefly the line of argument to be pursued, and explain the architecture of the report. A clear and emphatic thesis statement is particularly important. It is not necessary, however, to preview the research findings. The intent is to introduce the reader to the research project, thereby establishing a context for what is to come and an enticement to read the entire report.

Although in many respects the introduction to the research report will resemble the abstract or executive summary, it will generally not provide an overview of the research findings. The similarity between the two will be less disconcerting to you, the author, if you keep in mind that the abstract or executive summary is meant to stand alone; it should be intelligible even if the report itself is never read. The introduction, however, is a part of the research report. It sets the stage for the larger project and is not meant to stand alone.

Literature Review

The importance of this component of the research report will be a function of the report's audience. Reports written as course assignments or submissions to academic journals must include a **literature review**, although not necessarily labelled as such. The literature review serves a number of important functions. First, readers will expect to see how your research project grew out of the existing literature. What are the holes, lacunae, or contradictions it was designed to address? Are you replicating research done before in a different setting or at a different time? If so, are you incorporating significant innovations in your research design beyond the spatial or temporal change? In short, you must demonstrate how your research fits into the larger body of literature but is still unique.

Second, the literature review may provide the foundation for many of the empirical measures embedded in your report. For example, if you are exploring the relationship between globalization and support for neoliberalism, you must explain the literature roots of your measures of these terms. As was observed in Chapters 3 and 4, there are many alternative conceptualizations and operationalizations for any given term. If your measure fits with the existing body of literature, its roots within that literature should be acknowledged. If your measure differs from conventional practice, this too should be noted.

Third, readers will want to know how your findings fit into the established knowledge in the field. Have you confirmed, reinforced, challenged, expanded, or contradicted existing knowledge? Have you pushed back the boundaries of knowledge or altered what we thought we knew? All these questions are important and interesting, and none of them can be addressed unless a literature review has been put into place.

A good literature review is more than a description of what has come before. It should present a *critical* overview of the existing literature, including an identification of problems, omissions, and contradictions. After all, if the existing literature has 'said it all', the value of your own report will be thrown into question. Thus, the literature review helps establish the rationale for your research project. It shows how you are improving rather than reinventing the wheel.

Nonetheless, literature reviews tend to be quite abbreviated in reports that are not targeted at an academic or a scholarly audience. For example, a report prepared for the Ontario Liberal party on gender differences in partisan support would be unlikely to include an extensive literature review. The client commissioning the report will be more interested in the current landscape than in what came before. Even here, however, a brief summary of existing knowledge could be useful to the client. If nothing else, it provides some handle on change over time.

EXPAND YOUR KNOWLEDGE
Reading Critically

Although students are urged to 'read critically', it may not be clear what this exhortation means in practice. By asking the following questions, your skill as a critical reader may be improved:

- Is the methodology adequately explained? Would you be able to replicate the research if you had the resources and inclination to do so?
- Is there a clear thesis statement? Does the author provide a road map for the analysis to come?
- Is there a literature review? Is the research project given a context within social science research on the same or similar topics conducted to date?
- Does the argument proceed logically? Is there a connection between the evidence provided and the conclusions drawn?
- Are the conclusions overstated?
- Is the analysis balanced? Does the author deal with contradictory evidence? With alternative explanations?

Research Design

In our earlier discussion of the scientific method, we stressed that good science must be capable of replication. If Professor Perrault finds X through method Y, then it should be possible for Professor Santini to come to the same conclusions if she follows the same method. This means that the research method must be clearly identified in the research report. This is done through a detailed explication of the project's **research design**.

But what exactly should be covered in this component of the report? If the research project included the collection of new data, the collection procedures should be described in detail. What ethical issues were encountered, and how were they addressed? Was sampling used? If so, what were the population, the sampling frame, the respondent selection procedures, the possible sources of bias, and the response rate? Were empirical measures constructed for theoretical concepts? If so, how were they constructed? What reliability and validity checks were used? It is not enough, for example, to say that levels of Western alienation were higher among native-born British Columbians than they were among recent migrants to the province unless you also indicate how Western alienation was measured and how 'recent' was defined.

The research design component should cover the study's theoretical points of departure, the hypotheses used to frame the study, and the operationalization of key concepts. It may also provide an explanation for the types of data analysis employed. Perhaps the key thing to remember is that the research design is more than a description of what you did. It is also an *explanation* and a *justification*. If readers are to have confidence in your findings and conclusions, they must first have confidence in your research design.

Presentation of Findings

This is the core of the research report. It is here that your contribution to the existing knowledge in the field is made. Given the importance of this component, there are a number of strategic choices to be made:

- Given that all the possible findings cannot be presented, which findings should you select and emphasize? Remember, if you try to present everything, the reader may be overwhelmed or lose interest. You must be selective.
- Which findings are important enough to warrant detailed presentation in the form of tables, graphs, and figures? Which findings might be mentioned more in passing?
- What level of methodological sophistication is best for your target audience? Will your audience expect the use of advanced techniques, or would the use of such techniques lose the readers?

Graphical elements can be an important part of a well-designed research report. The old adage that 'a picture is worth a thousand words' certainly applies. However, you must remember that figures do not always speak for themselves; they generally require explanatory text. Also remember that graphs and figures can be presented in a variety of ways and that only some ways are appropriate for certain kinds of data. For example, pie charts and bar graphs are appropriate for nominal data, whereas line graphs are not. Complex tables can be difficult for many readers. If they are included, it is essential that you walk the reader through by providing an interpretative guide. Tables are even less likely than charts or graphs to 'speak for themselves'.

Given that empirical research reports are often 'number-rich', you must be careful to use the appropriate numbers. Do not overstate the precision of your data; if the average age of your respondents is 46.253 years, for example, round to 46 years. If a Pearson correlation coefficient is +0.3763, round to +0.38. Be sure to use the appropriate correlation coefficients and to report tests of significance in a consistent manner. Do not, for instance, reject one finding as insignificant at the .01 confidence level while accepting another as significant at the .05 confidence level.

Also keep in mind the potential importance of negative findings, instances where the null hypothesis was not rejected. Sometimes students and scholars are inclined to stress only positive correlations, the relationships that are found to exist rather than the ones that do not. It may seem uninteresting to report what didn't happen, to note expectations that were not met. However, in many cases negative findings—the absence of a relationship—can be theoretically significant. Imagine, for example, that you were testing for the existence of class differences in partisan support within the Atlantic Provinces or for the existence of regional differences in public opinion in the national electorate, and you found there were no statistically significant differences. Such findings could be important in a substantive sense for our understanding of the contemporary political scene. Thus, you should be no quicker to reject negative findings as uninteresting than you should be to accept positive findings as interesting. It may all depend upon your theoretical point of departure and the hypotheses that frame your research.

Discussion

Research reports are often, although not always, constructed so that the data findings are first presented or described and then discussed. In the discussion section the author steps back from the details of the data presentation and tries to explore, usually in more qualitative language, just what the empirical findings might suggest. In many respects, the discussion section involves stepping back from the trees and examining the forest.

It is in the discussion section that you have the opportunity, indeed the obligation, to tie your findings back to the literature review and back to the study's guiding hypotheses. As a general rule, the discussion section should be accessible even to those readers who may not be able to follow the details of your statistical analysis. Many readers will rely upon you to make sense of the data analysis for them; they may read the literature review and research design, and then skip to the discussion.

Conclusions

The conclusions should take the reader back to the report's introduction. Recap the research problem and the thesis statement. Remind the reader what you set out to do, and then discuss to what extent those objectives have been accomplished. Remember, data seldom speak for themselves. You cannot assume that the reader will draw the same conclusions from the data analysis that you yourself have drawn. You need, therefore, to provide some interpretation of the findings.

Some readers will read only your conclusions; they will skip to the bottom line. As a consequence, your conclusions should be strongly and clearly stated. At the same time, you should not ignore nuances that may have emerged in the data analysis or discussion sections. If some readers are to carry away only the concluding paragraph or two of your report, you want to be sure that they do not have a distorted impression of your findings.

The concluding section of the research report often contains recommendations for action, for the next steps that should be taken. If the report is aimed at the scholarly community, such recommendations might be suggestions for future research.

If you could do the research again, what might you do differently, and why? Has your research closed off some doors for future research while opening others? If the report is aimed more at a nonacademic audience, the recommendations are more likely to be policy recommendations than suggestions for future research: 'In light of the findings of this report, we recommend that your organization take the following steps if it wants to accomplish . . .' . In both instances, the same question applies: 'Are your findings actionable?'

References

The list of references at the end of the research report serves two primary functions. First, it provides specific bibliographical details for any theoretical or empirical citations in your report. It therefore allows your reader, should he or she be inclined to do so, to backtrack through the literature foundation for your research. Second, it provides readers with leads they can follow if your findings spark interest. Thus the reference section is an essential complement to the literature review.

Sometimes authors will inflate the reference section by including works that played a peripheral role at best in the research project. While it is essential to include full bibliographic references for any works directly cited in the research report, avoid excess padding. Research reports are seldom judged by the number of references; thoughtful readers expect you to be as selective in your references as you were in the presentation of your findings.

THE FINAL POLISH

We live in a time when personal computers and sophisticated printers mean that even the shoddiest piece of research can be presented in a *very* impressive way. Although we would never suggest that style can substitute for content, it is essential to pay close attention to the manner in which research findings are presented. Is the layout of the research report as attractive as possible? Does it have an attractive cover, a useful table of contents? Have you carefully checked for spelling and grammatical mistakes? Remember, if you get the small things wrong, if the report is poorly written or presented, the reader may assume that you have the big picture wrong as well. Packaging is critically important, for it conveys a sense of how careful you have been and how seriously you take the report. Sloppy work is quickly dismissed.

Remember, the report is the capstone. This is where it all comes together. A great deal of painstaking work can be discounted if it is poorly presented. The theoretical import of your work can be lost, along with the implications of your empirical evidence. Thus you owe it to yourself, and to others who may be involved in the research enterprise, to put as much effort into the presentation of your research as you did into gathering the empirical evidence.

WORKING AS A TEAM

1. If you are preparing draft research reports as course assignments, try exchanging drafts and writing up an abstract of no more than 100 words. Read the abstract back to the original author. Does the author accept the abstract as a reasonable distillation? Could you reduce the abstract to 75 words? To 50 words?

2. Have your group pull together a variety of research reports prepared in different formats and for different audiences. You might, for example, use royal commission reports, stories in news magazines, articles in academic journals, and reports in trade books. How do these different research reports compare with respect to format and components? Do they do the same things in different ways, or do they have little in common?

SELF-STUDY

1. Take one or more of your old term papers, and prepare an abstract of 150 words. Were you successful in capturing the core of the paper? What important elements, if any, were lost? What do you feel needed to be said, but was squeezed out? Now see if you can trim this abstract to only 100 words. Can you trim it to 75 words? How low can you go before the abstract becomes useless?

2. Select two articles from a recent volume of the *Canadian Journal of Political Science* or *Canadian Public Policy*. What similarities and differences exist between the two? Do they present their findings in a similar way? Do they use abstracts in a similar fashion? Do they both include explicit research designs and thesis statements?

GLOSSARY

abstract a brief summary of an article or a research paper that helps the reader quickly understand the purpose and findings of the research.

accidental sample a nonprobability sample technique in which the researcher gathers data from individuals whom she 'accidentally' encounters or who are convenient; also known as a *sample of convenience* or *haphazard sample*.

action research a reflective and iterative process of research focused on solving specific 'real world' problems.

advocacy research a type of policy research, typically practised by individuals who are deeply committed to an issue, often with a goal of marshalling evidence to heighten public debate and discussion of the issue, and to influence the policy process.

aggregate data grouped data for a specified geographic area.

alpha (α) level *see* confidence level.

alternative hypothesis the statement of a possible causal relationship, in contrast to another statement, often the research hypothesis; the use of an alternative hypothesis can be helpful in assessing the relative magnitude of the relationship in the research hypothesis.

ambiguous questions the phrasing of response items in survey research in which there is some uncertainty in the meaning of an individual's response; a question with multiple stimuli is an example.

analysis of variance (ANOVA) a statistical technique in which the observed variance is partitioned into components (within group and between group variances); in political science, this may be used when the dependent variable is measured at the nominal or ordinal level (particularly the former), and the independent variables are measured at the interval level.

anonymity the personal identity and personally identifying features of a person are not known; in research conducted on individuals, respondents must be informed whether their identity will be revealed, or whether they will remain anonymous.

applied research a term that is often used in contrast to 'pure research' or 'basic research', to indicate that the research is directed to addressing a topic or problem in the 'real world'.

audit trail a record of decisions made when gathering and analyzing data.

authenticity the extent to which the analysis of a phenomenon corresponds with reality.

axial coding the second stage of qualitative data analysis, during which specific passages are labelled as belonging under certain themes; see also *tagging*.

bandwagon effect a phenomenon in political science that observes that a number of people hold a certain belief or act a certain way because many other people think or act in that way; a type of group normality.

basic linear regression *see* ordinary least squares regression.

basic research research is carried out to increase understanding of the world, whether or not the results of the research have immediate or obvious applications; often used in contrast to applied research.

bivariate involving two variables.

Canadian Election Studies (CES) a series of academic surveys conducted on a sample of the Canadian electorate at the time of federal elections. The Canadian Election Studies series was first conducted in 1965, following on similar studies administered in the United States beginning in 1952. The Canadian Election Studies have been conducted during every federal election since 1965, with the exception of 1972, and provide a rich source of data for academic research on political beliefs and voting behaviour.

case a single unit of analysis.

case identification a number, or combination of numbers and letters, used to identify the case.

case study a method of analysis that involves an in-depth investigation of a single individual, group or event. In political science, the case study method is generally used with the intent of identifying general causal principles.

categorical a level of measurement in political science, also referred to as nominal measurement; a categorical variable is one in which the numerical values of a variable (1, 2, 3, etc.) represent a difference in kind, rather than a difference in degree: the regions of Canada can be included in a categorical variable in which 1 = Atlantic, 2 = Quebec, etc.; in this instance, the value of 2 is not higher than 1; it is simply different.

causal effect the difference between the value of an outcome when a subject receives a treatment and when a subject does not receive the treatment.

causality the relationship between two events, in which one event is a consequence of another event; the relationship between the events is referred to as cause and effect.

Census an enumeration or a record of the full population.

central tendency the centre of a data distribution; measures of central tendency include the mode, median, and mean.

central value the numeric representation of the centre of a data distribution; also known as measure of central tendency.

chunks passages of text that serve as indicators of a given theme.

closed questions (close-ended questions) a question format in which respondents are provided with the full set of acceptable responses.

cluster sampling a probability sampling technique in which the researcher divides the population into a number of subgroups, known as clusters, and then randomly selects clusters within which to randomly sample.

codebook an instrument developed to guide coding; it lists the elements of the text that will be observed (variables) and itemizes how they will be categorized (values).

coding the systematic categorization of different aspects of communication.

coding sheet a sheet on which coders can record the values for each case.

comparative research a research design that seeks to compare phenomena across different political systems or cultures.

complex multiple indicator some concepts in political science comprise more than one quality and to provide a complete measure of such concepts, variables may also consist of more than one aspect; an example would be the measurement of a person's political participation, which may comprise a variety of different aspects.

computer assisted qualitative data analysis software (CAQDAS) computer programs designed to assist researchers in coding, retrieving, storing, and analyzing qualitative data.

concept an abstract idea that represents or symbolizes a quality; it can be contrasted with a variable, which is the specific and concrete measurement of a concept for a particular research project.

concordant pairs pairs of cases that exhibit similar ordering on the independent and dependent variables.

confidence interval the estimated range of values within which the population parameter is likely to fall.

confidence level the probability that the sample statistic is an accurate estimate of the population parameter; also known as alpha level.

confidentiality information is made available only to those who are authorized to have access to it; in political science research, subjects typically are provided with a guarantee of confidentiality and to ensure this, in survey research names and other identifying features of respondents are not included in the data set used for analysis.

confirmability the extent to which the results of a study may be verified by an independent researcher.

confounding the presence of some unobserved difference between groups that is correlated both with the outcome of interest and with the independent variable of interest, thereby making causal inference impossible.

content any message that can be communicated, including words, meanings, symbols, or themes.

contingency table a table that presents data for two variables, with the location of a particular case being contingent upon its values for each of the two variables; also known as cross-tabulation or cross-tab table.

continuous a variable in which responses can be arrayed along the entire range of the measure, with no gaps or breaks in the distribution.

continuum a continuous series or event, no part of which is distinguishable from other parts.

control group a group of subjects randomly assigned not to receive the treatment in an experiment; the control group in a randomized experiment is identical in all respects to the treatment group, with the exception that the control group does not receive the treatment.

convergent validity in measuring a concept with multiple indicators, where the indicators reveal the same or similar qualities, they have convergent validity.

correlation the measurement of, or the observation of, a common variation among multiple concepts or measures; a correlation can exist without a causal relation.

Cramer's V a chi-square based measure of association for nominal-level data.

credibility the extent to which the results of an analysis 'fit' with the reality being depicted.

critical value the number that the calculated inferential statistic must meet or exceed if we are to reject the null hypothesis.

cross-sectional data the data collected from individuals at one point in time.

cross-sectional studies a type of research design in which the intention is to gather empirical evidence on an entire population, or a representative sample of the population, at a particular point in time.

decennial Censuses Censuses taken at the start of a decade (for example, 1991, 2001, 2011).

deductive reasoning a type of reasoning that shows or attempts to show that a conclusion necessarily flows from a set of premises; in political science, often used in rational choice analysis, where individuals are assumed to be utility maximizers, and their actions are assessed in relation to what they would be if this premise is true.

dependability the extent to which a researcher has produced accurate results, based on precise methods.

dependent variable the outcome event, or the event to be explained, in a research project; the research hypothesis is that an independent variable or variables act on or effect the dependent variable.

descriptive research a study that aims to chronicle or describe some aspect of reality; involves questions of who, what, where, and when.

determinism the view that a certain outcome is inevitable.

difference of means a statistical test to determine if the difference in mean scores for two subgroups from the sample population is statistically significant.

direction identifying the type of message by situating it along some sort of continuum or classification scheme.

discordant pairs pairs of cases that exhibit dissimilar ordering of the independent and dependent variables.

discriminant (divergent) validity the assessment of a measure in which those elements or factors that are expected to be different from the measure are shown in fact to be different; the opposite of convergent validity (see above).

dummy variable a measure in which a quality is dichotomous and is represented by the presence and the absence of the quality, usually using the values of 0 and 1; for example, gender can be a dummy variable of 1 = female and 0 = not female; a more complex example is to measure region of residence in Canada with a set of dummy variables, such as Atlantic = 1 for Atlantic resident and 0 for not Atlantic resident; Quebec = 1 for Quebec resident and 0 for not Quebec resident; and West = 1 for West resident and 0 for not West resident; in this instance, one category (Ontario) is suppressed, and consequently the effect of each region is interpreted to be in relation to Ontario.

ecological fallacy the assumption that group-level patterns imply individual-level patterns.

elite interviews interviews of individuals or groups with access to specialized information.

empirical research the reliance on observation of the real world to test theories and gain knowledge.

endogenous a set of variables that are included within the model being assessed.

epistemology the study of knowledge (or 'how we know what we know').

equivalent measures indicators that measure the same concept across different countries, political systems, or cultures.

equivocal having the possibility of several different meanings; ambiguous.

executive summary a short document that attempts to identify the key elements from a larger report or set of reports, such that the reader can become familiar with the latter without reading the longer report(s).

exhaustive including all of the possible causal factors in an explanatory model. It is often useful to consider whether the analysis is assisted by using an exhaustive model, with many variables, or a parsimonious model, that attempts to maximize explained variation with a limited number of variables.

exogenous a set of variables that are excluded from the model being assessed.

experimental design a research design in which the researcher has intervened in some way to randomly assign some subjects to a treatment group and others to a control group before an event takes place.

explained variance the amount of variation in the dependent variable that is accounted for by the independent variables.

explanatory research a study that aims to account for or explain some aspect of reality; involves questions of why or how.

exploratory research a study that aims to discover factors relating to a subject about which very little is known.

external validity the extent to which the findings drawn from the cases under examination may be used to make generalizations about phenomena outside the original study.

face validity as the name implies, face validity provides a validity test based on the fact that the outcome 'looks like' it is expected to look.

falsifiable the idea that a hypothesis is not true by definition and is stated in such a way that empirical data could demonstrate that it is not true.

feasibility the extent to which a study is capable of being completed, given the researcher's skills and resources.

feeling thermometer a type of measure in which the metaphor of a thermometer is used to assist respondents identify their beliefs, feelings, or thoughts as relatively 'warm' or relatively 'cold'; often used with a 100-point scale.

fieldnotes detailed descriptions of events observed during observation research.

frequency whether or not something occurs, and if it does, how often.

frequency distribution a list of the number of cases for all possible values of a variable.

gamma a proportional reduction of error measure of association for ordinal-level data.

hard-to-reach population a population that is difficult for researchers to identify and/or that is less likely to participate in research studies.

Hawthorne effect when subjects under observation alter their behaviour because of the presence of the researcher.

heteroskedastic two variables are related, but the strength of relationship varies throughout the range of the variables; put another way, the variances are not consistent along the full distribution of data.

heterogeneity how dissimilar a population is with respect to the variable of interest.

highest reliable level of measurement when designing survey questions, this principle suggests that the goal is to obtain data with a relatively high level of precision in measurement. For example, when asking about the age of respondent, it is better to use the precise age in years, or year of birth, rather than categories such as 'young, middle age, and old'. Precise measures can always be reclassified in less precise terms, but imprecise measures cannot subsequently be made more precise.

homogeneity how similar a population is with respect to the variable of interest.

homoskedastic two variables are related, and the strength of relationship is consistent through the range of the variables; ordinary least squares regression assumes a consistent error terms across the full range of the variables.

hypothesis a statement of a proposed causal relationship between two concepts.

hypothesis-testing a method used in statistics to test the validity of a statement, by comparing expected results with empirical or observed results. Formally we typically test the null hypothesis that the independent variable has no effect on the dependent variable, and based on the results decide whether to accept or reject the null hypothesis. Rejecting the null hypothesis lends support to the research hypothesis that the independent variable affects the dependent variable.

idea the issue or a message being communicated.

ideal type the formulation of a concept based upon a notion of its 'true form', rather than in relation to how it operates in the real world.

impartiality the extent to which a study offers findings based on observation and evidence, as opposed to opinion or conjecture.

independent variable the measure used as the proposed causal influence in a relationship between two measures.

index a complex measure that combines responses from more than one question in the creation of the new measure.

indicator a variable that is used to represent the presence of a quality.

inductive reasoning a type of reasoning that bases conclusions on the presence of empirical evidence; evidence is used for theory development.

inferential statistics statistics used to determine if sample statistics are representative of population parameters.

informed consent the idea that respondents in a research project fully understand the nature of the project, the extent of their participation, and agree to participate based on these understandings.

intensity the strength of the message.

intercept in regression analysis, the point at which the regression line crosses the Y-axis.

intercoder reliability the extent to which different coders reach the same conclusions (that is, assign the same values when coding); a high level agreement indicates the coding instrument is reliable.

internal validity the extent to which the researcher has produced results reflective of reality, as measured within the confines of the study.

interpretivism also referred to as anti-positivism, it is the view that reality does not exist independent of individuals and that all knowledge is socially constructed. According to this view, there is no such thing as 'objective reality' that can be understood by all observers, and measured through techniques such as survey research. Instead, interpretivism is associated with the view that reality is socially conditioned and understood, and methodologically was associated with more qualitative approaches.

intersubjectivity a phenomenon is experienced by more than one person; a situation in which two people, acting independently, perceive the same thing.

interval a level of measurement in which all values have a numerical category, the categories are ranked from highest to lowest, and there is a consistent range between each of the values.

intervening variable a situation in which a third variable comes between an independent and dependent variable; the independent variable influences the intervening variable, which in turn influences the dependent variable.

investigator triangulation the use of multiple researchers in a single research study, as a means of ensuring the trustworthiness of the examination.

interview framework a written list of questions that the interviewer intends to ask of the respondent.

interviewer effect a respondent provides a response because it is what he or she expects the interviewer to desire.

knowledge mobilization a term used, for example by the Social Sciences and Humanities Research Council (SSHRC), to describe the practical application in society of research.

lambda the proportional reduction of error measure of association for nominal-level data.

large-N study research involving a large number of cases.

latent content the underlying or implied meaning of the message.

levels of measurement the precision used in the interpretation of the numerical values of the measures used in the research; distinction is made among nominal, ordinal, and interval measures.

Likert scale a psychometric scale of measurement based on a five-point scale ranging from strongly disagree to strongly agree.

linear regression a statistical technique used to assess the strength of relationship between two or more variables measured at the interval level, in which the model assumes a consistent (linear) relationship across all values of the dependent variable.

literature review a text that attempts to identify the current state of knowledge in a given subject area, with a particular focus of the main substantive understandings and theoretical approaches.

longitudinal data the data collected from the same individuals over time.

manifest content the literal, or surface meaning of the message.

margin of error a range around the estimate, expressed in percentage terms (for instance, ±5 per cent), that likely contains the population parameter; used by researchers to state their sample statistics as a confidence interval; also known as random sampling error.

marginals the total number of cases in a row (row marginal) or column (column marginal) of a table.

mean the arithmetic average, calculated by adding together all scores in a distribution and dividing by the total number of cases.

measurement validity the extent to which the measurement of a particular concept matches its operational definition.

measures the ways in which concepts are measured; for example, the importance of a political actor within a news story could be measured by whether or not he or she is named in the headline of the news story, or by the frequency with which he or she is referred to in the story, or by the length of direct quotes (if any) attributed to this actor within the story.

measures of association statistical measures of the strength of a relationship between two variables; also known as 'coefficients of association' or 'relationship measures'.

measures of variation statistical measures for the dispersion of scores around the central tendency.

median the value above which and below which 50 per cent of the cases fall.

member checks the process of verifying the results of a study in consultation with its subjects.

memoing the process of writing notes to oneself regarding the coding process.

metadata the technical documentation that accompanies secondary data.

microdata nonaggregated data that allows the researcher to consider individual units of analysis (such as individuals or households).

minimal risk a term used in the research ethics review process to indicate that the risks associated with participating in a research project are no greater than risks encountered in everyday life.

minimize defensive reactions when designing survey questions, frame the questions in such a manner that respondents do not provide an automatic emotional, and negative, response.

mixed-methods research the use of a variety of qualitative and quantitative methodologies in the confines of a single study.

mode the most frequently occurring value in a distribution of scores.

moderate relationship a change in the independent variable is to some degree correlated with change in the dependent variable.

most-different-systems design a comparative research design in which the researcher compares very different systems, seeking to explain similarities between them.

most-similar-systems design a comparative research design in which the researcher compares very similar systems, seeking to explain differences between them.

multicollinearity a relationship exists between the independent variables in a model, which in general violates the assumption of linear regression that independent variables should be unrelated to one another; the existence of multicollinearity leads to unstable estimates of the effect of the relationships.

multidimensional a concept comprises different elements or dimensions, each of which must be captured in the definition and measurement.

multiple regression including more than one independent variable in a regression model.

multivariate involving three or more variables.

mutually exclusive two elements cannot co-exist.

negative correlation two variables are related, with increases in one variable associated with decreases in another variable.

no relationship perfect independence between two variables: change in the independent variable is not correlated with change in the dependent variable.

nominal a level of measurement, also referred to as categorical, in which values have different numerical categories, but the values indicate a difference in kind, not in degree; party choice is a nominal variable, with Conservative = 1, Liberal = 2, NDP = 3, etc.; although the values of 1, 2 and 3 are different, in this nominal variable one is not larger than the other.

nonparametric statistics statistics whose use is not contingent on the parameters of the data distribution.

nonrandom error systematic error; nonrandom error can occur for a variety of reasons, for example, because of people not telling the truth; many surveys overreport voter turnout, since this variable suffers from nonrandom error, in which some people who don't vote don't want to admit that they don't vote, and consequently report voting when they did not vote.

nonsingular a model that does not have one and only one correct solution, but rather is open to different possible interpretations.

normal curve a curve that represents the normal distribution.

normal distribution a bilaterally symmetrical curve in which the mean, median, and mode are all equal, and which meets other mathematical conditions; mathematical distribution of cases.

normative analysis a type of analysis that is value-laden, in which indications of ought or should are often used.

null hypothesis the statement of the inverse of the research hypothesis; the null hypothesis states that there is no relationship between the independent and dependent variables, and formally we typically are empirically testing the null hypothesis.

objectivity the extent to which the results of a study are unbiased by the predispositions of the researcher.

observation research a research design in which the researcher observes actual behaviour; also known as field research or ethnography.

observation schedule a checklist for recording behaviour in observation research.

observational design a research design in which researchers have not intervened to randomly assign a treatment but instead observe an event and analyze the data after the event has taken place.

obtrusive observation research observation research in which the subjects are aware that they are being observed.

omnibus surveys surveys that are not dedicated to examining one specific issue or to focusing on the concerns of only one sponsor, but rather are more general in character and often involve multiple sponsors.

one-tailed test an inferential statistical test used when the direction of difference is relevant to the hypothesis testing.

open coding the first stage of qualitative data analysis, during which general patterns or themes are identified.

open questions (open-ended questions) questions are framed in such a way that respondents can state their position without any cueing from the researcher.

operationalization the process of moving from a conceptual definition (an abstraction) to an measure or a set of measures (concrete) that enables a researcher to empirically observe the construct in his or her particular research project.

operational definition the way in which a variable is defined by a researcher for a particular study. This often involves very specific issues, such as how to deal with non-responses, 'don't knows', and the like. It involves taking an abstract concept and providing a way to measure it for all cases in a study.

optical character recognition (OCR) software designed to translate nonelectronic text into machine-readable format.

ordinal a level of measurement in which values represent differences, and the values can be rank-ordered from lowest to highest; however, unlike interval variables, there is not a consistent unit across the range of values; Likert scores (see above) are a good example of ordinal variables.

ordinary least squares (OLS) regression a form of regression analysis in which the slope (or regression coefficient) is estimated on the basis of a technique that minimizes the squared variations between the observed and predicted values of the dependent variable.

panel studies *see* cross-sectional data.

paradigm a theoretical framework within a discipline in which there is general agreement on the laws, theories, conceptual definitions, and manner of measuring variables.

parametric statistics statistics that have assumptions about the distribution of the data that must be met if they are to be used and interpreted correctly.

participant observation an unobtrusive observation research design in which the researcher becomes part of the community that she is observing.

passages labelled as belonging under certain themes; *see also* tagging.

Pearson's r the Pearson product moment correlation coefficient that examines the strength of relationship between two variables, ranging from -1 to $+1$.

peer evaluation process a very common practice within the scholarly community that subjects new research findings to a double-blind review by the members of the scholarly community; the major academic journals use the peer evaluation process to assess whether an article merits publication.

perfect correlation a change in the independent variable is always and systematically correlated with change in the dependent variable.

pilot study a preliminary investigation intended to test and refine the methodology employed in the main study.

plausibility when compared with alternative accounts, the extent to which the results of a study offer a reasonable, believable account of reality.

policy analysis the analysis of public policy processes or outcomes.

population in research, the group that we wish to generalize about (for example, citizens of Canada in 2010); in content analysis, the texts most appropriate for answering the research question.

population parameter population characteristics, expressed in numeric terms when the responses of each and every member (or case) of the population are measured.

portability the extent to which the results of a study may be used to draw conclusions about other cases not immediately under investigation.

positive correlation two variables are related such that an increase in one variable is associated with an increase in the other variable.

positivism a philosophical position that the scientific approach is the best way to gain knowledge.

postmaterialism a social theory developed by Ronald Inglehart in the 1970s that postulated that advanced industrial societies were moving from a division based on material wealth and physical security to one based on individual autonomy, concern for the environment, and self-expression.

postmodernism a philosophical position that it is not possible to identify 'objective' knowledge, since all knowledge is embedded within the power, class, gender, and racial structure of society.

postulates a proposition that is viewed as self-evident.

precision the extent to which a study offers an accurate account of reality, based on the ability of other researchers to reach similar conclusions under similar circumstances.

predictive validity a measurement of a concept is affirmed in part because it leads consistently to accurate predictions.

prior conditions the nature or status of a situation before the inclusion of an independent effect.

probability the mathematical likelihood that the results of a study apply beyond the cases under examination, to cases under the same general category.

prominence the placement and importance of a message in a text.

proposition a statement expressing the truth or falseness of a situation.

proportional reduction in error (PRE) **measures** a special class of measures of association that compare the amount of error we have without knowing the independent variable with the amount of remaining error after knowledge about the independent variable is taken into account.

purposive sampling a nonprobability sampling technique in which the researcher uses his judgment to select cases that will provide the greatest amount of information; also known as judgmental sampling.

qualitative research the nonnumerical examination of reality, typically through the use of verbal depiction.

qualitize the process of supplementing quantitative data with nonnumerical evidence.

quantitative research the numerical examination of reality, typically through the use of statistical analysis.

quantize the process of supplementing qualitative data with numerical evidence.

question order the order in which questions are posed in a survey questionnaire.

quinquennial Censuses Censuses taken mid-decade (for example, 1996, 2006, 2016).

quota sampling a nonprobability sampling technique in which the researcher combines purposive or accidental sampling with stratification: the researcher identifies a number of target groups (strata), and then sets a quota number that must be met for each group.

random assignment the process of assigning some members of a population to a treatment and others to a control; random assignment ensures that the two groups are identical in all respects aside from the receipt of treatment.

random errors inaccuracies caused by factors that are not systematic and/or intentional; for example, all samples contain random error simply by virtue of the fact that the sample includes less than the full range of possible respondents; fortunately, we can estimate the amount of random error in a probability sample.

random selection a selection technique in which all cases in a population have an equal opportunity for selection for the sample.

range the difference between the lowest and highest values in a distribution of scores.

research design the manner in which the research question has been structured in light of the literature review of the topic, including the way in which data are to be gathered and analyzed to test the major hypothesis or hypotheses of the study; it is not uncommon for researchers to prepare a written document that presents the research design, in advance of the data being analyzed.

regression line the line that corresponds to the slope in a regression model, adjusted by the intercept; in ordinary least squares regression, it minimizes the errors in predicting the dependent variable.

reliability the extent to which the measurement of a particular variable yields consistent results.

replicability the extent to which a study is repeatable or duplicable.

replication the repeating of a study in an attempt to duplicate and confirm results from a previous study.

representative sample a sample that accurately reflects the larger population from which it was drawn.

residual the amount that is left over, or unexplained.

response set the group of response categories that comprise all responses to a particular question.

right to withdraw for research on human subjects to receive ethical approval, there is a condition that respondents must be given the right to withdraw from the study at any time, and also that they be informed of this right.

rigour the validity and reliability of the research.

sample a record of a subset of a population.

sampling the process of drawing a number of cases from a larger population for further study.

sampling distribution the theoretical distribution of a sample statistic (for example, the mean) for a given sample size.

sampling error the difference between the sample statistic and the population parameter.

sampling frame a list of all the units in the target population.

scatter plot a graphical presentation of the relationship between all cases on a dependent and independent variable, typically where these variables are measured at the interval level.

science a systematic approach to gaining knowledge and understanding based on a method of formulating hypotheses and testing these hypotheses with empirical data.

scientific analysis analyses that use the scientific method, in whichever discipline the study is taking place.

scientific approach to politics the application of the scientific method to the study of political phenomena.

secondary data data that are not collected directly by the researcher; examples include government data, such as Statistics Canada and Elections Canada data, and data collected by other research teams, such as the Canadian Election Studies.

selective coding the third and final stage of qualitative data analysis, during which the researcher verifies the accuracy of earlier coding decisions.

self-selection individuals select themselves for participation in the sample (for example, radio call-in programs).

simple random sampling the process by which every case in the population is listed, and the sample is selected randomly from this list.

size of a message how much space or time a message takes up within the text.

skew the opinion an uneven distribution of opinion on a topic, in which a disproportionate percentage of the respondents hold an opinion on one side of the issue.

slope sometimes described as the rise over the run, the amount of change in the dependent variable for a one-unit change in the independent variable.

small population the population for which there are relatively few members (for instance, cabinet ministers).

small-N studies research involving a small number of cases.

snowball sampling a nonprobability sampling technique in which the researcher begins by identifying a few cases and from these cases gets referrals for other cases and continues to branch out; also known as network sampling.

spurious the relationship between the independent and dependent variables, while initially thought to be causal, is noncausal and instead is a function of the presence of a third variable, which causes the variation in both variables.

standard deviation a number that represents the average of how cases vary from the mean.

standardized scores scores expressed in terms of the number of standard deviations they fall from the mean of the total distribution of scores; also known as z-scores.

statistic a numeric estimate of the population parameter.

statistical power the ability of a research design to detect effects should such effects exist; a power analysis can give researchers an idea of the sample sizes necessary for an experiment to be sensitive enough to detect effects of certain sizes.

stimulus *see* treatment.

stratified sampling a probability sampling technique in which the researcher breaks the population into mutually exclusive subgroups, or strata, and then randomly samples each group.

structural features how the message is conveyed by and/or within a text; for instance, structural features of a newspaper story include the headline, lead paragraph, author, length, type of story, etc.

substantive features the substantive meanings being communicated by a text.

sum of squares the sum of the squared deviations from the mean.

systematic selection a probability sampling technique in which the researcher calculates a selection interval and uses this interval to select cases from the sampling frame.

tagging the process of labelling specific passages as belonging under a given theme.

tau-b a proportional reduction of error measure of association for ordinal-level data; requires square tables.

tau-c a measure of association for ordinal-level data; requires nonsquare tables.

temporal order the arranging of the sequencing of events based on the order in which they occur.

text any form of communication (written, visual, spoken, etc.).

theories statements of the reasons for the causal relationship between two variables.

ties pairs of cases that differ on one variable but are tied on the other.

total variance the full amount by which the observed occurrences of the dependent variable differ from the estimated or predicted value based on independent variable.

transferability the extent to which researchers may export the lessons drawn from one investigation to develop conclusions about another set of cases.

treatment the intervention of interest; also known as stimulus.

treatment group a group of subjects randomly assigned to receive the treatment—some intervention of interest—in an experiment; the treatment group in a randomized experiment is identical in all respects to the control group, with the exception that the control group does not receive the treatment.

triangulation the use of multiple approaches to data collection and analysis as a means of drawing trustworthy conclusions about reality.

trustworthiness the extent to which a study produces legitimate knowledge.

two-tailed test an inferential statistical test used when the direction of difference is not relevant to the hypothesis testing.

Type I error the error made when the null hypothesis is incorrectly rejected; also known as 'false positive'.

Type II error the error made when we incorrectly fail to reject the null hypothesis; also known as 'false negative'.

typology the classification of things on the basis of their characteristics. For example, one could devise a typology of political party systems based on the number of competitive parties in the system.

underdog effect a phenomenon in which respondents hold views or perspectives based on the perception that a group or individual is trailing a leader, as in a party or candidate getting additional support because of sympathy toward his or her position.

unexplained variance the total amount of deviation between the observed and predicted values of the dependent variable that is not due to the presence of the independent variable.

unit of analysis the portion of text that will be coded (for example, the headline of a news story).

univariate involving a single variable.

universe synonymous with population.

univocal having one meaning; unambiguous.

unobtrusive observation research observation research in which the subjects are unaware that they are being observed.

valid a concept, conclusion, or measurement that corresponds accurately to the real world. A concept that is valid has no random or nonrandom error.

validity the extent to which the results of a study reflect reality.

values categories that capture the variance between observable characteristics of phenomena; for coding to be effective, values should be collectively exhaustive (include all possible variations) and mutually exclusive (that is, they should not overlap).

variables the observable characteristics of phenomena that can take on more than one value.

variance the sum of the squared deviations from the mean, divided by the number of cases.

variation ratio the number of cases that are not in the modal category.

z-scores *see* standardized scores.

REFERENCES

Abu-Laban, Yasmeen and Linda Trimble. 2010. 'Covering Muslim Canadians and Politics in Canada: The Print Media and the 2000, 2004 and 2006 Federal Elections.' In Shannon Sampert and Linda Trimble, eds., *Mediating Canadian Politics.* Toronto: Pearson Education: 129–50.

Akeroyd, Anne V. 1991. 'Personal Information and Qualitative Research Data: Some Practical and Ethical Problems Arising from Data Protection Legislation.' In Nigel C. Fielding and Raymond M. Lee, eds., *Using Computers in Qualitative Research.* London: Sage Publications: 89–106.

Alberts, Sheldon and Rebecca Eckler. 1996. 'Income Gap Widening.' *Calgary Herald.* 26 July: A1.

Albrow, Martin. 1970. *Bureaucracy.* London: Pall Mall Press.

Alcantara, Christopher. 2007. 'Explaining Aboriginal Treaty Negotiation Outcomes in Canada: The Cases of the Inuit and the Innu in Labrador.' *Canadian Journal of Political Science* 40, 1 (March): 185–207.

Almond, Gabriel and Sidney Verba. 1965. The *Civic Culture,* abridged ed. Boston: Little Brown.

Altheide, David L. 1996. *Qualitative Media Analysis.* Thousand Oaks, CA: Sage Publications.

Ambrose, Jay. 1996. 'We're Smart Enough to Know How Dumb IQ Tests Are.' *Globe and Mail,* 3 August: D1.

Andrew, Blake C. 2007. 'Media-generated Shortcuts: Do Newspaper Headlines Present Another Roadblock for Low-Information Rationality?' *Press/Politics* 12, 2: 24–43.

Angus Reid Strategies. 2008. *Conservatives Close Campaign Ten Points Ahead of Liberals.* http://angusreidstrategies. com/uploads/pages/pdfs/2008.10.13_Final.pdf, accessed 17 November 2009.

Arceneaux, Kevin and David Nickerson. 2005. 'Even If You Have Nothing Nice to Say, Go Ahead and Say It: Two Field Experiments Testing Negative Campaign Tactics.' Paper presented at the American Political Science Association Annual Meetings, Washington, DC.

Archer, Keith and Alan Whitehorn. 1990. 'Opinion Structure Among New Democratic Party Activists: A Comparison with Liberals and Conservatives.' *Canadian Journal of Political Science* 23, 1 (March): 101–13.

Archer, Keith and Faron Ellis. 1994. 'Opinion Structure of Party Activists: The Reform Party of Canada.' *Canadian Journal of Political Science* 27, 2 (June): 277–308.

Archer, Keith and Roger Gibbins. 1997. 'What Do Albertans Think? The Klein Agenda on the Public Opinion Landscape.' In Christopher J. Bruce et al., eds., *A Government Reinvented: A Study of Alberta's Deficit Elimination Program.* Toronto: Oxford University Press: 462–85.

——, Rainer Knopff, and Les Pal. 1995. *Parameters of Power: Canada's Political Institutions.* Toronto: Nelson Canada.

Atchade, Yves F. and Leonard Wantchekon. 2007. 'Does Ethnic Solidarity Facilitate Electoral Support for Nation-Building Policies? Evidence from a Political Experiment.' NYU Mimeo.

Atkinson, Michael M. and Maureen Mancuso. 1985. 'Do We Need a Code of Conduct for Politicians? The Search for an Elite Political Culture of Corruption in Canada.' *Canadian Journal of Political Science* 28, 3 (September): 459–80.

Avio, Kenneth L. 1987. 'The Quality of Mercy: Exercise of the Royal Prerogative in Canada.' *Canadian Public Policy* 13, 3 (September): 366–79.

Babbie, Earl. 1989. *The Practice of Social Research,* 5th ed. Belmont, CA: Wadsworth.

——and Lucia Benaquisto. 2002. *Fundamentals of Social Research,* Cdn ed. Scarborough: Thomson-Nelson.

Bahry, Donna L. 1981. 'Crossing Borders: The Practice of Comparative Research.' In Jarol B. Manheim and Richard C. Rich, *Empirical Political Analysis: Research Methods in Political Science.* Englewood Cliffs, NJ: Prentice-Hall: 230–41.

——and Rick K. Wilson. 2006. 'Confusion or Fairness? Rejections in the Ultimatum Game Under the Strategy Method.' *Journal of Economic Behavior and Organization* 60, 1: 37–54.

Bailey, Kenneth D. 1978. *Methods of Social Research.* New York: The Free Press.

Bakvis, Herman and Laura G. Macpherson. 1995. 'Quebec Block Voting and the Canadian Electoral System.' *Canadian Journal of Political Science* 28, 4 (December): 659–92.

Banks, Russell. 1989. *Affliction.* Toronto: McClelland & Stewart.

Barbolet, Herb, Vijay Cuddeford, Fern Jeffries, Holly Korstad, Susan Kurbis, Sandra Mark, Christiana Miewald, and Frank Moreland. 2005. *Vancouver Food System Assessment.* http://www.sfu.ca/cscd/publications/documents/final_draft_compress.pdf, accessed 7 January 2010.

Bardach, Eugene. 2009. *A Practical Guide for Policy Analysis: The Eightfold Path to More Effective Problem Solving,* 3d ed. Washington, DC: CQ Press.

Baxter-Moore, Nicolas, Terrance Carroll, and Roderick Church. 1994. *Studying Politics: An Introduction to Argument and Analysis.* Toronto: Copp Clark Longman.

Becker, Howard S. 1998. *Tricks of the Trade: How to Think About Your Research While You're Doing It.* Chicago: University of Chicago Press.

Bedford, David. 2003. 'Aboriginal Voter Participation in Nova Scotia and New Brunswick.' *Electoral Insight.* www.elections.ca

—— and Sidney Pobihushchy. 1995. 'On-Reserve Status Indian Voter Participation in the Maritimes.' *Canadian Journal of Native Studies* 15, 2: 255–78.

Bell, Edward, Harold Jansen and Lisa Young. 2007. 'Sustaining A Dynasty in Alberta: The 2004 Provincial Election.' *Canadian Political Science Review* 1, 2: 27–49.

Belson, William A. 1986. *Validity in Survey Research*. Aldershot: Gower Publishing.

Berdahl, Loleen, Christopher Adams and Greg Poelzer. 2009. 'Aboriginal Provincial Party Support in Manitoba,' Paper prepared for the 2009 Canadian Political Science Association Annual Meetings, Ottawa, 27 May 2009.

Berg, Bruce L. 1989. *Qualitative Research Methods in the Social Sciences*. Boston: Allyn & Bacon.

——. 2004. *Qualitative Research Methods for the Social Sciences*, 5th ed. Toronto: Pearson Education.

Berry, William D. 1993. *Understanding Regression Assumptions*. Newbury Park, CA: Sage Publications.

Bibby, Reginald W. 1995. *The Bibby Report: Social Trends Canadian Style*. Toronto: Stoddart.

Black, Conrad. 1977. *Duplessis*. Toronto: McClelland & Stewart.

Blais, André, Pierre Martin, and Richard Nadeau. 1995. 'Attentes économiques et linguistiques et appui à la souveraineté du Québec: une analyse prospective et comparative.' *Canadian Journal of Political Science* 28, 4 (December): 637–57.

——, Elisabeth Gidengil, Richard Nadeau, and Neil Nevitte. 2002. *Anatomy of a Liberal Victory: Making Sense of the Vote in the 2000 Canadian Election*. Peterborough, ON: Broadview.

Bouchard, Lucien. 1994. *On the Record*, trans. Dominique Cliff. Toronto: Stoddart.

Boyatzis, Richard E. 1998. *Transforming Qualitative Information: Thematic Analysis and Code Development*. Thousand Oaks, CA: Sage Publications.

Brady, Henry E., David Collier, and Jason Seawright. 2004. 'Refocusing the Discussion of Methodology.' In D. Collier and H. E. Brady, eds., *Rethinking Social Inquiry: Diverse Tools, Shared Standards*. Boulder, CO: Rowman & Littlefield.

Brannen, Julie. 1988. 'Research Note: The Study of Sensitive Subjects.' *Sociological Review* 36: 552–63.

Broadhead, Robert S. 1984. 'Human Rights and Human Subjects: Ethics and Strategies in Social Science Research.' *Sociological Inquiry* 54: 107–23.

Brodie, Ian and Neil Nevitte. 1993. 'Evaluating the Citizens' Constitution Theory.' *Canadian Journal of Political Science* 26, 2 (June): 235–59.

Brodie, M. Janine and Jane Jenson. 1980. *Crisis, Challenge and Change: Party and Class in Canada*. Toronto: Methuen.

Brown, Douglas. 2002. *Market Rules: Economic Union Reform and Intergovernmental Policy-Making in Australia and Canada*. Canada: McGill-Queen's University Press.

Brown, Steven D., Andrea Perrella, and Barry J Kay. 2010. 'Revisiting the Local Campaign Effects: An Experiment Involving Literature Mail Drops in the 2007 Ontario Election.' *Canadian Journal of Political Science* 43, 1 (March): 49–67.

Brown, Steven D., David Docherty, Ailsa Henderson, Barry Kay, and Kimberly Ellis-Hale. 2006. 'Exit Polling in Canada: An Experiment.' *Canadian Journal of Political Science* 39, 4 (December): 919–33.

Bryman, Alan. 2001. *Social Research Methods*. Toronto: Oxford University Press.

——. 2004. *Social Research Methods*, 2d ed. Toronto: Oxford University Press.

Budd, Richard W., Robert K. Thorp, and Lewis Donohew. 1967. *Content Analysis of Communication*. New York: Macmillan.

Budge, Ian and Judith Bara. 2001. 'Introduction: Content Analysis and Political Texts.' In I. Budge, H.-D. Klingermann, A. Volkens, J. Bara, and E. Tanenbaum. *Mapping Policy Preferences: Estimates for Parties, Electors and Governments 1945–1998*. New York: Oxford University Press: 1–18.

Burden, Barry C. and Casey A. Klofstad. 2005. 'Affect and Cognition in Party Identification.' *Political Psychology* 26, 6: 869–86.

Burnham, Peter, Karin Gilland, Wyn Grant, and Zig Layton-Henry. 2004. *Research Methods in Politics*. London: Palgrave.

Cairns, Alan C. 1975. 'Political Science in Canada and the Americanization Issue.' *Canadian Journal of Political Science* 8, 2 (June): 191–234.

——. 1993. 'A Defence of the Citizens' Constitution Theory: A Response to Ian Brodie and Neil Nevitte.' *Canadian Journal of Political Science* 26, 2 (June): 261–67.

Callahan, Daniel and Bruce Jennings. 1983. *Ethics, the Social Sciences, and Policy Analysis*. New York: Plenum Press.

Camerer, Colin F. 2003. *Behavioral Game Theory: Experiments in Strategic Interaction*. Princeton: Princeton University Press.

Campbell, Angus, Philip E. Converse, Warren E. Miller, and Donald E. Stokes. 1960. *The American Voter*. New York: John Wiley and Sons.

Canache, Damarys, Jeffrey J. Mondak, and Ernesto Cabrera. 2000. 'Voters and the Personal Vote: A Counterfactual Simulation.' *Political Research Quarterly* 53, 3: 663–76.

Canadian Press. 1996. 'Public Jittery About Pensions.' *Calgary Herald*. 20 June: A1.

Carbert, Louise. 2006. *Rural Women's Leadership in Atlantic Canada: First-Hand Perspectives on Public Life and Participation in Electoral Politics*. Toronto: University of Toronto Press.

Carroll, James. 1996. 'Uncle Sam's New Stinginess.' *The Boston Globe*. 23 July: A13.

Carroll, Lewis. 1990. *Alice's Adventures in Wonderland and Through the Looking Glass*. Notes by Martin Gardner. New York: Random House: 126.

Carty, R. Kenneth and Munroe Eagles. 2006. *Politics Is Local: National Politics at the Grassroots.* Toronto: Oxford University Press.

Chadwick, Bruce A., Howard M. Bahr, and Stan L. Albrecht. 1984. *Social Science Research Methods.* Englewood Cliffs, NJ: Prentice-Hall.

Chan, Alfred L. and Paul Nesbitt-Larking. 1995. 'Critical Citizenship and Civil Society in Contemporary China.' *Canadian Journal of Political Science* 28, 2 (June): 291–309.

Chong, Dennis, and James N. Druckman. 2007. 'Framing Public Opinion in Competitive Democracies.' *American Political Science Review* 101, 4: 637–55.

Chrétien, Jean. 1994. *Straight From the Heart.* Toronto: Key Porter Books.

Clarke, Harold D. and Allan Kornberg. 1993. 'Evaluations and Evolution: Public Attitudes Toward Canada's Federal Parties, 1965–1991.' *Canadian Journal of Political Science* 26, 2 (June): 287–311.

Clarke, Harold, Jane Jenson, Lawrence LeDuc, and Jon Pammett. 1979. *Political Choice in Canada.* Toronto: McGraw-Hill Ryerson.

Clarkson, Stephen and Christina McCall. 1990. *Trudeau and Our Times, vol. 1: The Magnificent Obsession.* Toronto: McClelland & Stewart.

Constantatos, Christos and Edwin G. West. 1991. 'Measuring Returns from Education: Some Neglected Factors.' *Canadian Public Policy* 17, 2 (June).

Copsey, Nathaniel. 2008. *Focus Groups and the Political Scientist.* European Research Working Paper Series, Number 22. http://www.eri.bham.ac.uk/documents/research/wp22-copsey.pdf, accessed 7 January 2010.

Creswell, John W. 1998. *Qualitative Inquiry and Research Design: Choosing Among Five Traditions.* Thousand Oaks, CA: Sage Publications.

———. 2003. *Research Design: Qualitative, Quantitative, and Mixed Methods Approaches.* Thousand Oaks, CA: Sage Publications.

——— and Vicki L. Plano Clark. 2007. *Designing and Conducting Mixed Methods Research.* Thousand Oaks, CA: Sage Publications.

Dahl, Robert. 1961. *Who Governs? Democracy and Power in an American City.* New Haven: Yale University Press.

———. 1989. *Democracy and Its Critics.* New Haven: Yale University Press.

Davis, James A. 1985. *The Logic of Causal Order.* Newbury Park, CA: Sage Publications.

DeKeseredy, Walter. 1994. 'Addressing the Complexities of Woman Abuse in Dating: A Response to Gartner and Fox.' *Canadian Journal of Sociology* 19, 1: 75–80.

——— and Katherine Kelly. 1993. 'The Incidence and Prevalence of Woman Abuse in Canadian University and College Dating Relationships.' *Canadian Journal of Sociology* 18, 2: 137–59.

Denzin, Norman K. and Yvonna S. Lincoln. 1994. 'Entering the Field of Qualitative Research.' In N.K. Denzin and Y.S. Lincoln, eds., *Handbook of Qualitative Research.* Thousand Oaks, CA: Sage Publications.

Dewan, Torun, Macartan Humphreys, and Daniel Rubenson. 2009. 'The Impact of Leaders and the Messages They Convey: Evidence From a Field Experiment in British Columbia.' Paper presented at the annual meetings of the American Political Science Association, Toronto, ON.

Dolence, Michael G. and Donald M. Norris. 1995. *Transforming Higher Education: A Vision for Learning in the 21st Century.* Ann Arbor, MI: Society for College and University Planning.

Downs, Anthony. 1957. *An Economic Theory of Democracy.* New York: Harper & Row.

Driscoll, Kathleen and Joan McFarland. 1989. 'The Impact of a Feminist Perspective on Research Methodologies: Social Sciences.' In Winne Tomm, ed., *The Effects of Feminist Approaches on Research Methodologies.* Waterloo, ON: Wilfrid Laurier University Press.

Druckman, James N., Donald P. Green, James H. Kuklinski, and Arthur Lupia. 2006. 'The Growth and Development of Experimental Research in Political Science.' *American Political Science Review* 100, 4: 627–35.

Duelli-Klein, R. 1983. 'How to Do What We Want to Do: Thoughts About Feminist Methodology.' In G. Bowles and R. Duelli-Klein, eds., *Theories of Women's Studies.* London: Routledge & Kegan Paul.

Duffy, Andrew and Brad Evenson. 1996. 'Canadians Seek Truth, Integrity from Leaders.' *Calgary Herald.* 29 June: A8.

Duverger, Maurice. 1964. *Political Parties.* London: Methuen.

Eagles, Munroe. 1993. 'Money and Votes in Canada: Campaign Spending and Parliamentary Election Outcomes, 1984 and 1988.' *Canadian Public Policy* 19, 4 (December): 432–49.

Edwards, Allen L. 1969. *Statistical Analysis.* New York: Holt, Rinehart and Winston.

———. 1990. *Statistical Analysis,* 3d ed. New York: Holt, Rinehart and Winston; McGraw-Hill: 235–38.

Eldersveld, Samuel J. 1956. 'Experimental Propaganda Techniques and Voting Behavior.' *American Political Science Review* 50, 1: 154–65.

Elifson, Kirk W., Richard P. Runyon, and Audrey Haber. 1990. *Fundamentals of Social Statistics,* 2d ed. New York: McGraw-Hill.

Elkins, David J. 1978. 'Party Identification: A Conceptual Analysis.' *Canadian Journal of Political Science* 11, 2 (June): 419–21.

Esterberg, Kristin G. 2002. *Qualitative Methods in Social Research.* Boston: McGraw-Hill.

Eulau, Heinz. 1964 (c. 1963). *The Behavioral Persuasion in Politics.* New York: Random House.

Everitt, Joanna and Michael Camp. 2009. 'One Is Not Like the Others: Allison Brewer's Leadership of the New Brunswick NDP.' In Sylvia Bashevkin, ed., *Opening Doors Wider: Women's Political Engagement in Canada.* Vancouver: UBC Press: 127–44.

Finch, Janet. 1984. '"It's Great to Have Someone to Talk To": The Ethics and Politics of Interviewing Women.' In Colin Bell and Helen Roberts, eds., *Social Researching: Politics, Problems, Practice.* London: Routledge & Kegan Paul: 70–87.

Flanagan, Tom. 1995. *Waiting for the Wave: The Reform Party and Preston Manning.* Toronto: Stoddart.

Fowler, James H. 2006. 'Altruism and Turnout.' *Journal of Politics,* 68: 647–83.

Fox, Bonnie J. 1993. 'On Violent Men and Female Victims: A Comment on DeKeseredy and Kelly.' *Canadian Journal of Sociology* 18, 3: 321–4.

Freedman, David A. 2009. *Statistical Models: Theory and Practice,* rev. ed. Cambridge, UK: Cambridge University Press.

Frohlich, Norman and Irvin Boschmann. 1986. 'Partisan Preference and Income Redistribution: Cross-National and Cross-Sexual Results.' *Canadian Journal of Political Science* 19, 1 (March): 53–69.

Gadd, Jane. 1996. 'AIDS Spreading Among Canadians.' *Globe and Mail.* 3 July: A6.

Gartner, Rosemary. 1993. 'Studying Woman Abuse: A Comment on DeKeseredy and Kelly.' *Canadian Journal of Sociology* 18, 3: 313–20.

George, Alexander L. 2006. 'Quantitative and Qualitative Approaches to Content Analysis.' In J. Scott *Documentary Research,* vol. 1. Thousand Oaks, CA: Sage Publications.

Gerber, Alan S. and Donald P. Green. 1999. 'Does Canvassing Increase Voter Turnout? A Field Experiment.' *Proceedings of the National Academy of Science* 96, 19: 10939–42.

———. 2000a. 'The Effect of a Nonpartisan Get-Out-the-Vote Drive: An Experimental Study of Leafletting.' *Journal of Politics* 62, 3: 846–57.

———. 2000b. 'The Effects of Canvassing, Direct Mail, and Telephone Contact on Voter Turnout: A Field Experiment.' *American Political Science Review* 94, 3: 653–63.

———. 2001. 'Do Phone Calls Increase Voter Turnout? A Field Experiment.' *Public Opinion Quarterly* 65, 1: 75–85.

——— and Christopher W. Larimer. 2008. 'Social Pressure and Voter Turnout: Evidence From a Large-Scale Field Experiment.' *American Political Science Review* 102, 1: 33–48.

——— and Edward H. Kaplan. 2004. 'The Illusion of Learning from Observational Research.' In Ian Shapiro, Rogers Smith, and Tarek Massoud, eds., *Problems and Methods in the Study of Politics.* New York: Cambridge University Press: 251–73.

——— and Matthew N. Green. 2003. 'The Effects of Partisan Direct Mail on Voter Turnout.' *Electoral Studies* 22: 563–79.

——— and Ron Shachar. 2003. 'Voting May Be Habit-Forming: Evidence from a Randomized Field Experiment.' *American Journal of Political Science* 47, 3: 540–50.

Gerber, Linda M. 2006. 'Urban Diversity: Riding Composition and Party Support in the Canadian Federal Election of 2004.' *Canadian Journal of Urban Research* 15, 2: 105–18.

Gerring, John. 1998. *Party Ideologies in America, 1828–1996.* Cambridge, UK: Cambridge University Press.

Gibbons, Jean Dickinson. 1976. *Nonparametric Methods for Quantitative Analysis.* New York: Holt, Rinehart and Winston.

Gidengil, Elisabeth. 1992. 'Canada Votes: A Quarter Century of Canadian National Election Studies.' *Canadian Journal of Political Science* 25, 2 (June): 219–48.

——— and Joanna Everitt. 1999. 'Metaphors and Misrepresentation: Gendered Mediation in News Coverage of the 1993 Canadian Leaders' Debates.' *Press/Politics* 4, 1: 48–65.

———. 2000. 'Filtering the Female: Television News Coverage of the 1993 Canadian Leaders' Debates.' *Women & Politics* 21, 4: 105–31.

———. 2003. 'Conventional Coverage/Unconventional Politicians: Gender and Media Coverage of Canadian Leaders' Debates, 1993, 1997, 2000.' *Canadian Journal of Political Science* 36, 3 (September): 559–77.

Gill, Jeff. 1999. 'The Insignificance of Null Hypothesis Significance Testing.' *Political Research Quarterly* 52, 3: 647–74.

Gingras, Anne-Marie, Shannon Sampert, and David Gagnon-Pelletier. 2010. 'Framing Gomery in English and French Newspapers: The Use of Strategic and Ethical Frames.' In Shannon Sampert and Linda Trimble, eds., *Mediating Canadian Politics.* Toronto: Pearson Education: 277–93.

Glaser, Barney G. 1992. *Emergence vs. Forcing: Basics of Grounded Theory Analysis.* Mill Valley, CA: Sociology Press.

Goldberg, Michael A. and Maurice D. Levi. 1994. 'Growing Together or Apart: The Risks and Returns of Alternative Constitutions of Canada.' *Canadian Public Policy* 20, 4 (December): 341–52.

Gosnell, Harold F. 1927. *Getting-Out-The-Vote: An Experiment in the Stimulation of Voting.* Chicago: University of Chicago Press.

Grant, Judith. 1993. *Fundamental Feminism: Contesting the Core Concepts of Feminist Theory.* New York: Routledge.

Green, Donald P., and Alan S. Gerber. 2004. *Get Out the Vote.* Washington, DC: Brookings Institution Press.

——— and David W. Nickerson. 2003. 'Getting Out the Vote in Local Elections: Results from Six Door-to-Door Canvassing Experiments.' *Journal of Politics* 65, 4: 1083–96.

Green, Donald P. and Jonathan S. Krasno. 1988. 'Salvation for the Spendthrift Incumbent: Reestimating the Effects of Campaign Spending in House Elections.' *American Journal of Political Science* 32: 884–907.

Griffin, John Howard. 1977. *Black Like Me,* 2d ed. Boston: Houghton Mifflin.

Guba, Egon G. and Yvonna S. Lincoln. 1985. *Naturalistic Inquiry.* Thousand Oaks, CA: Sage Publications.

———. 1994. 'Competing Paradigms in Qualitative Research.' In N.K. Denzin and Y.S. Lincoln, eds., *Hand-*

book of Qualitative Research. Thousand Oaks, CA: Sage Publications.

Guérin, Daniel. 2003. 'Aboriginal Participation in Canadian Federal Elections: Trends and Implications.' Electoral Insight. www.elections.ca

Habyarimana, James, Macartan Humphreys, Daniel N. Posner, and Jeremy M. Weinstein. 2007. 'Why Does Ethnic Diversity Undermine Public Goods Provision?' American Political Science Review 101, 4: 709–25.

———. 2009. Coethnicity: Diversity and the Dilemmas of Collective Action. New York: Russell Sage Foundation.

Hackett, Robert A., William O. Gilsdorf, and Philip Savage. 1992. 'News Balance Rhetoric: The Fraser Institute's Political Appropriation of Content Analysis.' Canadian Journal of Communication 17, 1: html version accessed 8 December 2009.

Hartz, Louis. 1964. The Founding of New Societies: Studies in the History of the U.S., Latin America, South Africa, Canada and Australia. New York: Harcourt, Brace, and World.

Hayslett, H.T., Jr. 1968. Statistics Made Simple. New York: Doubleday.

Heard, Andrew D. 1991. 'The Charter in the Supreme Court of Canada: The Importance of Which Judges Hear an Appeal.' Canadian Journal of Political Science 24, 2 (June): 289–307.

Hesse-Biber, Sharlene Nagy, and Patricia Leavy. 2006. The Practice of Qualitative Research. Thousand Oaks, CA: Sage Publications.

Hill, Carey Anne. 1998. 'New Technologies and Territorial Identities in Western Canada.' M.A. thesis, Department of Political Science, University of Calgary.

Hite, Shere. 1976. The Hite Report: A Nationwide Study of Female Sexuality. New York: Macmillan.

———. 1981. The Hite Report on Male Sexuality. New York: Ballantine Books.

Hodder, Ian. 1994. 'The Interpretation of Documents and Material Culture.' In N.K. Denzin and Y.S. Lincoln, eds., Handbook of Qualitative Research. Thousand Oaks, CA: Sage Publications.

———. 2003. 'The Interpretation of Documents and Material Culture.' In N.K. Denzin and Y.S. Lincoln, eds., Collecting and Interpreting Qualitative Materials, 2d ed. Thousand Oaks, CA: Sage Publications.

Holland, Paul W. 1986. 'Statistics and Causal Inference.' Journal of the American Statistical Association 81, 396: 945–60.

Holliday, Adrian. 2007. Doing and Writing Qualitative Research, 2d ed. Thousand Oaks, CA: Sage Publications.

Horowitz, Gad. 1966. 'Conservatism, Liberalism and Socialism in Canada: An Interpretation.' Canadian Journal of Political Science and Economics 32, 2 (June): 143–71.

Humphreys, Macartan, William Masters, and Martin E. Sandbu. 2006. 'The Role of Leadership in Democratic Deliberations: Results from a Field Experiment in São Tomé and Principe.' World Politics 58, 4: 583–622.

Hyde, Susan. 2007. 'The Observer Effect in International Politics: Evidence from a Natural Experiment.' World Politics 60, 1: 37–63.

Iyengar, Shanto. 1996. 'Framing Responsibility for Political Issues.' Annals of the American Academy of Political and Social Science 546 (July): 59–70.

Jackson, Winston. 1995. Methods: Doing Social Research. Scarborough: Prentice-Hall.

Jahoda, Marie. 1981. 'To Publish or Not to Publish?' Journal of Social Issues 37: 208–20.

Jenson, Jane. 1975. 'Party Loyalty in Canada: The Question of Party Identification.' Canadian Journal of Political Science 8, 4 (December): 543–53.

———. 1978. 'Comment: The Filling of Wine Bottles Is Not Easy.' Canadian Journal of Political Science 11, 2 (June): 437–8.

Johnston, Richard. 1992. 'Party Identification Measures in the Anglo-American Democracies: A National Survey Experiment.' American Journal of Political Science 36, 2: 542–59.

———, André Blais, Henry E. Brady, and Jean Crete. 1992. Letting the People Decide: Dynamics of a Canadian Election. Montreal: McGill-Queen's University Press.

Jones, Susan R. and Marylu K. McEwen. 2002. 'A Conceptual Model of Multiple Dimensions of Identity.' In S.B. Merriam, ed., Qualitative Research in Practice. San Francisco: Jossey-Bass.

Kelly, Katherine D. 1994. 'The Politics of Data.' Canadian Journal of Sociology 19, 1: 81–5.

Key, V.O. 1966. The Responsible Electorate. Cambridge, MA: Harvard University Press.

Kimmel, Allan J. 1988. Ethics and Values in Applied Social Research. Newbury Park, CA: Sage Publications.

King, Gary, Robert Keohane, and Sidney Verba. 1993. Designing Social Inquiry: Scientific Inference in Qualitative Research. Princeton: Princeton University Press.

Kinnear, Michael. 2003. 'The Effect of Expansion of the Franchise on Turnout.' Electoral Insight. www.elections.ca

Krippendorff, Klaus. 2004. Content Analysis: An Introduction to Its Methodology, 2d ed. Thousand Oaks, CA: Sage Publications.

Krueger, James S. and Michael S. Lewis-Beck. 2008. 'Is OLS Dead?' The Political Methodologist 15, 2: 2–5.

Kuhn, Thomas. 1962. The Structure of Scientific Revolutions. Chicago: University of Chicago.

———. 1970. The Structure of Scientific Revolutions, 2d ed., rev. Chicago: University of Chicago Press.

Kulisheck, Michael R. and Jeffrey J Mondak. 1996. 'Candidate Quality and the Congressional Vote: A Causal Connection.' Electoral Studies 15, 2: 237–53.

Lane, Robert E. 1962. Political Ideology: Why the American Common Man Believes What He Does. New York: The Free Press.

Lanoue, David J. 1991. 'Debates That Mattered: Voters' Reaction to the 1984 Canadian Leadership Debates.' Canadian Journal of Political Science 24, 1 (March): 51–65.

Lather, Patti. 1988. 'Feminist Perspectives on Empowering Research Methodologies.' *Women's Studies International Forum* 11: 569–81.

Laver, Michael. 2001. 'Why Should We Estimate the Policy Position of Political Actors?' In M. Laver, ed. *Estimating the Policy Positions of Political Actors.* London: Routledge.

Lazerwitz, Bernard. 1968. 'Sampling Theory and Procedures.' In Hubert M. Blalock, Jr. and Ann B. Blalock, eds. *Methodology in Social Research.* New York: McGraw-Hill: 278–328.

LeDuc, Lawrence, Harold Clarke, Jane Jenson, and Jon Pammett. 1984. 'Partisan Instability in Canada: Evidence from a New Panel Study.' *American Political Science Review* 78: 470–83.

Lee, Raymond M. 1993. *Doing Research on Sensitive Topics.* London: Sage Publications.

——— and Claire M. Renzetti. 1990. 'The Problems of Researching Sensitive Topics.' *American Behavioral Scientist* 1, 33 (May–June): 510–28.

Leo, Christopher and Jeremy Enns. 2009. 'Multi-Level Governance and Ideological Rigidity: The Failure of Deep Federalism.' *Canadian Journal of Political Science* 42, 1 (March): 93–116.

Lewis, Jane, and Jane Ritchie. 2006. 'Generalizing from Qualitative Research.' In J. Ritchie and J. Lewis, eds., *Qualitative Research Practice: A Guide for Social Science Students and Researchers.* Thousand Oaks, CA: Sage Publications.

Liemohn, Wedell. 1979. 'Research Involving Human Subjects.' *Research Quarterly* 50, 2: 157–63.

Lijphart, Arend. 1994. *Electoral Systems and Party Systems: A Study of Twenty-Seven Democracies, 1945–1990.* New York: Oxford University Press.

Lipset, Seymour Martin. 1990. *Continental Divide: The Values and Institutions of the United States and Canada.* New York: Routledge.

Loewen, Peter John. 2008. 'Experimentation and Political Science: Six Applications.' PhD thesis, Université de Montréal.

——— and Daniel Rubenson. 2011. 'For Want of a Nail: Direct Mail and Negative Persuasion in a Leadership Campaign.' *Party Politics.*

——— and Leonard Wantchekon. 2010. 'Help Me Help You: Conducting Field Experiments with Political Elites.' *Annals of the American Academy for Political and Social Science* 628 (March): 165–75.

Lowe, Graham S. and Harvey Krahn. 1995. 'Job-Related Education and Training Among Younger Workers.' *Canadian Public Policy* 21, 3 (September): 362–78.

Lublin, David and D. Stephen Voss. 2002. 'Context and Francophone Support for the Sovereignty of Québec: An Ecological Analysis.' *Canadian Journal of Political Science* 35, 1 (March): 75–101.

Luntz, Frank. 1994. 'Focus Group Research in American Politics.' *The Polling Report.* http://www.pollingreport.com/focus.htm, accessed 7 January 2010.

Mackie, Richard. 1996. 'Quebeckers Feel Sovereignty Will Bring Greater Prosperity.' *Globe and Mail.* 24 August: A5.

Maclean's. 1997. 'False Positive and False Negative.' 17 February: 70.

Manheim, Jarol B. and Richard C. Rich. 1981. *Empirical Political Analysis: Research Methods in Political Science.* Englewood Cliffs, NJ: Prentice-Hall.

——— and Lars Willnat. 2002. *Empirical Political Analysis: Research Methods in Political Science,* 5th ed. Toronto: Longman.

——— and Craig Leonard Brians. 2008. *Empirical Political Analysis: Quantitative and Qualitative Research Methods,* 7th ed. New York: Pearson Education.

Marshall, Catherine and Gretchen B. Rossman. 1989. *Designing Qualitative Research.* Thousand Oaks, CA: Sage.

———. 2006. *Designing Qualitative Research,* 4th ed. Thousand Oaks, CA: Sage Publications.

McCall, Christina and Stephen Clarkson. 1994. *Trudeau and Our Times, vol. 2: The Heroic Delusion.* Toronto: McClelland & Stewart.

McCall, Robert B. 1986. *Fundamental Statistics for Behavioral Sciences,* 4th ed. New York: Harcourt Brace Jovanovich.

McIlroy, Anne. 1996. 'Dingwall Pledges Tests Will Include Women.' *Globe and Mail.* 10 August: A1.

Merriam, Sharan B. 2002a. 'Assessing and Evaluating Qualitative Research.' In S.B. Merriam, ed., *Qualitative Research in Practice.* San Francisco: Jossey-Bass.

———. 2002b. 'Introduction to Qualitative Research.' In S.B. Merriam, ed., *Qualitative Research in Practice.* San Francisco: Jossey-Bass.

Michels, Robert. 1962. *Political Parties: A Sociological Study of the Oligarchical Tendencies of Modern Democracy.* New York: The Free Press.

Milbrath, Lester. 1965. *Political Participation.* New York: Rand McNally.

Milgram, Stanley. 1963. 'Behavioral Study of Obedience.' *Journal of Abnormal and Social Psychology* 67: 371–8.

Moehler, Devra C. 2007. 'Private Radio and Public Information: An Experimental Study of Radio Campaigns in Africa.' Paper presented at Annual Meeting of the American Political Science Association, Chicago, IL.

Mondak, Jeffrey J. and Robert Huckfeldt. 2006. 'The Accessibility and Utility of Candidate Character in Electoral Decision Making.' *Electoral Studies* 25, 1: 20–34.

Monroe, Kristen Renwick, ed. 2005. *Perestroika!: The Raucous Rebellion in Political Science.* Princeton: Yale University Press.

Morse, Janice M. and Lyn Richards. 2002. *Read Me First for a User's Guide to Qualitative Methods.* Thousand Oaks, CA: Sage Publications.

Morton, Becky, and Kenneth Williams. 2008. 'Experimentation in Political Science.' In Janet M. Box-Steffensmeier, Henry E. Brady, and David Collier, eds., *Oxford Handbook of Political Methodology.* Oxford: Oxford University Press.

MRC, NSERC, and SSHRC. 1994. *Integrity in Research and Scholarship: A Tri-Council Policy Statement.* January.

Mutz, Diana C. 2006. *Hearing the Other Side: Deliberative Versus Participatory Democracy.* Cambridge, UK: Cambridge University Press.

———. 2007. 'Effects of "In-Your-Face" Television Discourse on Perceptions of a Legitimate Opposition.' *American Political Science Review* 101, 4: 621–35.

Nachmias, David and Chaua Nachmias. 1987. *Research Methods in the Social Sciences,* 3d ed. New York: St. Martin's Press.

Nesbitt-Larking, Paul. 2007. *Politics, Society, and the Media,* 2d ed. Peterborough, ON: Broadview Press.

Neuendorf, Kimberly A. 2002. *The Content Analysis Guidebook.* Thousand Oaks, CA: Sage Publications.

Neuman, W. Lawrence. 1994. *Social Research Methods: Qualitative and Quantitative Approaches,* 2d ed. Boston: Allyn & Bacon.

———. 1997. *Social Research Methods: Qualitative and Quantitative Approaches,* 3d ed. Boston: Allyn & Bacon.

———. 2000. *Social Research Methods: Qualitative and Quantitative Approaches,* 4th ed. Toronto: Allyn & Bacon.

———. 2007. *Basics of Social Research: Qualitative and Quantitative Approaches.* Boston: Pearson Education.

———. and Karen Robson. 2007. *Basics of Social Research: Qualitative and Quantitative Approaches,* Cdn ed. Toronto: Pearson Education.

Nevitte, Neil and Roger Gibbins. 1990. *New Elites in Old States: Ideologies in the Anglo-American Democracies.* Toronto: Oxford University Press.

Nickerson, David W., R.D. Friedrichs, and D.C. King. 2006. 'Partisan Mobilization Campaigns in the Field: Results from a Statewide Turnout Experiment in Michigan.' *Political Research Quarterly* 59, 1: 85–97.

Nie, Norman, Sidney Verba, and John Petrocik. *The Changing American Voter.* Cambridge, MA: Harvard University Press, 1976.

Norusis, Marija J. 1990. *SPSS Introductory Statistics Student Guide.* Chicago: SPSS Inc.

Ornstein, Michael D. and H. Michael Stevenson. 1981. 'Elite and Public Opinion before the Quebec Referendum: A Commentary on the State in Canada.' *Canadian Journal of Political Science* 14, 4 (December): 745–74.

Paluck, Elizabeth Levy. 2009. 'Reducing Intergroup Prejudice and Conflict Using the Media: A Field Experiment in Rwanda.' *Journal of Personality and Social Psychology* 96: 574–87.

Panagopoulos, Costas. 2009. 'Partisan and Nonpartisan Message Content and Voter Mobilization: Field Experimental Evidence.' *Political Research Quarterly* 62, 1: 70–6.

Patton, Carl V. and David S. Sawicki. 1993. *Basic Methods of Policy Analysis and Planning,* 2d ed. Englewood Cliffs, NJ: Prentice-Hall.

Pedhazur, Elazar J. 1982. *Multiple Regression in Behavioural Research,* 2d ed. Orlando, FL: Harcourt Brace.

Pierce, Roger. 2008. *Research Methods in Politics.* London: Sage Publications.

Pilon, Dennis. 2009. 'Investigating Media as a Deliberative Space: Newspaper Opinions About Voting Systems in the 2007 Ontario Provincial Referendum.' *Canadian Political Science Review* 3, 3: 1–23.

Pitsula, James M. 2001. 'First Nations and Saskatchewan Politics.' In Howard A. Leeson (ed.), *Saskatchewan Politics: Into the Twenty-First Century.* Regina: Canadian Plains Research Centre.

Platt, Jennifer. 2006. 'Evidence and Proof in Documentary Research: Part II, Some Shared Problems of Documentary Research.' In J. Scott, ed., *Documentary Research,* vol. 1. Thousand Oaks, CA: Sage Publications.

Punch, Keith F. 2005. *Introduction to Social Research: Quantitative and Qualitative Approaches,* 2d ed. Thousand Oaks, CA: Sage Publications.

Putnam, Robert. 1993. *Making Democracy Work: Civic Traditions in Modern Italy.* Princeton: Princeton University Press.

Putt, Allen D. and J. Fred Springer. 1989. *Policy Research: Concepts, Methods, and Applications.* Englewood Cliffs, NJ: Prentice-Hall.

Reinharz, Shulamit. 1992. *Feminist Methods in Social Research.* New York: Oxford University Press.

Richards, Lyn. 2005. *Handling Qualitative Data: A Practical Guide.* Thousand Oaks, CA: Sage Publications.

Richerson, Peter J. and Robert Boyd. 2004. *The Origin and Evolution of Cultures.* London: Oxford University Press.

Riffe, Daniel, Stephen Lacy, and Frederick G. Fico. 2005. *Analyzing Media Messages: Using Content Analysis in Research.* Mahwah, NJ: Lawrence Erlbaum Associates.

Ritchie, Jane, Jane Lewis, and Gillian Elam. 2003. 'Designing and Selecting Samples.' In Jane Ritchie and Jane Lewis, eds., *Qualitative Research Practice: A Guide for Social Science Students and Researchers.* London: Sage Publications: 77–108.

Roberts, Alasdair and Jonathan Rose. 1995. 'Selling the Goods and Services Tax: Government Advertising and Public Discourse in Canada.' *Canadian Journal of Political Science* 28, 2 (June): 311–30.

Roberts, Helen. 1984. 'Putting the Show on the Road: The Dissemination of Research Findings.' In Colin Bell and Helen Roberts, eds., *Social Researching: Politics, Problems, Practice.* London: Routledge & Kegan Paul: 199–212.

Roethlisberger, F.J. and W.J. Dickenson. 1939. *Management and the Worker.* Cambridge, MA: Harvard University Press.

Rubenson, Daniel, and Peter John Loewen. 2008. 'Both Sides Now: A Field Experiment with Competing Messages.' Working paper.

Ryan, Gery W. and H. Russell Bernard. 2003. 'Data Management and Analysis Methods.' In N.K. Denzin and Y.S. Lincoln, eds., *Collecting and Interpreting Qualitative Materials,* 2d ed. Thousand Oaks, CA: Sage Publications.

Sampert, Shannon and Linda Trimble. 2010. 'Putting It into Practice: A Primer on Content and Discourse Analysis.' In Shannon Sampert and Linda Trimble, eds., *Mediating Canadian Politics.* Toronto: Pearson Education: 326–37.

Sauvageau, Florian, David Taras, and David Schneiderman. 2005. *Last Word: Media Coverage of the Supreme Court of Canada.* Vancouver: UBC Press.

Scientific American. 2007. 'The Genetics of Politics.' http://www.scientificamerican.com/article.cfm?id=the-genetics-of-politics, accessed 12 January 2009.

Seidman, I.E. 1991. *Interviewing as Qualitative Research.* New York: Teachers College Press.

Shapiro, D.M. and M. Stelcner. 1987. 'The Persistence of the Male-Female Earnings Gap in Canada, 1970–1980: The Impact of Equal Pay Laws and Language Policies.' *Canadian Public Policy* 13, 4 (10 December): 462–76.

Shea, Christopher. 1996. 'Psychologists Debate Accuracy of "Significance Test."' *The Chronicle of Higher Education.* 16 August: A12, A17.

Sieber, J.E. and B. Stanley. 1988. 'Ethical and Professional Dimensions of Socially Sensitive Research.' *American Psychologist* 43: 49–55.

Sieber, Sam D. 1973. 'The Integration of Field Work and Survey Methods.' *American Journal of Sociology* 78, 6: 1335–59.

Simon, Julian. 1995. 'Earth's Doomsayers Are Wrong.' *The Next City* 1, 2: 10–11.

Singer, Eleanor. 1978. 'Informed Consent: Consequences for Response Rate and Response Quality in Social Surveys.' *American Sociological Review* 43: 144–62.

———. 1983. 'Informed Consent Procedures in Surveys: Some Reasons for Minimal Effects on Response.' In Robert F. Boruch and Joe E. Cecil, eds., *Solutions to Ethical and Legal Problems in Social Research.* New York: Academic Press: 183–211.

Singleton, Royce, Jr., Bruce C. Straits, Margaret M. Straits, and Ronald J. McAllister. 1988. *Approaches to Social Research.* New York: Oxford University Press.

Skocpol, Theda. 1979. *States and Social Revolutions: A Comparative Analysis of France, Russia, and China.* Cambridge: Cambridge University Press.

Small, Tamara. 2007. 'Canadian Cyberparties: Reflections on Internet-Based Campaigning and Party Systems.' *Canadian Journal of Political Science* 40, 3 (September): 639–57.

Smiley, Donald. 1980. *Canada in Question: Federalism in the Eighties,* 3d ed. Toronto: McGraw-Hill Ryerson.

Smith, Denis. 1995. *Rogue Tory: The Life and Legend of John G. Diefenbaker.* Toronto: Macfarlane, Walter & Ross.

Soderlund, Walter C., Ronald H. Wagenberg, and Ian C. Pemberton. 1994. 'Cheerleader or Critic? Television News Coverage in Canada and the United States of the U.S. Invasion of Panama.' *Canadian Journal of Political Science* 27, 3 (September): 580–604.

Soroka, Stuart. 2002. 'Issue Attributes and Agenda-Setting by Media, the Public, and Policymakers in Canada.' *International Journal of Public Opinion Research* 14, 3: 264–85.

——— and Blake Andrew. 2010. 'Media Coverage of Canadian Elections: Horse-Race Coverage and Negativity in Election Campaigns.' In Shannon Sampert and Linda Trimble, eds., *Mediating Canadian Politics.* Toronto: Pearson Education: 113–28.

———, Erin Penner, and Kelly Blidook. 2009. 'Constituency Influence in Parliament.' *Canadian Journal of Political Science* 42, 3 (September): 563–91.

Statistics Canada. 1989. *The Labour Force* (71-001, December).

Statistics Canada. 2009a. *Data Liberation Initiative: DLI Survival Guide. Section 4: Data.* www.statcan.gc.ca/dli-ild/guide-trousse/guide-trousse/toc-tdm/3000276-eng.htm, accessed 5 January 2010.

Statistics Canada. 2009b. *Overview of the Census: A brief history.* www12.statcan.ca/census-recensement/2006/ref/dict/overview-apercu/pop1-eng.cfm, accessed 5 January 2010.

Statistics Canada. 2009c. *Overview of the Census: Taking a Census of Population.* www12.statcan.ca/census-recensement/2006/ref/dict/overview-apercu/pop2-eng.cfm, accessed 5 January 2010.

Statistics Canada. 2009d. *2006 Census reference materials, Aboriginal Peoples Technical Report, Data quality measurement.* www12.statcan.ca/census-recensement/2006/ref/rp-guides/rp/ap-pa/p5-eng.cfm#toc5_4_2, accessed 5 January 2010.

Statistics Canada. 2009e. *Statistics Canada: About Us.* www.statcan.gc.ca/about-apercu/about-apropos-eng.htm, accessed 5 January 2010.

Statistics Canada. 2009f. *2006 Census reference materials, Aboriginal Peoples Technical Report, Concepts and Variables.* www12.statcan.ca/census-recensement/2006/ref/rp-guides/rp/ap-pa/p1-eng.cfm, accessed 5 January 2010.

Steinem, Gloria. 1983. *Outrageous Acts and Everyday Rebellions.* New York: Holt, Rinehart and Winston.

Strauss, Anselm and Juliet Corbin. 1994. 'Grounded Theory Methodology: An Overview.' In N.K. Denzin and Y.S. Lincoln, eds., *Handbook of Qualitative Research.* Thousand Oaks. CA: Sage Publications.

Strauss, Stephen. 1996. 'Landmark Male Bisexuality Survey Seeks Basic Truths.' *Globe and Mail.* 2 April: A6.

Studlar, Donley T. and Richard E. Matland. 1994. 'The Growth of Women's Representation in the Canadian House of Commons and the Election of 1984: A Reappraisal.' *Canadian Journal of Political Science* 27, 1 (March): 53–79.

Sumser, John. 2001. *A Guide to Empirical Research in Communication: Rules for Looking.* Thousand Oaks, CA: Sage Publications.

Tashakkori, Abbas and Charles Teddlie, eds. 2003. *Handbook of Mixed Methods in Social and Behavioural Research*. Thousand Oaks, CA: Sage Publications.

Tavris, Carol. 1992. *The Mismeasure of Woman*. New York: Touchstone.

Thomas, Paul. 2008. 'Leading from the Middle: Manitoba's Role in the Intergovernmental Arena.' *Canadian Political Science Review* 2, 3: 29–50.

Tocqueville, Alexis de. 1863. *Democracy in America*. New York: Amereon House.

Tremblay, Manon, 1998. 'Do Female MPs Substantively Represent Women? A Study of Legislative Behaviour in Canada's 35th Parliament.' *Canadian Journal of Political Science* 31, 3 (September): 435–65.

Trimble, Linda. 1997. 'Feminist Politics in the Alberta Legislature, 1972–1994.' In Jane Arscott and Linda Trimble, eds., *In the Presence of Women: Representation in Canadian Governments*. Toronto: Harcourt: 128–53.

———. 1998. 'Who's Represented? Gender and Diversity in the Alberta Legislature.' In Manon Tremblay and Caroline Andrew, eds., *Women and Political Representation in Canada*. Ottawa: University of Ottawa Press: 257–89.

———. 2007. 'Gender, Political Leadership and Media Visibility: *Globe and Mail* Coverage of Conservative Party of Canada Leadership Contests.' *Canadian Journal of Political Science* 40, 4 (December): 1–25.

——— and Joanna Everitt. 2010. 'Belinda Stronach and the Gender Politics of Celebrity.' In Shannon Sampert and Linda Trimble, eds., *Mediating Canadian Politics*. Toronto: Pearson Education: 50–74.

——— and Shannon Sampert. 2004. 'Who's in the Game? Framing of the Canadian Election 2000 by the *Globe and Mail* and the *National Post*.' *Canadian Journal of Political Science* 37, 1 (March): 51–71.

———, Laura Way, and Shannon Sampert. 2010. 'Drawn to the Polls? Representations of Canadian Voters in Editorial Cartoons.' *Journal of Canadian Studies* 44, 2: 70–94.

Turcotte, André. 2007. *'What Do You Mean I Can't Have a Say?' Young Canadians and Their Government: Charting the Course for Youth Civic and Political Participation*. Ottawa: Canadian Policy Research Networks.

Verba, Sidney and Norman Nie. 1972. *Participation in America: Political Democracy and Social Equality*. New York: Harper & Row.

Vipond, Robert. 2008. 'Introduction: The Comparative Turn in Canadian Political Science.' In Linda A. White, Richard Simeon, Robert Vipond, and Jennifer Wallner, eds., *The Comparative Turn in Canadian Political Science*. Vancouver: UBC Press: 3–16.

Walker, James. 1996. 'Charest Would Boost Merged Reform, Conservative Parties: Poll.' *The Financial Post*. 18 May: 5.

Wantchekon, Leonard. 2003. 'Clientelism and Voting Behavior: Evidence from a Field Experiment in Benin.' *World Politics* 55.

———. 2008. 'Expert Information, Public Deliberation and Electoral Support for "Good" Governance: Experimental Evidence from Benin.' NYU Mimeo.

——— and Christel Vermeersch. 2005. 'Information, Social Networks and the Demand for Public Goods: Experimental Evidence from Benin.' NYU Mimeo.

Warwick, Donald P. and Thomas F. Pettigrew. 1983. 'Towards Ethical Guidelines for Social Science Research in Public Policy.' In Daniel Callahan and Bruce Jennings, eds., *Ethics, the Social Sciences, and Policy Analysis*. New York: Plenum Press: 335–69.

Watts, Ronald L. 1989. 'Executive Federalism: The Comparative Context.' In David P. Shugarman and Reg Whitaker, eds., *Federalism and Political Community: Essays in Honour of Donald Smiley*. Peterborough, ON: Broadview Press: 439–59.

Weimer, David L. and Aidan R. Vining. 2005. *Policy Analysis: Concepts and Practices*, 4th ed. Upper Saddle River, NJ: Pearson Prentice Hall.

Wente, Margaret. 1996. 'The Feminine Olympics.' *Globe and Mail*. 3 August: D7.

Wesley, Jared J. 2011. *Code Politics: Campaigns and Cultures on the Canadian Prairies*. Vancouver: UBC Press.

Wetstein, Matthew E. and C.L. Ostberg. 2003. 'Strategic Leadership and Political Change on the Canadian Supreme Court: Analyzing the Transition to Chief Justice.' *Canadian Journal of Political Science* 38, 3 (September): 653–73.

White, Linda A., Richard Simeon, Robert Vipond, and Jennifer Wallner, eds. 2008. *The Comparative Turn in Canadian Political Science*. Vancouver: UBC Press.

White, Louise G. 1994. *Political Analysis*, 3d ed. Belmont, CA: Wadsworth.

Woliver, Laura R. 2002. 'Ethical Dilemmas in Personal Interviewing.' *PS: Political Science & Politics* 35, 4: 677–8.

Wright, R.L.D. 1976. *Understanding Statistics*. New York: Harcourt Brace Jovanovich.

York, Geoffrey. 1996. 'Russian Media Accused of Bias.' *Globe and Mail*. 6 July: A1, A12.

INDEX